TRANSFORMATIVE BEAUTY

TRANSFORMATIVE BEAUTY

Art Museums in Industrial Britain

AMY WOODSON-BOULTON

Stanford University Press
Stanford, California

Stanford University Press
Stanford, California

This book has been published with the assistance of Loyola Marymount University.

Printed in the United States of America on acid-free, archival-quality paper

Library of Congress Cataloging-in-Publication Data

Woodson-Boulton, Amy, author.
  Transformative beauty : art museums in industrial Britain / Amy Woodson-Boulton.
    pages cm
  Includes bibliographical references and index.
  ISBN 978-0-8047-7804-6 (cloth : alk. paper)
    1. Art museums—Great Britain—History—19th century. 2. Art museums—Great Britain—History—20th century. 3. Art and state—Great Britain—History—19th century. 4. Art and state—Great Britain—History—20th century. 5. Art and society—Great Britain—History—19th century. 6. Art and society—Great Britain—History—20th century. I. Title.
  N1020.W66 2012
  708.209'034—dc23
                    2011030708

Typeset by Bruce Lundquist in 10/15 Minion

For my family, who believe in the arts

CONTENTS

FIGURES

ACKNOWLEDGMENTS

It is a pleasure to be able to thank all of the institutions and individuals who have helped me to research, write, and publish this book over the course of many years. I am sincerely grateful for the administrative and moral support of the History Department at Loyola Marymount University; for publishing grants from the History Department, from Bellarmine College of Liberal Arts Dean Paul Zeleza, and from Chief Academic Officer Joseph Hellige at LMU; for support from the LMU Sponsored Projects Office, particularly from Cynthia Carr; for a Robert R. Wark Fellowship from the Huntington Library, Art Collection, and Botanical Gardens; for a Summer Stipend from the National Endowment for the Humanities; for summer writing grants and a Bellarmine Research Grant from Loyola Marymount University; for a summer writing grant from Juniata College; for an Edward A. Dickson Fellowship in the History of Art from the UCLA Art History Department; for a Walter L. Arnstein Prize from the Midwest Victorian Studies Association; for grants from the UC Centers for German and Russian Studies and European and Russian Studies, respectively; and for a Pauley Fellowship and other support from the History Department at UCLA.

Many librarians, archivists, and curators helped in the research for this book. Deep thanks go to Jane Farrington, Martin Ellis, Brendan Flynn, Zelina Garland, Victoria Emmanuel, and Tom Heaven at the Birmingham Museum and Art Gallery; to the staff at the Birmingham Central Library; to Christine Penney at the University of Birmingham Special Collections; to Melva Croal, Andrea Martin, Vincent Kelly, Sarah Skinner, and Tracey Walker at the Manchester City Art Gallery; to the staff at the Manchester Central Library Local Studies, Archives, and Art Library, especially David Taylor, Judith Baldry, Sarah Sherratt, Katherine Taylor, and David Govier; to Joseph Sharples and Nathan Pendlebury at the Walker Art Gallery; to Mark Pomeroy at the Royal Academy Archives; to the staff at the Tate Archives and Amelia Morgan at Tate Images; to Carmen Pérez Gutiérrez at the Museo Nacional del Prado and to Juan Luis Sanchez for his assistance; and to the staffs of the Liverpool Central Reference Library, the National Art Library, the British Library, the Colindale Newspaper

Archive, the Huntington Library, and the Interlibrary Loan offices at UCLA's Young Research Library and at LMU's William Hannon Library.

Many scholars have been very helpful at all stages of this project. In Britain I was helped in particular by Gordon Fyfe, Kate Hill, Rohan McWilliam, Edward Morris, Susan Pearce, Giles Waterfield, James Moore, and Dungo Chun. At UCLA, I am grateful to participants in the European History and Culture Colloquium, where I presented my first drafts; my particular thanks go to Professors Lynn Hunt, Margaret Jacob, Muriel McClendon, Peter Reill, Geoffrey Symcox, Teo Ruiz, Russell Jacoby, and Gabi Piterberg, and to Drs. Gabriel Wolfenstein, Eric Johnson, John Mangum, Andrea Mansker, Ben Marschke, Kelly Maynard, Britta McEwen, Peter Park, Courtenay Raia, Patricia Tilburg, and Claudia Verhoeven. Additional scholars who advised and helped to shape the project at the earliest stages, and deserve great thanks, include Sylvia Lavin, Robert Wohl, Anthony Vidler, David Sabean, and Dianne Sachko Macleod. Since I joined the faculty at LMU, the British History Reading Group in Los Angeles has been a welcoming and generous source of professional support, and special thanks go to Erika Rappaport, Lisa Cody, and Philippa Levine for mentoring and hospitality. Vanessa Schwartz, Peter Stansky, Jordanna Bailkin, and Lara Kriegel gave me sound advice and thoughtful comments along the way, for which I am very grateful. My students, teaching assistants, and student researchers at LMU have performed multiple, much-appreciated tasks and pushed me to consider the big picture. My LMU colleagues have attended presentations and provided many ideas, hallway listening sessions, and (best of all) friendship. I also thank the many conference attendees who allowed me to test-run much of this material over the years. Finally, I am profoundly obliged to three stellar champions, whom it is difficult to thank sufficiently: Debora Silverman's work has been a constant inspiration, and I deeply appreciate her support of my career generally and of this project specifically. Tim Barringer has become an invaluable source for thinking about art history and history, and I have felt extremely lucky to have his assistance, advice, and encouragement. Tom Laqueur has been an unbelievably buoyant and attentive ally, reading drafts and book proposals and galvanizing me into finishing the manuscript (particularly when he heard I was pregnant *again*).

My friends in Britain have been more valuable than perhaps they realize in supporting my research and writing. They have of course deepened my understanding of British culture, but they have also given me emotional sustenance, many nights of lodging, and countless meals. Thanks to Claire and Mark Johnston,

Helen and Andrew Scott, Stephen Metcalfe and Mark Ford, Dominic Wilson, Paul and Anna Spyropoulos, Rachel Board, Andrew and Emma Watson, Matt and Wendy Turner, Daniel Castle, Zelina Garland, and David Rowan (who supplied last-minute photographs of Birmingham institutions). I cannot thank my English family enough: Charonne and Jeremy Boulton, Hannah Boulton, Richard and Ava Rose Jones, and Marje Aston.

Norris Pope, Sarah Crane Newman, and Carolyn Brown at Stanford have been delightful to work with, and copyeditor Jessie Dolch performed a wondrous job of polishing this text that I have been poring over for so long. I am especially grateful to the two anonymous readers of the manuscript, whose comments enabled me to see how, finally, I could finish it to my own satisfaction. Of course, as ever, any errors or omissions remain my own.

I dedicate this book to my American and English families, who have quite simply made this long project possible, and who have helped me to think about the public role of culture and the arts. Charonne and Jeremy Boulton have provided much good humor, marvelous hospitality, and outstanding generosity. My mother, father, and brother have commented on countless drafts and maintained a remarkable and consistent enthusiasm. (Now that I am myself a mother, it is a bit staggering to realize how much I owe my parents; how can I ever thank them enough?) Finally, my husband, Luke, deserves (like all faculty spouses) an honorary degree and at least one really nice night out. He saw me through graduate school and tenure, and his coparenting has allowed me to revel in my two rambunctious and wonderful boys, Felix and Leo, while still engaging in historical scholarship. I am so grateful to these three for giving me the time to work, and for always insisting that I find time to play.

TRANSFORMATIVE BEAUTY

INTRODUCTION

Recovering Victorian Ideas
About Art, Beauty, and Society

In 1885, James McNeill Whistler gave a brilliant and caustic speech attacking the then-pervasive habit of understanding art as a means to an end: "the people have acquired the habit of looking, as who should say, not *at* a picture, but *through* it, at some human fact, that shall, or shall not, from a social point of view, better their mental, or moral state."[1] Indeed, late-nineteenth-century civic reformers used this idea of art as the experience of its subject matter to support art galleries as part of a profound reimagining of their industrial cities. Alongside libraries, schools, town halls, sanitation works, drainage systems, food inspection, and the panoply of state-sponsored reactions to industrialization, municipal art museums and galleries of contemporary art became a fixture of city life. Inspired by social critics such as John Ruskin, who connected aesthetics and ethics, middle-class civic leaders worked to rectify the moral and physical ugliness of industrial capitalism through access to art. As Whistler complained, "Beauty is confounded with Virtue, and, before a work of Art, it is asked, 'What good shall it do?'"[2]

A generation later, this understanding of a purposive social role for art persisted, predicated on looking "through" paintings: for example, in 1911, Professor Michael Sadler gave a lecture to the Royal Manchester Institution, which in 1883 had given its building and collection to the city to become the Manchester City Art Gallery. Sadler was an important art collector and professor of education at the University of Manchester; in various posts from Oxford to Calcutta, he developed an internationally influential, sociological approach to education.[3] In this talk, "Pictures in a Great City," he explored the relationships between urban space, nature, art, and beauty, with particular reference to the city art museum in Manchester. Sadler understood the art collection in terms of its urban location: "Those who live in Manchester have their sense sharpened for the beauty and refreshment of unspoiled landscape. We are hungry for it. Through separation from it, we understand what it means to us. And the pictures in the gallery reveal its delights and prepare us for a deeper delight in it."[4] For Sadler, the city was defined by separation from the beauty of nature, and while some could—

and did—go to the countryside themselves, others had access to such beauty only through art. Indeed, exposure to art could "prepare" viewers to understand nature more profoundly.

Whistler and Sadler, cosmopolitan modern artist and imperial educator, separated by a generation, present in a nutshell the argument of the Victorian museum movement: art is not important for itself, but for the experience it provides, made possible by viewing paintings as windows; further, this encounter is directly related to the daily deprivations of the modern industrial city and something called "nature," its imagined opposite. *Transformative Beauty* tells the story of this idea and how citizens turned it into city art museums—bricks and mortar, pictures on walls, and visitors to galleries—in Birmingham, Liverpool, and Manchester. In doing so, this book explores the complex relationship between a period's governing aesthetics and its public use of art. In tracing the reformers' attempts to beautify their cities, we come up against fundamental questions about culture, money, and power: who should pay for art? what is it for? how can society generate the wealth that pays for it without also causing suffering and poverty? are art museums equally open to all, regardless of education level?

In his 1885 speech, Whistler blamed many of the errors of his time period's ideas about art on an unnamed critic, offering a searing portrait of his old rival Ruskin: "Sage of the Universities—learned in many matters, and of much experience in all, save his subject. Exhorting—denouncing—directing. Filled with wrath and earnestness. Bringing powers of persuasion, and polish of language, to prove nothing. Torn with much teaching—having naught to impart. Impressive—important—shallow. Defiant—distressed—desperate. . . . Gentle priest of the Philistines."[5] Like Whistler (although not sharing his disdain), I have observed Ruskin's importance to the people who helped make art public in the city museums of Birmingham, Liverpool, and Manchester. Certainly, multiple voices connected art and morality in the late nineteenth century, deriving ideas from such figures as A. W. N. Pugin, Thomas Carlyle, William Morris, Matthew Arnold, Prince Albert, George Eliot, and Ruskin himself, to name just a few.[6] What is remarkable, however, is the extent to which reformers who wanted to make art public engaged with Ruskin's work, and often with Ruskin personally, even when he himself disagreed with their attempts to put his ideas into practice. Indeed, during the 1870s, largely through his publication *Fors Clavigera*, Ruskin emphasized that the entire system of Liberalism, free markets, and industrial capitalism, divided as it was into separate and unequal social classes, worked against his understanding of God and morality.[7] He tried to make his well-intentioned followers, correspondents, and students see the suffering around them and exhorted them to action: "Children should have enough to eat, and their skins should be washed clean. It is not *I* who say that. Every mother's heart under the sun says that, if she has one."[8] To put his ideas into practice, Ruskin began or participated in several projects, such as teaching at the Working Men's College in London, building roads with his Oxford undergraduates, and establishing the Guild of St. George. All of these combined art, education, and manual labor in varying degrees, enacting his particular criticisms of industrial society and his understanding of the close relationships among meaningful work, beauty, and morality.[9]

Alongside these efforts, however, most of the many men and women inspired by Ruskin worked during this same period to do what they could to bring art, beauty, and nature to their own cities and towns and to address social problems without wholesale revolution or radical economic restructuring to an imagined preindustrial ideal. As we will see in Chapter 1, reformers in all three cities explored in this book engaged with Ruskin personally on some level, and all received similar exhortations to take on more radical social change. Even though Ruskin criticized their projects, however, his followers were deeply committed to translating his writings into action; indeed, Ruskin inspired a worldwide audience, as for example described in Gandhi's autobiography, the Mahatma being one of the few people who converted Ruskin's ideas into radical social experimentation.[10] Part of the larger, international Arts and Crafts movement, such reformers founded Ruskin Societies that presented lectures, produced pamphlets, and organized meetings; created paintings that attempted to achieve "truth to nature"; gave sermons to inspire individual and civic reform; began new communal housing and work ventures to alleviate poverty; designed buildings, furniture, and everyday objects with a new craft aesthetic and philosophy; and founded museums and wrote exhibition catalogues to redeem industrial capitalism using methods inspired by Ruskin's art and social criticism.[11] Collectively, these enthusiasts created a vision of art and meaningful labor as experiences necessary for counteracting the debilitating and dehumanizing effects of industrial capitalism in general, and the ugliness of modern cities in particular. Thus, as Whistler perceived, the art museums in these industrial cities were not intended to teach viewers about art itself, either in terms of established modes of connoisseurship or as showcases for the history of art—in contrast, for example, to the National Gallery at the time, or to nearly all art museums today.

However, as *Transformative Beauty* also shows, these goals of bringing a wider public to beauty and morality through art were complicated by multiple actors striving to use art in different ways: art could represent philanthropy or civic pride, and museums could be important venues for the display of middle-class (including lower-middle-class) cultural aspirations. Close research into the histories of these art museums shows them as sites of vibrant cultural debate—over the role of government (should taxes support public art?), over the meaning and role of art (is it a necessity or a luxury?), and over what kinds of art, what kinds of audience, and what kinds of interpretation should go into public institutions. Debates led to extreme positions on both sides, as those in favor of art as part of the betterment of society claimed powers for it akin to religious awakening, and those against public art mocked these claims in favor of traditional religion, self-help, or different kinds of public intervention. These institutions, therefore, although largely created from middle-class initiative, did not form a unified cultural imposition. Rather, public art remained a fraught and hotly contested issue, as interested parties sparred over the museums' founding, financial support, institutional structure, collecting policies, educational programs, and opening hours.

Likewise, the art itself brought all of the tensions and debates of late Victorian culture into the sanctuary of the museums. Nineteenth-century British art, eclipsed for several generations by the criticism and aesthetics of modernism, has recently reemerged as worthy of sustained scholarly investigation and interpretation.[12] Far from being simplistic escapism into rural idylls or nostalgic historicism, the paintings in these museums, and the criticism they generated, raised fundamental concerns of the Victorian age, including the relationship between the material and the spiritual, the meaning of labor and wealth, the mystery of faith and the gnawing cancer of doubt, and the historical significance of the Industrial Revolution and the British empire. By the end of the nineteenth century, modernists such as Whistler had thrown out the basic premise that painting was primarily a medium through which to engage with subject matter. Despite this sea change in aesthetic standards, however, the idea that art can be a force for moral regeneration, and the institutions this idea inspired, have continued to shape our own conceptions of beauty, the urban experience, and the public role of art.

I find two distinct foundational assumptions behind the new libraries, parks, and museums supported and run by local governments. The first was the cult of domesticity, or ideology of "separate spheres," that celebrated the home as a benign, healing sanctuary from industrial capitalism. This topic has of course received a great deal of attention in recent years, particularly from historians of gender and the family. Writers have emphasized that the cult of domesticity arose in reaction to the physical and moral conditions of industrial labor.[13] New forms of public space such as museums, libraries, and parks took on the qualities associated with the domestic sphere: separate from industrial capitalism and offering refuge, beauty, and morality.[14] For instance, longtime Birmingham Museum and Art Gallery curator Whitworth Wallis explained that his museum hoped to create a space outside of everyday experience: "Ruskin says that the word museum means 'Belonging to the muses,' and that all museums ought to be places of noble instruction, where, free from the distractions of the outside world, one can devote a portion of secluded and reverent life to the attainment of divine wisdom, which the Greeks supposed to be the gift of Apollo or of the sun, but which the Christian knows to be the gift of Christ."[15] Like a civic version of the ideal Victorian home—a place of moral refuge and repose, outside the hurly-burly of the marketplace—city art museums would provide a domesticated public space for beauty. Art museums could thus bring middle-class ideals to the center of industrial cities, part of the wider response to industrial capitalist society and its perceived ugliness. The cover image of this book, an illustrated map of Birmingham by H. W. Brewer from 1886, highlights this idea, showing the new cultural center architecturally distinguished from the smokestacks that stretch to the horizon.

A second idea behind the museum movement, as the Sadler lecture showed, was that the beauty of nature (and nature through art) was a necessary counterpart to cities, particularly industrial cities. This idea developed out of three related aspects of Victorian society and culture: first, the rapidity of urbanization, and the lucid memory, preserved in literature and art, of village life and country traditions; second, the resulting, often nostalgic, articulation of clear dichotomies in society and culture between the country and the city, even if these differences ignored continuities of exploitation; and third, the understanding that art acted as a window that could provide an experience of beauty within the ugliness of the city.[16] As we will see, advocates linked the set of ideas associated with "home" and those connected to "nature," both signifying opposition to industrial, commercial cities, in order to bolster their arguments for public art museums.

The prominence of art museums in late-nineteenth-century (and contemporary) cities has made them, as Jesús Pedro Lorente phrased it and titled his 1998 book, "cathedrals of urban modernity." However, much of the historiography has understood Victorian museums as hodge-podge collections of contemporary British art, the result of more or less clumsy middle-class attempts at "social control" combined with civic or personal boosterism.[17] In contrast, detailed archival research shows the complex beliefs behind these new urban institutions, which embodied the possibilities for local government action and city leaders' attempts to contain the chaotic forces of industrialization. In other words, when we examine the Victorian ideas and aesthetics behind the museums, we uncover as a major impulse both a serious dissatisfaction with industrial society and a reasonable hope for mitigating its worst effects. Viewed in this light, the art collections and educational policies of these museums make sense because they were amassed and organized not in terms of art history or art education, but to provide art as experience. Whether understood as pursuing fine craft and self-expression or as presenting through art the beauty of nature and God's creation, these art museums came out of romantic and natural theological conceptions about the universal language of, and need for, beauty, most particularly in the context of industrial cities. In supporting such institutions, reformers echoed the dominant cultural trope about the possibilities for the home as refuge. When museums developed as city-run institutions, they enshrined a new type of public, urban space, a domesticated ideal supported by an increasingly powerful government that thereby took on new responsibilities for its citizens. Their educational, opening, and collection policies were certainly ad hoc and often contradictory, but they were usually premised on these fundamental assumptions and were not simply accidental.

Ultimately, in the successes and failures of these Victorian museums, their histories reveal a tragic fact of the modern age: thriving cultural institutions such as city art museums arose out of the same wealth that caused or profited from, at least in part, the very inequalities they were meant to alleviate. We still cannot solve this basic conundrum. On the one hand, industrial capitalism and its attendant forms of imperialism and globalization create vibrant cities, people, and cultural institutions, such as public museums. On the other, the same forces give rise to tremendous suffering, poverty, and conflict, ills that no art collection, regardless of size or quality, can hope to abolish. In his fantasy *News from Nowhere*, William Morris imagined a utopia of joyful labor where all workers were artisans and all artisans were artists, thus actually ending "art" in the European tradition: "Many of the things which used to be produced—slave-wares for the poor and mere wealth-wasting wares for the rich—ceased to be made. That remedy was, in short, the production of what used to be called art, but which has no name amongst us now, because it has become a necessary part of the labour of every man who produces."[18] Morris lectured to Birmingham reformers and helped choose acquisitions for Manchester's city art museum; like Ruskin, however, his mighty imagination sought some larger, more beautiful, more complete—and perhaps, therefore, impossible—solution to the iniquities of the machine age.

THE GRECIAN URN VERSUS RUSKIN'S WINDOW: BEAUTY AND TRUTH

How did art become a tool for ameliorating industrial cities? To understand this, we have to go back to an earlier generation's concept of art. In 1819, both the future Queen Victoria and future art critic John Ruskin were born—both would live until 1901 and, in their own ways, define the age. That same year, John Keats wrote his five "great odes," including probably the most famous, "Ode on a Grecian Urn." This ode, using ideas derived from Joshua Reynolds, the first president of the Royal Academy and most influential British eighteenth-century painter and art theorist, contained what became a near-ubiquitous statement of the equation of beauty and truth. This poetic proclamation would echo throughout the nineteenth century and become the standard by which and against which artists, art critics, and the art-buying public would try to judge artworks and their social role.

Keats considers the urn as an example of perfect artistic expression, its figures preserving unblemished the ideal forms of youth, love, and beauty:

Bold Lover, never, never canst thou kiss,
Though winning near the goal—yet, do not grieve;
She cannot fade, though thou hast not thy bliss,
For ever wilt thou love, and she be fair![19]

Most famously, the poem imagines that the urn's ultimate statement to humanity is Reynolds's equation of beauty and truth:

When old age shall this generation waste,
Thou shalt remain, in midst of other woe
Than ours, a friend to man, to whom thou say'st,
"Beauty is truth, truth beauty,"—that is all
Ye know on earth, and all ye need to know.[20]

Reynolds had equated beauty and truth in his "Discourse VII" (1776), which made an argument (similar to that previously advanced by John Locke and Locke's pupil the Earl of Shaftesbury) for the "uniformity of sentiments among mankind," which results in "the reality of a standard in taste, as well as in corporeal beauty." He concluded that beauty and truth are "formed on the uniform, eternal, and immutable laws of nature, and . . . of necessity can be but one."[21] Keats's poem, then, participated in an understanding of art as essentially about the uncovering of universal truths through the search for ideal beauty, both being based on unchanging natural law. While the artist alone could reveal the essential harmonies of nature, all of humankind could recognize them. However, fine art still seemed to demand some education or culture; could one exhibit a classical nude, however beautiful, to all classes?[22]

In the middle decades of the nineteenth century, a complex combination of artistic movements, art criticism, and the rise of new art buyers challenged this established understanding of art and paved the way for the idea of art as an experience that would counteract the ills of urban, industrial capitalism. This revolution would find beauty in the particular rather than the general, and in the eager use of nature by early Renaissance artists, rather than in the perfection of Raphael that had been conventionalized in the academies. In the works by what became the Pre-Raphaelite Brotherhood, and in the writings of Ruskin—their most famous defender—beauty could be achieved only by absolute truth to nature, a fidelity that ignored received conventions of color, composition, or style; instead, these artists sought to portray universally recognizable truths through a meticulous realism and attention to (symbolic) detail. The Pre-Raphaelites reviled "Sir Sloshua," targeting the abstract idealizing and muted palette of Reynolds's portraits, and they avoided the generalities and long gaze of the romantic landscape artist. Instead, they developed an intense focus on foreground detail, used vivid color from painting outdoors, adopted explicitly moralizing and narrative subjects, and emphasized medieval rather than classical models of beauty. This revolution in the relationship between beauty and truth, and a concomitant change in the purpose and understanding of art—as a mimetic representation of imperfect nature, rather than the expression of beautiful, ideal forms—made art appear to many viewers and collectors both moral and appropriate for all classes, and hence part of a new approach to addressing social and economic disparity.

In defending and explaining this new approach to art, Ruskin combined the romantic idea of the artist as revealing the "invisible world" with an evangelical language that no doubt comforted his many middle-class readers.[23] Yet Ruskin's oeuvre was enormous, contradictory, and dense, and his ideas changed throughout his lifetime. His middle-class upbringing combined strict evangelical doctrine, family trips in Europe, and art collecting, and from an early age he began developing a new mode of visual interpretation that would justify visual pleasure in terms of religious experience and, eventually, social relations.[24] His five-volume work *Modern Painters* (1843–1860) brought a new urgency to art criticism, as he combined the campaigning zeal of A. W. N. Pugin and Thomas Carlyle with his own religiously inflected aesthetics.[25] From the first book of *Modern Painters*, what we might call Ruskin's new "visual evangelism" emphasized the continuity of beauty and morality; he argued that the joy derived from beauty was based not on sensuality, but on the perception of the divine.[26]

Ruskin put forward an influential interpretation of paintings in the chapter "Of the Use of Pictures" in the third volume of *Modern Painters* (1856). Here, he tried to explain his ideas about beauty and "truth to nature," which some readers had apparently found somewhat confusing. If, he wrote,

it were offered to me to have, instead of [works of art], so many windows, out of which I should see, first, the real chain of the Alps from the Superga; then the real block of gneiss, and Aiguilles Rouges; then the real towers of Fribourg, and pine forest; the real Isola Bella; and, finally, the true Mary and Elizabeth; and beneath them, the actual old monk at work in his cell,—I would very unhesitatingly change my five pictures for the five windows; and so, I apprehend, would most people, not, it seems to me, unwisely.[27]

Ruskin thus encouraged his readers to see a key source of art's greatness as its subject, even to the point of preferring the subject over the painting, and to understand the painting not in terms of representation or surface, but in terms of its engagement with subject matter. Throughout his writings, he led his readers to judge art by asking themselves whether paintings represented nature faithfully, not by convention or preconceived ideas of beauty. Indeed, at its best, for Ruskin, art could unite the divine in God's creation, the creative process, and the viewer. He argued that it was the role of the artist to act as an "*eye*-witness" whose sight testified to the glory of nature as God's creation: "Nothing must come between Nature and the artist's sight; nothing between God and the artist's soul."[28] Thus art, because of these properties, became a key index of social justice; Ruskin's famous essay "The Nature of Gothic" measured beauty not only in terms of aesthetics, but also in terms of morality, judged again through connections to the real world, that is, to conditions of production.[29]

Using these ideas, reformers worked to bring art and the beauty of nature to the public, primarily through museums but also through country walks, settle-

ment programs, local exhibitions and world fairs, publications, and design reform. For example, in 1895 Manchester reformer T. C. Horsfall argued that the
city art museum there could provide "the inhabitants of the poorer parts of the
town knowledge of the beauty and wonderfulness of the world and of the nobler
works of Man."[30] By the end of the century, when Horsfall was writing (here,
advocating the Sunday opening of the Manchester City Art Gallery), this had
become an established trope.[31] Indeed, art had been incorporated as part of the
governing structure of most British towns in the form of city museums, often
using a version of this argument that the visual arts were universally accessible
and could offer a restorative experience of beauty.

The movement to bring art to the people thus came out of a nineteenth-
century British aesthetic ideology distinct from both what preceded and what
followed. Born of romanticism, natural theology, the reification of "nature," and
changes in artistic practice and art criticism, the new approach allowed, even
encouraged, artists, critics, and audiences to participate in defining the social
role of art and dominant modes of representation.[32] In other words, nineteenth-
century British art itself helped make it possible for reformers to think that it
would be beneficial to make art accessible to the masses. Trying to understand
the relationship between art, ideas, and the movement to make art public allows
us to take seriously the profound dissatisfaction with their cities that spurred
many museum advocates to action. This book is thus part of the larger scholarship that has recently tried to understand nineteenth-century art and art institutions not simply as instruments of social control, but as emerging out of complex
negotiations among a disunited middle class that deployed art for multiple (and
often contradictory) purposes.[33] As Dianne Sachko Macleod has convincingly
argued in *Art and the Victorian Middle Class* (1996), the broad middle classes,
active as new art patrons and civic leaders in late-nineteenth-century British
towns, helped to create an eclectic art that reflected their values. But they did
not agree on how the resulting works should be used.

A substantial body of scholarship has emphasized that middle-class patrons'
entry into the art market in the 1830s and 1840s had several significant conse-
quences, creating what Robert Hewison has called a new "visual economy."[34] The
new class of collectors bought contemporary British art and shunned old masters—limited in number and hence out of the price range of most buyers—not
least to differentiate themselves from aristocratic connoisseurs.[35] As artists lost
their traditional sources of patronage, an exhibition system developed in London

and the great regional cities to connect artists to their new, anonymous public.[36] Capitalizing on increasing public interest, the press reported on art exhibitions, guided the new buyers in aesthetic decisions, and explained the merits of the rapidly multiplying numbers of artists.[37] The explosion of museum-building in the last half of the nineteenth century arose out of, and in turn fuelled, a new enthusiasm for contemporary British art; the most important regional art museums, such as those in Manchester and Liverpool, held annual exhibitions of new works for sale to raise revenue and often bought from these exhibitions (see Chapter 1). The Royal Academy, commercial galleries, and regional art museums, in concert with the national press, all participated in the diffusion and popularization of contemporary British art and the discussion of new ideas about art's social role.

Over the course of the nineteenth century, these interconnected developments had a profound impact on the use and prominence of art in British society. Many individual choices by single collectors gradually created a new art market and a new visual language. The new practice of professional art criticism was not only a sign of art entering mainstream culture, but also a continuing catalyst, as art critics helped to justify and popularize art in new ways. In this context, Ruskin's enormous influence becomes more understandable. In the relationship between Ruskin and the Pre-Raphaelites, art criticism, practice, and patronage combined to redefine categories of traditional aesthetics. Artists, art critics, and collectors continued to explore the relationship between beauty and truth, and museum advocates strove to create public spaces for both.

VICTORIAN MUSEUMS IN CONTEXT

What economic and social aspects of late-nineteenth-century society spurred museum proponents to advocate art as a restorative experience? How was the museum movement part of the larger story of reactions to the new realities of economic depression, urbanization, democratization, imperialism, and mass production of the late nineteenth century? For many observers, it was obvious that there was something wrong with an economic system that created not only air blackened with soot and farmland grown into slums, but terrible suffering and poverty, a pervasive erosion of established social relations, and an empty materialism and consumerism. This increased markedly after the Great Depression of the early 1870s, as the economic slump spurred on an active press and increasingly proactive local governments to describe the depth of suffering and poverty across Britain.[38] At the same time, British fears of competition from the United States and Germany (like American anxiety about China and India today) led to initiatives to improve industrial design, while fears of revolution and degeneration prompted action to ameliorate workers' living conditions and their opportunities for education and "improvement." By the end of the century, imperialist and nationalist ideologies suffused discussions of culture and society, as Victorians and Edwardians increasingly saw themselves in a larger international and even racial competition for survival. The city art museums in Liverpool, Manchester, and Birmingham began to develop in the last third of the nineteenth century, a period of intense social, cultural, and economic pressure. The museums opened in purpose-built, permanent structures within eight years of each other: the Walker Art Gallery in Liverpool in 1877, the Manchester City Art Gallery in 1883, and the Birmingham Museum and Art Gallery in 1885.

It is a particular aspect of this period that reformers looked to art as one of the key methods that were slowly and haphazardly devised to deal with the problems of the emergent modern, secular, industrial age. The municipal art museums embodied a new version of the Liberal ideal, in which individuals could—through self-education, hard work, and discipline—participate in ever-increasing numbers in the democratic process. They harnessed together private and public wealth. Built with donations of money and objects, administered by elected councilors, and maintained through public funds, the museums helped to strengthen and extend the idea of local government. Cities developed art galleries alongside a number of other, related beautification and educational projects, such as libraries, parks, and museums of natural history and anthropology (these last two were often combined, as during this period curators understood artifacts of many other cultures through racist categories). Often the same active citizens advocated for all of these improvements, and the resulting institutions were frequently combined administratively—for example, Liverpool's Free Libraries, Museum, and Arts Committee.[39] Yet it is notable that unlike free public libraries, the art museum projects in these cities were not successful in the immediate wake of the roaring sensation of the Great Exhibition of 1851 and the boom years that followed. Instead, they came out of a distinctly more anxious period.

The last quarter of the nineteenth century witnessed a raft of technological marvels—the telephone, the cinema, the bicycle, the telegraph—that compounded, in the age of the railroad and steamboat, an ever-increasing pace and sense of displaced traditions.[40] Despite the economic depression of the 1870s, which hit agricultural sectors especially hard, new opportunities proliferated, particularly for the broad middle and even working classes; in fact, falling prices helped urban workers, who increasingly participated in new leisure cultures, including sport, music halls, and workingmen's clubs.[41] Urbanization continued to depopulate the countryside, mass production and a proliferating mass press offered an unprecedented consumption of goods and images, department stores and large corporations began their steady domination of the economy, and nations entered an intense competition for world markets and resources.[42] Museums thus operated in an increasingly saturated visual culture and as one option among many for middle- and working-class leisure and consumption.[43]

Out of all of these various social and economic transformations, the political economy of the last decades of the nineteenth century was marked by a constant search for elusive consensus and stability. Museums, and the art they contained, offered important venues for attempting such resolution, in the process prompting multiple debates and struggles between interested parties. Successive Conservative and Liberal governments managed to pass significant reform legislation that expanded the electorate, created a mandatory national system of primary education, and standardized the political process.[44] These moves toward the democratization of politics and culture changed the political landscape less through their direct effects—workers voted Conservative more often than not—than through the new political culture of partisan competition and the threat of new political groupings that might claim workers' allegiance as legitimate parties, as the socialist movement eventually generated the Labour Party. During the years before World War I, the women's suffrage movement, massive strikes and demonstrations, acts of violence against people and property, and urban poverty threatened the balance that maintained Britain's class- and gender-divided society. These developments also increased the pressure to bring the working and lower middle classes into a common culture with dominant middle-class values, a goal that gave further impetus to the movements to establish domesticated public spaces such as libraries, museums, and parks.

Museum advocates achieved success in making public art a key issue of debate in a particular moment of great change in the constitution of local governments, which faced the same tensions between forces of traditional authority and increasing democracy.[45] Indeed, local governments themselves had been subject to significant reform, as over the course of the nineteenth century, older institutions of local administration had proved inadequate to deal with the problems of modern industrial cities or the needs of mass populations.[46] Through a series of parliamentary acts from 1835 to 1894, feudal privileges and positions in local government haphazardly gave way to elected bodies of officials and central oversight boards, as, piece by piece, local government in Britain gained new powers, responsibilities, and administrative structures. The beginning of this new role for local government was the 1835 Municipal Corporations Act, part of the same broad transformation of the practice and administration of British governance initiated with the Reform Act of 1832 (which began the long process of widening the franchise and election reform) and the New Poor Law Act of 1834 (which created a new administration for poor relief, a system separate from and parallel to local governments). The 1835 act established town councils as the unit of local governance and granted the right to vote to all ratepayers (taxpayers) who had lived in the city for three years.

Parliament gradually added both permissive and mandatory legislation, creating a body of law that reflected the concern of the time to strike a balance between traditional elites and elected authorities, and between central and local administration. This process left many important aspects of governance in the hands of the town councils and allowed for a wide range of engagement and activity, as different cities created different styles of municipal government. Over the course of the century, local governments adapted and expanded to tackle many problems that became more acute as cities grew, such as sanitation, health, education, housing, care for the poor, transportation, lighting, policing, and recreation. In the case of public museums and libraries, Parliament passed the Museums Acts of 1845, 1850, and 1855, which allowed local governments to assess rates (property taxes) to maintain public libraries and museums.[47] Parliament tried to standardize the provision of basic services at the local level, and to create a simplified administrative structure, through legislation passed between the late 1860s and the middle of the 1890s. At the same time, regional cities struggled during this period to cope with their new responsibilities.

The continuing pace of urbanization in the wake of the economic crisis of the 1870s, new political movements, and the mass press combined not only to make poverty more visible than ever to citizens and civic leaders, but also to convince many contemporary observers of the unhealthy influence of the cities themselves.[48] The glaring distance between rich and poor had long been studied and publicized in the industrial cities, forming a core part of earlier reform efforts from the 1840s on. From the novels of Elizabeth Gaskell and Benjamin Disraeli to the inquiries of Owen Chadwick and Frederick Engels, fiction, official studies, and exposés did much to create the image of the (especially northern) industrial city as one of masters and men, of great wealth and abject poverty. The awareness that London harbored comparable inequality thus came relatively late, but the capital's discovery of the horror of the slums of the East End spurred a national debate on the need for major social reform and the best means of accomplishing it.

New cultural amenities such as art museums, funded by local government and the donations of wealthy industrialists, represented a novel approach to government intervention in British society and a new vision of social reform— social change through aesthetic experience.[49] Because of the gradual move to state-run institutions, the story of the erection and funding of museums in nineteenth-century Britain is part of the larger story of the haphazard and of-ten-faltering development of government intervention after the mid-century triumph of laissez-faire. Museums were not simply passive receivers or products of new ideas about culture and governmentality, but were active agents of this transformation. They were part of a concurrent movement that rebuilt urban centers with libraries, concert halls, and parks for new and expanded publics, a creative solution using ideals of domesticity and the morality of art to create domesticated public spaces dependent on, but positioned in deliberate contrast with, the wider capitalist economy.

TRANSFORMATIVE BEAUTY

In this book I argue that the art museums of Liverpool, Manchester, and Birming-ham were part of a broad reaction to industrial, capitalist society. Research into the history and origins of Victorian museums gives us a glimpse of a culture deeply self-conscious about the very leisure time, wealth, and material abundance that allowed their production.[50] Civic art museums were one of many new institutions that proliferated during the second half of the nineteenth century because they helped Victorian society to negotiate and even reconcile the apparent extremes of evangelical religion and the new productivity of the industrial economy, and, in doing so, to imagine a new relationship with material culture. They were part of the great transformation by which the wide middle class deeply affected by evangelical Christianity came to think, as Deborah Cohen has recently put it, of "morality and materialism . . . as mutually reinforcing propositions."[51] Public museums emerged as material prosperity grew, taking particular objects out of the market—or into a very special part of the marketplace—for a variety of purposes.[52] By doing so, Victorians evinced a great belief in the didactic and morally transformative potential of objects, whether art or natural specimens, even as mass production was revolutionizing labor relations, consumption patterns, the domestic interior, the urban environment, and traditional practices of all kinds. Ultimately, museums both celebrated the new dogma of progress and hoped to mitigate the worst effects of urbanization, industrialization, and capitalism.[53]

When "the museum" is understood as a conceptual category, it is tempting to see it as a metaphor for modern society as a whole.[54] It is easy to see the museums around us (whether of art, history, natural history, or other, more idiosyncratic types of collections) as powerful symbols and generators of Western culture since the Enlightenment. After all, they—like the Enlightenment project in general—make objects of study visible, categorize them, and submit them to rational inquiry. In this light, scholars have understood both nineteenth-century European imperial kleptomania and historicism (artistic, architectural, or philosophical) as being "museal," "the museum" becoming both product and producer of a larger cultural drive.[55] Yet museums did not always present their collections in a "rational" or disciplined way; these late-nineteenth-century city art museums had in fact a rationale very different from that of the scientific or "disciplined" study of art history. *Transformative Beauty* thus contributes to recent work that has shown Victorian museums to be far less universalizing or powerful than earlier, abstract studies might have suggested.[56] The museum movement in Britain and its empire was widespread, but—in contrast to continental cultural provision—was locally driven, without any central administration.[57] Similarly, this book agrees with other recent scholarship in finding that museums had no single cause, method, public, or constituency.[58]

To reinterpret museums in this way, *Transformative Beauty*, like other recent works, considers museums in their specific contexts, with sensitivity to the complex relationships between culture, class, and agency. Its five chapters investigate the city art museums in Birmingham, Liverpool, and Manchester: their founding (Chapter 1), opening policies (Chapter 2), collecting practices (Chapter 3), art and educational materials (Chapter 4), and subsequent embrace of the value of art for art's sake (Chapter 5). I focus on these cities because contemporaries most frequently mentioned these city art museums, comparing them with each other and with museums in London. This is not unexpected; after all, in addition to Dublin and Glasgow, these were the major British cities outside of the metropolis, and they might be expected to have the biggest and most important cultural institutions. At the same time, these cities embodied the Industrial Revolution and all of the cataclysmic social, economic, political, and cultural transformations it wrought. There are no scholarly published histories of the Birmingham Museum and Art Gallery, the Manchester City Art Gallery, or the Walker Art Gallery in Liverpool, so this project thus rectifies serious lacunae in both museum studies and British cultural history.[59] Although I present evidence that each urban context was unique, I also show a unified museum movement that operated through the art, ideas, and social networks of the late nineteenth century, a profound response to industrial society in general, and industrial cities in particular.

Chapter 1 follows the men who tried to put Ruskin's ideas into practice—even though he exhorted them to more radical reform—to bring art to these industrial cities: architects making illuminated, calligraphic Ruskin bibliographies; city councilors lecturing on beauty; preachers inspiring city councilors to think of themselves as municipal Medicis. Chapter 2 addresses the question of whether art could draw people out of the pub, and—since they were generally not going to church or chapel—whether the working classes needed a government-supported alternative to their own homes for rest and recreation. Chapter 3 looks at the contested development of the museums' art collections, showing that all three museums collected art with the understanding that they were providing essential experiences rather than representative historical or educational collections. Chapter 4 considers how the three museums continued the idea of art as providing a means of engaging with subject, story, and morality through public lectures and through published catalogues and guidebooks, and examines the relationship between these readings of art and the works themselves. Finally, Chapter 5 explores how new ideas in the early twentieth century gradually transformed the museums, as a new generation of directors and city councils reconceived of the collections as primarily existing to educate citizens about art rather than to provide an antidote to industrial ugliness. Modernist art and art criticism, with their rejection of beauty, truth, and morality as artistic measures, would ultimately revolutionize the public role of civic art museums.

Although modernism brought in its wake radical changes in art and ideas about its purpose, the idea of art as experience, and of beauty as social transformation, created lasting institutions and social policy. These institutions continue to reinvent themselves, often recalling earlier goals and methods. By the end of the twentieth century, modern art museums had again created a public space for the exhibition of everyday objects that could radically challenge viewers' perceptions. In unexpected ways, installation and conceptual art have brought back the idea of art as subject and the idea that an encounter with everyday objects in a museum might transform our experience of the city outside. Indeed, these institutions continue to thrive; at the beginning of the twenty-first century, art museums still, more often than not, form the central foci of urban renewal schemes. While standards for beauty have changed, the Victorian idea of art (and beauty itself) as reforming, refreshing, and inspirational has continued to influence contemporary policy. The Victorian museums are thus not just testaments to a past visual culture, but keystones for the central place of art in the modern city and in industrial capitalist society itself.

1 RUSKIN, RUSKINIANS, AND CITY ART GALLERIES

Birmingham, Liverpool, and Manchester established city art museums in 1867, 1877, and 1883, respectively.[1] By the middle of the nineteenth century, exposés and novels had stereotyped industrial cities as driven by greed and intractably divided by class; Manchester, the epicenter and leader of these changes, became known as "Cottonopolis." Against this still-powerful image, the museum movement reveals the complexities and contradictions of people striving to improve a system of profound structural inequality. In Birmingham, leaders embraced sermons on the sanctity of civic service and made culture central to their larger project of municipal reform, while the Society of Art applauded lectures by its president, William Morris, and put his ideas into the city art museum's collection and catalogues. Meanwhile, in Liverpool, class divisions and a parsimonious town council forced the art reformers to be creative, under the guidance of one city councilor who sought John Ruskin's approval and another who was determined to bring nude sculptures and paintings to the people. And in Manchester, a close network of ambitious and radical reformers oversaw the gifting of the Royal Manchester Institution to the city, while also trying to bring art to the poorest in the slums of Ancoats on principles explicitly derived from Ruskin. They engaged deeply with Ruskin's writings and often with the man himself, but, as we will see, he did not share their hopes for liberal reform and civic projects. These museum advocates held many of the same assumptions about the role of art in reforming industrial society, but each city had its own politics and economy, and each found a different way of creating a new public space for art.

The histories of these three museums show the extent to which they owed their founding to several (sometimes overlapping) groups: highly motivated reformers convinced of art's efficacy and of industrial society's glaring deficiencies; others who felt that museums would provide excellent models for both working-class behavior and industrial design; and the many citizens who enjoyed art museums' prestige and cultural capital. Indeed, in this historical moment, "art" as a concept meant many things to many people, and could fill many different social roles;

this is ultimately why cities built art museums. Reformers believed that art could effect social healing, promote moral and cultural regeneration, and train workers to become alive to beauty in the world and in design. Even those who did not accept art's reforming potential, however, felt that art had a particular ability to raise the civic profile and provide a key arena for genteel sociability. Most supporters associated the resulting public spaces with the domestic sphere, set apart from the corrosive effects of industrial society, and emphasized the importance of art for the experience it offered of beauty, morality, and narrative. Yet these new public collections, like the homes they emulated, depended on the wealth generated from the same rampant commercialism they sought to beautify and soften.

Because of the very multiplicity of art's possible uses and champions, the histories of these three regional art museums allow us to examine the conflicts that emerged over the use and meaning of art. These political battles show us the extent to which middle-class museum advocates acted out of differing motives; the depth of many reformers' discontent with industrial, capitalist society; and, finally, the way that ideas played out in different local circumstances. In practice, financial and social pressures often overwhelmed the idealists, and those reformers most firmly committed to using art as a means of promoting real social change for workers frequently saw their pet projects subsumed into the "ritual" spaces of middle-class use and display.[2] Thus, as others have recognized, museums emerged in the nineteenth century as vital sites for class expression: the middle classes showed their cultural uniqueness—their difference from both the aristocracy and the working classes—through precisely this kind of cultural project.[3] Yet at the same time, these museums were not the product of a unified middle class but emerged out of continual debates between groups with conflicting visions of art's purpose.

Reformers overcame a long-standing British aversion to taxation, and an even longer-standing suspicion of art as foreign, idolatrous, and aristocratic, to make cities provide art to their citizens.[4] This use of art helped to expand and extend the role of government to include new aspects of citizens' welfare, thereby forming a key part of the remaking of British government that had begun earlier in the century.[5] Indeed, in Birmingham, Manchester, and Liverpool, the movements to establish municipal art museums faced considerable opposition precisely because to do so meant a significant redefinition not only of art, but also of the role of the local city council and of the very idea of government in British society. In turn, however, governments transformed the meaning of art, putting it on the municipal payroll in order to proclaim the achievement of local self-rule and the success of their industrial cities. Reformers such as George Dawson, John Henry Chamberlain, and Whitworth Wallis in Birmingham; James Allanson Picton and Philip Henry Rathbone in Liverpool; and Thomas Coglan Horsfall and John Ernest Phythian in Manchester hoped that art museums would both represent and realize a new relationship between the government and the governed, between the middle and the working classes, between beauty and the industrial city. Ultimately, these histories show the development and enactment of a particular understanding of art as providing an experience of beauty that could counteract the moral and physical ugliness of industrial society. This powerful idea created lasting institutions that, perhaps unsurprisingly, rarely lived up to their founders' hopes.

BIRMINGHAM: MAKING THE CITY BEAUTIFUL

In Birmingham, art became a dominant metaphor in civic development as the municipal government remade itself and rebuilt much of the city center over the course of the 1860s and 1870s. Birmingham was a manufacturing town with relatively stable employment and many small workshops, and the municipal art museum played a crucial role in embodying both the town council's new goals and the ruling elites' hope to connect all classes in the pursuit of beauty and good design. Debates about art focused on the extent to which good government might solve society's problems without prohibitively heavy rates of taxation and on how to make art accessible and useful for the greatest number of people. In the end, the city got an art museum through a clever use of the wealth and civic space created (literally) by Birmingham's municipal socialism.

Until the middle of the nineteenth century, the Birmingham Town Council met in a pub and had a reputation for penny-pinching narrow-mindedness.[6] Three influential Birmingham ministers—Unitarians George Dawson and H. W. Crosskey and Congregationalist R. W. Dale—helped to create a new "civic gospel" by arguing that, as Dale put it, "perhaps a strong and able Town Council might do almost as much to improve the conditions of life in the town as Parliament itself."[7] All three men gave municipal reform a spiritual meaning; although from different traditions of Dissenting Protestantism, they shared an emphasis on the duty of public service and the interpretation of Christianity as the emulation of Christ's work in the world.[8] Crosskey preached that "there is no distinction between that which is practically useful and that which is divinely good," and thus on the possibilities for "divine service" in working to improve the conditions in a large town.[9] Dale brought an eloquent and respectable zeal to the continuing reform in Birmingham local government; as a dedicated minister and scholar, he built on Dawson's approach and brought it to the wider evangelical Nonconformist community.[10]

George Dawson set the tone for much subsequent municipal reform. Like later advocates of government cultural provision, he understood the experience of beauty in terms deeply influenced by the works of John Ruskin. As the *Spectator* wrote, Dawson was "a kind of literary middleman between writers like Carlyle and Ruskin and those ordinary English manufacturers, or merchants, or tradesmen, who like thought but like it well illustrated."[11] Like Ruskin, he argued for the importance of beauty in everyday life; he judged the accomplishments of a society in terms of the quality of its arts and the quality of its citizens' lives, and he believed that art could bring people closer to God through nature. In his sermon "Beauty and Purity in Towns," Dawson interpreted scripture in ways that show Ruskin's influence, particularly his idea of artistic truth to nature.[12] Just as Ruskin had described art as a window on nature, which he conceived as a kind of sacred scripture,[13] Dawson made nature into a mirror reflecting God's glory: "No man can see God and live, and therefore we have, as it were, our backs to Him, and Nature has spread out a mirror, so that we may see as much as possible for us without being dimmed with glory."[14] His reading gave new social meaning and importance to the artist, who, Dawson said, "has a great vocation—to hold up the glass to Nature until man can behold the glory, and, looking into the picture, be tempted to go back to its original, and see, perchance for the first time, how glorious it is."[15] Nature is God's mirror; art is nature's.

If, as Dawson concluded, "pursuit of beauty becomes a duty to all," this also meant that the municipality had to ensure that everyone had the opportunities and abilities to perceive beauty, which could only come as a result of education: "To a well-taught man everything is beautiful. There are no ugly things in the world but ourselves—nothing but the unruly working of carnality." Also, it was the government's responsibility to give its citizens beautiful surroundings since, as he further explained, "he who would get and keep within himself the sense of beauty must look upon things that are beautiful, in order that the law of assimilation may be carried out." Dawson even suggested the formation of a "Beauty Society," which would be made up of "educated men, artists, and all true patriots, and it should have for its object the seeking after beauty"—everything from limiting the smoke pouring out of manufacturers' chimneys to providing architectural advice to homebuilders.[16] Echoing Ruskin's discussions of the role of the artist as an interpreter of God's creation, Dawson gave these ideas new meaning as the inspiration for civic activism.

Heavily influenced by Dale, Crosskey, and Dawson, Liberal reformers believed in the importance of art and culture, and in civic activism as a Christian duty, as they worked to improve their city. The Birmingham Liberal Party thus expanded both the power of the town council and the council's role in providing cultural and educational opportunities as mutually reinforcing aspects of the same project.[17] One sign of Dawson's impact is that the first four chairmen of the Free Libraries Committee were members of his congregation, as were others intimately involved in art education.[18] Other evidence comes from Crosskey's church, which included many of those who would most influence the cultural policy of the new municipal administration.[19] The resulting preponderance in the city's Liberal leadership of a Nonconformist, active Christianity was not lost on contemporaries; one critic wrote in 1871 that the town council was being taken over by "Unitarians, Dawsonites."[20]

Birmingham's new Liberals reshaped city and national politics by combining large secular educational and political reform goals with local organizing. Indeed, many of the most influential political leaders, including minister Dale, city councilors George Dixon and Jesse Collings, and mayor and then member of Parliament Joseph Chamberlain, first worked together and learned their organizational skills through founding the Liberal Association in Birmingham in 1865 and extending it to a national scale in 1867.[21] In that same year, they and others founded the Birmingham Education Society, and in 1869 they created and ran the National Education League to campaign for secular national education administered through local governments.[22] This culminated with the successful passage of the Forster Education Act in 1870, which first established elementary education throughout England and Wales. The takeover of municipal politics by the Liberal Party—specifically, the wing of it dominated by Joseph Chamberlain—effected a sea change in the kind of people serving on the Birmingham Town Council (more large employers and professionals, fewer small masters and shopkeepers) and in their understanding of the goals and powers of municipal government.[23] This local-level political organizing became the backbone of political party development in Britain in the late nineteenth and early twentieth centuries.[24] It aided the growth of cultural institutions as members put their ideas into practice and consolidated their power.[25]

Alongside the congregations, the Liberal Party, and the National Education League, another point in the Birmingham art-as-reform network was local architect John Henry Chamberlain (no relation to the other important family of Chamberlains in Birmingham, which included Joseph, Arthur, and Richard). According to Warwickshire historian Samuel Timmins, J. H. Chamberlain was a "fellow-worker" and "devoted friend" of George Dawson; he developed Ruskin-inspired Italian Gothic redbrick architecture for both public and private commissions.[26] Like Timmins, J. H. Chamberlain was also a member of Ruskin's Guild of St. George; he formed a remarkable collection of Ruskin's works, and his manuscript bibliography of this collection—*A Catalogue of the Works of Mr. John Ruskin*..., beautifully written in a free calligraphy and decorated with illuminations and designs—is a wonderful expression of his close engagement with Ruskin's vast literary output. J. H. Chamberlain participated in almost all possible aspects of the transformation of art, architecture, and art education in Birmingham until his death in 1883 and had a lasting effect

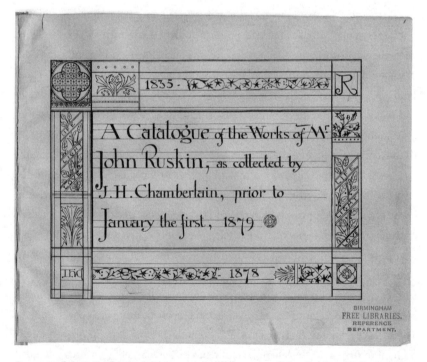

Cover page from J. H. Chamberlain's manuscript bibliography of his collection of John Ruskin's works. Reproduced with the permission of Birmingham Libraries and Archives, Inner Iron Room 74/78126, 1879.

as the architect of many municipal libraries, Board Schools, the Central Reference Library, and the School of Art.[27] He spoke of the adoption of "Italian Renascence" architecture as leading to the death of native English art (that is, the art of the Middle Ages), encouraging English artists to "lay aside the supreme folly of clothing our own ideas in the worn-out garments of other nations."[28] He embraced Gothic architecture as an ancient, living, and native tradition that had never ceased practice.[29]

J. H. Chamberlain particularly worked to expand the audience for art; as he said in a lecture the night before he died, "[in 1851] no one wanted Art, now we want Art for all." He understood art as arising out of admiration for "the beauty and the glory of this marvelous world," and with the greater availability of art, "the man and woman of to-day see more to admire in the universe that surrounds them than their immediate ancestors."[30] His son, Arthur Bensley Chamberlain, became assistant keeper of the Birmingham Museum and Art Gallery in 1890 and served in that position until he retired in 1927.[31] Interest in Ruskin and art reform also connected J. H. Chamberlain to the hydraulic engine manufacturer Richard Tangye, donor with his brother George of the £10,000 that put the Museum and Art Gallery on a permanent footing and of another £10,000 that built the Municipal School of Art. Tangye Bros. was one of the largest employers in Birmingham, and Richard had an extensive collection of Ruskin's works, as well as a copy of J. H. Chamberlain's Ruskin bibliography; he also specifically named J. H. Chamberlain as the most appropriate architect for the School of Art.[32] J. H. Chamberlain's architecture brings us back to the political and social circles that ruled the city, as he designed meticulously rendered houses in an early Arts and Crafts style for both Joseph Chamberlain and his brother-in-law, William Kenrick (a room of Kenrick's house, "The Grove," is now part of the British Galleries at the Victoria and Albert Museum in London; Joseph Chamberlain's house, Highbury Hall, now belongs to the City of Birmingham).[33] Kenrick was "a great admirer of Ruskin" and "a friend of Edward Burne-Jones," owning paintings by Edward Burne-Jones, Alfred Hunt, Henry Wallis, J. W. North, John Everett Millais, William Holman Hunt, and Albert Moore.[34] He chaired the Museums and School of Art Committee from its inception in 1884, through its change into the Museum and Art Gallery Committee in 1912, until his death in 1918. In their private and public lives, these reformers believed that beauty could and should be part of any project of municipal improvement, not as an addition or afterthought, but as its essential and ultimate goal.[35]

William Morris also brought ideas about the need for beauty to Birmingham through his role as president of the Birmingham Society of Arts in 1879 and 1880. In speeches to that body, later published as "The Art of the People" and "The Beauty of Life," Morris presented many of the ideas for which he is now best known.[36] He made Ruskin-inspired connections between beauty, art, nature, and labor: "beauty, which is what is meant by *art*, using the word in its widest sense, is, I contend, no mere accident to human life, which people can take or leave as they choose, but a positive necessity of life, if we are to live as nature meant us to; that is, unless we are content to be less than men." He urged his audience to transform the injustice and brutality of the industrial age, repeatedly promoting "art made by the people and for the people as a joy to both the maker and the user." He questioned the idea that the highest form of civilization means "conventional comforts" that enslave others by their production and gave his audience words to live by as part of a wider solution: "*Have nothing in your houses that you do not know to be useful, or believe to be beautiful.*"[37] What is remarkable here is not just that Birmingham art supporters had opportunities to hear such iconic speeches firsthand, but that these ideas ultimately made it directly into the planning, collecting, and educational policies of the Birmingham Museum and Art Gallery.

The cause of civic reform and municipal improvement had developed a language and achieved some concrete goals by the mid-1860s. However, it was in the 1870s, and especially during the mayoralty of Joseph Chamberlain (1873–1876), that the town council accomplished the most dramatic changes in municipal government.[38] In 1895, the Reverend R. W. Dale, looking back on these years of active city government, remembered that town councilors "spoke of sweeping away streets in which it was not possible to live a healthy and decent life; of making the town cleaner, sweeter, and brighter; of providing gardens and parks and music; of erecting baths and free libraries, an art gallery and a museum."[39] Under Joseph Chamberlain, the council municipalized the gasworks and waterworks and, under the terms of the Artisans' Dwellings Act of 1875, cleared and improved a large central area of the city.[40] Cultural and political structures reinforced each other; for example, in 1875, Joseph Chamberlain (then mayor) stated explicitly that he gave £1,000 to the Industrial Museum "to show, in some practical way, my confidence in our Municipal Institutions."[41] His Liberal Party caucus also came to control the new school board (created through the 1870 Forster Education Act, which many of them had worked to put into law), expanding local government authority into elementary education. Through these measures, the new

Liberals in local government established what came to be known as "municipal socialism," a new era in the radical tradition in Birmingham.[42]

The elementary schools provided through the Municipal School Board, the "Board Schools," became a prime example of the use of architecture to simultaneously beautify the town, raise the prestige of the local government that built them, and improve the taste of those who viewed and used the buildings.[43] Indeed, the campaign to build Board Schools in the 1870s was a good test case for the "new economy" of the town council—proponents such as Jesse Collings and Joseph Chamberlain often described this as "wise economy" against the old "false" school of economists who wished at all costs to keep property taxes low. As Joseph Chamberlain argued:

If [the Board Schools] are beautiful, it is because the outline is noble, because the grouping is harmonious and pleasing, and because the general appearance is graceful; but not because they have been overladen with any superimposed ornament without meaning and without use. All ornament which is worthy of the name must be derived in part from the necessity of the construction, and it is absurd to suppose that everything which is ornamental may therefore necessarily be assumed to be useless, and everything which is graceful may be taken as extravagant.[44]

This argument seems heavily influenced by Ruskin, who in *The Seven Lamps of Architecture* discussed the use and meaning of architectural ornament at great length and in punctilious detail, defining architecture as "the art which so disposes and adorns the edifices raised by man for whatsoever uses, that the sight of them contribute[s] to his mental health, power and pleasure."[45] In fact, one architect of many Board Schools was none other than J. H. Chamberlain, for whom, as for Joseph Chamberlain, the use of ornament itself was a declaration of the new political ideal—of "wise" as against "false" economy—of a municipality willing to pay for the education and improvement of its citizens. The Board Schools' redbrick Italian Gothic was again part of a larger transposition of the idea that beauty could and should be an intrinsic aspect of municipal improvement.[46]

In the summer of 1877, immediately after Joseph Chamberlain's mayoralty and as these many changes were under way, Ruskin in fact came to Birmingham to meet with a group of the leading municipal reformers at the home of the next mayor, and member of Ruskin's Guild of St. George, George Baker.[47] This moment highlights all of the tensions between Ruskin, with his Cassandra-like calls to arms against the ills of his time, and the men earnestly attempting

The Birmingham Municipal School of Art (completed 1885; J. H. Chamberlain, architect), 2011. Photograph by David Rowan.

to follow his advice. After this meeting, Ruskin admitted in *Fors Clavigera* that he felt like a "good ship . . . struck by a heavy sea," but that he was "most clearly impressed by . . . the right-mindedness of these men, so far as they see what they are doing . . . nor, under the conditions apparent to them, do I believe it is possible for them to act more wisely or faithfully."[48] He then succinctly described his disagreement with those who sought to improve their industrial cities, even when they had been inspired to do so by his own work:

all they showed me, and told me, of good, involved yet the main British modern idea that the master and his men should belong to two entirely different classes; perhaps loyally related to and assisting each other; but yet,—the one, on the whole, living in hardship—the other in ease;—the one uncomfortable—the other in comfort; the one supported in its dishonourable condition by the hope of labouring through it to the higher one,—the other honourably distinguished by their success, and rejoicing in their escape from a life which must nevertheless be always (as they suppose,) led by a thousand to one of the British people.[49]

Here is a succinct summary of the continuing debate over the reform or radical revolution of industrial society. Despite the good intentions of the Liberal reformers, Ruskin rejected their efforts because they accepted the fundamental fact of their society, that is, its class divisions and intrinsic, structural inequalities.

Ruskin's basic disagreement with those who believed themselves to be putting his ideas into action came up again in his response to the death of George Dawson. Again and again in *Fors Clavigera*, Ruskin exhorted his readers to consider Christian doctrine as driving them to immediately help those in need, to take on squalor and hunger, and to reimagine their society that—to him—so calmly accepted massive, seemingly intractable poverty and suffering. He would later write that he "went mad" and had endured "humiliation" because "nothing came" of his work and "nobody believed a word" of his manuscripts.[50] But it was not simply that no one believed; Ruskin could get frustrated with those who seemed to only partially understand. For example, in his sermons, Dawson seemed to equate civic reform projects with Christian duty. Ruskin was willing to praise Dawson's ideas about the steadfastness of the "spiritual universe" but also complained that Dawson's civic gospel missed the point: "As a Christian, I believe prayer to be, in the last sense, sufficient for the salvation of the town; and drainage, in the last sense, insufficient for its salvation. Not that you will find me, looking through the back pages of *Fors*, unconcerned about drainage. But if, of the two, I must choose between drains and prayer—why, look you—whatever you think of my wild and whirling words, I will pray."[51] Ruskin, in other words, did not want to simply reduce faith to secular government interventions to fix a basically unjust (and thus unchristian) system. Yet Birmingham, Liverpool, and Manchester all had strong Liberal movements, often inspired by Ruskin himself, to improve their cities—to build drains and establish art museums, that is, to better a social, economic, and political system that Ruskin understood as inherently flawed.

Despite Ruskin's misgivings, new Liberal councilors took many of his ideas about art, beauty, and justice to heart; indeed, it is a testament to the change in the general attitude toward government provision of culture that Birmingham's first attempt to adopt the Free Museum and Libraries Act failed to pass the town council in 1852 but succeeded eight years later with a new, reform-minded council.[52] Just three months after the act had been adopted, the newly created Free Libraries Committee had developed an ambitious scheme: a "central Reference Library with Reading and News Rooms, a Museum and Gallery of Art, and four District Lending Libraries with News Rooms attached."[53] While the town council worked on this, supporters of the plan set up the Birmingham and Midland Institute to privately address the same goals. Indeed, the institute in many ways assisted the development of later municipal institutions, in the sense of forming an audience and constituency for reading, art, and education. But it also helped in very practical terms: the new municipal committee literally built on the work of the voluntary institute by attaching rooms to its buildings for the new municipal institutions.[54] By 1867 the last part of the scheme was finished when one large room of the library was designated the municipal art gallery, exhibiting fifty-one paintings.[55]

This one-room art museum was enormously successful, perhaps more so than even its founders had hoped. Through gifts from individuals and several semipublic bodies, the museum's collections and annual attendance rate grew until, by 1872, the Free Libraries Committee was urging the town council to increase the museum's size.[56] At first, the council attempted to expand the original buildings, but when this proved impossible, it tried to find a site and the funds to erect a temporary art gallery in the center of town.[57] In fact, over the next eight years, the art gallery was stymied by its own success and that of the other cultural institutions with which it shared space. Private gifts and support had apparently outstripped the town council's ability to provide adequate physical housing for what it had established.[58] In 1880, the town council received private donations amounting to about £17,700 (including the £10,000 from Richard and George Tangye) for objects for an art gallery and industrial museum *if* the council provided a suitable structure. This finally propelled the council to look for a way to build a permanent museum and art gallery.

The council found an ingenious way to use the profits of the city's recently municipalized gasworks, which allowed an elegant statement of the civic gospel and of Birmingham's municipal socialism: the Gas Committee built its own offices with an art gallery and museum on top, at its own expense, on land appropriated through the Free Museum and Libraries Act.[59] Thus, by owning the gasworks, the town council could build a more magnificent gallery than it otherwise could have afforded, with guaranteed year-round free entry and without raising local property taxes.[60] The council ultimately approved a total cost of £92,500 out of the Gas Committee's funds for the Gas Offices and Art Gallery, which still adjoin the Italianate Council House in the center of town.[61] The new, permanent Birmingham Museum and Art Gallery opened on Saturday, November 28, 1885, with a celebration at the Town Hall and an address by the Prince of Wales (the future Edward VII).[62]

The Birmingham Museum and Art Gallery would be significantly shaped by the knowledge, prominence, connections, and longevity of its curator, who effectively acted as a director; the council appointed Whitworth Wallis in 1885, and he

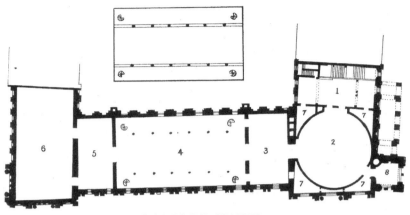

PLAN OF THE GALLERIES.

Scale—50 feet to One Inch.

1. VESTIBULE.
2. CIRCULAR PICTURE GALLERY.
3. ITALIAN GALLERY.
4. INDUSTRIAL HALL, WITH SIDE GALLERIES.
5. WEDGWOOD GALLERY.
6. PICTURE GALLERY.
7. OFFICES, ETC.
P.   8. MUSEUM KEEPER'S OFFICE.

Plan of the Birmingham Museum and Art Gallery, from Whitworth Wallis, *Handbook, with Descriptive Notes, to the Collections of Industrial Art Objects in the Museum and Art Gallery* (Birmingham, 1886), front matter. From the collection of the Birmingham Museum and Art Gallery.

The Birmingham Museum and Art Gallery (completed 1885; Yeoville Thomason, architect), 2011. Photograph by David Rowan.

retained the position until his death in 1927. Wallis was the second son of George Wallis, keeper of the art collections at the South Kensington Museum (and formerly the headmaster of the Birmingham School of Art) and was at the time of his appointment to Birmingham employed at South Kensington in the Indian department.[63] Educated in London and Germany, and having worked in Paris at the 1878 Exposition Universelle, Wallis came to the post with a broad knowledge of a wide variety of art forms and with connections to the metropolitan, European, and imperial art worlds. With these strengths and a purchasing fund raised to nearly £20,000, Wallis shaped the Birmingham Museum and Art Gallery into a model combination of applied and fine art, with frequent loan exhibitions and a discerning collections policy.[64]

When the museum opened, the penny catalogue of the permanent collection emphasized the purpose of its particular combination of fine and applied arts and the extent to which the project had been shaped by the ideas of both John Ruskin and William Morris. Visitors must try to learn from the exhibits, Wallis wrote, "to make, if only at first in a small way, our manufactures, candlesticks, coal-boxes, spoons, or *whatever* it may happen to be, more and more beautiful. It is to our interest (to look at it in its most mercenary sense) to do so, and life will thus become more interesting both to the man who makes the article and to the one who uses it."[65] (Note the echo of Morris's lecture five years before.) With its portico, campanile, and Italianate finishing, the building was a clear statement of the goals set up earlier by Dawson, Dale, and Crosskey and their followers that Birmingham might someday compete with Florence, Venice, and Pisa and make such cultural achievements available to all.[66] Funded by a municipalized gasworks and filled with private wealth generated from the industries of the town, the museum aimed at making social relations and industrial design more harmonious. Physically embedded within the Council House and the Gas Offices, the Birmingham Museum and Art Gallery established the connections that also appear in the administrative records: the gallery pronounced in stone the expanded responsibilities and prestige of the town council.

LIVERPOOL: LUXURY AND NECESSITY

As in Birmingham, the men most active in promoting a municipal art museum in Liverpool did so largely inspired by ideas derived from Ruskin that connected art, beauty, nature, and society. However, Liverpool's reformers were far more isolated within their community. Ultimately, the constraints of the city's po-

litical and economic situation, as well as the ideas about art that these reformers embraced, created a very different kind of institution. Is art a luxury that
should be maintained through private wealth and the free market? Or is it an
engine of civilization and economic improvement, which should therefore receive public support? In ways very different from Birmingham, Liverpool ultimately found a compromise, using exhibitions of art for sale to generate funds
and gifts and creating a museum of fine art whose policies mirrored the city's
stratified class structure.

One of the world's greatest ports, Liverpool has looked as much to its trading
partners in Europe, America, and Africa as to London; it is a city that still feels
as if it turns its back on England to face the sea.[67] That most basic fact about
Liverpool, that it is a port city, led both to its great wealth and to many of its
most intractable problems. Growing enormously during the eighteenth century
through the African and West Indian slave trade, Liverpool had such a vast international commerce that the end of that trade in 1807 had little effect on the
city's economy.[68] The development of the textile industry in Lancashire further
boosted the city; between 1820 and 1850 Liverpool brought in four-fifths of all
British cotton.[69] However, it lacked the strong manufacturing base that fostered
small-scale workshops in Birmingham or the variety of factory sizes and skilled
trades that we will see in Manchester. Instead, Liverpool contained a small number
of extraordinarily wealthy merchants and ship owners, a larger number of struggling lower-middle-class clerks and traders, and a vast pool of dock laborers and
builders with varying degrees of skill but all suffering chronic unemployment.

As a major center of immigration, Liverpool served as the entry, departure,
and often final destination point for many of Britain's most desperate, especially
after the mid-century Irish potato famine. As in Manchester, rapid and sustained
growth led to horrible overcrowding and high mortality rates from the lack of
sanitation. As the city's population swelled, the city's system of courts and alleys
turned into a densely packed warren, with usually only a few feet between buildings. This kind of opportunistic "jerry-building" (a term that emerged first in
Liverpool to describe the largely Welsh-controlled building trade) became nox-
ious and even deadly because of Liverpool's acute water shortage, which meant
that waste could not be properly washed out of the courts.[70] At its worst, the
center of Liverpool suffered the highest death rate, the most unsanitary conditions, and the direst poverty of anywhere in Britain. In addition, this swelling
population of the poor and hungry brought with it extremes of Catholic and

Protestant identification, which the city's politicians exploited.[71] Civic leaders' fears of charity to the "undeserving" poor, combined with sectarian divisions, prevented a consensus on the need to educate or provide culture for the working classes and therefore frustrated the development of municipal socialism or reformist educational schemes.[72] Indeed, despite its art museum advocates, unlike Birmingham, Manchester, or London, Liverpool had no significant movements to bring art to the poor.

In place of a unified and active city government, therefore, private organizations developed to mitigate Liverpool's poverty or provide culture.[73] Despite the city having a smaller and less dominant class of professionals and manufacturers, in Liverpool, as in Birmingham and Manchester, networks developed that brought people together who were interested in social reform through education and culture. They often organized projects through Nonconformist Sunday schools,[74] and the same pattern emerges of the importance in promoting municipal cultural institutions of Nonconformist families, particularly the Rathbones, and their congregation, the Renshaw Street Unitarians.[75] However, the strongest voice in city government remained that of ratepayers such as clerks and traders who had limited incomes, were the hardest hit by increased property taxes, and who therefore argued for economy. In fact, both the Liberal and Conservative parties included many who wished to limit rather than encourage government expansion and spending and who consistently voted against such perceived luxuries as a municipal gallery of art.[76] At the same time, the lack of manufacturing meant that there was no demand in Liverpool for the education of artisans in skilled trades; at one point the municipal Library, Museum, and Arts Committee argued that the town council should establish a municipal art gallery precisely in order to *bring* manufacturing to Liverpool.[77]

It was in this highly stratified, contentious, sectarian, and partisan climate that three town councilors, Liberals James Allanson Picton and Philip Rathbone and Conservative Edward Samuelson, voiced their support for municipal cultural projects.[78] Both Picton and Rathbone championed a municipal art museum as fulfilling the town council's duty to reform and improve the city, and both were deeply influenced by the ideas of Ruskin, emphasizing the importance of art, beauty, and nature as means of creating a good and just society.[79] Although they both came from Dissenting, Liberal backgrounds, Picton and Rathbone had very different upbringings and personalities. Picton was a self-made architect and lifelong Nonconformist, while Rathbone, an underwriter in the family insurance company, enjoyed the wealth and prestige of being a member of one of Liverpool's oldest and most established Unitarian families (he later joined the Church of England).[80] Picton's difficult early years of poverty made him steadfastly earnest in his attempts to better himself and to encourage others to do the same.[81] Although later a Congregationalist, Picton had been deeply involved as a youth in the Sunday school at the Wesleyan Leeds Street Chapel, and he wanted to provide others with greater opportunities than he had enjoyed. As his son wrote, Picton "picture[d] the Sunday school, not as a sectarian or theological propaganda, but as a sort of secondary academy for the promotion of culture—or rather, perhaps, a sort of gymnasium for exercise in the arts of self-government and mutual improvement."[82] Rathbone, on the other hand, was a "bohemian" to most of his contemporaries; an 1881 caricature in the often-critical *Liberal Review* shows a character in the council chamber swooning over "a dingy, cracked old plate," saying, for example, "'Take it, worship it, and be one of us,'" and again, "It is High Art. It is the Ideal of the truly Lovely; the aesthetically quite too Purely Pure."[83] He himself wrote in 1875 that the "people can but accept or reject, it requires a happy combination of the men of genius, with those of leisure, culture, and wealth, to initiate the intellectual and artistic life of a nation."[84] Having grown up in Liverpool's intellectual and social elite, Rathbone was a thorough patrician with a correspondingly patronizing attitude to culture.[85]

For Picton, as for the Birmingham reformers, cultural institutions were part of a larger program of municipal reform and improvements such as street widening and slum clearance. As he wrote in 1853—echoing Ruskin in *The Seven Lamps of Architecture*—if a town attempted to embellish itself with fine architecture before seeing to the necessities and convenience of its citizens, it risked becoming a "whited sepulchre—beautiful to the eye at a distance, but festering within with corruption and rottenness."[86] In order that the council might successfully tackle Liverpool's severe problems, Picton steadfastly argued for a stronger city government, whether through better funding via a new form of municipal bond or by consolidating power in a single, representative local authority.[87] In recommending physical improvements or cultural goals, Picton invoked posterity, consistently comparing Liverpool to other great centers of trade and commerce of the past.[88] Liverpool was to Picton "the modern Tyre," and he urged his fellow Liverpudlians to "render the external aspect of their town worthy [of] the exalted rank she seems destined to fill in the commerce of the world."[89] He worked for libraries, a museum, and an art gallery from the understanding that cities—especially cities of commerce—were the basic nesting ground of civilization, and that as such their governments should be active in promoting moral and intellectual progress.[90] Moreover, he argued that municipal cultural institutions should never aim at the lowest common denominator but should provide the best examples available, because "a craving thirst for intelligence and enlightenment pervades all classes."[91] When Picton died in 1889, Rathbone wrote a poem to mark the passing of a fellow spirit with whom he had worked closely for twenty-two years. In this poem Rathbone described Picton as

Broad, brave, yet cautious, with a calm, wise soul,
Hasting not, resting not, pressing towards his goal,
From passing ages gathering fading light
To cast before and make the future bright.[92]

For Rathbone, as for many other social reformers who hoped to use art to improve Victorian society, three key ideas were the morality of art, its ability to work this influence on a wide audience, and its status as an index of its society.[93] He directed the founding of the city art museum, organized its annual exhibitions, and lectured and published widely on art, often in terms he adapted from Ruskin, particularly the idea of artists striving to achieve "truth to Nature." In an 1875 lecture given at the Liverpool library, he spoke "of Art as the embodiment of the highest thought and aspiration of a nation," arguing that through art, "a perfect civilisation" would give individuals an understanding of their role and place within this "living organic whole" and of their contributions to the "grandeur and nobility of [the] community." Art could do this—could bring the citizens of Liverpool together and connect them to the wider world—because "the universality of Art forms a bond between all nations, causing us to feel and sympathise with all that is common to our human nature with a force not otherwise easily attainable."[94] He explicitly rejected the ideas prevalent in Liverpool that culture was the enemy of democracy, that art was a luxury, and that it led to moral corruption.[95] He blamed this suspicion of art on the fierce anti-Catholicism and iconoclasm of the Reformation (and, one might add, of nineteenth-century Liverpool): "I was standing on the bridge at Wakefield, where rises a Gothic chapel (such as we now dream of but cannot build), when a working man came up to me and said, 'This is all very beautiful, but it's Popery.' I couldn't help saying, 'I am no Catholic, but if this be Popery, I wish there were more Popery in England.' 'Art and Religion oughtn't to be mixed; it's idolatry,' was the reply."[96]

In their belief in the possibility of real reform through city government, Picton and Rathbone faced the problem of putting Ruskin's contradictory ideas about art and society into practice and in fact operated in urban conditions that, in his later years, Ruskin himself often seemed to despair of ameliorating through anything but wholesale political and economic transformation. We can see these contradictions in letters between Ruskin and Picton sent in the mid-1880s.[97] Ruskin inspired Picton for decades, and the two actually met, exchanged books, and entered into a brief correspondence on various topics of Liverpool history and architecture.[98] Picton invited Ruskin to attend the opening of the new extension to the municipal art gallery; Ruskin declined.[99] Picton shared his writings on Liverpool, and Ruskin responded with suspicion and distaste for industrial cities: "Your book on Liverpool is a model of such records. I only wish it had been of Carnarvon, or Conway, or Flint instead!" (July 21, 1884) and then again: "You and I feel exactly alike about what is pretty and proper—we agree about the disagreeableness of chemical works and the delightfulness of antiquities. . . . But I consider Liverpool the cause of the destruction of Flint, and of most of Lancashire!" (July 26, 1884).[100] Picton engaged with Ruskin's ideas and with the man himself, but—as with Ruskin's criticisms of George Dawson and others in Birmingham—he clearly did not receive encouragement for his attempts to put those ideas into practice in Liverpool.

From the beginning, Picton had grand ambitions; as soon as he joined the town council in 1849, he began advocating for municipal libraries and museums and initiated negotiations with the Liverpool Royal Institution over a transfer of their buildings and collections to the town (this ultimately took place in 1892, after Picton's death).[101] Already in 1852, a gift of natural history collections from the Earl of Derby prompted the council to raise property taxes in order to open the "Library, Museum, and Gallery of Art" in small rooms in the city center (although the gallery contained only the few paintings already owned by the city).[102] When the allocated building quickly became overcrowded, Picton urged the council to erect a purpose-built library, natural history museum, and art gallery. He had limited success; the council did eventually agree to purchase land for the project but balked at providing the funds to build. In 1857 the town was saved further expenditure when the wealthy merchant and Liberal member of Parliament William Brown paid to build the new Brown Library and Derby Museum of Natural History, which would not, however, contain an art gallery.[103]

This was an important first step for Picton, but he continued to try to get the town council to allocate funds for a separate, purpose-built city art museum;

however, the council continued to insist that art, as a luxury, should be provided through private effort. Picton did not try to refute this assumption; instead, he pointed out that the city would have to create an infrastructure in order to take advantage of private munificence: an art gallery needed the backing of the municipality to give collectors and donors enough confidence to support it.[104] (Indeed, this was very much part of the rationale behind the Birmingham scheme that was developing at roughly the same time.) Picton urged the council to build an ambitious institution that would allow room for the permanent display of painting and sculpture, for a school of design, and for annual exhibitions.[105] The Library, Museum, and Arts Committee pursued this grand scheme doggedly, particularly after 1867, when the city received the Mayer collection of applied art and ethnography, and newly elected Councilor Rathbone joined the committee. Still, the basic problem was money; art remained defined as a luxury, and there was simply no political will to allocate city funds for a public art museum.

Throughout the late 1860s and 1870s art became a point of heated debate, at least among Liverpool's chattering classes. The press discussed the proposed city art museum in terms of the role of government, the status of art, and, as the *Liberal Review* put it, "the work that there is for [art] to perform."[106] Liverpool art dealer B. H. Grindley argued in an 1875 lecture that "one of the greatest levers in refining and improving mankind is undoubtedly Art. . . . True art does not tend to luxury, which is extravagance: but to simplicity, which is but another name for truth."[107] Three years later, in disputes over public funding for the newly built city art museum, the dubious *Liberal Review* attacked the "art-maniacs": "If we were to believe all that we are told, we should arrive at the conclusion that the world is only to be regenerated by an acquaintance with Art [but that] it should always be borne in mind, that Art is luxury. As such it should and must be secondary to necessities."[108] The *Liberal Review* rejected the claims of the "art enthusiasts" and insisted that, as a luxury, art must come second to more pressing needs and should not receive government support.[109] One *Liberal Review* author found "laughable" the supporters' alleged ideas that under art's influence, "wife-beaters" would (as he put it) "turn into angels of sweetness and light," couples living in sin would "fly to the parish church or the registrar's office," or drunks would "be redeemed from the thraldom of the Drink Demon" and go to church socials ("which are, unhappily, at present called by the irreverent folks of these inartistic, not to say barbarous times, muffin struggles"!). He saw this "fashion of modern philosophers—or of those who set up for being philosophers—to enthrone Art upon an imaginary altar" as a fad like "the Colorado Beetle scare, the Tichborne Claimant worship, and the passion for the delightful and euphonious word, 'Whoa, Emma' which have in turn seized upon the popular fancy." He assumed that eventually "the exaggerated notions which are at present entertained in regard to Art, the absurd worship of the aesthetic side of human nature, will be treated by public opinion in a like fashion, and will be made to give place to more healthy and true ideas on the position which Art ought to occupy in the world and the work that there is for it to perform."[110] The *Liberal Review* gives us the art movement in negative (and a glimpse of the "Whoa, Emma" fad).

In contrast, the art museum plan did find support in the much smaller and more specialized satirical journal the *Porcupine,* edited by working-class advocate Hugh Shimmin.[111] An 1868 *Porcupine* article argued that a "gallery for the display of works of art [was] not only desirable but indispensable" for improving industrial design and assured its readers that the "general voice of the public has proclaimed the necessity, and the carrying out of the project is merely a matter of time." Shimmin and his writers also bluntly stated that it was "discreditable to a large and opulent community like that of Liverpool that she has no Gallery of Art."[112] Shimmin argued in favor of a municipal art gallery as a necessity rather than a luxury but, unlike Picton and Rathbone, did so largely on the grounds of economy and civic pride.

By the end of 1870, when Picton and Rathbone's efforts had failed to get the town council to act, the Library, Museum, and Arts Committee held a special session to approve holding municipal autumn exhibitions in the library and museum building.[113] The committee had not given up on realizing a city art museum; in fact, the autumn exhibition was a way of working on a city art museum despite the council's inaction. The following year, the committee reported that the first exhibition was a great success and that its modest profit had allowed for the purchase of works from the exhibition "for the Permanent Collection."[114] The experiment worked. In 1873, just two years after the first autumn exhibition under municipal control, the increasing popularity of these exhibitions and a growing consensus that the city needed an art museum forced the town council to take up the question again.[115] However, Conservative brewer Andrew Barclay Walker preempted the council when, upon his election as mayor in November, he announced that he intended to give the city an art gallery.[116]

The prominence of brewers in the ranks of the Conservatives, and the political fights over temperance and the Conservatives' use of liquor in elections (perennial Liberal issues), made Walker's gift of an art gallery part of a larger battle to find ways to legitimately court voters after the Reform Act of 1867 expanded the franchise.[117] Liverpool gained a municipal art museum, at least in part, out of Walker's profits from alcohol, ironically one of the social ills such an institution was intended to ameliorate. If the most vocal politicians in support of municipal spending on cultural institutions were often Liberals, Walker's gift showed that the Conservatives could also use art and culture to enhance their prestige, turning pints into pictures. The following year, the Duke of Edinburgh laid the foundation stone of the new Walker Art Gallery, and that year the Liverpool Town Council allocated a small fund for purchases for its permanent collection.[118] The Walker opened to the public on September 6, 1877, with a public holiday, processions, speeches, and grand banquets for the city's elite. Through municipal art sales and private generosity, the government became responsible for just the kind of cultural patronage that it had previously avoided.

The Walker Art Gallery's origins, however, had a lasting effect on the institution. Despite Picton and Rathbone's idealism, and perhaps Mayor Walker's intent, the extent of the Walker's commercial activities—which Picton and Rathbone helped devise as a means of getting around the town council's reluctance to spend money on art—meant that the gallery was not equally open and accessible to all classes. The Walker did not have the liberty that the Birmingham Museum and Art Gallery enjoyed to put on free-entry loan exhibitions and provide consistent free entry to the permanent collection. Entry fees for the autumn exhibition and other events meant that for much of the year only those who were able and willing to pay a fee could take advantage of Liverpool's art museum.[119] Rather than striving to bring even the humblest worker into contact with the benefits of civilization, as Picton and Rathbone hoped, or exposing workers to examples of industrial design, as Shimmin had advised, the Walker became a very visible means of enhancing the reputation of the city and its government through high-profile social events and exhibitions.[120] With their neoclassical architecture and imposing siting above the city center, the Brown Library, Derby Museum, and Walker Art Gallery embodied in stone Picton and Rathbone's references to the "great commercial cities of antiquity."[121] However, the art museum's policies, like its architecture, created a solemn temple of the fine arts for the educated rather than bringing "enlightenment [to] all classes." In Liverpool, perhaps Ruskin's suspicions were justified, as art remained a luxury rather than a necessity.

THE WALKER ART GALLERY, LIVERPOOL.

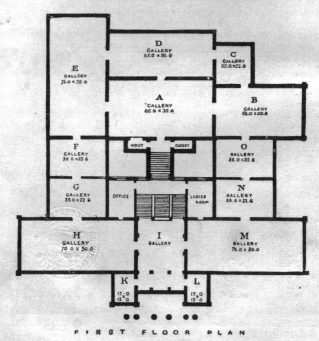

The Gallery is open free to the Public daily, from 10 a.m. till dusk (Fridays excepted). Friday being Students' day, Sixpence each is charged to the Public for admission. The Gallery is also open free on Sundays, during eight months of the year, from 2 to 4.30 p.m.

The Walker Art Gallery (completed 1877; Sherlock and Vale, architects), ca. 1900. From *Catalogue of the Walker Art Gallery; Ed. with introduction and notes by Charles Dyall, Gems of the Galleries, No. 3* (Liverpool, 1900), front matter. Galleries A–E were added in 1884. Liverpool Central Library, H 708.5 WAL. Courtesy of the Liverpool County Record Office.

MANCHESTER: CIVIC PRIDE AND SOCIAL REFORM

In Manchester, discussions about art and its social role revolved explicitly around the status of art as it related to industrial society itself. Was art a symbol of the success of industrialization, which brought benefits to all made possible by the wealth of a few? Or could art be a call to reform the society created by industry, reform that would make culture and beauty not a privilege but a right, and even transform conditions of production? That this is the case is not surprising; by the middle of the nineteenth century, Manchester had become the world's first model of unfettered industrial capitalism.[122] Recent scholarly work has considerably complicated the picture of the city's culture and society by refuting the stereotype of the "Manchester man," interested only in personal gain at the expense of vast numbers of degraded workers.[123] Indeed, although the Liberal Manchester City Council never developed the rhetoric of Birmingham's civic gospel, the city experimented far earlier than Birmingham with municipal ownership of its gasworks and waterworks and undertook massive improvement schemes throughout the century. At the same time, Manchester's middle class debated what should and should not be a matter of state interference and, as in Birmingham and Liverpool, tended to give generously to crisis-driven philanthropic schemes while vigorously opposing local government projects that would increase taxes.[124] The stereotype of Cottonopolis remained important for people at the time and influenced how they worked to change their city.

Although schemes to establish a city art museum did not begin until the second half of the nineteenth century, the city's central arts institution—which in fact eventually turned itself into the Manchester City Art Gallery—had emerged a generation earlier. Founded in 1823, the Royal Manchester Institution (RMI) was one of many middle-class cultural institutions established across Britain during that period (for instance, the Liverpool Royal Institution was founded in the same year).[125] In Manchester in particular, the RMI established the crucial role that art could play in the development of a common civic culture.[126] The RMI, indeed, proved to be an institution especially important to the burgeoning Manchester middle classes, for social events, the articulation of a new cultural confidence, and the development of shared values and aesthetics.[127] Although it was originally begun as an artists' society, nonartist "gentlemen" controlled the RMI's Board of Governors from the outset.[128] From the beginning, the RMI aimed at the diffusion of high culture (among the middle class, not the working classes) through exhibiting past and contemporary art.[129] It was well funded through a system of governorships set at prices to attract the elites of the town; several months after the granting of royal patronage, memberships had raised £23,000.[130] The RMI used these substantial funds to secure a permanent home for lecture theaters, exhibition space, and meeting rooms; it sought and acquired land suitably central and free of any associations with other political or religious entities, and solicited plans from six architects, eventually choosing the Greek Revival design of Charles Barry.[131]

The RMI came to serve as a meeting place and a kind of clearinghouse for the cultural societies of Manchester.[132] Its annual exhibitions of new works for sale, begun in 1827, became an important part of the city's social calendar and served as the source of both some of the RMI's profits and of its slowly growing permanent collection of art. Measures like gas lighting for evening openings and six-penny tickets increased attendance, but the RMI remained primarily a middle-class society for appreciating the arts, rather than an active force for bringing art and culture to the uneducated.[133] Its collection reflected the tastes of the day, showing a gradual shift from old masters (of often dubious provenance) to works by con-

The Manchester City Art Gallery (completed in 1829 as the Royal Manchester Institution, Charles Barry, architect), 1890. Courtesy of the Greater Manchester County Record Office (with Manchester Archives), m58920.

temporary British artists, a transition that many have interpreted as part of the growing cultural confidence of the British middle classes.[134] This confidence would find ultimate expression in the great exhibition of art that Manchester held in 1857.

Building on the success of the RMI and inspired by the Great Exhibition of 1851, the Manchester Art Treasures Exhibition of 1857 successfully harnessed individual wealth for a grand public cultural project and led to the first effort to establish a city art museum. Aided by Prince Albert, the Manchester exhibition of privately owned old masters and contemporary art brought the then-notorious industrial city a new kind of fame as being able to wield cultural as well as economic and political power. Building on this triumph, Thomas Fairbairn—chairman of the Art Treasures Exhibition organizing committee, partner in his father's large engineering firm, and active art enthusiast and patron—convened a meeting in 1860 to establish a Manchester city art museum.[135] This spin-off project planned to take advantage of the new interest in art generated by the 1857 exhibition and to follow a similar model, hoping to build a collection from the wealth and generosity of local art patrons and to raise money locally from both workers and manufacturers. The 1860 scheme also looked to refashion the city's image, as one supporter of the city art museum project argued: "Do not let it be said that Manchester men have no higher pursuit than making money; but let us leave behind us some evidence, that while we were exercising our energy and industry in promoting our own interests, we were not unmindful of the source from which our benefits sprung, and that we tried by our influence and means to leave the community in every respect better than we found it."[136] Such enthusiasm, however, did not outlive the next economic crisis. Support for Fairbairn's Free Art Gallery and Museum plan was never unanimous, but it might have gotten further than it did if not for the severe bout of layoffs and closures that hit Manchester in the wake of both overproduction and the end of U.S. cotton imports during the Civil War.[137]

The Cotton Famine of the 1860s helped create a more active city government and a new generation of reformers more interested in using art as a means of social outreach to the poor than as a tool in civic boosterism.[138] As one of these reformers, Charles Rowley, later explained, the crisis opened his eyes to the suffering around him:

When on the larger public relief committees we saw as visitors the interiors of the very homes of those neighbours in a familiar manner which one could never hope to obtain in any other way. The memories of the squalor and the potency of the odours of those appalling, stinging slums can never be effaced. We had been living next door to them all our lives, and yet were not aware of their bestial condition. This is always going on; people guess, or glance at things from the outside, but they cannot imagine what the inner state is of such dwellings where crowds live day in day out.[139]

Instead of Prince Albert's patriotic and proindustrial projects, it was Ruskin's cultural and social criticism that inspired the individuals who would in fact help make Manchester responsible for providing art. Their proposals came not from a sense of boundless optimism in unstoppable historical progress, but from a fear of the reality of industrial capitalism and its degrading effects on both the workers and those who consumed mass-produced goods.

A network of like-minded reformers took part in the boards, committees, and societies that aimed at making art available to the public, including in some of the most deprived areas of Manchester, such as Ancoats. These people came from different areas and social backgrounds, but worked together on a series of projects to bring art, nature, and beauty into the lives of Manchester's workers.[140] This group included Thomas Coglan Horsfall, son of a card manufacturer of moderate wealth; architect Thomas Worthington; picture framer Charles Rowley; lawyer John Ernest Phythian; and cotton spinner Charles James Pooley, who all left some record of an intense engagement with art as social reform. This work could have a more radical side: as William Morris wrote to Horsfall, "Educate your workmen into general discontent."[141]

Thomas Coglan Horsfall grew up spending time in a variety of spas and re-sorts to improve his weak health; ironically, because of this, he developed a keen sense of the injustice of the society that created spas for the wealthy and slums for the poor.[142] In later life, he devoted all his time and most of his fortune to a variety of reforming projects. These included bringing artworks and museum exhibits to schoolchildren, opening the Manchester Art Museum in Ancoats, working for cleaner air, sponsoring municipal art prizes for watercolors of the local landscape, and helping to transfer the RMI to the city. His ideals and their origins are not hard to find; he wrote of his Manchester Art Museum project that it was "formed for the purpose of giving effect to Ruskin's teaching."[143]

Charles Rowley grew up, and continued throughout his life, working in his father's frame-making workshop in New Cross, one of the "respectable" parts of Ancoats. He was not formally educated but benefited from his father's love of literature and dedication to self-improvement through the Manchester Mechanics Institute. Like Picton in Liverpool, his commitment to institutions that would provide education and culture for the working classes came from his experience as an autodidact.[144] Rowley eventually used his connections with the city government and the art world to take charge of many of the municipal art museum's framing needs. However, he was involved in art reform efforts not only as part of his business; he was also deeply concerned with what he saw as the "warfare" and separation between the classes in modern society, and with the materialism of the age: "The real danger of our materialistic success is that we get divorced from Nature and have no capacity for art. Everything becomes ludicrously artificial, which artificiality is the foe to every real enjoyment that is true and sound and lasting."[145] Rowley put his energies into bringing art to Manchester through private and public means; he served on the city council from 1875 to 1884, and again in the 1890s, and had a direct hand in getting the council to hire Frederic Shields and Ford Madox Brown to paint the great series of murals (eventually completed by Brown alone) in the new Town Hall in 1877.[146]

Thomas Worthington was an architect from an old and established Unitarian family; his father owned a warehouse in the city center, and the family lived in the fashionable Salford Crescent until Thomas Sr. died and they moved to the comfortable suburb of High Broughton.[147] He enjoyed the benefits of a good education, placement as an articled pupil in a local architecture firm, and eventually the opportunity to travel to the Continent in the momentous year of 1848. After a period of intense work as an architect, entering local and national competitions (including for the Great Exhibition of 1851), he returned to Italy in 1858, this time with Ruskin's great work *The Stones of Venice* to guide him through that city. Deeply affected by Ruskin's teachings, Worthington moved his architecture toward a decorated Gothic style, and he increasingly concentrated on the physical and moral improvement of Manchester. He participated in the activities of the RMI, the School of Art, and the Statistical Society and was a founding member of the Sanitary Association. He seriously and scientifically studied the state of Manchester's slums, worked on housing for the poor, designed the city's first public baths and washhouses, contributed to improving the area around the Town Hall (he designed Manchester's Albert Memorial, which predated Sir Giles Gilbert Scott's London version by more than a year), gained Florence Nightingale's praise for his hospitals, and helped to make art more accessible to all by spearheading the effort to transfer the RMI to the city government. In 1860 he read a paper before the Manchester Statistical Society in which he wrote, "We are apt to boast of our polished civilisation, of our refined intellectual culture, of our advance in social progress and political science, forgetting for the moment how dark is the reverse of the picture, how harsh the contrast with our own luxurious ease and abundance."[148] Like John Henry Chamberlain in Birmingham and James Allanson Picton in Liverpool, Worthington was an architect inspired by Ruskin to improve his profession and to encourage his profession to improve modern industrial society.

Less has been written about Charles James Pooley and John Ernest Phythian. Pooley was a "cotton spinner," a manufacturer who participated in many of the art reform movements in late Victorian Manchester, collected art, corresponded with artists Ford Madox Brown and Frederic Shields, and was a constant and important presence on both the RMI Council and then on the city council's Art Gallery Committee.[149] He has left few direct statements of his ideas or influences, but his activities show his commitment to widening the audience for art, and the collections he lent to exhibitions in Ancoats show that his tastes tended toward the Pre-Raphaelite Brotherhood and their later followers. He was the major factor in getting the Manchester City Art Gallery to purchase its now emblematic painting, Brown's *Work*, in 1884.[150]

A younger man, J. E. Phythian did not take a leading role in the transfer of the RMI to the city, but he was involved in setting up the Ruskin Society in Manchester in 1879 and later became a principal figure on the Manchester City Art Gallery Committee. Phythian made a succinct connection between studying the writings of Ruskin and his active art museum work in a series of "Reminiscences" that now exist as undated manuscripts in the Manchester Central Reference Library Archives:

Before this [1881] I had made acquaintance with Ruskin by picking up "The Crown of Wild Olive" at the house of Marshall Mather, a Methodist minister at the chapel with whom I had a close & enduring friendship. I was completely carried away by the book. In 1879 The Ruskin Society was formed in M/C & I became a member. In the following year, on January 14th & 15th, four or five of us met Ruskin, by his invitation, at St. George's Museum, Sheffield, and had a never-to-be-forgotten experience. About this time I joined T. C. Horsfall's Art Museum Committee, & so began the kind of work that was to supersede the law. The collection he had formed, largely educational, was first at Queen's Park Museum, & then at Ancoats Hall.[151]

Trained as a lawyer, in 1880 Phythian sought advice on his choice of a career from Ruskin, who helpfully replied, "Be *anything* rather than a Lawyer or a Clergyman" and admonished Phythian to "get your living by direct labour of some kind.

Then Preach—and do justice—gratis as you will—and when you can."[152] Ruskin thus had a small direct as well as a great indirect influence on Phythian and the gradual devotion of his time to lecturing on art and ideas about society, nature, and religion and to working on free temporary loan exhibitions of Ruskin, the Pre-Raphaelites, and their followers at the Manchester City Art Gallery during the early years of the twentieth century.

When the Manchester City Art Gallery eventually opened in 1883, it did so as a result of the persistent campaigning and behind-the-scenes work of these men and others interested in expanding public access to art. Inspired by Ruskin, they participated together in a variety of public and private projects sharing general goals of art education for the working classes. The first of these projects in Manchester received attention and impetus in 1877, when Horsfall wrote to the *Manchester Guardian* with a proposal for a Manchester art museum explicitly based on Ruskinian principles.[153] Horsfall sent a copy to Ruskin, who included his favorable reactions in *Fors Clavigera*, quoting and analyzing Horsfall's proposal at some length.[154] The Manchester Art Museum's siting and liberal opening policies would benefit the working classes, its loan policies to schools and workingmen's clubs would increase the accessibility of exhibits, and it would make each exhibit understandable to the uneducated with a series of explanatory labels.[155] However, as with Dawson in Birmingham and Picton in Liverpool, Ruskin both appreciated Horsfall's work and questioned the basic social relations that prompted the art museum project.

Several of Ruskin's comments on the Manchester Art Museum in particular parallel his reactions to the art museum movements in Birmingham and Liverpool. First, Ruskin noted—and, by implication, disagreed with—Horsfall's assumption that the present society was a given: "In his presently following proposals for 'a better system,' the writer [Horsfall] leaves many of these calamitous conditions unspoken of, assuming them, presumably, to be irretrievable. And this first one, that we do not meet in temples, etc., he passes in such silence." Then again, Horsfall's proposal for the Manchester Art Museum took the haste and ugliness of the modern world as its starting point; in Horsfall's words, "We have far less leisure than the contemporaries of Raphael or of Praxiteles. Our eyes rest patiently on the unmeaning and ugly forms of modern furniture, on soot-begrimed and hideous houses, on a stratum of smoke-laden air that usurps the name of sky." Ruskin responded again with a systemic question: "What are all our machines for, then? Can we do in ten minutes, without man or horse, what a Greek could not have done in a year, with all the king's horses and all the king's men?—and is the result of all this magnificent mechanism, only that we have 'far less leisure'?" Finally, Ruskin took the whole project as so much whitewashing:

From the point where my last note interrupted it, the preceding letter is all admirable; and the passage respecting choice and explanation of pictures, the most valuable I have ever seen printed in a public journal on the subject of the Arts. But let me strongly recommend the writer to put out of his thoughts, for the time, all questions of beautiful furniture and surroundings. Perfectly simple shelter, under the roughest stones and timber that will keep out the weather, is at present the only wholesome condition of private life. Let there be no assumptions of anything, or attempts at anything, but cleanliness, health, and honesty, both in person and possession. Then, whatever you can afford to spend for education in art, give to good masters, and leave them to do the best they can for you: and what you can afford to spend for the splendour of your city, buy grass, flowers, sea, and sky with. No art of man is possible without those primal Treasures of the art of God.[156]

Once again, here is Ruskin admonishing a passionate follower to rethink art as a means to bring nature and beauty to an industrial city, or meaning to workers' lives and labor. Instead, he urges, rethink the system that makes such remediation necessary, and bring nature into the city directly; first work for basic standards of living, including access to the beauty of nature, and then agitate for art.

However, Ruskin's Manchester adherents were not deterred, and in fact, while this project got under way, city librarian and reformer W. E. A. Axon, Horsfall, and Phythian participated in the first Ruskin Society, founded in Manchester in 1879. This "Society of the Rose" (the name suggested by Ruskin, with echoes of English history and of his beloved, deceased Rose de la Touche) gives us a good example of the close connection between Ruskin's works and reformers' efforts.[157] The Manchester founders imagined a remarkably religious engagement with Ruskin's ideas and active social work based on those, as stated in the "Aims of the Society":

To promote the study and circulation of Mr. Ruskin's writings; to exemplify his teachings; and to aid his practical efforts of social improvement.
The Society offers Public Readings and Expositions of Mr. Ruskin's Works to Institutions, Mutual Improvement and other Associations.
Its members desire to place Collections of his Works in Public Libraries and elsewhere, accessible to all readers, and will welcome material co-operation to this end.[158]

The "Ruskin Society Scrapbook," which remains in the Manchester library archives, testifies to twenty-five years of the energy and output of the men who participated in the society. Members gave lectures at churches, the city library, and mechanics' institutes on Ruskin's works and related fields (such as art, architecture, history, political economy, and morality), published essays on Ruskin, and investigated the Ruskin holdings in British municipal libraries; some members met with Ruskin at his newly formed St. George's Museum in Sheffield.[159] In doing so, they used his ideas and intentions as a starting point and moved beyond them, adding texts and interpretations of their own. From 1880, others interested in promoting the experience of art and beauty (including Horsfall, Phythian, Pooley, and Rowley) organized a series of art exhibitions in the slum district of Ancoats (eventual home of Horsfall's Manchester Art Museum) through the Ancoats Recreation Society.[160] The Recreation Society's exhibition catalogues announced their reforming and moralizing intentions with epithets like Ruskin's "Life without Industry is guilt; Industry without Art is brutality."[161]

As the Manchester Art Museum, the Ruskin Society, and the Ancoats Recreation Society were gaining momentum, reform-minded members of the private RMI began to think of it, as Ruskinian architect Thomas Worthington wrote, as "the future permanent Art Gallery of Manchester."[162] In 1880, these RMI members proposed to their governing body that they "transfer the entire property *as a public gift to the City of Manchester* and to the custody of the Corporation [the city council]."[163] The men interested in using art as a philanthropic and educational tool, many of them simultaneously working on the other, related projects around Manchester, were involved in the committees that promoted, and ultimately oversaw, the transfer of the RMI to the city.[164]

These idealists were able to succeed in this project as well as they did because of two important factors: the declining profile of the RMI and the simultaneous rise in prestige and visibility of city art museums, especially Liverpool's Walker Art Gallery, which piqued Manchester's civic pride and opened up possibilities for the municipal subsidization of art. They found that the RMI's "narrowing sphere of usefulness" contrasted with developments in Liverpool, where the art museum "seem[ed] to derive its chief strength from association with its rich and powerful Corporation [the town council]."[165] The reformers believed that, being under municipal control, the Walker Art Gallery was attracting "through its power of purchase, more attractive and prominent Works," and more visitors, as "the property of the People, who recognise that it is maintained for their advantage and enjoyment."[166] They thus characterized Manchester's institution as private, narrow, and unable to grow but found a successful model in the new municipal art museums, particularly that of Manchester's main rival. The reformers' request led to negotiations and a successful transfer scheme by which the RMI presented its entire property, including land, building, and collections, to the City of Manchester as a public gift. The major achievements of the RMI's reformers lay in persuading the city council to spend £2,000 annually on the purchase of works of art to form a permanent collection (although the city reduced this to a commitment of twenty years) and to allow one-third of the Manchester City Art Gallery Committee to be RMI members.[167] The new art museum would also continue the RMI's autumn exhibitions. The renamed and remodeled Manchester City Art Gallery officially opened—in Charles Barry's original neoclassical building of 1829—with the now municipally run autumn exhibition of works for sale on Friday, August 31, 1883.

Despite the ideals of the men who had initiated the transfer, however, tensions between the use of art to enhance the city's national standing and the ideals of bringing art to the people were readily apparent in the museum's content, organization, and accessibility. This conflict would become only more pronounced in later years; as in Liverpool, the Manchester City Art Gallery's paid-entry exhibitions of works for sale competed with the growth of the free permanent collection for space and resources. Apparently, the old wish to remove the stigma of the "myth of Manchester" had not entirely disappeared; the Manchester City Art Gallery sought to obtain, in the curator's words, the "big names" in the art world to increase the popularity and prestige of its exhibitions.[168] (According to one artist, this actually increased the influence of London and the Royal Academy, to the noticeable detriment of locals.[169]) Ironically, perhaps, the members of the old, private RMI on the Manchester City Art Gallery Committee continued to push the city to create an educational museum for all that would incorporate copies of great works, lectures, applied art, and clear labels. With their prodding, the committee did acquire a collection of applied art, portions of which were chosen by William Morris, Charles Rowley, Frederic Shields, and Ford Madox Brown. However, the Manchester City Art Gallery primarily developed as a space for the collection—and annual sale—of popular contemporary painting, and the applied art aimed at the working classes remained in the dark lower galleries year-round, showing the place they held in the priorities of the museum's civic trustees. Ultimately, the Manchester City Art Gallery could not avoid friction between its stated mission of giving workers access to fine art and artisanship and its frequent use as a space of middle-class entertainment and sociability.

CONCLUSION

In Birmingham, Liverpool, and Manchester, Ruskin's ideas inspired citizens to work to make art available to a broader public. However, local circumstance and personality encouraged different goals, and these differences were only magnified when reformers, city administrators, and benefactors tried to put their ideas into action. Birmingham's developing municipal socialism, which emphasized aesthetics as part of the wider mission of "improvement," placed the art museum in the center of city administration, with free entry to the permanent collection, loan exhibitions, and a collection that emphasized both fine and applied arts. Liverpool's class divisions and parsimonious council forced art museum supporters to be creative, ultimately using annual, paid-entry autumn exhibitions of art for sale to raise funds and interest among the city's elites. This strategy, combined with generous private funding, did ultimately give the city an art museum, but it remained encumbered with annual exhibitions that made most of the museum a paid-entry reflection of the city's stratified class structure. Likewise, despite the high ambitions and radical politics of Manchester's Ruskinian reformers, their use of the RMI as the basis of the city art museum left the new institution as oriented as Liverpool's toward the city's middle class.

The major advocates of these city art museums connected art, beauty, social justice, labor, and morality in slightly different ways, but all argued that art was a necessity for the improvement and amelioration not simply of the working classes, but of industrial society itself. Yet when Ruskin engaged with the reformers who were trying to put his ideas into action, he questioned the efficacy of their proposals and plans and emphasized the need for major social change rather than bettering what he saw as an essentially toxic system. At the same time, even similar ideas led to very different results in different local contexts. Horsfall and Rowley, as idealistic as any Ruskinian reformers anywhere, found that the Manchester City Art Gallery, which they helped to establish as a municipal institution, failed in its duty to provide examples of the best work or to elucidate what it did contain with labels and lectures for the uneducated.[170] Similarly, in Liverpool, Picton and Rathbone argued that municipal cultural institutions should aim to make the highest possible standard accessible to all classes, but they ended up creating an institution that shut up the free, permanent collection for much of the year.[171] Following the Ruskinian ideal of the time, and the demands of its skilled workforce, the Birmingham Museum and Art Gallery concentrated on applied and industrial art to an extent far beyond Liverpool's Walker Art Gallery or the Manchester City Art Gallery. Yet this very success would become a burden to the Birmingham museum in the twentieth century, as aesthetic standards and ideology changed.

Besides the contradictions of failed good intentions, we can observe another key conflict as these cities put ideas into practice. The Ruskinian museum advocates never could have developed these museums on their own; they relied on private benefactors and city councils willing, for a variety of reasons, to put up the money. Art held a peculiar and liminal position such that by building art museums, cities could apparently help both themselves and the underprivileged at the same time. The idealists who argued and worked behind the scenes were successful only because others, such as Andrew Walker in Liverpool or the engineering Tangye brothers in Birmingham, supported their projects financially. The movement to make art public and the use of art for civic pride could work together to get a museum built, but often these aims conflicted once committees actually started to run their institutions—establishing opening hours, forming collections, and writing catalogues.

2

THE PUBLIC HOUSE VERSUS THE PUBLIC HOME

The Debate over Sunday Opening

"O lift the workman's heart and mind
Above low sensual sin;
Give him a home, a home of taste,
Outbid the house of gin."

Ebeneezer Elliott, quoted in a sermon by Rev. Bernard J. Snell
on the Sunday opening of free libraries, 1888

Is there a "right" to culture or beauty? If so, should the government provide it? What is the official or public role of religion? Should the religious objections of a minority impede majority rights? All of these questions, and more, came up in the heated debates over whether or not to open the new city art museums on Sundays. Museum advocates' arguments for the use of art for moral regeneration reached an apotheosis during these debates. Their claims put museums in direct competition with traditional religion and thus at the heart of debates about secularization. The most radical argued that art museums might serve as places of worship, and beauty might convey the lessons of church or chapel. Most reformers, however, framed their argument on the understanding of museums and libraries as a new kind of domesticated public space, made up of collections that could offer the same benefits as the art and books in individual middle-class homes, but "posses[ed] in [a] corporate capacity" (in the words of Birmingham councilor Jesse Collings).[1] Indeed, the debate over opening museums and libraries on Sundays was a disagreement among generally middle-class adherents who envisioned different models for modern society. Advocates of traditional religion saw moral instruction as the fundamental purview of church and chapel, and argued that worship needed to remain both public and supported by the state through closure laws and other measures. In contrast, public art museum supporters imagined an active, liberal state, supported by a citizenry moralized through private worship and the operations of the domestic sphere and, where this was impossible, through public spaces offering education, beauty, and refuge from the industrial city. The Sunday-opening debates pushed forward the arguments for public domestic space, as middle-class reformers came up against adherents of organized religion. However, as we will see, truly opening the new art museums to all classes still faced considerable institutional challenges, illustrating the difficulty of redirecting elite culture to a wider public for new purposes.

The Religious Census of 1851 had given an indication of the irreligion of the great majority of the urban population, particularly in the rookeries and slums where the poorest eked out a miserable existence.[2] As reports and exposés of the late nineteenth century opened up new "dark continents" of despair, it became clear that the mid-century church-building movement had had little effect. Indeed, by the 1870s, threats to traditional religion had increased, in the forms of Darwinism, urban culture, and commercial society, and were combining to form a new, secular morality.[3] At the same time, reformers began to question the idea of simple missionary expeditions into working-class life and culture. Some began to articulate the thought that, if the masses were not attending religious services, the government should provide suitable instruction and edification as a means of bringing them into religion, or at least out of the public house.[4]

As debates about the Sunday opening of museums show, during the last decades of the nineteenth century many of art's supporters began to claim roles for art that were traditionally given to organized religion. In the public debates about museums' goals and methods, in their architecture and siting, and ultimately in the way audiences used them, nineteenth-century art museums carved out a particular social space. In the end, these museums played both a quasi-religious and spiritual role *and* a secularizing one. As recent historians of religion have noted, it was precisely this kind of civic project, which transcended denominational differences but incorporated higher moral or spiritual aims, that undermined traditional religion.[5]

In the drive to establish city art museums during the 1860s and 1870s, the most fervent supporters of the museum movement began to use a Ruskinian, religiously inflected language to describe the benefits of these new civic institutions. This became even more pronounced during the debates over whether or not to open museums on Sundays, the traditional Sabbath and day of rest.[6] In order to persuade the majority that this would not abrogate the biblical Fourth Commandment to keep the Sabbath day holy, museum supporters found a variety of ways to argue that cultural institutions could confer moral benefits comparable to those provided by traditional religion and hence were compatible with Sunday opening. They connected museums and libraries with the morality of the domestic sphere, and they even began to argue that visiting art museums could serve as a form of religious observance. The basic problem was this: the museums' supporters justified them in terms of their broader social mission (without which there would have been no call to have rate-supported cultural institutions), and this mission would be effective only if the museums were open and accessible to mass audiences. This, in turn, was possible only if the art museums opened on the traditional day of rest, Sunday, the only day that workers would generally be able to attend a library, natural history museum, or art museum. In order to call for the opening of cultural institutions on Sundays without tearing down all restrictions on Sunday labor and business, however, reformers had to claim that the libraries and museums were compatible with the general religious purposes for which the day was in theory set aside and which many individuals enjoyed privately in their own homes. The debate over Sunday opening of the art museums thus directly compared the goals and claims of art and religion and distinguished between domesticated and "brutal" public space.

At the same time, both Anglicans and Nonconformists also urged that social issues were a core part of religious work, not only as part of an active interpretation of religion (the "social gospel"), but as a means of combating the crisis of faith. Even the official report of the Religious Census of 1851 suggested "better dwellings" for workers—that is, housing comparable to that of the middle-class, the "peculiar isolation" of which encouraged "solitude" and thus "habits of reflection."[7] In this context, clergy also harnessed the domestic ideal to combat what they saw as debased and irreligious forms of working-class leisure. For example, in Bristol in the 1890s Baptist clergyman F. B. Meyer created a "People's Drawing Room" for working women and a "Pleasant Sunday Afternoon" for working men.[8] Meanwhile, the Church of England and Nonconformist denominations battled for parishioners and influence. Issues such as Sunday leisure often divided the middle class along sectarian lines; these battles derived not just, or even primarily, from doctrinal differences but were part of a larger struggle for social power in Victorian cities.[9] However, as J. H. S. Kent argues, this conflict only helped to weaken what increasingly became a "religious subculture . . . slowly separating itself institutionally from the dominant, largely secular culture."[10] Throughout this process, both secular and religious voices utilized visions of domesticated public space, part of the larger conflict within the middle class about how to make cities more livable and how to bring the working classes into their own orbit, that is, either into secular citizenship or into the fold of a particular denomination.

For art museum supporters, art had a profound moral and social role; for the clergy, art might even lead *away* from "holiness." Working in one of the poorest sections of Manchester, industrial Ancoats, T. C. Horsfall advocated art museums as a key means of bringing the beauty of the world and of human endeavor to those who had seen little or none of either:

I had long been convinced that unless children gain knowledge of beautiful and inter-esting country things, and of beautiful and interesting things made by men, they will have in later life little religious feeling, and little knowledge of the better part of the human nature common to them and their fellow creatures; and that, moreover, unless the same conditions are fulfilled, nearly all the most wholesome kinds of recreation must be without attraction for them.[11]

This argument, however, rested on a connection between art and religion that was deeply suspect to many members of the clergy and their congregations, as can be seen in this passage from an anti-Sunday-opening pamphlet: "Christian-ity will humanize; we are not so sure that humanizing will Christianize. Let us be clear upon the matter: aesthetics are not religion. It is one thing to civilise, to polish, it is another to Christianize. The worship of the beautiful is not the worship of holiness. Nay, I know not whether the one may not have a tendency to disincline from the other."[12] To these Christians, the art-as-reform group was in danger of making a religion of art itself, and mistaking what was essentially sensual entertainment or coarse materialism for that spiritual nourishment available only through scripture-based worship.

When historians have addressed the Victorian crisis of faith, they have made much of the conflict between science and religion and of the ways in which doubt and faith coexisted (and perhaps even strengthened each other).[13] In addition, scholars have acknowledged the ways in which secular projects that co-opted previously religious activities (such as moral reform) and religious movements that emphasized the social rather than the metaphysical aspects of religious prac-tice *both* tended to deemphasize the monopoly that religion had had on central social, philosophical, and moral issues. All of this suggests that, for a little while, for certain reformers, and at the height of doubt and worry about the status of organized religion, art museums provided an exceptionally unified alternative to traditional religion. Using a combination of romantic ideas and the zeal of the social gospel, and bolstered by the highly developed set of assumptions about domesticity and morality that took shape throughout the Victorian period, art museum supporters provided a rationale, an institutional base, and a physical experience. Reformers imagined that art museums would be accessible to all, reaching each at his or her own level of education and comprehension, and ideally serving to bring beauty and meaning into lives short on both.

The Sunday-opening debate made explicit a series of questions about the role of evangelical Christianity in British government and society, about what kinds of secular institutions or models might provide substitutes for the universalizing claims formerly made by the Church of England, and about the role of government in providing domesticated public spaces to those who lacked the ideal private space that formed the ideological basis for the formation of the (public) citizen. Those in favor of Sunday opening consistently compared the art museums and libraries to what was then currently available, namely, the public house—taken here in the full meaning of the term. The question of whether or not to open city art museums on Sundays thus became a site of real and profound conflict among a variety of groups—within the middle class and, increasingly, within the working class—because it touched on distinctions between public and private, on the rights of majorities and minorities, on the role of religion in contemporary Britain, and on the definitions of both art and religion.

One possible compromise between opening art museums on Sundays and keeping them locked to the mass of potential visitors was to open them in the evenings, an option made possible by improvements in artificial illumination (gas and electric lighting). The question of whether to use artificial lighting in museums, however, was not a simple one, because of conservation concerns, namely, the potential damage to delicate works, especially watercolors, in gaslight and the danger of fire thought to increase with electrical wiring. Indeed, the National Gallery, which became an important lender to the regional art museums for temporary exhibitions, would not send works to museums that used gas lighting to stay open in the evenings.[14] Thus, museums might have the choice of borrowing art to make their exhibitions more interesting (often explicitly for the benefit of local "artizans"), using new, expensive, and potentially dangerous electric lighting, or being open with gas lighting when large audiences could attend. Sunday afternoon opening could thus seem to many museum committee members to be the best and easiest means of widening the audience for art.

In attempting to open on Sundays, the Birmingham, Liverpool, and Manchester art museums each faced a different set of challenges. In Birmingham, the dominant ideas of the "municipal gospel" led the town council to open the city's new civic institutions on Sundays at a very early date (1872). The Sunday-opening debate led to attacks on the prominently Unitarian city leadership and raised the question of the rights of the citizen and the civil authority, particularly regarding religious minorities and in terms of the relationship between private and public ownership. In Liverpool, where sectarian differences and the Irish question loomed large in city life, the issue became deeply politicized and connected to Liberal attempts to gain control of the Conservative city council. There, the debate centered in particular on the role of the city in providing alternatives to, or simply containing, "vice" in the form of drinking establishments. In Manchester, where a private institution became the city art museum, radical reformers came up against the traditions of art collecting and connoisseurship that supported a large local art market. The debates there thus raised the questions of who the art museum was for and what its purpose was. Did the art museum exist to help the poor or to continue the enlightened discourse of the educated classes? Note that all of these questions, about art, citizenship, religion, and governance, are still relevant today.

Ultimately, all three of these city art museums opened on Sundays by the middle of the 1890s, before the Sunday opening of the national institutions in London in 1896. The fierce battles waged over this issue reveal yet another rift between the rhetoric of art to improve and inspire workers and the reality that limited the access of the masses to these ostensibly public institutions: the same art market and collecting habits that fed the belief in art also threw up considerable institutional barriers to making art and art education available to everyone. However, Sunday openings and accessibility to free permanent collections did lead to increased attendance figures and became central to the idea of public collections. These victories for the art reformers show the zenith of the conception of art as a public good and of museums as spaces that could offer all of the moral and aesthetic refuge of the ideal middle-class home.

THE NATIONAL DEBATE:
THE LORD'S DAY VERSUS SUNDAY

The debate over whether to open government-run public educational institutions on the traditional day of rest was a national one, and was a particularly modern problem. However, it bears remembering that Sunday observance was a fraught issue in British society even before such innovations as municipal art museums.[15] The question of how to mark the Sabbath in a Christian way, in fact, goes back to the early history of the church and concern over the continued relevance of Jewish law to the new Christian faith.[16] English Sabbatarianism aimed to reinstate a "Sabbath," following the injunctions of the Fourth Commandment to "remember the Sabbath and keep it holy," that is, to restrict all activity to religious observance of the "Lord's Day." The origins of this movement are intimately connected with the history of the English Church itself. Early versions of Protestant Sabbatarianism emerged during the Reformation to differentiate Protestant and Catholic belief and practice, as the new Anglican Church dismantled Catholic customs such as the celebration of myriad saints' holy days.[17] Indeed, nineteenth-century Sabbatarians' use of precedent and arguments for a return to old values speak to a modern "invention of tradition."[18] The mid-century Sunday-opening movement followed, and was in large part a reaction to, a nearly thirty-year Sunday-closing movement, during which evangelicals agitated for a reinvigoration of Sunday observance, campaigning for the Sunday closure of any and all businesses that demanded labor on that day. The earliest Sabbatarian society, the Lord's Day Observance Society, founded in 1831, helped to promote a new vision of Sunday observance; it enjoyed only mixed legislative success, but did make the issue of Sunday practice and worship prominent during the 1830s and 1840s.[19]

The debate over Sunday opening reveals underlying tensions between deeply ingrained Victorian ideals: individual freedom and the greater good, religious duty and self-improvement, the right to education and the need to regulate labor and industrial production. The debate thus created strange bedfellows: evangelicals and socialists railed against the Sunday opening of libraries and museums, while radical reformers, Catholics, and members of the Anglican clergy defended it. The question of the opening hours and days of municipal and national institutions had far-reaching implications. Who owned such institutions? For whose benefit did they exist? Would the working classes be most aided through religious or secular means?[20] For the most part, both proponents and opponents of Sunday opening assumed that the middle classes needed to help bring the working classes into their newly achieved citizenship, the key question being the means. As the century wore on, more working-class voices entered the debate, pressing for Sunday opening in terms similar to their middle-class counterparts.

Although Sunday had traditionally been a day of worship, rest, and relaxation, the combined effects of evangelical revival and the emerging cultural power of the middle classes in the first half of the nineteenth century had redefined Sunday as strictly for religious activities.[21] In the middle of the century, however, largely following the huge, peaceful working-class attendance of the Great Exhibition of 1851, a new movement began to loosen some of those strictures to enable institutions of education or rational recreation to open for the working classes on Sundays. In this nearly fifty-year national debate, the main actors were organizations of varying membership, who lectured from pulpit and lectern, published arguments in pamphlets, wrote to the national press, and attempted to change public policy through deputations to government officials and many presentations of petitions.[22] By the early 1850s, Sabbatarian interests generally controlled Parliament on Sunday issues; however, in reaction to attempts at Sabbatarian legislation that would restrict Sunday trading, three Sundays in July 1855 witnessed the worst rioting in London in decades.[23] Indeed, in addition to the Hyde Park riots, there had been further evidence of a new *anti*-Sabbatarian trend when, in 1854, a parliamentary Select Committee on Sunday Trading of Public Houses actually recommended that the British Museum, the National Gallery, and the Crystal Palace should be opened on Sundays. Questions were raised in the House of Commons about this recommendation, and petitions were sent in on both sides; votes were taken (and lost) to open the national institutions on Sundays in 1856, 1869, 1874, and 1878.[24]

Like the Sabbatarian movement before it, the Sunday-opening movement began as a metropolitan phenomenon but became national in scope. The debates about opening libraries and museums took place across the country, both about the national institutions in London—particularly whenever Parliament debated this issue—and about the opening of specific local ones. Opening the National Gallery, British Museum, and Crystal Place became the purpose of the National Sunday League, founded in 1854.[25] Local chapters of the league formed, and a national confrontation emerged between those supporting the use of cultural institutions for social reform and evangelical Sabbatarians wishing to either maintain the status quo or close down any and all Sunday trading and amusement. Through the 1870s and 1880s, when great numbers of cities founded libraries and museums, the problem became more acute: the new municipal institutions were often explicitly created for the moral and practical education of the working classes, but if workers were to benefit from such institutions, they would need the time to do it. When the National Sunday League began working on other Sunday issues—excursion trains, lectures, music in the parks, the opening of for-profit ventures—a splinter group founded the

Sunday Society in 1875 to redirect reformers' energies toward specifically opening libraries and museums.[26] As it turned out, the advent of city institutions
meant that cities such as Birmingham, Liverpool, and Manchester in fact led
the capital in opening their cultural institutions on Sundays.

Sabbatarians and Sunday-openers fought over three major topics: the religious nature of the day, and how a Christian's duty to keep it must be fulfilled;
the rights of workers, and how these might best be served; and the practical
problem of Sunday drinking, and how this might most effectively be ended.
Through these issues, the Sunday-opening debate projected municipal art museums into the center of major political differences. The controversy shows both
the continued strength of religion in Victorian political life and the emergence of
a new vision—one of shared civic culture, universal education, and an increased
role for government—predicated on domesticated public space.

BIRMINGHAM: THE CIVIC GOSPEL AT WORK

As we have seen, the city art museum in Birmingham defined itself for a broad
audience as part of a radical program of civic renewal. With a curator heavily
influenced by John Ruskin and William Morris, the museum aimed to connect
artists and artisans, employers and workers, by showing fine and applied art, by
placing great emphasis on developing a large free permanent collection, and
by hosting innovative free themed loan exhibitions. The museum had a clear
acquisitions policy directed by curator Whitworth Wallis, enhanced through
the efforts of many leading citizens to further the museum's work with gifts
and bequests. It is no surprise, then, that the Birmingham Corporation Free Art
Gallery, as it was then called, opened to the public on Sundays for the first time
on April 28, 1872, after several months of debate and deputations in the town
council, well before most other cities had even opened municipal art museums.
After initial disagreement, the gallery remained open on Sundays without incident—indeed, with markedly increased attendance and seemingly widespread
approval. The Sunday opening of Birmingham's art museum did not go un-
contested, however. In fact, the Liberal politics of the city in the 1870s, and the
dominance of secularists—particularly Unitarians—made opening the gallery
on Sundays a political as well as a religious issue.[27]

One strong reason for the town council to open the art gallery on Sundays
might have been local glass manufacturer Thomas Clarkson Osler's creation
in 1871 of the Public Picture Gallery Fund, with an (anonymous) initial gift of

£3,000.[28] One prominent proviso of that gift was that the pictures so granted must be shown in a gallery open free to the public on Sundays.[29] As well as perhaps inducing the council to take action, the stipulation on his gift shows that members of the council were not alone in wanting the public collections to be more accessible. Another impetus for opening the gallery on Sundays—perhaps related to or coming out of the first—came with the election of Liberal councilor Jesse Collings, first to the town council in 1868 and then as the chair of the Free Libraries Committee in 1872.[30] Collings was a Liberal iron merchant interested in education and reform, especially the rights and economic status of agricultural workers; he was deeply involved in the Liberal Party and the effort to establish the Forster Education Act of 1870 and became a vice president of the National Sunday League in 1876.[31] He left the Birmingham Town Council when he became member of Parliament for Ipswich in 1880 and then served as Bordesley's Liberal Unionist MP from 1886 until 1918.[32] As chairman of the Free Libraries Committee, he later described being "struck . . . that it was not right for those great institutions to be closed on Sundays, the only days on which the working-classes could visit them."[33] The idea passed from the committee to the town council in its report of January 2, 1872, and the debate continued over two more council meetings, on March 26 and April 2, when it finally won approval by a vote of twenty-seven to fifteen.[34] Compared with what would turn into a forty-year fight to open the national institutions in London, Birmingham moved with lightning speed.

The debate pitted numerous religious organizations, including the Sunday School Union and the Lord's Day Defence Association—representing both Anglican and Nonconformist members and ministers—against the Liberal town council, the Birmingham Trades Council, and the Labour Representation League.[35] City residents presented memorials on both sides of the question (although the council did not record in what numbers), but the town council seems to have been remarkably unswayed by the strong opposition that religious groups mustered. The debate revolved around four key issues: first, can art or culture be religious? Second, how can workers best be helped—by providing alternatives to the pub or by preventing any and all employment on that day? Third, can the civil authority be limited by the conscientious objections of minorities? And fourth, what rights do citizens have to public property? The religious opposition sought to make it a religious debate—about the status of art and culture, and about the nature of the day of rest—while Collings, as the primary spokesman for Sunday opening, turned the debate to questions of rights. In particular, he moved the question from the spiritual to the domestic, positioning the art museum as a kind of public drawing room, owned in a "corporate capacity."[36]

The religious lobby first put forward its arguments through an anonymous pamphlet, issued late in 1871 (presumably in response to the Free Libraries Committee's discussions of the issue as it prepared its end-of-year report), and then in oral arguments at the meeting of the town council on January 2, 1872.[37] The lobby presented both religious and practical arguments against Sunday opening: first, that art and religion are fundamentally different, and second, that opening "places of recreation" would in fact hurt rather than help the working classes. The pamphlet *The Sunday Question Again: Shall the Free Libraries and Art Gallery Be Open on Sunday?* at first explained that it would only argue in practical terms, but then slipped into the religious debate by quoting one F. W. Robertson at length. For Robertson, the idea that art and culture could heal industrial society was fundamentally flawed; as quoted in the pamphlet, Robertson denied "the assumption that public places of recreation, which humanize, will therefore Christianize the people . . . that architecture, sculpture, and the wonders of nature and art which such buildings will contain, have a direct or indirect tendency to lead to true devotion."[38] Many Sabbatarians and anti-Sunday-openers felt that the pro-Sunday-opening campaigners, in justifying their position, had moved to extreme arguments that had begun to conflate art and religion. After emphasizing the danger of confusing aesthetics and religion, the worship of the beautiful and the worship of the holy, Robertson argued that this sort of logic in fact led to decadence and decline: "Greece was the home of the arts; the sacred ground on which the worship of the beautiful was carried to its perfection. Let those who have read the history of her decline and fall; who have perused the debasing works of her later years, tell us how music, painting, poetry, the arts, softened and debilitated, and sensualized the nation's heart."[39] The passage shows the specific challenge that those in favor of the Sunday opening of museums posed to Sabbatarians, even mild or tolerant ones such as Robertson claimed to be. The use of art for social reform had not, until then, conflicted with evangelical Christianity. However, in trying to justify the Sunday opening of art galleries, supporters had begun to slip between "humanizing" and "Christianizing," treating the social and spiritual benefits of religion as equally important, or even as identical. To Robertson, in fact, art represented just the opposite: the sensual, feminized pleasure and decadence of Greece, not the purity and manly spirituality of Christianity. At the January 2 town council meeting the Reverend Isaac Spooner, vicar of Edgbaston Old Church, also argued in primarily religious terms, objecting to the Sunday opening because "taking the Word of God as their guide, they [the Sabbatarians] believed the observance of the Sabbath to be a perpetual obligation."[40] Ultimately, both Robertson and Spooner took the position that those speaking for art as a positive force in society had begun to use a fuzzy and utilitarian definition of religion in order to make claims for art. A Mr. Vince, arguing in front of the council, also sought to make the issue a religious one, putting the question in terms of the need for religious coexistence. Vince proposed that as Sunday opening violated the religious feelings of some citizens—who, as ratepayers, were "proprietors" of the reference library and art gallery—it would be best for the institutions to remain on "common ground" (that is, not offending any group or sect).[41]

The religious lobby, however, also attacked Sunday opening on practical grounds, and in terms of workers' rights and benefits. The 1871 pamphlet argued that traditional Sunday observance allowed the silence and contemplation, the physical and mental rest, required for both worldly and spiritual health, and framed these in terms of workers' rights: "The effort and tendency of the labours of the true working man, are everywhere to shorten the hours of toil; but these spurious friends of the working class now wish to add to them."[42] By this argument, opening municipal institutions on Sundays was the thin end of the wedge that would lead to a seven-day workweek. Further, the author reasoned that the current opening hours of the library were more than sufficient without making others work on Sunday.[43] To this author, even the fact that the art gallery was *not* open during hours convenient for workers did not justify its opening as being "necessary" work. He also dismissed the argument that government provision of alternative places of recreation would diminish Sunday drinking or that the people who frequented pubs would benefit from the public library or art museum; the Reverend Spooner would also repeat this argument.[44]

In contrast, Councilor Collings moved the question away from religious issues, framing it instead in terms of rights and of the nature of domesticity. He first argued that the question was *not* a religious one: against Rev. Spooner he pointed out that the Bible forbade a great many things performed on the Sabbath, and urged that it remained an open question whether Sunday opening would in fact violate any of God's laws.[45] Against Mr. Vince, he again stressed the nonreligious nature of the debate, reasoning that just because some felt it was a religious issue did not necessarily make it so and that religious arguments were by their nature outside the scope of the town council.[46] Collings proceeded to take Mr. Vince at his own argument, pressing, like Vince, for a consideration of the common good in making the decision. Collings held, however, that it was precisely in matters when an individual's belief system was violated that it must not be allowed to dictate against the general welfare: "the moment a man's conscience interferes with the rights and liberties of his fellow citizens, then, though it might be respected, it ought not to be obeyed."[47] Against Mr. Vince's warning of religious conflict if Sunday opening proceeded, Collings placed the question of Sunday opening firmly on secular ground: "in our day it is the civil power which governs, both in imperial and local affairs, and which will in this instance, I am sure, consider only what is just and right to all, without regard to any ecclesiastical demands or threats whatever."[48] Having thus dismissed the religious argument, Collings shifted the debate: it was a question of citizens' rights to culture and public property, and a question of efficacious public policy on the issue of Sunday drinking—but more than both of these, it was a question of harnessing the power of the domestic ideal for a wider public.

Collings questioned a policy that would allow private citizens to enjoy books and pictures on Sunday if they owned them privately, while preventing the public collections from opening—when the only way for many to own such things was in just such a "corporate capacity":

if you are rich enough to become sole proprietors of books, and gardens, and pictures, nay, if you are rich enough to hold a share in a company that has such possessions, the law will not be against you, public opinion will be with you, and a religious scandal will not be created. If you can buy a share in the Crystal Palace, or if you can subscribe a guinea to the Edgbaston Botanical Gardens, you can enjoy art and nature righteously; but if you are so poor that you can possess books, and pictures, and gardens, in the only way in which the poor can hope to possess them, namely, in their corporate capacity, then such enjoyments become oppressive to the consciences of certain other men, many of whom by their own confession, derive the utmost delight in doing in their own homes that which they so strongly object to be done in the Public Libraries and Art Gallery of the town. I cannot see either the justice or the logic of such arguments.[49]

He highlighted this with a passage "from a letter on the subject by a working man":

I trust the Council will in the discussion of this question keep this fact before their eyes; that the Reference Library being established by the rate-payers for the good of the town cannot at present be used by the bulk of the town, because the majority of them have to work from morning till night on week days, and are at the close of those days too weary to avail themselves of those privileges which their money has helped to purchase.[50]

He used the worker's letter to question the assumption that evening openings were good enough, and to legitimate the argument that true study of literature or art demanded energy that one simply could not expect after a hard day's work.

Collings also addressed the issues raised by the deputation—and others against Sunday opening, such as the author(s) of the pamphlet *The Sunday Question Again*—on the subject of Sunday drinking. He had two main points: first, that Sunday pub-going was *not* an issue of respectability, but rather of the options open to most of the poor:

There are young men in lodgings, men in crowded houses; what are they to do with them-selves on Sundays, on wet days especially? The practice of public house going begins with an occasional visit, and only gets confirmed into a habit by time; and a single visit to the libraries on Sunday may, as we know it has done on week days, create an interest in the place, leading to further visits, and into a habit of reading and study. At any rate, let it be no longer said that in Birmingham there is no choice but the streets or the public houses.[51]

Collings questioned the constant call that Sabbatarians made for a Sunday of cozy, private domesticity; for many, the only domesticity available was the public house.

Second, Collings invoked the idea that through a public form of domestic-ity, art and culture could change society. If Sunday drinking among the working classes was a problem, he argued, it was so—for the majority, in any case—only because they had no viable alternatives. Art and culture had transformed the middle classes; let it work the same change on the working classes:

I would remind these gentlemen that at one time the upper and middle classes of England, the men of the class now sitting in this chamber, were slaves to drinking habits, that they have freed themselves from these habits, not by Acts of Parliament, but by social and edu-cational influences, by better culture and a higher standard of taste; and I am persuaded that the same results will be seen by a similar process among the poor and working classes; and that process will be aided and hastened by such measures as we propose to-day.

He had "just received a very thoughtful letter from a working man on the same subject," who concluded:

if the opening of these places should only be the means of drawing fifty men from the public houses, (which next to the street is their only place of resort,) and make them more thoughtful and enquiring men, it will be sowing a seed that may bring forth a hundred fold, and would I am sure be gratifying to those who now oppose the measure. I for one have no misgivings as to what may be the result of the experiment.[52]

Here Collings imagined that the changes wrought by the middle class in individual households might be replicated for a mass public through government provision of the same cultural amenities, reiterating through his correspondent the absence of domestic comforts for so many, who could choose only between street and pub.

Finally, Collings brought the argument back to the nature of the proposed changes to Sunday observance and leisure, and back to the compatibility of art, literature, and religion. Increasing the availability of art and culture would not open the floodgates to Sunday trade, but in fact would increase religiosity and improve society: "those who have seen the magnificent Art Collections in some of the towns in Europe, and have noticed the behaviour and the interest of the multitudes who go to them on a Sunday, will agree with me, that the religious feelings are rather heightened than depreciated by such visits."[53] As the anti-openers presented arguments on both scriptural and practical levels, Collings also attempted to argue that it was *not* a religious question and that even if it were, access to culture was compatible with spiritual aims.

Whether they were swayed by the workers' deputations or Collings's speech, or would have voted for the proposal in any case, the members of the town council approved the measure, and the Birmingham Corporation Free Art Gallery opened to the public for the first time on a Sunday on April 28, 1872. The Free Libraries Committee reported that 1,042 people visited the art gallery (then just one thirty-by-seventy-foot room) on the first day of Sunday opening, and that a "number of persons were waiting for admission at the time of opening [4 p.m.] and shortly after, the Art Gallery was well filled. . . . Whole families appeared to attend, parents bringing their children."[54] In emphasizing the healthy domesticity of the scene, the report implicitly contrasted this with the public house. After the initial debate, the Birmingham Museum and Art Gallery remained open, and subsequent reports of the Free Libraries Committee continued to note increasing attendance and interest. Ultimately, a strong Liberal town council, including many members who belonged to nonevangelical denominations, successfully framed the issue as one of rights to public property and public domesticity, rather than of religion and the rights of conscientious objectors.

LIVERPOOL: THE POLITICS OF SUNDAY OPENING

Unlike in Birmingham and Manchester, the Liverpool City Council was dominated by Conservatives, although the Liberals generally controlled (even if a Liberal did not often chair) the Library, Museum, and Arts Committee.[55] Liverpool's
large Irish population meant that politics there through the last quarter of the
nineteenth century revolved around the issue of Ireland, as Home Rule Liberals
and Irish Nationalists combined and the Conservatives depended on both Liberal
Unionists and the fiercely Protestant Orangemen.[56] This particular mix of politics
and sectarian strife meant that the issue of Sunday opening in Liverpool, like most
issues there, became a bone of contention between Liberals and (mostly Catholic)
Irish Nationalists on the one hand (for Sunday opening) and (mostly Protestant)
Sabbatarian Unionists on the other (against Sunday opening). Liberals consistently brought up the issue, particularly through the press, arguing in terms of
the public's right to city property and stating that the library, museum, and art
gallery were essentially comparable to the "domestic resources" held privately in
middle-class homes. Complicating the situation further, the brewing interest
in Liverpool was a strong part of the Conservative Party, and any measures to
limit licensing or control public drinking—claims that Sunday-openers made
for their cause—generally remained unenforced.[57] This portrait of the politici-
zation and a deliberate policy by the Conservative town council is substantiated
in the recollections of the Reverend Charles F. Aked, minister for the Pembroke
Baptist Chapel in Liverpool, 1890–1906: "Law is one thing, but the enforcement
of it is another. The experience of Liverpool by this time is well known. . . . The
civic authorities protected vice . . . the policy of concentration was the one followed. Two districts were given up to the trade in vice. If the evil-doers opened
business in other neighbourhoods they were prosecuted, but so long as they kept
within the infected areas they were safe."[58] Clearly, the Conservatives had to walk
a fine line to appease the Sabbatarian Unionists, the working class, and powerful brewing families. Such a policy of "containment" had effected a compromise
but left Liberals, workers, and even Sabbatarians unsatisfied. The Conservatives
generally voted to please the Sabbatarian Unionists, although their disunity on
the issue and growing weakness during the late 1890s eventually led to the Walker
Art Gallery opening on Sundays in 1891.[59] The twenty-year battle over Sunday
opening in Liverpool shows again the powerful idea of museums as domesticated
public space, and the extent to which both the use of art as a means of social reform and evangelical Sabbatarianism could become politicized.

Liverpool society was highly stratified, with an extremely wealthy merchant class above and the periodically employed masses of unskilled dockworkers below. Over the course of the last three decades of the nineteenth century, as education and the franchise expanded, as the Labour Party began to be a political factor, and as cultural institutions took on an established role in municipal life, pressure grew to open Liverpool's libraries, museums, and art collection to a wider public. The city's first experiment with increased access to its cultural institutions occurred during 1863–1871, when the Derby Museum of Natural History opened on Monday evenings.[60] At first, this appeared to be a success, but increased visitors also meant more possibilities for improper behavior; the museum committee reported visitors "spitting on the floors, lounging about and obstructing the passages . . . preventing proper inspection of the cases," and seats "occupied by idlers; persons wandering around without any object."[61] When the Derby Museum began evening openings again in 1888, the committee noted a marked change in behavior; during the intervening seventeen years, those attending evening openings had apparently learned what kind of behavior middle-class authorities expected in public places.[62] Many have read this emphasis on appropriate behavior as an attempt by the middle class to exert control over and influence workers, but it can also be seen as contemporaries saw it, that is, that this kind of public cultural space was essentially the public version of the middle-class home, and thus demanded certain forms of decorum. (Clearly, provision of such spaces meant that middle-class reformers were providing behavioral norms to working-class visitors; this does not mean, however, that workers were ultimately controlled by such tactics.[63]) Indeed, by 1888, pressure was mounting to open the library, museums, and Walker Art Gallery permanently on Sundays and to increase public access to the gallery's permanent collection.

The annual autumn exhibitions began in 1871 as a way to expand the audience for art and to raise funds for a permanent art collection. As early as 1873, these exhibitions offered cheap (three-penny) evening tickets, which greatly increased attendance; the Library, Museum and Arts Committee eventually authorized free admission on a limited number of Sundays beginning in 1889. The development of Liverpool's municipal art museum (opened in 1877) was thus closely tied to the history of its autumn exhibitions, where local and national artwork was sold, as the committee depended on the revenue the exhibitions generated for acquisition funds. At the same time, however, the autumn exhibitions, although a primary means for the Walker Art Gallery to support itself, acted to maintain social distinctions in the use of the museum: there was a charge for admission, staggered by price and time of day, and the free-entry permanent collection was displaced for a great part of the year by the hanging and display of the temporary exhibition. So even though the autumn exhibition opened on Monday evenings for a reduced fee from 1873, its very existence was an obstacle to free public access to the permanent collection. This point—and its connection to the Sunday-opening issue—was made explicitly by the acerbic editor and art critic of the Liberal *Liverpool Lantern*, K. C. Spier, in 1880:

At present, to the vast majority of the population of Liverpool, the art of the day is a sealed book, and neither the pictures of the town nor the splendid Art Gallery which the generous donor meant to bestow upon the people, are their own. The public pictures are locked up from them during the only periods when they have an opportunity of seeing them, and for nearly half the year the gallery is illegally monopolised by an art speculation to which only the paying class can be admitted.[64]

To Spier, the Walker Art Gallery's purpose was the free exhibition of a permanent collection, the autumn exhibition being an "art speculation" held only for the benefit of the "paying classes"—clearly not the people for whom the free art gallery had been intended.[65]

The Liberal papers consistently called for an end to Sabbatarian control of the Sunday-opening issue and framed it as one of private versus public domesticity. As early as 1876, when the Social Science Association held its annual congress in Liverpool and its program included a paper on Sunday opening, the Liberal *Daily Post* embraced the idea, and a local Sunday Society was formed.[66] Events in 1879 illustrate both the strength of the Sabbatarian faction in Liverpool and the feeling of the Liberal press against it. In July, the mayor and leader of the Conservatives, A. B. Forwood, gave his support to the Sabbatarian Sunday Closing Bill, which sought to restrict all Sunday trade and was specifically aimed at closing the public houses. This piqued the *Liberal Review*: "working men may well feel inclined to ask whether it is altogether good taste on the part of gentlemen with their domestic resources to seek to impose upon their poorer countrymen sacrifices and inconveniences to which they would happily not be called upon to submit themselves?"[67] Here again we see the idea that public institutions made the "domestic resources" and refuge from the city provided by middle-class homes available to all. The paper concluded its tirade against the "sabbatical dogma" and "dominion of a tyrannical Puritanism" that the Sunday Closing Bill represented by arguing that

in our opinion there is at present but one way which affords any substantial hope of stopping Sunday drinking, of making West Derby-road "fit and decent for respectable people to walk along," and generally of realising all the aspirations expressed at the town's meeting on Saturday. It is to put the Art Gallery, the Museum, the Library, and the Concert-hall in competition with the public-house—to empty the grog-shop by refining the tastes of the people, instead of arbitrarily closing it by Act of Parliament.[68]

In the rhetoric of the Liberal press in Liverpool, then, as in Birmingham, the issue was one of rights to a kind of "public home" that was fundamentally opposed to the "public house." The Liberal press in Liverpool agitated for further action when, later in 1879, the RMI opened its autumn exhibition for the first time on some Sundays, and the papers continued to argue in favor of opening Liverpool's institutions throughout the 1880s.[69]

Pressure stepped up in 1885, when a Liverpool Sunday League formed, the Trades Union Council considered the issue at its annual meeting, and the Library, Museum, and Arts Committee ordered a comprehensive report on the extent of Sunday opening in the rest of the country.[70] What is most striking about the information the committee gathered is how many city art galleries it contacted (142); how few institutions were actually open on Sundays (17, or 12 percent); and that despite the continuous agitation by various Sunday-opening societies and vociferous complaints of Sabbath desecration by Sabbatarians, the issue had been raised at only about one-third (43) of the responding institutions.[71] Ultimately, the 1885 report tells us that the committee—which was itself deeply divided—faced a great deal of opposition over Sunday opening, and it wished to back up any action with clear precedent; across most of the country, however, it was still the unusual municipal institution that opened against the general Sabbatarian pressure.

After 1885 the question became only more politicized in Liverpool. The Trades Union Council, which had voted against endorsing Sunday opening in 1885, reversed that decision in 1887.[72] As labor struggled to organize itself in Liverpool, and the Liberal Party slowly gained ground, the Sabbatarians could no longer control the vote. In the municipal elections of 1890, the Liberal John Lea won a seat on the city council against a Conservative candidate undecided on Sabbatarianism, and Liberals and Irish Nationalists combined to win another seat; by that year, the Conservatives maintained their majority only through their control of the aldermen.[73] The Irish Nationalists on the council raised the issue in each of the three councils from 1888 until the eventual victory of Sunday opening in 1891.[74] Dissension within the Conservative Party, and the strength of the Liberal–Irish Nationalist alliance, meant that in 1892 the Liberal Party gained control of the Liverpool Town Council for the first time in fifty years.[75]

At the end of 1891, the Library, Museum, and Arts Committee reported that, "acting upon a resolution of the Council, the Committee have opened the Permanent Gallery on Sunday afternoons; the attendance has been large and very orderly, and the opportunity of seeing our picture galleries has been largely availed of by the artizan classes."[76] The report also recorded that on the first thirteen Sundays that the Walker Art Gallery was open, between the hours of 2:30 and 5:30 p.m. the average attendance was 1,773.[77] However, the controversy was not entirely over. The minutes of the Arts and Exhibitions Sub-Committee record that the Walker Art Gallery was the subject of the Sunday-opening debate that continued in the rest of the country, as correspondents from both sides of the issue wrote asking for the results of Liverpool's Sunday-opening experiment.[78] Then, following the decision to open the gallery on Sundays, the subcommittee recommended each year to *close* it on Sundays during the months of June, July, and August—"for cleaning and other purposes."[79] Thus the working classes had the option of seeing the permanent collection only during the autumn, winter, and spring—when for the most part special exhibitions were taking place and displacing a significant portion of the art gallery. However, the principle had been granted: that the municipal art museum existed for the benefit of the people of Liverpool, as a domesticated public space, and if the vast majority could attend only on Sundays, it should be open to them on that day.

MANCHESTER: FROM ART FOR THE PRIVILEGED TO ART FOR THE PEOPLE

In Manchester, where the RMI gifted itself to the city, we see a clear debate about the nature of working- and middle-class homes and whether or not the Sunday opening of civic institutions would change the "brutal" nature of the city.[80] Were working-class homes places of rest and recuperation, or did the public house offer the only comfort possible? Would those who had a decent home go to a pub, and would those at the pub ever step into a library or an art museum? In other words, was there a separate "public-house-going class" within the working class, whose drunkenness and violence stemmed not from their conditions of life, but from their very natures? At the same time, opening the RMI to new audiences challenged the meaning and scope of the institution. Who was art for, and what was the purpose of the collection? In the course of these debates, Manchester reformers harnessed the now-familiar associations with the domestic sphere, arguing that civic cultural institutions made available to all publicly what the privileged already enjoyed privately. However, several reformers also stressed the spiritual nature of art, conflating beauty, nature, and religion in ways that reconceived the art museum as comparable not only to a private home, but also to a house of worship.

In Manchester, as elsewhere, the city libraries opened on Sundays before the art gallery, simply because the city built libraries first. The city council received a memorial to open the municipal libraries on Sunday afternoons as early as 1873, but considerable opposition from religious organizations prevented any success until 1878, when the Manchester Sunday Society successfully mustered the support of a broad coalition that included religious representatives: "a memorial was presented in favour of the proposal to open the Reference Library and the Reading rooms on Sundays, signed by 1776 clergymen, ministers of religion, merchants, manufacturers, and other ratepayers."[81] Soon after, in 1879, the RMI first opened its exhibition for several free Sundays, which again prompted consternation from the religious community.[82] When the RMI transferred itself to the city as the new Manchester City Art Gallery in 1883, the practice of opening the autumn exhibition for free on at least four Sundays continued; eventually, this meant that the permanent collection was also open for certain Sundays. Under pressure from reforming members of the Art Gallery Committee, particularly RMI representative and radical Ruskinian T. C. Horsfall, the committee finally approved free opening on all Sundays in 1895. In the case of Manchester, then, we see the complications created by an institution designed to provide art for the educated elites opening itself to a wider public. In contrast to the free libraries, the private RMI had been founded—according to the catalogue to its autumn exhibition of 1880—"to foster and encourage Literature, Science, and Art, in all their branches."[83] That is, it was interested not in bettering people through art, but in bettering art through collective patronage. Perhaps because of these internal contradictions, supporters of Sunday opening such as Horsfall pushed themselves to rhetorical extremes in arguing for their very different vision of the role of art and of government in the city.

In June 1878, Horsfall pushed a familiar argument in a socialist direction when he wrote to the Manchester *Guardian* to argue that as it was the very labor of the working classes that made possible the "conditions under which [the "educated rich"] live," those privileged classes had a "duty to make the conditions of life of the poor as far as possible like those to which they owe their own best life—in other words, it is their duty to at once help to get museums, picture galleries, libraries and gardens opened on Sunday afternoons."[84] However, for the most part, both pro- and anti-Sunday-openers in Manchester used the arguments that were used in Birmingham and Liverpool. In the 1878 debate over opening the free libraries, many opponents of Sunday opening emphasized political-economic as well as religious affiliations. Members of congregations signed as, for example, "Ratepayers attending the Collyhurst Wesleyan Chapel" (implying that they disapproved of this use of public funds to which they contributed, that they were influential voters, and that they disapproved on religious grounds).[85] The Manchester Sunday Society urged the opening of "Libraries, Museums and Art Galleries" for familiar reasons: the institutions should open, it wrote, as "instruments for the promotion of intellectual and moral well-being, and as agencies opposed to ignorance and vice; and that it is therefore of the highest importance that they should be made available on the only day when large sections of the community can benefit by them." The society members rather pithily used the drinking and religious arguments, as they "further urge[d] their strong conviction that the Sunday opening of these Institutions would prove a powerful safeguard against dissipation caused by enforced idleness and the temptations of the public-house, and be a valuable auxiliary to the work of the Church, the Chapel, and the Sunday School."[86] Once again, we see the arguments for publicly owned property and for alternatives to the pub.

The debate over whether to open the RMI on Sundays took on the issue of drinking, and the nature of the "drinking classes," even more explicitly. Proponents of Sunday opening portrayed the working classes as simply wanting to enjoy publicly what the middle classes already could privately and stressed that conditions of life, not inherent brutishness, led many to Sunday drinking. Thus, when in the late 1870s a small but influential group of RMI members persuaded the august institution to become a more active force for promoting and widening public access to art, this included opening the RMI's autumn exhibitions to the public for free on Sundays in 1879, the year after the Manchester free libraries had done the same. According to contemporary accounts, this was so outside the original mission of the RMI that it seemed a revolutionary act, a veritable—if peaceful—storming of the palace of art. As Mrs. Jane Axon, wife of councilor and Ruskinian art supporter W. E. A. Axon, wrote for the *Sunday Review*:

The governing body of the Royal Institution, whilst always credited with good intentions, has never been regarded as very revolutionary in spirit, and many persons would be agreeably surprised at the news that, by a majority of thirteen to two, the Council had decided to open the galleries on Sunday afternoon from two to five o'clock, absolutely free. The stimulating motives to this act, as wise as it is generous, were in all probability the quiet but unmistakable success of the Sunday opening of the Free Libraries in this city, and the example of Sir Coutts Lindsay, who has so munificently placed the Grosvenor Gallery [in London] at the disposal of the Sunday Society.[87]

In fact, this "revolutionary" spirit was the beginning of the major change in the mission and audience of the RMI that came about just five months later when on March 1, 1880, a group of RMI members urged the RMI Council to give the institution to the city to become the municipal art museum.[88]

Mrs. Axon, as a supporter of Sunday opening, emphasized in her account of the free Sunday admission to the RMI on October 19, 1879, that it was a "dull, cold, and cheerless day, over which wind and rain held alternate rule." She brought out the "patience" and "forbearance" of the "overflowing" crowd; she guessed that they were "undoubtedly men and women who had to fight very hard in the struggle for existence." She summarized the success of the experiment:

The intelligent honest interest shown by the people in the pictures, the thankfulness for any explanation as to the meaning of some of the incidents represented, their perfect decorum, and their expressions of gratitude to those who had given them the opportunity of this glimpse into the fairy land of Art, all showed that the time is quite ripe for the exertion of a very real educational influence by the Sunday Art Gallery.[89]

To Mrs. Axon, the meeting of Art and the People was both magical—a "fairy land"—and the beginnings of a practical educational program—"a very real educational influence." She reports that forty-five hundred people attended the RMI on those first three hours of Sunday opening and that "certainly not less than five hundred more were unable to gain admission."[90] Here, she emphasizes that these are patient, grateful, decorous people who only needed opportunities to better themselves; they were not brutal, but were brutalized by the "struggle for existence."

In contrast, also in 1879 the Working Men's Lord's Day Rest Association published a pamphlet against Sunday opening which argued that increasing opportunities for amusement would in fact increase Sunday drinking. Writing of the Sunday Society's advocacy of music in parks, Charles Hill wondered, "Can anyone doubt that many of the hundreds who . . . go to public-houses after their visit to the Sunday bands would be quietly resting in their homes, or perhaps attending a place of worship, but for the attraction of the Sunday bands?"[91] Here, the quiet rest of home is a pleasant alternative, from which the amusement of music and drink have torn the wayward. Further, he drew a clear distinction between those who would attend a pub and a museum: "Those who know anything of the classes who spend their time in public-houses also know that these classes have no taste whatever for the objects of interest in museums, galleries, and libraries."[92] Hill gave multiple statistics from both Birmingham and Manchester to cite the apparent fact that Sunday opening lured non-pub-going men away from their homes; for instance, quoting the *Daily News*, he cited the bishop of Manchester, who, upon visiting a local library, "found 'only about twenty men there. These men were all reading newspapers, which they might have read on Saturday. He did not think they were of the public-house-going class.'"[93] To dismiss the argument that workers needed an alternative public space to the public house, he argued that pub-goers were quite simply a different "class" of men.

In contrast, ten years later, in 1889, the Reverend Bernard J. Snell gave a sermon in Salford (later published in Manchester and London) which argued that the very conditions of some workers' homes demanded action by both churches and governments to provide other options:

People are not necessarily blasphemous sinners because they do not care to spend all Sunday in church. "Then, let them stay at home." That, too, is easily said by comfortable citizens ensconced in their own easy chairs. Do they realise that there are thousands who do not know what a domestic life is? Do they realise the sordid, squalid circumstances of the homes of most of their fellow-citizens? How are these people to find distraction to pass the time pleasantly? All that is left to them is to walk freely in our grimy streets, and to drink freely in our too frequent public-houses.[94]

Snell thus insisted that these brutal domestic spaces required a public alternative:

A warm and well-lighted room on Sunday, where a man need not order something "for the good of the house" and the harm of himself, where he has some intelligent and interesting occupation, would be for many a successful competitor against the grog-shop. As it is, a man is fatigued with too much idleness on a Sunday, and in sheer desperation he drops in to drink with his companions. *The dismalness of Sunday is the great cause of Sunday intemperance.* It is an instructive fact that publicans, as a class, are opposed to the Sunday opening of museums and libraries: they know that the emptier the Sunday the fuller their bars will be.[95]

Since the working man in the pub did not have a quiet home where he might be at rest, Snell and other pro-Sunday-openers argued in favor of opening "public libraries and museums," as they were "among the finest results of civilisation" and "the property of the people."[96] Moreover, like Collings in Birmingham, Snell made it clear that such access would only be making public what the well-to-do could already enjoy:

I should like to inquire whether these well-to-do, double-chinned gentry, who opposed free libraries themselves as long as they could (and it is a delight to think of their being visited by the tax-gatherer in order that they may contribute, however unwillingly, to the cause of public education and enlightenment), and now oppose their full utilisa-tion on the plea of "Holy Sabbath"—I should like to know whether they are consistent and sincere in this business? Do they turn the key on *their* libraries on Sunday? Do they lock up their newspapers? Do they hang the pictures with their faces to the walls? Do they forgo their Monday morning's paper? These men who are so punctilious about the employment of one or two men for the sake of a thousand, do they never trouble their servants on Sunday? Nor ring the dining-room bell? Do they shave in cold water? These men, who without scruple have two or three domestics to minister to the necessities and comforts of their households, begrudge (in the name of piety) six men's toil for the sake of six thousand! "Oh, the offence is rank, and smells to heaven!"[97]

In both Hill and Snell, then, we can see how antagonists in the debate over Sun-day opening specifically focused on the domestic qualities of civic institutions, and on the nature of the "public-house-going-class."

The experiment at the RMI had been approved only for the autumn exhi-bition of 1879; the following year, it had to be proposed and approved again. Indeed, at the October 1880 monthly meeting of the RMI Council, the first mo-tion to open that year's exhibition lost. Some of the governors of the institutions evidently feared the same crush of people as the previous year, unsuccessfully proposing an amendment to the Sunday-opening motion that "admission be limited to such reasonable numbers as will admit of the seeing of the works of art with comfort."[98] Eventually, the new Sunday Committee devised a system of tickets to try to prevent the massive crowds of the previous year.[99] The RMI Council was evidently not unanimous about its new public role, or how that role might best be filled.[100]

There was a great deal of continuity between the old RMI and the new Manchester City Art Gallery, both in the people directing the institution and in the policies they put forward. In the case of Sunday opening, and accessibility issues in general, the transformation of the art gallery from a private to a corporate institution did not make so many changes as many might have hoped (or feared). The art gallery maintained the autumn exhibition and continued to provide a number of Sundays that were open free. During a limited number of Sundays in November and December, the exhibition—and consequently the permanent collection—would open free to the public, and charities could write in to request free admissions, which were granted on a case-by-case basis. However, beginning in 1889, two of the upper galleries were set aside for the permanent collection during the exhibition and were open free to the public (although these galleries were open only on the certain designated Sundays).[101] The Art Gallery Committee also provided cheap evening openings to the autumn exhibition.[102] In this series of compromises, we see the difficult balance between the aims of the old institution, to promote arts patronage, and the new, to bring beauty to the masses through art.

Ultimately, those RMI representatives in favor of making art more accessible to the public again made their voices heard on the Art Gallery Committee, the RMI Council recommending in 1894 that the Manchester City Art Gallery should open to the public free on all Sundays and evenings. Indeed, it was that unflagging proponent of art T. C. Horsfall who proposed the resolution.[103] By this point, however, the character of the art gallery was changing: more interested in public education, in putting on free loan exhibitions for the public (beginning with the very successful Arts and Crafts Exhibition in 1891), a new generation of people such as art enthusiast J. E. Phythian were coming onto the Art Gallery Committee and gradually shifting the focus of the institution. The committee approved the recommendation of its RMI members on January 31, 1895, and opened the gallery from 2 to 5 p.m. on Sunday afternoons, and until 9 p.m. on each weekday, beginning in September of that year.[104] The city council itself seems not to have voted on this decision, which apparently went unchallenged.[105]

In November 1895 Horsfall read his utopian fable *The Government of Manchester* to the Manchester Statistical Society. In it he propounded his ideas for a strong mayor and town planning reform, but he also defended the Sunday opening of art galleries. In his imaginary Manchester, the city council "decide that all service which makes known the wonderfulness of the works of GOD may rightly be done on SUNDAY."[106] Continuing the story, he has his mayor persuade the Sabbatarian deputation that the poor must be given the opportunity to see the beautiful creations of God and humanity, without which they would never "feel love and reverence for the Maker of the world and respect human nature." The deputation coming around to this point of view, the mayor assures them as they leave that "the places which the Town Council intended to open on Sunday should be as truly and fully Houses of God as any Churches or Chapels; and that the attendants would therefore be as much priests of God as any clergyman could be; so that they, like the clergy, if they profaned the Sabbath or Sunday would yet be blameless."[107] Horsfall stretched the idea of art as a source of meaning and as a tool for social progress to this extreme because of his frustration with the continued use of the art gallery for other purposes: for the aggrandizement of the city, the promotion of artists associated with the Royal Academy, and the continued exhibitions of works for sale, which made the gallery a gathering place of the privileged rather than the poor, who had up to that point gained access only through limited, charitable concessions. Those active Ruskinian art advocates such as Horsfall, who had worked through the RMI to create a municipal art museum that would seek to educate all classes rather than simply entertaining the well-to-do, continued to campaign for new acquisition, opening, and education policies that would widen the audience for art. Gradually, the permanent collection grew in importance, and free temporary exhibitions opened the Manchester City Art Gallery to increasingly large numbers; in 1902 the Art Gallery Committee ceased to charge for attendance at even the autumn exhibition.

In Manchester, we see the familiar struggle between Liberal reformers and workers supporting the opening of civic institutions free on Sundays and religious organizations opposing it on the grounds of both religion and protections against a seven-day workweek. However, in the arguments put forward by Axon, Hill, Snell, and Horsfall, we see the particular dynamics of how the museum functioned as a new kind of domestic space, and the issues this raised. Did the working class have access to a domestic sphere that provided refuge from the "struggle for existence"? How could the middle classes justify closing public cultural institutions when they could enjoy books and pictures in their own homes? As the RMI transitioned into the Manchester City Art Gallery, these issues came to the fore, as an institution designed for private enjoyment slowly became public, with moments of celebrating the new mass public (Axon's "fairy land of Art") and of fearing the crush of bodies (limiting admission to "reasonable numbers" so that one could see "the works of art with comfort"). Horsfall's socialist leanings and commitment to radical reform through access to beauty pushed the argument for public access to art on Sundays to rhetorical extremes, as the museum became for him not a public home, but a house of worship.

CONCLUSION

The Sunday-opening debate thus highlights a heretofore unremarked aspect of the Victorian museum movement: the nature of museums as a public vision of domesticity, shared among all and accessible as public property. Not only did the Sunday-openers, and the wider museum movement, propose a particular vision of art and culture—in which beauty could mitigate the brutality of the industrial city—they also harnessed ideas developed during the mid-Victorian period about the sanctity of the domestic sphere. Both sides of the debate attempted to use ideas about the character of domestic refuge and about the quality of urban life to make their points. In a wider sense, then, this debate pitted a new kind of secular morality—predicated on romantic conceptions of art and the home—against evangelical religion and strict interpretations of the Bible. Could beauty lead to morality? Would those people in the pub be tempted to change their ways by visiting an art gallery?

The debate also raised the issue of the waning power of religion against a secular morality in another sense, namely, the rights of citizens to public property and the rights of governments to ignore the religious objections of institutions and constituents. Could a local government act against the religious convictions of its citizens, particularly its important voters and taxpayers? Could a local government induce people to work against their religious beliefs? Some, like Birmingham councilor Jesse Collings, argued that the needs of the majority outweighed the demands of the offended minority and that as public, government-run art institutions, the municipal art museums had to be open to their constituents when those constituents could attend. In Liverpool, however, with its particular brand of sectarian conflict, this question of the relationship between government and religion became highly politicized and controversial.

Finally, the new voices of the working classes themselves began to emerge throughout the debate; the rise of the Labour Party and the threat of socialism led both sides to argue that they were working on the workers' behalf. Evangelical Protestants inside and outside of the Church of England had created new restrictions on Sunday trading and activities during the first half of the nineteenth century and fought hard to maintain or even to extend those restrictions (trying to close pubs on Sundays, for example). For others, however, such restrictions seemed increasingly class based, as the pleasures of leisure, culture, and recreation opened up to the middle classes in the domestic settings of the suburban villa or private club or association (such as the elite Edgbaston Botanical Gardens). Here, again, the art museum supporters and religious groups came into direct conflict. Who spoke for the interests of the working classes? What would help them most?—education, culture, and healthy recreation or religion? Religious groups argued that opening public cultural institutions on Sundays would be the beginning of a seven-day workweek. Sunday-opening advocates countered that by remaining closed on Sundays, the art museums were effectively locked to the very people for whom they were intended, and that workers had a right to publicly owned culture even as they had a right to leisure and limited working hours. This right, they argued, outweighed both claims that Sunday opening would erode Sunday as a universal day of rest (the universality of which they questioned in any case, noting the myriad jobs that continued on the Sabbath) and that it would offend certain religious beliefs.

Through the course of this debate over the nature of Sunday, the status of art as a mode of religious experience or secular recreation, the relationship between governance and faith, and the best means of improving workers' lives—through preserving a day devoted to religion or by opening new opportunities for education and entertainment—reached new rhetorical extremes. These debates, indeed, might mark the high-water point for the expressions of the belief that art could be an active and potent force for social reform. The Sunday-opening movement crystallized the arguments of art museum supporters, who advocated a new role for government as a provider of education and culture, who insisted on wide access to public collections, who envisioned the broadest possible audience for art, and who ultimately articulated hopes that art would provide the kind of spiritual experience and moral refuge comparable to both the ideal home and places of worship.

3 COLLECTING FOR ART AS EXPERIENCE, OR WHY MILLAIS TRUMPS REMBRANDT

The most striking thing about the collections of the city art museums of Birmingham, Liverpool, and Manchester is that for several generations after their founding, they were dominated by contemporary British art, particularly the Pre-Raphaelite Brotherhood. Very few foreign works of any period, or older British art, entered these collections until the 1930s.[1] This was not a coincidence, or the result of narrow parsimony or patriotism. Rather, the collecting policies of these museums show the confluence of ideas and institutional structure. The foundational idea behind these museums that art was socially valuable as experience, and the Liverpool and Manchester art museums' commitment to holding annual exhibitions of art for sale, created art collections that were, by and large, uninterested in art history. By examining how the museums' permanent collections developed out of contemporary ideas about art and its social role, we can see the distinct vision of art during this period, its relation to the evolution of industrial cities, and how the social use of art was shaped by class relations. Through the committee minutes, local lectures, writings on art, and acquisition records of these museums, I explore their choices about forming their permanent collections and debates about what kinds of art would be most appropriate for different audiences. The collections ultimately emerged out of negotiation and compromise among groups who differed on what kind of experience they felt would be most beneficial to the inhabitants of these industrial cities. We find that the question of what types of fine and applied art the museums should collect started from specific, fundamental assumptions about how paintings functioned as conduits of meaning and how applied art could train workers to improve industrial design.

These institutions developed in a society profoundly divided by class. This most basic fact about Victorian society shaped all aspects of museums' conception of art, arguments for public access, and acquisitions. What made art museums possible in these industrial cities was the understanding that they did not exist to focus on intellectual endeavor or connoisseurship, but to provide the direct perception of beauty. Speaking of middle-class efforts to "improve" the artisan class, Whitworth Wallis, the influential curator of the Birmingham Museum and Art Gallery, wrote in 1911, "In one case, that of the Free Library, the mind in its wider aspects is appealed to; in the other, that of the Museum, the eye is the organ through which the perception of beauty and proportion is conveyed to the mind."[2] The idea that art could communicate directly to even the unschooled mind justified these institutions and underlay their assumptions about public art. Beauty in this conception is an absolute category, apprehensible by all, and connected to morality in both its universality and its roots in divinely created nature.[3] Art museum supporters framed the moral and physical ugliness of the industrial city as directly opposed to the moral and physical beauty of art and nature, the latter including both wilderness and that charming concept "the English countryside."

As others have noted, the categories of "city" and "country" were part of the same exploitative economic relations that so many museum advocates hoped to alleviate through art and education.[4] The conception of art as experience, however, was rooted in this idea of the need for the beauty of nature (with its sense of deeper purpose, divine creation, and ultimate meaning) in the industrial city. When Professor Michael Sadler spoke to the Royal Manchester Institution in 1911 on the relationship between art and the refreshment of a trip to the countryside, he asked:

Who of us, after having been kept for weeks continuously in Manchester by the claims of absorbing and insistent work, has not felt the thrill of pleasure with which, as the train carried him at last into real country and beyond the drab film of the smoke-cloud, he looked out of the window into Cheshire fields, or on to Pennine moorland, or the delicate contours of the limestone landscape of the Peak? Was it possible that sky could be so blue, grass so green, clouds so white? But after all, so far as we consciously range our impressions of the beauty of it, so far as we see pattern in its landscape, balance in its structure and design, are we not seeing what we see through the vision of some dead and gone painter . . . ?[5]

Thus at the same moment as modernists pursued abstraction, and just a few years before World War I, Sadler conceives of painting as functioning to frame our experience of the beauty of nature in terms familiar to Victorian public art supporters. He does not make painting about form or representation per se, but rather understands it as a conduit to true experience, that is, of the beauty of nature.[6] In this sense, like many other Ruskinian advocates for art, Sadler imagines paintings as acting like his train's "window into Cheshire fields," through which the vivid colors of nature come to take him away from the "drab film of the smoke-cloud," the haze of the industrial city. As Keith Thomas, Wolfgang Schivelbusch, Timothy Barringer, and others have pointed out, the particular relationship between industrial modes of travel, capitalist economic relations, and the exploitative relationship between city and country can be hidden in reflections such as these that make art into nature and nature into an unproblematic balm on the ugliness of the city.[7] What is missing from this privileged account is both an awareness of how such relationships to the city and to nature were determined by class and education, and a recognition that the aesthetic experience of "countryside" and "nature" were products of a distinctly middle-class leisure. And yet, perhaps to their credit, reformers hoped that everyone could have that same experience of joy and release in the beauty of art acting as a substitute for nature.

The committees amassing art collections in the industrial cities of Birmingham, Liverpool, and Manchester did so from shared assumptions about the possibilities for the direct communication of beauty, subject, and narrative, and about the role of paintings as windows onto nature. Mainly middle-class professionals, traders, and factory owners, they struggled with how to reach the working classes who, they felt, so desperately needed an escape from the city. Reformers imagined museums as a means of making beauty accessible and therefore as part of the solution to the host of problems industrial capitalism created; this idea helped establish new institutions, museums of contemporary art, which have become so prominent and central in modern cities. Thus nineteenth-century reformist middle-class culture, which sought to control industrial capitalism and the chaos of the industrial city, founded these art institutions in a very different guise from how we know them today (that is, as primarily about art practice and art history). Instead, as we have seen, reformers imagined the experience of art as an antidote to these negative aspects of city life. The formation of public spaces for experiencing beauty, which became the basis of modern urban development and renewal, was imagined and fostered by middle-class leaders who supported contemporary British art with its emphasis on "readability," subject, and narrative. It is no accident, then, that these three collections converged on modern British art, which was both within budget and exemplified a clear connection between accessibility and social purpose, rather than the dubious classicism, Catholicism, or sensuality of older or foreign works.[8]

Aside from this basic idea about art, that it could provide the direct apprehension of subject matter, the public did not agree on what kind of art should, and what should not, be part of a public collection. Indeed, with this sense of art's power, the type of art that could be usefully presented to all classes became a matter of heated debate. Assuming that different types of art would interest and engage different audiences, reformers and museum officials questioned what kind of art to collect: fine or applied, contemporary or historical, original works or copies, narrative or nonnarrative. Museum administrators tended to connect applied art with the working classes, historical art with a broader educational mission, idealizing art with high moral purpose, and narrative art with simple entertainment. Their explicit discussions about collecting and acquisitions policies were framed within larger disputes about the basic functions and goals of art museums. Those directing the collections at the municipal art museums thus wondered how to spend their limited acquisitions funds, understanding that they were also implicitly (and sometimes explicitly) deciding the proper audience for and purpose of their institutions. Converging on contemporary British art, Victorian art museums could eventually include formal academicism, Ruskinian truth to nature, sentimental genre scenes, or sensual aestheticism precisely because the museums were interested in the experience of subject rather than telling the history of artistic practice, and because they understood different categories to appeal to different types of audiences.

In 1877, 1883, and 1885, respectively, the municipal art museums in Liverpool, Manchester, and Birmingham opened in purpose-built galleries with intact permanent collections, although of varying quality, representativeness, and scope. The art that the governing committees of these museums bought for their permanent collections formed a key way of expressing and fulfilling the museums' social missions. As we have seen, the idea that art deserved public funding rested on the premise that it could accomplish a variety of socially beneficial goals. The kinds of art that the municipal art museums collected was controversial precisely because different groups hoped that the museums would accomplish different things. At the same time, there was a wide consensus on what particular kinds of art were for and the audiences they might attract. Applied art would train workers in a variety of crafts and give examples of good design.[9] Popular, narrative art would make the museums attractive to all classes and help to bring workers out of the pubs and into the museums. Historical art would provide education on history, art, literature, and religion for those who would never take a Grand Tour. The "best" examples of art—whether historical or contemporary—would offer the beauty and hope that might help all classes unite to reform the ugliness, injustice, and alienation of modern, industrial, imperialist, capitalist society.

In the field of applied and decorative art, the most potent example and practical influence was the South Kensington Museum, which lent objects to and aided purchases for the municipal art museums. The museums and their displays developed under the simultaneous influence of Sir Henry Cole and John Ruskin, who advocated very different standards of design and art education. Cole's work came out of the select committees and concerns about artisanal training and industrial design of the 1830s and 1840s. His project, the Great Exhibition of the Works of Industry of All Nations of 1851, celebrated the productive capacity of British manufacturing even as it showed up the country's weaknesses in design. The South Kensington Museum and the Department of Science and Art's national system of art schools and examinations aimed to address these deficiencies in industrial production. Ruskin, meanwhile, attacked the very system of industrialization that forced people to become accessories to machines and destroyed the creative joy of artisans.

The many reformers who worked to create municipal art museums often cited the writings of Ruskin and William Morris on the need for beautiful products that would give joy to both the producer and the user. However, it is often unclear how they hoped this would work: whether, like Morris, they hoped that artisans would rediscover the skills to make and market handmade goods, or whether, like Cole, they thought the museums would provide design ideas for industrial, mass-produced items. Even the specimens considered to be industrial or applied art included both decorative art, such as casts of sculpture and architectural ornament, and functional items, such as textiles, guns, and metalwork. Again, "art" held multiple and often contradictory meanings, implications, and uses, which complicated the development of municipal art museums' permanent collections. However, at all three city art museums, purchasers tended to assume that applied art collections, like simple, narrative paintings, would be of especial use and relevance to workers, while more complex fine art would appeal to educated audiences.

A key point of debate arose regarding what kinds of subject and treatment, and therefore what kind of viewer response, museums should endorse. Did reading a painting for subject matter mean the contemplation of Platonic ideals or of scenes from everyday life? Both Ruskin and Thomas Greenwood supported art as a means of social reform and were influential in the museum movement of the late nineteenth century. Greenwood wrote and lectured widely as an advocate for free municipal museums and libraries, and maintained a wide correspondence both at home and abroad with many influential figures in the library and museum movements of the last decades of the nineteenth century.[10] As we have seen, Ruskin was especially influential in the museum movement, and many of the most active art advocates were avid followers of his ideas about aesthetic and social reform. Both of these men emphasized paintings as windows onto their subjects and public museums as a means of bringing beauty to all. They also agreed that most viewers tended to "read" paintings as stories; however, this fact led them to different conclusions about the kind of art that museums should collect, because they held opposing views on the experience that the museums should provide. Their views articulate the opposing positions of the debate that played out in each local context about the role of entertainment and accessibility in public collections.

Greenwood wrote that "Mr. Ruskin's influence on the age has been marked and beneficial," but noted that to some "he is known as an idealist with regard to Museums."[11] In contrast, Greenwood maintained that "Art is essentially democratic in its character," insisting that it could and should reach both educated and uneducated audiences through narrative. Thus, he wrote in 1888: "The multitude who visit Art Galleries and Museums . . . come not to criticise but to enjoy, and they like a good story on canvas or Bristol board well told. Their hearts and their interests are excited by the man who draws what he knows and not what he dreams. The 'Village Wedding' of Luke Fildes, is worth more to them than all the works of Rubens in the National Gallery."[12] For Greenwood, the paintings of a public collection would be most useful to most people if the stories they told were familiar and easily accessible. In discussing how he has "watched minutely the faces of visitors at many an Art Gallery and Museum, especially in the evening, and the faces of the working-class visitors," Greenwood found that "the eyes light up at some picture, where the 'one touch of nature makes the whole world kin,' and I have more than once seen a wife with a pale careworn face cling more closely to the arm of her husband as some picture of child life was being looked at, or something else suggestive to them, perhaps, of little fingers lying cold in mother earth."[13] Here, Greenwood wrote his own story about this tableau of workers connecting art to what he imagined to be their own deepest experiences of love and loss. In his fictional narrative, he placed the highest importance on the ability of art museums to allow people to see their own lives or wishes reflected back at them, giving them a way to connect familiar events with larger themes and meanings. He did not verify his imaginings. In the practice of using art as a means of bringing beauty to an urban audience, there were always at least two sets of narratives: the stories told by the paintings, and the stories that reformers told themselves about the lives of the disadvantaged who needed help of one kind or another.

Ruskin agreed that people tended to "read" pictures in this way but drew a very different conclusion: "A museum is not a theatre. Both are means of noble education—but you must not mix up the two. Dramatic interest is one thing; aesthetic charm another; a pantomime must not depend on its fine colour, nor a picture on its fine pantomime."[14] Ruskin's own interpretive habits tended to the literary, but he encouraged viewers to engage with art on the level of symbolism rather than plot.[15] He illustrated his discussion of the criteria for museum acquisitions with his reaction to the popular and sentimental picture *Sympathy* by Royal Academician Briton Riviere. Exhibited in 1878, the painting depicts a little girl and her dog sitting on a step of an interior staircase, evidently banished there for bad behavior. Ruskin wrote that it was "long" since he had been "so pleased in the Royal Academy" with a picture; the dog was "uncaricatured dogged-ness, divine as Anubis, or the Dog-star," and the "child [was] entirely childish and lovely. . . . A most precious picture in itself, yet not one for a museum." This was not because of the subject matter (a girl and a dog), but because of the way in which the painting invited viewers to approach it:

Everybody would think only of the story in it; everybody [would] be wondering what the little girl had done, and how she would be forgiven, and if she wasn't, how soon she would stop crying, and give the doggie a kiss, and comfort his heart. All which they might study at home among their own children and dogs just as well; and should not come to the museum to plague the real students there, since there is not anything of especial notableness or unrivalled quality in the actual painting.[16]

In this wonderful discussion of Riviere's quintessentially Victorian genre painting, we begin to see that Ruskin is making a clear statement about the purpose of the art in a museum, which is quite different from the enjoyment of art generally: Ruskin understood the experience of museum-going as precisely *not* that of the everyday. For Ruskin, museums offered art and natural history, as he wrote in another context, for visitors to devote time to "'the concerns of their immortal souls,' that is to say, to the contemplation and study of the works

Briton Riviere, *Sympathy*, 1877. © Tate, London, 2011.

of God."[17] While Greenwood advocated the way in which narrative art might allow museum visitors to connect the art to their own lives, Ruskin saw a museum's function as giving the public a chance to experience the truly beautiful and good.[18] Thus, rather than *Sympathy*, Ruskin would put Velázquez's painting of the family of Felipe IV in a public art museum:[19]

The child is doing nothing; neither is the dog. But the dog is absolutely and beyond comparison the best painted dog in the world . . . and the child is painted so that child *cannot* be better done. *That* is a picture for a museum . . . the museum is only for what is eternally right, and well done, according to divine law and human skill. The least things are to be there—and the greatest—but all *good* with the goodness that makes a child cheerful and an old man calm; the simple should go to learn, and the wise to remember.[20]

Ruskin envisioned the art museum as a special place, which did not contain the "dramatic or didactic art" that "should be universally national, the lustre of our streets, and treasure of our palaces, the pleasure of our homes."[21] For Ruskin, not everyone would necessarily approach museum collections to study the "quality of the painting"—this is only for "real students." However, it was precisely this characteristic of evincing "what is eternally right, and well done" that allowed viewers to contemplate the object-in-itself, the subject of the painting as an idea. As in his defenses of Turner and the Pre-Raphaelites, Ruskin consistently emphasized the goal of the artist as illustrating divine creation through truth to nature, of illuminating the artist's apprehension of reality. Ruskin, and the idealists who followed him, hoped that museums could communicate the wonder of nature as godly scripture, but believed that only the best artists could accomplish this;

Diego Rodríguez de Silva y Velázquez, *The Family of Felipe IV, or Las Meninas*, ca. 1656. Cat. no. P1174. Courtesy of the Museo Nacional del Prado, Madrid.

others, as he argued, were simply providing theatrical entertainment. Yet the sheer volume, density, and inconsistency of Ruskin's writings meant that many of his most avid followers, such as Greenwood, argued that art which presented people with familiar scenes could inspire just such a transcendent experience through narrative itself.

The realities of municipal art museums' acquisitions budgets meant that few of Ruskin's dicta on the ideal museum could be put into practice, yet he himself recognized that this was part of a larger cultural alignment. For instance, Ruskin told the art museum committee in Leicester that it should appoint "a well-informed gentleman of taste in your neighbourhood, to buy for the Leicester public just what he would buy for himself" while despairing that most art museums had filled with contemporary art that fell far short of his ideal: "What use is there in my telling you what to do? The mob won't let you do it. It is fatally true that no one nowadays can appreciate pictures by the old masters, and that every one can understand [William Powell] Frith's 'Derby Day.' That is to say, everybody is interested in jockeys, harlots, mountebanks, and men about town; but nobody in saints, heroes, kings, or wise men, either from the East or West."[22] Ruskin here disparages the position of Greenwood and those who agreed with him that museums should provide images of contemporary, everyday life that a wide audience could understand. He clearly distinguishes between appropriate subjects for public collections, revealing his well-known distaste for the modern era and much of the popular art depicting it. In his own St. George's Museum in Sheffield, Ruskin privileged copies of historical works over popular contemporary subjects like those painted by Frith. Several key Ruskinian art museum supporters, such as Charles Rowley and T. C. Horsfall in Manchester, Philip Rathbone in Liverpool, and Whitworth Wallis in Birmingham, tried to pursue these idealistic policies by acquiring works that would align with Ruskin's views: historical works (originals or copies), applied art, and nonnarrative paintings. Ultimately, however, if the museums did contain their fair share of "saints, heroes, kings, or wise men," these were by contemporary artists, not the old masters whom Ruskin proposed for museum collections. The associations between contemporary British art and respectable morality (something Ruskin himself had done much to create) were too strong, and it took a long time for public art institutions to begin to collect the art so long connected with Catholicism or the collecting habits of the aristocracy. Thus, for example, in 1892 the purchasing committee in Manchester chose to buy John Everett Millais's *Autumn Leaves* for £1,300 rather than a Rembrandt for £1,500 (see Chapter 4 for an illustration of *Autumn Leaves*).[23] Greenwood and Ruskin thus differed considerably in how to approach the problem of developing public art collections, and their battle was carried on in the many committee chambers and town halls where museum purchasing decisions got made.

BIRMINGHAM: ARTISTS AND ARTISANS

As we have seen, the Birmingham Museum and Art Gallery grew out of a "civic gospel" that emphasized the increased role of city government and the need to connect all citizens in a common work to improve and beautify the city. This heritage is evident in the artworks that the museum purchased. The art museum included industrial exhibits and applied art, which implied the hope for a large working-class audience; throughout its policies, the museum sought to combine art and craft as equal products of joyful labor. However, the two acquisition funds, the Public Picture Gallery Fund (semipublic, with the mayor and the chair of the Museums and School of Art Committee ex-officio trustees) and the Art Gallery Purchase Committee (a town council committee, part of the museum administration), differed in their emphases. Largely directed by Whitworth Wallis, the Art Gallery Purchase Committee allowed the museum to develop according to his particular vision, seeking out art and crafts that would exemplify his commitment to the ideas of William Morris.

The Public Picture Gallery Fund had been formed in 1871 with an anonymous donation of £3,000 (later revealed to be from local glass manufacturer Thomas Clarkson Osler), and it continued to give works to the Birmingham Museum and Art Gallery through the 1940s.[24] The second, council-run fund for acquisitions developed out of the private Art Gallery and Industrial Museum Fund, made up from individual donations, including the £10,000 gift of the Tangye Bros.; in 1882 this fund handed over more than £17,600 to the town council, which then established the Art Gallery Purchase Committee to spend this amount on works of fine and industrial art. Birmingham thus had two privately raised acquisition funds, both run by civic leaders, one in an unofficial and the other in an official capacity. The Art Gallery Purchase Committee bought a variety of applied and fine art, while the Public Picture Gallery Fund concentrated on popular contemporary British art, its acquisitions thus more closely resembling the purchasing patterns of the Manchester City Art Gallery and Liverpool's Walker Art Gallery.[25]

A valuable description of Wallis's role has been preserved in the minutes of the Manchester City Art Gallery Committee, in the form of a report made by Ruskinian reformer J. E. Phythian in 1894.[26] Phythian used Wallis as a model when he advocated appointing an art director in order to most efficiently develop a good permanent collection, a change that would only happen in Manchester twenty years later with the appointment of Lawrence Haward as director in 1914. Phythian went to Birmingham to interview Wallis, who in fact effectively acted as a director and was noted as running one of the most successful regional art museums. Phythian reported that the "Committee"—presumably the Art Gallery Purchase Committee—"reserves to itself the making of large purchases, but Mr. Wallis has power to make smaller purchases (£50 to £100) without consulting the Committee. When a sale is pending, he looks over the catalogue, calculates what he would like to spend, and gets authority to purchase up to a certain amount." Phythian noted that Wallis felt "purchase by Committee . . . to be a mistake; there must be one man, the life and soul of the work, if a good collection is to be formed." (Recall that this is exactly what Ruskin had also said in his advice to the Leicester art museum.) Phythian reported that the Birmingham Museum and Art Gallery bought very few contemporary pictures, "the purchase of works which have had no test of time being considered a mistake," but that the museum received "many such works" as gifts. He emphasized the extent to which Wallis acted as an agent and representative for the Birmingham Museum and Art Gallery: "being well known amongst collectors, he can influence loans and gifts; . . . the loans often become gifts of which quite a considerable part of their collection consists," and that Wallis had been able to acquire examples of applied art at relatively low prices by traveling to Egypt, Italy, France, and Germany.[27] In short, Birmingham's Art Gallery Purchase Committee worked largely as an extension of the curator's policies, and Wallis was given a great deal of freedom to direct the development of the permanent collection with the available funds.

Under Wallis's control, the committee concentrated its efforts on the decorative crafts and applied art, especially of the Italian Renaissance but including examples of ancient Peruvian pottery, Japanese cloisonné enamels, Indian metalwork, and Roman glass. The committee also bought pictorial art, emphasizing the works of the Pre-Raphaelite Brotherhood and its followers, including Dante Gabriel Rossetti, acquiring *Beata Beatrix* in 1891 for £600; Edward Burne-Jones, commissioning a work in 1885 that resulted in *The Star of Bethlehem* (delivered in

1892), price unknown; William Holman Hunt, buying *Two Gentlemen of Verona* in 1887 for £1,050; Ford Madox Brown, with the purchase of *The Last of England* in 1891 for £420; and Ruskin's favorite copyist (and Burne-Jones's former assistant) C. Fairfax Murray, purchasing *St. George and the Dragon* for an unknown price in 1900.[28]

In contrast, the Public Picture Gallery Fund mainly bought works by popular (if high-minded) contemporary artists working in Britain, including Royal Academy members Frederick Leighton, John Brett, Briton Riviere, Sir William Blake Richmond, Henry Moore, Frederick Walker, G. F. Watts, and William Dyce as well as Alphonse Legros, James McNeill Whistler, James Aumonier, and C. Napier Hemy. We thus see a clear division between the works bought by the Public Picture Gallery Fund and the Art Gallery Purchase Committee, the works acquired by the fund showing a distinct continuity with those bought at the museums in Liverpool and Manchester. In many ways, then, the distinctiveness of Birmingham's municipal art museum derived from the Art Gallery Purchase Committee, significant in that it was controlled to a large extent by Wallis, who more than any other figure at the three museums acted in the capacity of director. The committee's acquisition of works by the Pre-Raphaelites and their followers in addition to applied art seems to have continued the museum's policy of attempting to unite the artist and the artisan in the pursuit of fine work. As Wallis wrote: "The various collections have been mainly selected . . . for the Education of the Artisan, the improvement of his taste, and the extension of his knowledge of design, that these superb examples of the Art products of other times and other lands have been brought together. They are not formed for our *amusement* only, or for the gratification of an idle curiosity, nor have they been made for the benefit of the purely *artistic* classes."[29] The carefully crafted and meticulously painted works of the Pre-Raphaelite Brotherhood echoed the fine handiwork of the applied art of many periods and regions. Paintings and artifacts thus combined to create a museum with a clear aesthetic and definite goal: to provide a beautiful experience that would educate both worker and middle-class consumer so that, as Wallis wrote, echoing William Morris, "life will thus become more interesting both to the man who makes the article and to the one who uses it."[30] These comments are borne out in the purchasing decisions of Birmingham's Art Gallery Purchase Committee.

In the early twentieth century the policy of the Public Picture Gallery Fund to focus on contemporary British artists changed, perhaps in response to Joseph

Chamberlain's criticism that the art museum should avoid contemporary works that had not stood the test of time. The fund then began to concentrate on the works of older or deceased artists, notably early Victorian watercolorists William James Müller, William Henry Hunt, Samuel Prout, and John Ruskin, while in the years just before World War I the fund also bought works by Victorians Cecil Gordon Lawson and Alphonse Legros. Although the Public Picture Gallery Fund favored members of the Royal Academy, these works were often of nonnarrative, "high," or classical themes, judged appropriate to the ideals of a public art museum.

Birmingham's municipal art museum had, since its earliest incarnation in 1867, been both an "art gallery" (fine art) and an "industrial museum" (applied art).[31] In 1885 when the purpose-built art museum opened, Wallis prepared a "Report of the Curator on the Various Classes of Art Work Desirable to Be Procured for the Museum and Art Gallery," in which he outlined a clear and specific policy regarding applied art.[32] Looking back in 1911, Wallis characterized this policy as arising out of the industrial nature of the city: "It has ever been the object of the Committee to place before our visitors, notably in our decorative and industrial sections, all such objects having as far as possible a direct bearing upon the industries of the town, cultivating thereby the power of observation, and assisting also the education of the eye in its perception of form and style."[33] As we have seen, in the first catalogue of the permanent collection at the Birmingham Museum and Art Gallery's opening in 1885, Wallis linked the collection's moral and economic purposes in language clearly influenced by Morris (who had given several important addresses as president of the Birmingham Society of Art in recent years), showing the broader theory behind the combined emphasis on fine and applied art. Despite the increased mechanization of Birmingham manufactures, Wallis emphasized that providing beautiful objects for workers to study was part of a larger project of improving the beauty of goods and the fulfillment of the laborer.[34] This fits with Birmingham's wider goal of civic reform that aimed to use the power of local government to beautify the city and improve its citizens. Wallis later reported that his "desire . . . to make the Birmingham Art Gallery something more than a picture exhibition . . . may not have been popular with some people," citing as evidence that a "well-known, well-educated, and prominent citizen once asked me why money was wasted on the acquisition of 'earthenware platters,' meaning the beautiful majolica plates in the Italian Gallery."[35] Apparently, not everyone saw the connection between earthenware platters and industrial improvement (or a larger program of creating beauty for all), but Wallis followed a clear acquisitions policy that emphasized both applied and fine art and was connected to the museum's understanding of its social role.

LIVERPOOL: NARRATIVES AND NUDES

If Wallis pursued policies very closely related to the ideas of Ruskin on non-narrative art and Morris on applied art, Charles Dyall, curator of Liverpool's Walker Art Gallery, agreed with Thomas Greenwood that simple narrative pictures would appeal to uneducated viewers and that the museum had a duty to provide examples of these: "The Committee have borne in mind that the Collection is intended to improve and foster a taste for Art amongst the people, and with this view they have frequently chosen subjects of a popular character, such as appeal to our common sympathies and delineating domestic scenes and every-day incidents of life."[36] The Walker thus aimed to acquire works that, "by appealing to common feelings and sentiments of our daily life, have afforded a fine moral lesson, and given great pleasure to the numerous visitors to the Gallery who are uninitiated in the higher forms of Art."[37] Dyall boasted in an 1888 report that the Walker Art Gallery's collection "is fairly representative of Modern British Art; and although at present the names of many Artists of great repute are absent from the Catalogue, yet many eminent men are seen at their best in the works displayed; and in numerous instances the money value of the purchases has trebled since their acquisition by the Corporation."[38] Dyall and Greenwood associated narrative art depicting contemporary scenes with lower-class, uneducated visitors, both in terms of what those visitors could understand and what they should be getting out of their museum experience (a "fine moral lesson"). They believed that anyone could look through the painting's frame as he or she would look into a proscenium-arch theater, provided the picture told a clear story or reflected a world (real or imagined) that the viewer would recognize. They distinguished between popular narrative pictures and art that used classical or nonnarrative symbolism, understood to speak to essentially different audiences in distinct ways.

As we have seen, the Library, Museum and Arts Committee relied on profits from the annual autumn exhibitions of works for sale—from ticket receipts, commissions on sales, catalogue sales, and later, refreshments—for acquisition funds. The committee was then in charge of purchases (largely made from the autumn exhibition), although this was always pending approval by the full town council, which occasionally led to conflict. Councilor Philip Henry Rathbone largely directed purchases, although Alderman Edward Samuelson was nominally in charge of the committee. From the opening of the Walker Art Gallery in 1877 until 1912, the profitability of the autumn exhibition experienced a steady decline, from a high of a £2,300 profit in 1878 to a low of a £219 *loss* in 1912.[39] This obviously directly affected the Walker's ability to purchase works for the permanent collection. The most significant difference between purchases and receipts occurred in 1890, when the total reported receipts amounted to £1,400, but that year the Walker bought William Holman Hunt's *The Triumph of the Innocents* for £3,516. However, private subscriptions offset the total cost with contributions of £2,016 for that unique purchase, showing how a major acquisition of a large and famous Pre-Raphaelite painting, exemplifying moral narrative and an easily readable, intensely detailed style, could combine with civic pride to garner local support (see Chapter 4 for more discussion of this painting). Because the autumn exhibition generally brought in about £1,800, from 1890 on, the Art Gallery Purchase Committee contributed £300 annually to the Walker's general fund to support activities and expenses other than acquisitions.

The Walker Art Gallery had a difficult relationship with a town council and city ratepayers generally hostile to spending public funds on art. Because the Art Gallery Purchase Committee overwhelmingly bought from the autumn exhibition itself, the gallery necessarily emphasized contemporary artists over historical or representative works. Within this group, as Curator Dyall noted, the committee attempted to balance "high" and "popular" works, apparently meaning (like Ruskin and Greenwood) collecting both nonnarrative and narrative paintings. The autumn exhibition, combined with the influence of aesthete Rathbone on the committee, meant that the museum occasionally bought from the exhibition the work of young and unknown artists who later became established and successful, such as C. Napier Hemy in 1877, Hubert von Herkomer in 1878, Stanhope Forbes in 1882, and E. A. Hornel in 1892. (All of these artists, in contrast to most popular artists, used the loose brushwork and unsentimental observation of the lower social strata associated with the social realist and Newlyn School movements.) In 1893 the museum also purchased from the autumn exhibition its only foreign work acquired before the war, Giovanni Segantini's remarkable symbolist painting *The Punishment of Luxury*.

One controversy that showed Rathbone's dedication to going against popular opinion and narrative painting was his decision to include Lawrence Alma-

Tadema's nude work *The Sculptor's Model* in the 1878 autumn exhibition. The storm that followed led Rathbone to lecture and publish in the painting's (and his own) defense, arguing that the museum had a duty to lead public taste by exhibiting the painting.[40] He even went so far as to claim that public morality in fact *depended* on the exhibition of the human figure. Three years previously, while campaigning for a city art museum in 1875, Rathbone had posited that a Puritan influence kept the English thinking of art as a luxury and corrupter of morals. However, in the 1878 essay defending the nude he resorted to Orientalism, blaming the public distrust of the "undraped figure in art" as primarily due to "Turkish" and "Asiatic" influence.[41] Rathbone used all the arguments available in support of art at the time—industrial competitiveness, morality, religiosity—boldly claiming that not only the "future of English Art," but the future "of English morality" itself rested on "the right of the nude to a place in our galleries." He forthrightly brought up the issue most pressing to those collecting art for public museums: "Now, although the source of the prejudice against the nude is a thoroughly unhealthy and impure one, yet it is still shared by many pure-minded and honest, if somewhat uneducated, people. Is it worth while to shock their prejudices, or ought we to respect them?"[42] That is, to what extent should art institutions lead or follow the tastes of the public who both maintain them and form their audiences? Rathbone qualified this, however, by saying (as Ruskin might) that "no crude or incapable representation, in fact none but the highest the age can produce, ought to be allowed in any public gallery or exhibition."[43] It is a commonplace to think of the Victorians as prudes, but this misses the point; if art was the experience of subject matter, a nude painting became particularly problematic.

Representations of the naked human form were controversial in the municipal art museums precisely because these institutions aimed at mass audiences made up of uneducated visitors who, many middle-class observers feared, would not be able to distinguish between the nude form as a representation of purity and idealism, and the naked body, subject to prurient desire. Was Alma-Tadema's picture (explicitly of an artist's model, that is, a naked woman in front of a strange man) about nakedness or about ideal form and the search for beauty? The number of articles in local newspapers about law cases involving the abuse of female models, the possibilities for exploitation, and the politicized nature of the relationship between artists and their working-class models—the payment for nakedness seeming little better than prostitution—show us another perhaps unexpected aspect of reading paintings as windows, and another clue to the outrage of a nude painting to Victorian sensibility. The nude form itself was problematic for the lust it might inspire, but it was also a record of nakedness and possible impropriety. When art was treated as the experience of subject matter, in other words, viewers could not avoid the persistence of the physical object represented. In spaces conceived as embracing all classes, all ages, and both genders, nude paintings brought up too many problems of representation, propriety, and imagination. It was impossible, in other words, particularly in the case of Alma-Tadema's picture, to refrain from imagining the conditions of the painting's production, the actual naked woman who had stood before an actual painter in order to represent a nude model standing before a sculptor. Ultimately, the Walker Art Gallery did not purchase the picture.

Nine years later, Rathbone again showed his ambitions for public art by supporting the development of a representative gallery of casts of architectural ornament and famous sculpture, to be aimed primarily at the working classes. Rather than making the case for improving public morality, this time he made a directly economic case for acquisitions. He argued that because "everywhere coal and steam are superseding unskilled labour," the future of Liverpool, and indeed of England, rested on possessing a skilled workforce, and he worked to bring a "Museums of Casts, Architectural and Sculptural," to the Walker Art Gallery in 1887.[44] The catalogue to that collection explained that the casts came to the Walker for "training up a body of skilled artisans, which will enable them to tide over the trying period of transition in the industries of the world upon which we are now entering."[45] Bought throughout the 1880s, the collection of "Casts from Carvings and Sculpture of the French Schools, Chiefly Renaissance" would provide the necessary models to create a "supply of skilled labour capable of producing artistic architectural details."[46] This rather feeble connection between art and industry, however, was the Walker Art Gallery's only effort in this direction, and the Mayer Museum of applied art remained housed with the Derby Museum of Natural History, eventually becoming incorporated into Social Darwinist, racially categorized anthropological displays.[47] Industrial design and applied art on the South Kensington model did not fit into the merchant port of Liverpool, and the Liverpool Town Council and Walker Art Gallery leadership did not share a vision of art, beauty, and labor as in craft-rich Birmingham. The one foreign picture, one exhibited nude, and small collection of applied art were the exceptions that proved the rule. The Walker Art Gallery developed a collection of

contemporary British art that occasionally challenged popular taste but generally aimed at a mix of popular narrative pictures, to appeal to the uneducated;
"high" aesthetic, nonnarrative, or classical works, to appeal to the educated; and
celebrated Pre-Raphaelite works, hoped to be for everyone. Despite the high-
mindedness of Philip Rathbone, the class stratification of Liverpool thus found
its way into the collecting ethos at the Walker Art Gallery.

MANCHESTER: "BIG NAMES" AND RADICAL REFORMERS

In the formation of the permanent collection at the Manchester City Art Gallery,
we have a particularly clear debate between the followers of Ruskin and those of
Greenwood, as well as a notable preponderance of Royal Academicians in the
gallery's exhibitions and purchases. As we have seen, early proponents of a municipal art museum in Manchester hoped to rid the city of lingering associations
with the excesses of poverty and urban misery wrought by industrialization. In
contrast, another group strove to bring art to the poor explicitly to heal the industrial city with art using Ruskinian ideas. These reformers worked through
the RMI to create the municipal art museum in 1883, while also supporting
other venues such as the Manchester Art Museum in Ancoats and the Ancoats
Brotherhood, which aimed to bring beauty to the slums. However, they had only
marginal success in directing the collecting policies at the new city institution.
Indeed, we see the general ascendancy of the first group in the development of
the permanent collection of the Manchester City Art Gallery, which ultimately
concentrated on the most expensive works and the biggest names from the Royal
Academy and the new London galleries.

As the workings of the city-controlled art museum became more apparent,
artists and reformers noted these tendencies and the prevalence of popular Royal
Academy works in the collection. Thus, already at the end of 1883, the Manchester painter Frederic Shields (codesigner with Ford Madox Brown of the Town
Hall murals and follower of the Pre-Raphaelite style) complained to his friend
C. J. Pooley about the Manchester Art Gallery Purchase Committee and the effect of its patronage:

I content myself with wishing all prosperity to the New Institute [the Manchester City
Art Gallery], & confusion to the present Constitution of the Academy—for it is the
greatest obstacle to the true prosperity of the Fine Arts in this country—for by the ac-

tion of your own & the Liverpool Corporations, it is made as supreme over the provincial Exhibitions as it is over its own annual Shows—so that nowhere is there an escape from its power for those who will not submit to its dictation—[48]

Charles Rowley was also a friend of Shields and active both in the working-class district of Ancoats and with the Manchester City Art Gallery. In an 1889 lecture to the Manchester Athenaeum Graphic Club, he likewise bemoaned the gallery's choice of popular narrative works rather than pursuing higher ideals of bringing applied or educational art into the permanent collection: "For two years I was on the Art Gallery Committee of the Manchester Corporation. Nothing would induce me to undergo that experience again. I found myself, a poor, unlettered, enthusiast for art, with no authority among richer men, and with only one other person striving for the same objects, constantly outvoted because we wanted to teach, and show Art and not to let the Institution be drawn into a merely popular course."[49] Here again is the debate between Ruskin and Greenwood. In Manchester, increasingly radical Ruskinians attempted to influence policies at the same time that the annual autumn exhibition became a crucial regional showplace for the Royal Academy. As part of the handover of the RMI to the city, the new municipal Manchester City Art Gallery was committed to holding those annual exhibitions and, until 1903, to spending £2,000 per year on acquisitions—often purchased from the exhibition. Against the reformers' intentions, but perhaps not surprisingly, this resulted in a collection that became—as Shields and Rowley complained—heavily weighted toward expensive Royal Academy pictures.

While Manchester, the quintessential industrial city, thus developed a museum of contemporary British art, a number of Ruskin- and Morris-inspired advocates worked to include nonnarrative and applied art—nonnarrative art to provide, as Ruskin wrote, an experience of beauty and contemplation, and applied art for the benefit of artisans and designers who might therefore have a sense of greater fulfillment in their work and create more beautiful objects. In his 1889 lecture Rowley articulated the vision of many reformers whose imaginations and righteous outrage had been fired by Ruskin and by Rowley's friend Morris. Rowley argued that the contemporary world was full of a "materialism which is good for neither man nor beast, [a] ceaseless yearning after riches, which are not wealth, or well being, and [a] glorification of quantity instead of quality." He excoriated the imperialist capitalism that destroyed the native arts it most admired: "Indian Art, in the future, will only be found in

Museums, Commercialism will have killed it. So with Japan also." He blasted the rich who hoarded beauty by closing traditional walking paths across their land and patronized art only for their private pleasure rather than public enjoyment.[50] Like many at the time, he connected the ugliness of nineteenth-century mass-produced goods with the failure of the fine arts, and both with the squalid urban environment, the degradation of workers, and the separation of classes. Yet, like Ruskin and Morris, Rowley argued that the creation of a beautiful environment and the education of the workers might change this state of affairs, and he ended his diatribe with the hope of making a just and beautiful society: "I believe that our ordinary British workfolk are still the finest in the world and that we have nothing to fear if we only give them a chance by education of a real kind, by improved surroundings, and more joy in life and work."[51] Similarly, as T. C. Horsfall developed policies for his proposed Manchester Art Museum to bring art to the poor in Ancoats (see Chapter 1), he described its purpose as "giving the mass of the people knowledge and admiration of nature and of the most beautiful and interesting forms of human work."[52] For Horsfall and Rowley, the various projects they supported were part of a wider vision of social transformation.

In order to put all of these ideas into practice, these two men constantly argued for high standards for public art; by this they meant, like Ruskin, art that would avoid popular sentiment in favor of the eternal verities of nature and that would connect the artist and the artisan through beauty and expressive, meaningful labor. Rowley maintained that coming down to the level of the people by telling simple, sentimental, or melodramatic stories (as advocated by Greenwood and practiced by Dyall in Liverpool) ruined the museums' potential for effective educational work. In contrast to Dyall, Rowley said:

of this I am quite certain, the first duty of such a body [the Manchester City Art Gallery] is to provide classics in every branch of industrial, and fine art, and then, endeavour to make them understood. These objects should be constantly vivified by oral demonstration. On no account should a merely popular demand rule the policy. The defeat, as far as I can see, in all our Education—religious, literary, or artistic—is this constant bad habit of coming down to the people.[53]

As we have seen, Wallis in Birmingham and Rathbone in Liverpool also tried to apply high standards to municipal institutions that would not condescend to popular taste but elevate it, with varying ideas of what this meant and different degrees of success. Rowley quickly became disillusioned from his experience working on the Manchester City Art Gallery Purchase Committee. The presence on the committee of art dealer Thomas Agnew, along with the apparent desires of many of the other local bigwigs, brought the Manchester City Art Gallery into the center of the art world; this meant London, the new art societies, and the Royal Academy. Although Ruskinian reformers had been the driving force behind giving the RMI to the city, they did not have a strong institutional role and found that their idealism lost out to those who believed, like Greenwood, that narrative art would be best for the working classes, and who wanted the grandest and most expensive Royal Academy works to prove that Manchester could compete with London.

This battle between reformers and the "popular party" also played out in the conflict over the place of applied art in the Manchester collection. Reformers like Rowley consistently tried to include applied art in order to achieve the wider social goals of "education of a real kind, . . . improved surroundings, and more joy in life and work." In 1883, as the RMI was transferred to the city, Rowley and Morris helped acquire the Bock collection of textiles for £300, but thereafter acquisitions concentrated heavily on painting. Indeed, we see the continued low priority of applied art at the Manchester City Art Gallery in two unofficial pamphlets (from 1889 and 1912) and an official Art Gallery Committee Report of 1905, which all stressed the lack of, and need for, an industrial art museum. These documents give us a glimpse into the state of the Manchester City Art Gallery, pointing out over twenty-three years that lack of space at the art gallery meant that what industrial collections it did possess were either in storage or scattered in other facilities.[54]

Finally, we can understand the development of the Manchester collection through the actual record of purchases. The Manchester City Art Gallery was unique among the three museums in having a dedicated sum of £2,000 per year allocated by the city council to the Art Gallery Committee for acquisitions, part of the RMI's conditions for giving itself to the city (with a commitment of twenty years). Despite this uncommon fund for collecting, however, the Manchester City Art Gallery still concentrated on contemporary, popular, and narrative works. Occasionally, the gallery spent this on unusually expensive works, including Frederick Leighton's *Captive Andromache* for the incredible amount of £4,000—nabbed, in fact, out from under the nose of Liverpool's Walker Art Gallery, which had commissioned a work from Leighton but whose council (not surprisingly) refused to contribute any money to its purchase. (Probably because of the opportunity to trump its rival council, the Manchester City Council contributed an additional £2,600 to the annual acquisitions fund.[55]) This purchase was emblematic of Manchester's acquisitions. Manchester bought fewer young artists than Liverpool did; the Manchester City Art Gallery tended to wait until an artist's reputation was secure before acquiring a representative work. Although Manchester maintained an annual autumn exhibition, and attempted to get the "big names" to exhibit there, it did not purchase from its own exhibition as extensively as the Walker Art Gallery did. Instead, the Manchester City Art Gallery purchased from many auctions and sales. This is perhaps due to the strong influence of art dealer Agnew, who along with cotton manufacturer, art museum advocate, Pre-Raphaelite collector, and Ruskinian reformer Pooley was most often involved in purchasing decisions. (This could also lead to important non–Royal Academy acquisitions; Pooley was instrumental in the purchase of Ford Madox Brown's manifesto-like *Work* from Thomas Plint in 1884 for £400, as well as various works by Shields in subsequent years.[56])

The Manchester City Art Gallery's emphasis on Royal Academy works meant that it absorbed all the heterogeneity of that body during this period. In 1892, the gallery did purchase a nude work, the classical, idealizing single-figure painting *Syrinx* by Royal Academy associate Arthur Hacker, for £400, which was unusual for a public collection at the time. The gallery did not emphasize the work of the Pre-Raphaelites as early as did the other museums. It bought many works by Millais but primarily *after* his Pre-Raphaelite phase: *A Flood* in 1891, *Autumn Leaves* in 1892, *Victory, Oh Lord!* in 1894, *Stella* in 1908, and *Wandering Thoughts (Mrs. Charles Freeman)* in 1913; some of the most important works by William Holman Hunt, long after their creation: *The Hireling Shepherd* in 1896, *The Scapegoat* in 1906, and the most famous image created by that artist, *The Light of the World*, in 1912; and two works by Rossetti, *Astarte Syriaca* in 1891 and *The Bower Meadow* in 1909. Thus the museum in the 1880s and 1890s was indeed very much an outpost of the Royal Academy, with some important non–Royal Academy living artists, such as Edward Burne-Jones and Ford Madox Brown, also represented with a single work each. This kind of purchasing policy seems to have expressed the general desire of the Art Gallery Committee, which was to increase the artistic prominence of the city, connecting Manchester to the national art world in order to combat the common notion that Cottonopolis was a cultural desert. Despite the ideals of the Ruskinians who had helped transform the RMI into the Manchester City Art Gallery, the gentlemen who ran the gallery for the most part spent little time, money, or effort trying to educate or provide material specifically for the working classes and purchased only a few works that exemplified the "truth to nature" that Ruskin advocated. However, in its concentration on contemporary British art, the Manchester City Art Gallery still showed a commitment to art as experience. This is borne out in Professor Sadler's 1911 lecture, in which he claimed that the choices made had been part of a deliberate policy, which would benefit all the city's inhabitants: "Landscape and portraits are the great distinction of this collection. And has it not been a sagacious choice to make English landscape painting the central (though not the only) interest of a gallery set in the midst of a great industrial and commercial city?"[57] From the evidence we have, it is hard to find any deliberate policy of collecting landscapes that would fulfill this reformist argument for the purpose of art in industrial society. However, it underlines the continuing emphasis on art as experience of subject matter rather than art history or even the evolution of particular movements within British art.

CONCLUSION

Contemporary British paintings formed the bulk of the permanent collections at all three municipal art museums, through both institutional structure (buying from exhibitions of works for sale) and design (believing that art was socially redemptive through the power of narrative and subject rather than being educational through a representative collection of art history). William Arnold's 1889 essay on the state of the Manchester City Art Gallery bears this out, detailing "The Three Stages of the English Provincial Gallery": in the first, the museum was "a fortuitous *omnium gatherum* of trivial curiosities, without method, order, or purpose of any kind whatever"; in the second, it was "a development of the preceding one, more pretentious, but at bottom neither more scientific nor more useful"; by the third, "the provincial Gallery has devoted itself almost exclusively to the collection of contemporary British pictures; generally purchased from the autumn exhibitions, which are, in the main, made up of pictures that have already figured at an earlier period of the year in the Royal Academy, or the Grosvenor Gallery, and at the close of those exhibitions have remained unsold."[58] Arnold noted that "of the third stage, the existing City Art Galleries in Manchester and Liverpool are good, perhaps the best, instances." Arnold would push for the Manchester City Art Gallery to acquire a representative collection that could tell the full history of art, beginning the process of turning away from art as experience and toward art history (see Chapter 5).

Local politics and institutional structures led to some significant differences in emphasis and acquisitions policies of the art museums of Birmingham, Liverpool, and Manchester. However, in the end we can see strong similarities in assumptions about art and its social role: for all three museums, art was socially important and potentially beneficial because of its ability to present the experience of beauty, and applied art could be an important tool for improving industrial design. Both ideas rested on the notion of the universal perception of beauty through even the untrained eye and allowed middle-class reformers to claim public art as philanthropy. These assumptions led to collections that overwhelmingly favored contemporary British art and, in some cases, applied art aimed at the working classes. The alignments and affiliations within the art world were particularly complex during this period, when members of the Royal Academy exhibited alongside "outsider" artists at alternative art spaces such as the Grosvenor Gallery. The museums' choices to acquire a wide variety of styles and genres reflected the eclectic tastes of the day. However, their purchases also reflected the understanding that different styles would appeal to both educated and uneducated audiences. In the end, we see the evolution of institutions that could and did, from the outset, easily contain the entire, eclectic spectrum of Victorian artistic styles and subsume these within a rubric that understood art as essentially "refining and elevating" because style and technique were less important than subject matter.

4 TEACHING THROUGH ART
Beauty, Truth, and Story

Even as Victorian reformers sought to democratize art, contemporaries observed a surprising variety of styles, generally supported by the domestic art market and by multiple sites of cultural legitimacy. Indeed, the state offered only very limited patronage, the art-collecting royal family essentially acting in the capacity of model private buyers. This eclecticism and lack of clear standards led many to express a yearning for absolute methods of judgment and interpretation, weighing in particular the relative merits of beauty, truth, or story as the true aim of art. Victorian cities established art institutions that would house all the richness and contradictory impulses of their art world; their collections embodied the constant tensions in Victorian art—between truth and beauty, story and idealism, old masters and new artists. We can see such tensions by analyzing in detail exemplary paintings from each collection, using late Victorian art criticism, recent art historical analysis, and the museum catalogues. As we study particular works, and their Victorian and contemporary interpretations, we find again and again a conflict between an overwhelming "earnestness" (as one 1889 commentator phrased it) and a destabilizing doubt or fracture.[1]

The art that the city museums in Birmingham, Liverpool, and Manchester purchased and then explained to the public in lectures and catalogues had to justify public expenditure and the functioning of this peculiar new institution, the museum of (mostly contemporary) art. It is striking that each museum continued to express its wider policies of access, and its organizers' general philosophies of art, by consistently reading its paintings for narrative and subject. Lectures, pamphlets, and catalogues only rarely used the terms of Victorian art criticism—which was relatively limited by today's art historical standards. We have seen how the museum movement arose out of deep fears about the ugliness, moral and physical, of the industrial city and the society it created. The questions that Victorian paintings and their interpreters posed about beauty and truth were in fact central to the emerging role of art in contemporary society in complex and unpredictable ways. Despite the museums' efforts to read their collections in terms of the experience they offered—that is, like clear windows onto their stories and subjects—the paintings themselves carried the potential for multiple and even contradictory meanings.

The museums' emphases on narrative and moral readings stand out from other kinds of Victorian art interpretation. However, both kinds of Victorian discourse clearly illustrate the radical differences between the Victorians' art world and what was simultaneously developing into the modernist canon, mostly in France, or coalescing into the discipline of art history in Germany. Victorian art critics approached art by subject, treatment, and artist biography. They saw art as an index of its time (as Pugin, Carlyle, and Ruskin had argued in the early part of the century) but obviously did not conceive of art history as later theorists would, for instance, in terms of social context or economic relations or in terms of individual expression, pure color, or form, as in the nascent modernist movement. Victorian art critics lived in a profoundly modern world but felt a continuity with the early modern and even ancient periods that seems quite foreign to us, or to the generations after 1914; terms such as "truth" and "beauty" still meant something profound.

Given the museum administrators' assumptions about their audiences that we saw in Chapter 3, it is not surprising that few of the terms of Victorian art criticism made it into the museums' public educational materials. Many museum supporters believed that recognizable stories were essential for a public collection, and curators such as Charles Dyall at Liverpool's Walker Art Gallery deliberately sought to acquire a proportion of easily readable genre pictures. Indeed, more generally, because they purchased mostly contemporary British art, the institutions tended to amass paintings that lent themselves to narrative readings, a characteristic often noted in discussions of the British school.[2] As William Blake Richmond said in a speech at the Royal Academy in 1898, "where literary emotion is more or less absent from a work of art, in which form and colour are claimed to take precedence as the first essentials of the graphic or plastic arts, the English mind finds it difficult to appreciate; it is rather puzzled because form and colour in the abstract do not excite English sympathies, as do narrative and literary sentiment."[3] By the end of the century, the "moral" and "literary" nature of the British or English school (both terms were used) had become a commonplace. Nonetheless, compared with Victorian criticism, the museums' catalogues show us yet again that these cities did not display art in order to educate the public about form, color, or representation, but to allow visitors to experience beauty, truth, and story.

This chapter explores the problem of art interpretation and how to include the art itself in understanding the Victorian museum movement as embodied in Birmingham, Liverpool, and Manchester. The discussion focuses on two of the purchased paintings from each collection, works that received special notice and, sometimes, extensive interpretation in the museums' catalogues. The selections are paintings that critics and the museum thought were important at the time (on the basis of critical appraisal and purchase price, as well as space devoted to them in the catalogues), including one that is less known now but received notice then. Before addressing specific examples, I begin with a general introduction to the terms of late Victorian art criticism, followed by a brief examination of Victorian museums' educational methods in order to provide a sense of the context in which the catalogues emerged. I then examine what the works of art tell us about the Victorian museum movement, about the experience of going to a city art museum in the late nineteenth century, and about the disjunctions between the purposes for art imagined by museum supporters and the ungovernable and powerful nature of the works themselves. The differences between Victorian and modern criticism—and between general Victorian criticism and the museums' own experiential emphasis—will emerge by viewing the art through the refractions of three lenses: late-nineteenth-century English art criticism, the city museums' catalogues, and more recent, scholarly explorations of these representative works.

VICTORIAN ART CRITICISM AND
THE SEARCH FOR ABSOLUTES

Connecting the museum movement to the art and art criticism of the time helps to clarify the multiple dualities of Victorian culture—its bombast and anxiety, pomp and doubt, confidence and self-consciousness. Victorian art, and the criticism it inspired, shows us a yearning for absolute standards of judgment, debated in terms of the search for truth and beauty and negotiated through narrative and figurative art. Was the goal of art to realize ideal beauty or to present truth (what Ruskin called "stern facts")? The Pre-Raphaelites, and Ruskin in his defense of them, had emphasized a meticulous detail and unflinchingly honest portrayal of their generally nonprofessional models—as portraits rather than as idealized types—with the understanding that this would lead to a higher, spiritual beauty, revealing God's work in contrast to the conventional idealizations of Royal Academy artists. Yet the Pre-Raphaelite movement itself led to new forms of beauty, even new kinds of conventions, as in the works of Dante Gabriel Rossetti and Edward Burne-Jones, and indeed the aesthetic movement that emphasized beauty for its own sake.

Next to the question of beauty or truth as art's highest aim, another kind of tension in Victorian art derives from its oft-noted and multiple varieties of historicism. This use of the past could seem to some as an implicit criticism of the ugliness of the modern world. Yet at the same time, to some contemporaries these same works seemed absolutely "modern" in their approach and subject matter, even in their wistfulness and nostalgia. Meanwhile Victorian art achieved high levels of popularity across social strata.[4] Indeed, many Victorian commentators embraced their contemporary artists with extraordinary confidence and pride, in terms of the British school's position vis-à-vis both the Continent (particularly France) and the old masters, although this can sometimes come across as a bit defensive. For example, in 1899, the newly opened National Gallery of British Art (already known as the Tate Gallery) put out its first catalogue, which happily boasted that "in the closing years of the nineteenth century the nation is prepared to back its own country-men to produce paintings or sculpture, especially the latter, equal in merit, if not superior, to those of any other nation, France included."[5] The encomiums heaped upon Victorian artists and their works by Victorian art critics can sometimes surprise us; Ruskin, for instance, can seem very free and easy with his designation "one of the world's masterpieces."[6] I have come to understand Victorian historicism, and the nationalism that supported it, as an aspect of the particularly modern yearning for stability and (imagined) wholeness, for beauty, faith, and absolutes, that characterized the wider museum movement (and indeed many aspects of Victorian culture), in the face of industrial capitalism, Darwinism, imperialism, and secularization.

It was precisely this *lack* of clear standards, of an authoritative mode for judging art, that led both to the variety of Victorian artistic expression and to the confusion over how to judge it. For the Victorian art market did indeed drive a fantastic eclecticism that was only partially presided over by the Royal Academy, which famously neglected some of the era's most celebrated artists (notably William Holman Hunt, Burne-Jones, Rossetti, Albert Moore, and Whistler).[7] This market-driven variety made assessments of the British school extremely difficult, then and now (although generally the modernists could tell us quite explicitly what they disliked about Victorian art; see the Epilogue). British eclecticism became a commonplace of late-nineteenth-century art criticism, particularly as increasingly nationalist tendencies prompted critics to define the national school. In this context of artistic and critical eclecticism, powered by the growing middle class, the regional museums developed primarily as collectors, and exhibitors for sale, of contemporary or recent art. Thus they, along with other new exhibition spaces such as the Grosvenor Gallery and the New Gallery, became important new venues for bridging the gap between the market and the Royal Academy.

E. T. Cook, in his 1888 handbook to the National Gallery in London, asked:

Is there an English School at all? In the fullest sense of the term, there certainly is not. Every visitor who, after studying any one of the Italian Schools or the Dutch School, walks through the rooms devoted to the "English School," cannot fail to be struck by the absence of uniformity in the latter. Instead of one general type of picture, modified only by individual peculiarities, he will find in the English rooms almost as many styles as there are painters.[8]

Samuel Redgrave, in his introduction to the catalogue of the National Gallery of British Art at South Kensington of the same year, agreed, although he turned such an "absence of uniformity" into a blessing: "Unlike the Continental practice, our artists, both subject and landscape painters, mostly study art for themselves, and prefer nature to the painting-rooms of their eminent contemporaries. This habit has led not only to truth, but to variety and individuality, which are among the greatest charms of British landscape painting." Noting the lack of centralized state or religious patronage, Redgrave understood British art as

flourish[ing] from the demands of those who love it as a home delight; therefore our pictures are small, and suited to our private residences, while the subjects are such as we can live by and love; and hence, they have been largely illustrative of the feelings and affections of our kind, and of the beautiful nature of which we desire to be reminded as a solace in moments of rest from the hard labour of daily life.[9]

In Redgrave's patriotic account, the lack of established traditions of successful Academic history or religious painting becomes a sign of the strength of Britain's domestic sphere, the driving force behind the art market. In this formulation, similar to the justifications for city art museums, art comes out of the need for the beauty of nature as an antidote to modern society, and both are crucially connected to core middle-class values—"hard labor" and "home delight."

Victorian art and art criticism therefore developed during a period that, much like today, lacked clear standards for judgment. Unlike our own art world, however, this absence pained both artist and critic, and individuals sought their own resolutions to the problem. As we have seen, the defining terms of the nineteenth-century debate—taken from Reynolds and Keats, and revolutionized by Ruskin and the Pre-Raphaelites—were "beauty" and "truth," very different from our own concerns with politics and power. A primary question for many interpreters was the extent to which beauty and truth could be reconciled, a point that bears consideration in the context of the evolving landscapes of industrial society, and goes back to the questions of historicism and nostalgia. Could an artist create a beautiful painting of the modern world? What constituted truth—attention to detail or generalization? What role did the artist's hand, eye, or imagination play? Ruskin and his followers crusaded for "truth to nature" and the Pre-Raphaelite abandonment of idealization and convention. However, few painters other than J. M. W. Turner ever met Ruskin's simultaneously exacting, mercurial, and idio-syncratic standards, and Ruskin himself worked throughout his voluminous writings to resolve the question of the artist as witness or as poet—he tended to want both. (This issue was not limited to the visual arts, also being of primary concern in the context of literary realism and naturalism.)

The innovations of the Pre-Raphaelite Brotherhood, and Ruskin's justifica-tions in *Modern Painters* of both their works and those of Turner, had brought questions of truth and beauty to the fore in the middle of the century. These issues resurfaced in the 1880s and 1890s, as art critics sought to assess the British school in general and the influence of the Pre-Raphaelite school in particular. The debate hinged on the question of what kinds of truth, and what kinds of beauty, were the proper aim of art. Thus, in 1889 Kineton Parkes published a work in London and Birmingham on the Pre-Raphaelite school that argued, "Pre-Raphaelitism is in its essence truth to nature. . . . Its disciples sought not so much renown as for truth, and truth in which beauty resided—beauty which was true."[10] In an 1891 assessment of the Pre-Raphaelite school, William Morris was clear in his descrip-tion of what constituted "a great work of plastic Art"—as he put it, "presentation of nature and the telling of a story"—but he admitted that the

third side was both less considered by the public, and was much more difficult to put before it: that side was the ornamental function of the Art. No picture it seems to me is complete unless it is something more than a representation of nature and the teller of a tale. It ought also to have a definite, harmonious, conscious beauty. It ought to be ornamental. It ought to be possible for it to be part of a beautiful whole in a room or church or hall.[11]

For Morris, not surprisingly, his close friend and collaborator Edward Burne-Jones "complete[d]" the Pre-Raphaelite school, adding "the element of *perfect* ornamentation, the completely decorative side of the Art."[12] Both Morris and Parkes, then, understood Pre-Raphaelitism as aiming at both truth and beauty; in the words of Morris, "the naturalism of the Pre-Raphaelites . . . did not stop at the simple presentment of scientific fact but went further and conscientiously considered the due and proper incidents that were necessary in order to make a work of Art."[13] The movement created "genuinely *natural* conventions," art "addressed to us, the public, and not merely to artists prejudiced in favour of certain traditions," tempering truth with beauty through story and design.[14]

Not everyone, however, appreciated the Pre-Raphaelites' emphasis on readable detail or could see their truth to nature as beautiful. For example, Cosmo Monkhouse, art critic for *Scribner's Weekly*, the *Magazine of Art*, and the *Saturday Review*, wrote:

One practice to which they attached great importance was a minute imitation of Nature's detail. Far from the idea that painting should only imitate the general impression of the sight, they even set themselves against "generalization." Every leaf, every pebble, must be painted. So far was their theory carried that a microscopic accuracy was held to be a noble quality, and painting was thought to have reached superexcellence if all the facts which it represented could not be discovered without the aid of a microscope.[15]

Despite symbolist art critic Ernest Chesneau's criticisms of Ruskin and the Pre-Raphaelites, the English edition of his study *Peinture Anglaise* (1882, translated 1884) nonetheless included a preface by Ruskin assuring readers of his "own concurrence with M. Chesneau's critical judgement respecting all pieces of art with which we have been alike acquainted."[16] Chesneau, however, still gave his own, ultimately unfavorable interpretation of the role of detail, morality, and truth in painting:

The new school [the Pre-Raphaelite Brotherhood] ascribed to art, in direct terms, a distinctly moral purpose. Some of them thought to gain this object by representing, in as minute a style as possible, subjects in historical art, possessing a most precise and accurate character. Others proposed to attain their end in landscape painting, by carrying out faithfully the smallest details, and most insignificant particulars of the special spot in nature chosen by the artist. In both cases, in history and landscape, the system was one of microscopic analysis driven to the utmost extreme. By so strict a scrutiny they hoped to become closely united and incorporated with Truth, the beginning and end of all morality.[17]

Chesneau was deeply critical of this position, precisely because of its resulting lack of "artistic qualities" or "harmony": "Mr. Ruskin imputes to truth of detail, studied in a scientific manner (for that is really his idea), artistic qualities which it does not possess; he seems to me in direct contradiction with the evidence of facts when he asserts that this precision of detail is requisite and necessary in order to acquire the simplicity, seriousness, and harmony which characterise the general effect of natural scenes."[18]

Art critics Harry Quilter, Samuel Redgrave, and Ford Madox Hueffer (who later wrote as Ford Madox Ford) also argued against a minute attention to detail and truth over a sense of beauty, proportion, and what Hueffer called "charm."[19] As Quilter put it:

realism is not noble in itself, if it have no higher object. . . . The next step is the all-important one . . . the connection of material beauty with immaterial thought. . . . An artist must not only see more clearly than other people—he must also see more; he must, if he is to be an artist in anything but name, see those hidden significances in commonplace things, that poetry of the ordinary which, in another form, is revealed to us by the poet.[20]

Of course, in all of these debates Ruskin and the Pre-Raphaelites became caricatures of themselves, but what is most important is that at the end of the century there was still vibrant debate over the status of beauty, truth, and morality. In fact, Quilter's statement is actually a fair representation of what Ruskin said many times, and provides us with an excellent insight into the struggle both artists and critics were engaged in: the challenge of understanding the fraught relationship between the "material" and the "immaterial," the "hidden significances of commonplace things." As we will see, Victorian painters sought to overcome these contradictions in a wide variety of ways. The works collected in the city art museums grappled with the fundamental questions of appearance and reality, beauty and truth, materiality and transcendence, and with the paradoxes of faith and doubt, sentiment and the struggle for existence that lay at the heart of Victorian culture.

In addition to judging works in terms of their relative emphasis on "beauty" or "truth," Victorian art critics also measured contemporary work by the achievements of past ages. For example, William Richmond argued in an 1898 address that "there were during three decades of this century, pictures painted by Millais, Rossetti, Madox Brown, and Leighton, and others—I am not permitted to name living painters,—which are fit to hang side by side with the masterpieces of the 14th, 15th, and 16th centuries of Italian art."[21] M. H. Spielmann, editor from 1886 to 1904 of the influential *Magazine of Art*, felt it necessary in 1898 to argue that "the best Art of modern times is as good as any of its kind that has gone before," even while pointing out that "it is manifestly impossible to make just compari-sons between the widely divergent styles of the Ancient and Modern Masters, or to attempt to strike a balance between, say, Rubens and Hogarth." He referred to the continuing emphasis on old masters among connoisseurs, explaining that "to say that the old alone is good betrays great lack of judgment, and is an in-gratitude to the living," and noting that, in worshipping old works, people forget "the charm of mutilation or the fascination of decay." Instead, he urged, one must ask oneself, "What was that like when it was new?" Writing of how the freshly painted, perfectly finished Parthenon must have appeared at its grand opening, he imagines that "many of us, I venture to think, would cry at once, 'How exces-sively crude!'"[22] For many collectors, particularly among the titled gentry, "the charm of mutilation" and "the fascination of decay" had indeed been markers of worth and distinction. The development of distinct, class-differentiated pat-terns of collecting, as scholars have shown, derived equally from middle-class appreciation for the moral tone of much contemporary art, from the relative availability and affordability of that art, and from collectors' desire to distinguish themselves from earlier connoisseurs.[23] In much Victorian art criticism, then, even at the end of the century, the *Querelle* between ancients and moderns, and thus between aristocratic and middle-class patterns of collecting, was alive and well.

This has been a necessarily brief survey, but the examples above show that British art criticism at the end of the nineteenth century was concerned with some issues that were very different from later, modernist art history. The prominence of Victorian art overlapped with the search for refuge and morality in industrial society; the artistic search for beauty and truth helped bolster the museum move-ment, but also belied any easy resolution to the tensions and doubts of the age.

VICTORIAN "EDUCATION AND OUTREACH"

Two important museum educational tools were lectures and pamphlets, which generally supported the information and approach given in the catalogues. Lec-tures became a key means of mass education with the invention of the lantern slide and photographic reproductions. A brief example may illustrate how lectures continued the policy that appeared in both acquisitions and, to some extent, the catalogues, namely, the conception of separate art experiences for different audiences. In 1883, the year that the Royal Manchester Institution transferred itself to the city, Ruskinian reformer T. C. Horsfall delivered an address to the Manchester Literary Club, later summarized in the *Architect*, in which he advocated a regular system of lectures to make the gallery more accessible to the uneducated: "What is wanted is a system of training people to look carefully at pictures with the settled purpose of getting enjoyment from them. We need every year a series of lectures dealing in the simplest way with the elements of the subject and delivered in front of the pictures referred to."[24] At the same time, however, a different kind of art conversation than that proposed by Horsfall generally occurred at small clubs for the educated, such as the Manchester Literary Club itself. There, listeners might hear, for example, W. E. A. Axon speak about "Art in Lancashire," giving the history of collectors, of artists, and of the role of art in that county since the late eighteenth century, in terms similar to that of the art critical press.[25] This kind of historical information was not deemed important, or part of the museums' mission, for the general public.

As Horsfall had advocated, public lectures did gradually take on an important role in popularizing the contents of the museums. Councilor J. E. Phythian in Manchester began a series of midday talks at the Manchester City Art Gallery in 1903 and gave lectures on art to societies and associations throughout the area, eventually as part of the Workers' Educational Association.[26] In the last decades of the century, Birmingham curator Whitworth Wallis gave many lectures on art, and on the municipal art museum, in Birmingham and other cities, including Liverpool and Manchester.[27] Liverpool curator Charles Dyall gave municipal lectures on the contents of the Walker Art Gallery, and Liverpool councilor P. H. Rathbone gave lectures and published pamphlets on art, on the Walker Art Gallery, and especially on the annual autumn exhibitions.[28] Those interested in art, like Horsfall and Axon, gave talks at local clubs, societies, and congresses. Other interested parties (particularly nationally known figures) came to the art museums or local art societies to give lectures that were later published, some of which then entered the catalogues.[29] Gradually, these lectures came to include material on art appreciation previously deemed appropriate only for the educated classes, moving from simple narrative to include discussions of form, composition, and technique.

All three museums published a variety of catalogues, both of temporary exhibitions and of their permanent collections, at different prices. The Birmingham Museum and Art Gallery made the greatest effort to sell cheap, educational guides to the permanent collection and to its free temporary loan exhibitions, and included sales figures in the museum committee's annual reports. Liverpool's Walker Art Gallery and the Manchester City Art Gallery, in contrast, put a great deal of time and effort into catalogues for the annual autumn exhibitions and reported on sales of these in their committee records. These differed from permanent collection catalogues, in that they were intended for use in conjunction with exhibitions of works for sale and included only basic information—artist, title, price—with a brief accompanying text. Birmingham made a variety of inexpensive handbooks and catalogues available, many for one penny, while the cheapest catalogues available for the permanent collection or exhibitions in Liverpool and Manchester were three times as much, although still relatively inexpensive at threepence.[30] In all three cases many more people visited the museums than bought the guidebooks, leaving most visitors to their own devices to interpret the art they saw.[31]

While the catalogues of all three museums described the works in their collections in terms of subject matter, each also pursued particular emphases in line with their policies more generally. Thus, the Birmingham Museum and Art Gallery had essentially a strong director in curator Wallis and pursued a clear mandate to connect art and labor, part of a larger effort of municipal reform. In line with this, the art gallery's catalogues treated artists as artisans, focusing on their early training and development, and conceived of paintings as objects, sometimes giving a history of a work's creation and occasionally giving the artist's own interpretation. The connection between acquisition and interpretation is particularly clear in the case of the Birmingham Museum and Art Gallery, as the vast majority of works given attention in the catalogues had been purchased by the Art Gallery Purchase Committee, the fund that Wallis controlled.[32] The Walker Art Gallery, where curator Dyall advocated the acquisition of popular pictures that would hold interest for a broad and uneducated public, published catalogues in which Dyall composed imaginative literary interpretations of the works, with a clear emphasis on moral readings. Curator William Stanfield compiled the catalogues of the Manchester City Art Gallery, whose autumn exhibitions aspired to compete with London (particularly the Royal Academy)—this despite the protests of reformers such as Charles Rowley and Horsfall, who believed in a more didactic purpose and more democratic audience for the institution (see Chapter 3). Stanfield's descriptions judge works by their "vigor" and their "fidelity to nature," focusing on the artist's official status as well as the subject of the picture.

All three museums pursued definite collection and education policies as part of a project to bring beauty, truth, and story into the lives of their citizens, rather than art education as it came to be understood in the twentieth century, that is, dominated by art history. However, the paintings themselves could resist narrow or instrumental readings, and remain as potent reminders of the complex currents at work in these attempts to transform industrial society through public art collections.

BIRMINGHAM: PAINTINGS AS OBJECTS AND ARTISTS AS ARTISANS

The Birmingham Museum and Art Gallery, as we have seen, emerged with a particularly clear sense of purpose, as it was created by a town council that effected a remarkable reform effort and rebuilding plan and was overseen by a curator who was given many of the powers of a director. The collection combined the fine and applied arts, an expression of both the moral and aesthetic values of "joyful labor" espoused by the Arts and Crafts movement *and* the parallel, if contradictory, hope that improvements in design could help British manufacturers successfully compete in increasingly cutthroat global markets. The Art Gallery Purchase Committee gave Wallis a means of directing the development of this collection, a power admired by art reformers in Manchester.[33]

The museum displayed the collections of fine and applied arts in separate rooms, and from 1888 its "industrial art" was discussed in a separate catalogue, priced at just one penny. At the same time, however, the two-penny catalogue of works in oil and watercolors consistently framed the artists as artisans and came out in a penny version in 1889; all of the catalogue editions emphasized the maker over the object, describing every artist, at least briefly. By the 1901 edition, all of these artist descriptions included the artist's background and training, with detailed painting descriptions for only selected works.[34] In keeping with the goal of reaching a popular audience, particularly including artisans as well as the educated middle classes, Wallis created one-penny, two-penny, three-penny, six-penny, and one-shilling versions of his catalogues, the price primarily based on length of descriptions (of both artists and the works) and illustrations.[35] Wallis also assumed that the differently priced catalogues would appeal to different audiences, so the information in the various versions gives us a window on assumptions that even this idealistic and high-minded curator made about who needed to know what to learn from or enjoy a work of art.

The Birmingham Museum and Art Gallery catalogues of 1897 (one penny) and 1899 (twopence; illustrated) treated artworks as subjects to be read rather than as visual statements that related to a wider history of artistic representation. In 1892, the Art Gallery Purchase Committee bought Alfred East's landscape *Hayle, from Lelant* directly from the artist for the significant sum of £425. East had achieved acclaim as a landscape painter in the 1880s, which increased after the Fine Arts Society commissioned him to visit and draw Japan in 1889; he brought back some of the first modern views of that country that England saw after the Meiji Restoration.[36] The 1897 (one-penny) description of East's painting approaches it through the place it depicts and the interest this might hold for the citizens of industrial Birmingham:

This picture was painted from Lelant Station, on the St. Erth and St. Ives branch of the Great Western Railway, in the summer of 1891. The town of Hayle is celebrated as being the birthplace of railways although locomotives were not used. The railway was made to bring the ore from the mines, the full trucks as they came down pulling up the empty ones by cable. The town lies on a tidal port which finds its outlet in St. Ives Bay.[37]

Because the description uses ekphrasis—that is, it does not enter into the artist's portrayal of the scene, but into the scene itself—there are none of the debates about beauty and truth found in other Victorian art criticism; this is a very dif-

Alfred East, *Hayle, from Lelant*, 1892. © Birmingham Museums and Art Gallery.

ferent kind of approach to art, one consistent with the didactic idea of art as the experience of subject matter.[38] What is particularly remarkable about this description is that it bears virtually no relation to the scene that the painting depicts, being solely focused on the area's industrial history. In the more expensive six-penny catalogue, perhaps aimed at people who might consider themselves connoisseurs, or at least interested in the art world, the description retains the information about the industrial history but adds a discussion of light and color afterward—thick description that still employs ekphrasis: "The scene is represented under the warm light of the setting sun; the church, houses, workshops, and fishing boats are vividly lighted up by the last slanting rays of a summer sun, the pools of water on the sand reflecting the blue sky. The sun being at the back of the spectator there is scarcely any shadow except that thrown by the seagulls."[39] Here, we move directly into the beauty of the scene, apart from the history of mining and the innovative system of coal trucks that would later influence railway development.

East's painting is remarkable for its dominating expanses of water and sky, while he relegates to the periphery the human development, the harbor and manufacturing, which are indicated by the boats on the left and the small factory on the right, whose smoke blends into the hazy clouds, and which are modulated again by their reflections in the water. The painting, with its delicate color and loose brushwork, reflects East's training, mentioned in the brief biography: his time at the Glasgow School of Art and the Paris École des Beaux-Arts (and later in a French studio), and then his work at Barbizon, would have exposed East to the work of artists experimenting with light, color, and painterliness, particularly the Barbizon school and the French impressionists. The museum catalogues, however, direct the viewer to see the painting as a window onto both history (the industrial background) and nature (color and light). Although there is some distinction between the classes who might purchase the different catalogue editions, neither approaches the work in terms of contemporary art criticism, but in terms of its subject. The painting brings in another kind of experience, however—that of brushstrokes, color, and the overwhelming power of water, light, and sky over the small achievements of humanity. The catalogue celebrates the advent of industry, but the painting literally pushes it to one side and makes no allusion to the contribution to the railroad made there.

In the case of Edward Burne-Jones, the native son from whom the Birmingham museum in 1887 commissioned a major work—the enormous watercolor *The*

Star of Bethlehem[40]—we have a painter who received a great deal more attention, even at the time, and who received consistent reconsideration throughout the twentieth century despite the drastic changes to his reputation after World War I. At the end of the nineteenth century, several art critics wrote book-length considerations of him and his work, and many others explored him in more general discussions of the Pre-Raphaelite Brotherhood or the aesthetic movement. Two aspects of his work provoked particularly important points of debate. First, its unique combination of Ruskinian "truth to nature," closely observed detail, and careful drawing, even as it portrayed imaginary and usually mythic or spiritual subjects, presented a complex resolution to the art critical debate between beauty and truth. Second, this unreality, enhanced by Burne-Jones's idealization of both male and female figures and his distinct personal style, seemed to comment on the ugliness of the modern world in ways that contemporary observers could find quite disturbing (particularly the perceived "effeminacy" of his male figures).

Malcolm Bell wrote an influential assessment of Burne-Jones in 1892 that had gone into four editions by 1903. Bell defended the artist against multiple "common errors" made in interpreting his work, many of which, as Bell points out, were based on Ruskin's ideas about "truth to nature," even while Ruskin himself worked closely with Burne-Jones and praised his painting and design.[41] "No painter goes more constantly or reverently to nature," Bell wrote, "but he does not consider that to slavishly copy her is the be-all and end-all of art. . . . He has, indeed, no affinity with the modern realism which seems to exult in its triviality and emptiness, and which in the nature of things never can appear, let alone be real."[42] Symbolist Chesneau described Burne-Jones in glowing terms, and for similar reasons. Like Bell, Chesneau emphasized Burne-Jones's unusual, perhaps unique, technical facility and imaginative conception, which gave meticulous detail and finish to imagined scenes, calling him "the only artist whose high gifts in designing, arranging and colouring are equal to his poetical conceptions," praising the "feeling" of his work and "its poetical interpretation . . . allied to this devotion to truth and lofty imagination."[43] Like William Morris, Bell and Chesneau found in Burne-Jones's work an unusual solution to the seemingly intractable conflict between beauty and truth. Still, for many observers the fictional quality, the unreality, of his work made it beautiful but untrue. Recently, Stephan Wildman has given this same quality context in the larger (art historical) story of modernism, writing of Burne-Jones's efforts to "cut loose from the trammels of representation."[44]

This unreality was, indeed, Burne-Jones's intention, as Wildman has discussed: "'I don't want to pretend that this isn't a picture,' [Burne-Jones] would say; and when someone claimed that it was a mistake for an artist to paint 'out of his head,' he replied that, on the contrary, it was precisely 'the place where I think pictures ought to come from.'"[45] If this aspect of Burne-Jones's work raised problems of appreciation and interpretation in Victorian art critical terms, his close observation of natural forms in order to craft visions of worlds that were not only clearly imaginary, but often set in the distant past, also raised the problem of his relationship to the modern world.[46] Indeed, the fact that Burne-Jones was also a celebrated designer in tapestries and stained glass—two quintessentially medieval media—underscored his peculiar relation to his own era. For Julia Cartwright, one of his late Victorian interpreters, "The art of Burne-Jones from first to last has been a silent and unconscious protest against the most striking tendencies of the modern world." She goes on to connect this precisely to his abandonment of realism in favor of beauty:

In a period which is essentially prosaic, when realism has invaded both art and fiction, and material prosperity seems to be the end and aim of all endeavour, he has remained a poet and an idealist. In days when reverence has died out and no mystery is held sacred, the sense of wonder . . . is never absent from his creations. . . . From the dulness and ugliness of the present he turns with all the passionate ardour of his being to the forgotten past, and there, in the myths and fairy-tales of the old world, he finds the food after which his soul hungers.[47]

Cartwright read Burne-Jones's paintings as "silent" and "unconscious" protests, but she also saw in their anachronistic idealism a patent yearning that was absolutely modern: "These fair faces, in which the old and new world seem to meet and modern sentiment is as it were grafted onto a classic ideal, these sad eyes which haunt us with their look of unsatisfied longing, are laden with the burden and sorrow of the present day."[48] For her, then, these paintings were not just about reconciling truth and beauty, as for the other late Victorian critics, but about the comment they made—in both style and subject matter—on her own world.

In his opening address to the 1891 Pre-Raphaelite Exhibition at the Birmingham Museum and Art Gallery that included their new acquisition, Burne-Jones's *The Star of Bethlehem*, William Morris argued in similar terms that any beauty in modern art must studiously ignore the modern world: "When an artist has really a very keen sense of beauty, I venture to think that he cannot literally represent an event that takes place in modern life. He must add something or another to qualify or soften the ugliness and sordidness of the surroundings of life in our generation."[49] Wildman offers Burne-Jones's perspective:

The longing to "fashion a world that nothing could disturb" was fueled by a conviction that the real world was becoming uglier. There was much truth in this so far as his immediate surroundings were concerned. . . . Over the years, . . . the lanes and fields [around The Grange, the house/studio of Burne-Jones and his family] had been developed, until the house and its large garden, dominated by a huge mulberry tree, were an oasis of peace and beauty among the mean, jerry-built streets of late-Victorian Fulham. "All about us," Burne-Jones wrote in 1889, "the streets have grown so hateful—noisy, rowdy, blackguardly—it is often well-nigh unendurable."[50]

In Andrea Wolk Rager's recent persuasive discussion of Burne-Jones's *Briar Rose* series, she argues that "Burne-Jones deployed the fantastical dream as an epiphanic visionary mode, creating a liminal space from which to reflect back on the ills of the modern world rather than retreat from them."[51] What becomes clear is that far from simple, beautiful "dreams," Burne-Jones's works echoed with a host of questions about beauty, truth, the past, and the present.

The museum-commissioned watercolor *The Star of Bethlehem* brought with it all of these disturbances, but in contemporary criticism and catalogues these generally remained unarticulated, or referred to only obliquely. In keeping with his defense of Burne-Jones, Bell wrote that the picture avoided "petty precisions" of antiquarianism, noting the "broad suggestions" that give the Magi an "Oriental aspect," all three wearing exotic and imaginary costumes; "yet, individually and collectively, they are all exquisite, and the self-abasement of wealth and power before the weak majesty of a homeless mother and her babe has never found a truer or fairer expression."[52] Cartwright found that Burne-Jones's close observation of nature in the picture expressed the spiritual flowering of the nativity: "Tall white lilies blossom at [the Madonna's] side, red roses creep up the wattled fence, and flowers of every shape and hue spring up in the grass at her feet. The long-expected day has dawned upon the world, the Desire of nations is born and the wilderness has rejoiced and blossomed as the rose. . . . The kingdoms of this world and the flowers of the field alike bring their best to lay before the manger-throne."[53] At the New Gallery exhibition of the picture in 1891, before it went to Birmingham, the catalogue noted the spiritual dimension of Burne-Jones's depiction of the baby Jesus: "The Child turns towards His Mother, but

Edward Burne-Jones, *The Star of Bethlehem*, 1888–1891. © Birmingham Museums and Art Gallery.

looks round at the figures, the childish fear being overcome by the divine nature."[54] The *Art Journal* also commented on the central angel, "this strange, ra-
diant figure, resembling a statue from Chartres or Rheims, into which the glow
of life [has] been infused"—again, the particular quality of Burne-Jones's work
being his ability to bring imagined scenes alive and make them real.[55]

Wildman calls the watercolor "the finest religious painting by an artist whose
faith was of a personal, idiosyncratic kind," but, being an art historian, he also
notes the context and design history of the work. For instance, he points out that
the picture's origin as a tapestry for Exeter College, Oxford, woven by Morris &
Co., gave it a "distinctively two-dimensional feel" but that "Burne-Jones was able
to use its immense size to increase the areas of space between and behind the
figures, so as to give a greater sense of depth and atmosphere."[56] Indeed, I would
agree that the history of the painting as a tapestry gives particular emphasis in
the work on the textiles, which are almost more imposing and alive than the
statuesque figures and are as carefully designed as the original tapestry.[57] On its
own terms, however, the painting challenges the boundaries between painting
and weaving, artist and artisan, and beauty and truth.

In contrast, Wallis's 1897 one-penny and 1899 six-penny (illustrated) catalogues
to the Birmingham Museum and Art Gallery enter into the picture with empathetic narrative imagination: "The babe—a lovely chubby little fellow—is quite

nude, half shy and half afraid of the magnificent [*sic*] Magi; his little dimpled hands clutch at the blue robes which fall over the protecting bosom of the Virgin, but the sense of wonder and curiosity impels him to turn his dark lustrous eyes on the vision—these strange visitors that bend before him." In describing the Magi, the entry's author uses the painting to imagine story and character:

The first is an aged man. His eyes have looked on good and ill, and these have had, too, their war in his heart, not always, we judge, unequally matched, but good has triumphed. He has loved the right, and in his heart has cherished the love of what is beautiful and pure. . . . At his feet lies a gloriously gemmed crown. We could almost think that he had prepared this gift anticipating that the Star would lead him to some Shah or Sultan, some Prince or King, to whom the delight of the eye and the pride of life were all; but that when the Star stood still over that meek lady and that innocent chubby babe, he had cast it aside, feeling how poor and tame and common-place was his gift, and fallen back on the homelier offering in the little open casket in his hand.[58]

The catalogue copy brings the viewer into the picture through literary imagination, the character and his imagined history, and the stories behind the objects. The author does not comment on the making of the picture, its style, its combination of closely observed nature and idealization, its use of color, composition, design, or nostalgia. In turning to the dark-skinned figure at the far right, the author brings in the racist ideas of this period steeped in social Darwinism but foreign to the picture itself, choosing to read the three kings as allegories for Mind, Soul, and Body: "The third is a swarthy King, in Nubian cast of features. Do the other Kinds type Mind and Soul? If so, is this the animal nature of man which also shall bow to him? The colours of his dress are gayer and richer, and the face is less full of soul."[59] Both editions of the catalogue go on to describe the story of the Magi as told in two original sources, both the New Testament allusions to the "wise men" and the medieval "Three Kings of Cologne." The primary difference between the cheaper and more expensive versions is that the six-penny edition gives a great deal more information on Burne-Jones as an artist—the history of his work, exhibitions, and honors—although both describe his family background and training. It seems that curator Wallis imagined that both groups of catalogue purchasers would enter into the picture in the same way, in terms of story. However, he gave the audience buying the more expensive, illustrated catalogue additional information about the artist's most important works; his relationships with Ruskin, Morris, and Rossetti; and his work in tapestry and stained glass. Both editions gave a history of Exeter College's commission of the tapestry and of the museum's commission of the painting.

In these two examples from Birmingham, then, we see works that dealt in complex ways with their modern, industrial surroundings, which the catalogues framed in terms of story and subject. While late Victorian art criticism and twentieth-century art history interpreted Burne-Jones's work in particular in their own terms—the debate between beauty and truth and the narrative of modernism, respectively—they both found evidence in his work (as we found in East's) of a turn away from the ugliness of the modern, industrial age. Alongside the catalogues' interpretations, then, we need to put the paintings themselves, which offered complicated and ambivalent statements about the past as a place of beauty (and the present as a place of ugliness), the power of nature and faith, and the power and longevity of contemporary achievements. Together with the collections of Japanese, Chinese, Italian, and Indian handmade objets d'art, these paintings helped to create a collection in the museum that could seem to criticize as much as celebrate the "gains of industry" in the city outside.[60]

LIVERPOOL: NARRATIVE AND MORALITY

The Walker Art Gallery articulated a collecting policy with an even greater emphasis on acquiring examples of narrative art for the uneducated classes, and its catalogues also approached works through story and subject. In contrast to the Birmingham catalogues, however, which consistently described the artists in greater detail than the pictures—giving thorough descriptions of only the most notable works—the Liverpool catalogues gave literary descriptions for most of the pictures and only artists' names. Curator Dyall's *Descriptive Catalogues* engaged with the paintings in a lively, imaginative way, providing excerpts from relevant literary sources and occasionally dialogue and explicitly moral readings.[61] The two paintings considered here, Albert Moore's *A Summer Night* and William Holman Hunt's *Triumph of the Innocents*, differ in their aims and methods, but they bring out the multiple ideas at play in late Victorian art. Moore's work shows us the fractures between the Ruskin-inspired foundational assumptions of the museum about art and late Victorian aestheticism, formalism, and symbolism; Hunt's shows us how work deeply committed to Ruskinian ideas could embody contradictions of its own between the seen and the unseen, realism and wonder.

In a lecture at the Walker Art Gallery on the autumn exhibition of 1890, councilor, public art defender, and connoisseur Philip Rathbone spoke on

"Impressionism in Art." In the course of his lecture he makes interesting distinctions between types of art, specifically using the paintings by Moore and Hunt to exemplify divergent approaches to beauty and truth. He defends impressionism in terms of the ability to depict truth (the old Ruskinian goal): "This is the perfection of Impressionism; that is, painting exactly what the eye would see under the supposed circumstances, and leaving to the imagination the exact play which, in that case, it would be obliged to exercise. When the spectator comes to realise this, it gives a much greater sense of reality than if every detail, which he would not have seen at that distance, were painted." Rathbone contrasts the new method with the "old Pre-Raphaelite method,"

which was to paint every detail which existed, whether it could be seen or not by the spectator, of which we have a very fine instance in the "Triumph of the Innocents," in the next room; and that method, to many people, gives the idea of extreme hardness, because it ignores that the atmosphere is not an entirely transparent medium of sight. It must not be said that either of these methods are wrong; they are simply different.[62]

He takes this approach throughout the lecture, trying to explain the different goals of the various artists and the way to understand their works given their different motivations.

In addition to distinguishing between Pre-Raphaelitism and impressionism, Rathbone also contrasts the goals of a painting intended to be "a sort of window" with those of "a decorative picture . . . simply meant to give pleasure as part of a wall, and not to assert itself as a separate entity." The first, he explains, is "intended to give you somewhat of the impression of the real scene depicted," while the second's "chief purpose and aim" is a "bright restfulness" as part of a larger architectural scheme or interior design. In this context, he mentions Moore's *A Summer Night*: "The beautiful Albert Moore . . . [is] in the nature of a decorative picture."[63] Rathbone explicitly notes that he aimed at creating a "representative collection," and Hunt's *Triumph of the Innocents* and *A Summer Night* exemplify this, embodying very different kinds of art, with distinct goals: that of truth, "depicting a real scene" like a "window," or aiming at decorative flatness, part of a larger interior beauty that will give rest and repose.

The Walker Art Gallery purchased Moore's painting *A Summer Night* from the artist for £800, significantly less than the £1,500 he was asking for it.[64] Already in failing health, Moore was a friend of leading artists of the day, including outsiders Rossetti and Whistler, and president of the Royal Academy Frederick Leighton.

Albert Moore, *A Summer Night*, 1884–1890. Courtesy of National Museums Liverpool.

He was never voted into the Royal Academy, which some found a scandalous oversight; indeed, Moore never achieved great fame, during his lifetime or since his death.[65] Early in his career, Moore was influenced by the Pre-Raphaelites and Ruskin, particularly the latter's *The Elements of Drawing*, but as he trained in drawing, mathematics, and architectural drafting, Moore helped define the new aesthetic emphasis on formal qualities—color, composition, and rhythm—and the pursuit of beauty without concern for its moral implications.[66] Indeed, recently Elizabeth Prettejohn has described Moore's work as "represent[ing] the most rigorous example of 'art for art's sake' in its purest and simplest interpretation," since his paintings "offer a more limited presentation of the visible harmonies of the line and chromatic arrangement—a presentation that has a special integrity, at least, in its refusal to serve any other ends."[67] Contemporaries tended to explain Moore's nonnarrative approach to visual representation, also evident in the works of his friend Whistler, through analogies to music, as a nonnarrative and nondidactic form of art.[68]

A *Summer Night* is a meditation on beauty: in the bodies of the female figures, in the seascape beyond, in the garlands of flowers, and in the extraordinarily precise coloring and composition of the painting.[69] For contemporaries, the presence and treatment of the figures raised the question of whether Moore intended them as fully realized human beings in a naturalistic manner or as stylized representations of abstract beauty; as Prettejohn has described, Moore "concealed" the abstract organization of his pictures—particularly his use of a grid to develop color, pattern, and composition—"underneath figural compositions that *appear* fully representational."[70] As with the work of Burne-Jones, Moore's combination of careful draftsmanship and idealized and imaginary landscape perplexed contemporaries. In 1894, the *Magazine of Art* quibbled of *A Summer Night* that "the artist has in some measure departed from his usual decorative and flat treatment of the figures; and beautiful though the picture be, the more realistic painting of the flesh cannot be said to be altogether a gain."[71] Moore's student and biographer A. L. Baldry agreed that the figures of the painting were alive against their setting, and the *Art Journal* read the work as heralding a new symbolism and emotionality in Moore's work.[72] On the other hand, Baldry also criticized the painting for being too artificial: "If it has a fault, it is that in arrangement and grouping [*A Summer Night*] is somewhat too formal and deliberate."[73] Likewise, Rathbone forced the painting into his definition of "decorative," that is, "flat, and [making] no attempt to lead you to suppose you are looking at a real object. He explains: "The women and the overhanging garlands are pretty much all on the same plane, and the artist has taken care not to force the background, which is a lovely indication of a moonlight [*sic*] sea; so that the eye rests upon it without seeking to penetrate the distance, and see beyond the back of the wall."[74] Rathbone thus dismisses the effects of the background seascape and makes the picture completely abstract and flat, rather than offering any depth; what is odd about this discussion of Moore's painting is that the seascape is precisely where *A Summer Night* differs from Moore's other works, which mostly do feature flat walls or screens behind his figures. The seascape behind thus confounded people as much as the tension between the naturalism of the seminude figures and the formal qualities of the design, the rhythm of their placement and the play of horizontal and vertical elements. All of these combined to make the painting shimmer somewhere between received categories of "decorative" and "realistic" art, wall and window.

Late-twentieth-century critics have also brought out these disjunctions in the work. Edward Morris describes the work as "generally regarded as the last work by Moore in which formal qualities and the decorative use of colour are paramount; from 1890 onwards he was more concerned with emotion, with drama and with allegory and symbolism."[75] Robyn Asleson also brings up this tension, noting that the painting "constitutes Moore's most ambitious and seductive celebration of the female body. No longer indifferent elements in a decorative pattern, the figures here are rendered expressly as objects of desire."

Yet even while she notes the arrangement of the figures like "frames in a mildly erotic peepshow," she reads them as anonymous and distant: "Their blank stares, disjointed placement and chill, pearl-like pallor convey a dispassionate, almost inhuman quality, unwarmed by the sultry atmosphere. The delight is solely in looking, Moore seems to suggest; we are not encouraged to touch."[76] Asleson thus echoes the controversies in the original responses to the work.

With these contemporary and recent criticisms of the painting in mind, we come to the brief description in the Walker Art Gallery catalogue of 1896, repeated verbatim in 1901. Given the literary and didactic readings that Dyall tended to write, and given Moore's anomalous relation to the narrative tradition in British painting, the picture clearly posed something of a problem for the catalogue, as it did for other interpreters. The 1896 catalogue begins by explaining that the painting has no meaning: "A purely decorative picture. Composed to indicate beauty of line, delicate flesh tints, and harmonious colouring."[77] But the author then also engages with the debate over how to approach these women. Where Asleson sees "blank stares," the catalogue records a very different reaction: "A noticeable feature in the work is that the faces of the figures show refined animation, thus adding to the interest of the group—being a departure from the method adopted by many sculptors and painters of classical subjects, who leave the features of the figures in many cases almost expressionless."[78] Here we have a fascinating attempt to reconcile Moore's aestheticism with the museum's framing of art as primarily about the experience of its subject matter. The entry positions the work as "purely decorative" but then reengages with the figures in the work, reading them as evincing "refined animation" and looking for emotional cues about their inward experience rather than seeing them in terms of pure form. Indeed, the entry to some extent echoes (although not explicitly) the debate carried out in the art critical press about the picture, registering the tension in the work between the purely decorative elements and the (intentional?) treatment of the figures as real women in a real place. If Moore aimed at beauty only, the museum catalogue had a hard time not inscribing "truth" somewhere into the picture.

The Walker Art Gallery purchased Hunt's *The Triumph of the Innocents* in 1891 for the extraordinary price of £3,519 (although this was less than the 5,500 guineas Hunt asked for it).[79] The painting portrays the biblical story of the holy family on their flight into Egypt, but Hunt created a new image, surrounding them with the resurrected infants murdered by Herod. As Rathbone noted in his 1890 lecture, Hunt and Moore were radically different in their styles, subjects, and

William Holman Hunt, *The Triumph of the Innocents,* 1876–1887. Courtesy of National Museums Liverpool.

artistic goals. However, these paintings engaged with interestingly overlapping sets of problems in terms of materiality and transcendence, as Hunt brought his remarkable powers of verisimilitude to religious illustration.

Late Victorian critics routinely recognized Hunt as the last Pre-Raphaelite, the one founding member who had remained true to the Brotherhood's principles to the end. Chesneau argued that Hunt exemplified the fullest example of Ruskin's teachings:

Here [in Mr. Hunt's work] we see the most splendid—or most foolish—illustration of the principles so eloquently laid down by Mr. Ruskin. As I have already said, it is a system of microscopic analysis driven to the utmost extreme. . . . Its theory is governed by two ideas: a hatred of forms, appearances, and pretences, and a noble, passionate love of truth. [The Pre-Raphaelites] do not follow the Latin idea, and think that an artist's vocation is to please, but they look upon him as a man of higher ability than others, a prophet whose mission it is to set forth his own exalted revelations of nature's manifestations which have been granted him for this purpose.[80]

George Shepherd described Hunt's oeuvre in a similar vein, albeit in an approving tone: "In the works of Holman Hunt the principles of Pre-Raphaelitism find their faithful development, and his pictures mark a new era in religious art. We recognise in them an honest endeavour to depict what is most likely to have occurred, paying due regard to physiological and archæological facts, and reverently making them the suitable vehicles for the expression of pure and manly religious faith."[81] It was this attempt to portray "what is most likely to have occurred" that represents Ruskin's teachings. Critics described this as a "scientific" (Chesneau) or an "archaeological" (Sidney Colvin) approach in Hunt's paintings, which thus strove to present moral and religious truths. This tension between faith and realism is palpable in his works, which can seem too hard of line, ugly, and difficult to us now, with a strained solidity, an earnestness and intensity, and a didacticism that can appear so obvious as to be off-putting.[82] For contemporary observers, these qualities brought Hunt's work to the center of the Victorian debates over science and belief. As Frank Milner has written, "Hunt's interest in depicting scriptural episodes with geographical and historical accuracy was not merely scientific but designed to awaken the spectator's religious emotions and make him confront the problem of whether or not these biblical events had taken place."[83] Contemporary observers found this simultaneously wondrous and confounding; Hunt's work thus addressed both the essential problems of truth and beauty in art, and fact and faith in religion.[84]

Like the works of Burne-Jones and Moore, it was the way Hunt's paintings combined the categories of real and imaginary that particularly confused some viewers. F. G. Stephens rejected Hunt's use of naturalism to depict the supernatural, writing that *The Triumph of the Innocents* was a

strange mix of the real and the unreal. . . . An attempt to represent the unseen by substantial means and all too faithful methods which are self-contradictory and puzzling to the logical mind, is, so to say, heavily handicapped against itself. In this respect the picture fails completely, not, of course, through any defect of skill, studies, or power on the part of the artist, but simply because he has employed methods which could not succeed. He has endeavoured to represent spiritual essences with substantial appearances.[85]

Similarly, the critic of *Blackwood's Edinburgh Magazine* concluded that "the attempt to render the mind's intangible imaginings palpable to sense, is proved once more beyond the range of pictorial art," but at the same time acknowledged that "it cannot be said that the striving to pass from the material and the mundane to the realm of the spiritual and the divine fails entirely of reward. The mind somehow is led insensibly along the pathway of miracle. And wonder is awakened."[86] P. T. Forsyth also argued that the painting's problem lay in its exact depiction of the real and the spiritual, but he applauded the painter for raising the public's perceptions of both: "The difficulty in this picture is, that the painter is trying to raise us to do what, as an artist and seer, he habitually does—to see with two eyes at once, with the bodily eye and with the soul's; to gain one vision of two worlds; to read one system in two spheres. . . . Art has no higher function, when she can rise to it without over-strain, than this stereoscopic vision of the two-worlds."[87] Just as their Victorian counterparts, today's commentators have been undecided about whether or not the painting "works." For George Landow, "Hunt, in fact, succeeded magnificently in creating a new interpretation of the Flight into Egypt which combines the realistic and visionary, the physical and spiritual."[88] In contrast, Carol Jacobi writes that "the conception and execution of *The Triumph* represents a failed act of reparation of belief and self belief."[89] As the "last Pre-Raphaelite," Hunt attempted to create a believable spiritual experience through details and precision of both conception and execution.

For some observers, the painting made a clear theological statement by depicting the supernatural through meticulous realism. Charles Stubbs, dean of Ely Cathedral, gave a special lecture on the painting in Liverpool in 1891; he noted that the presence of the actual painting in the Church of St. Bridget, Bagot Street, "seemed to some timid members of our congregation a very dangerous, not to say idolatrous, experiment." Stubbs used Ruskinian terms to portray an artist's role as "striv[ing] to make clear to others what his keener sensibility and penetrative insight have made visible to him. He perceives, and then reveals the infinite."[90] He interpreted *The Triumph of the Innocents* as part of a broader move to a theology based on the "more comprehensive religion of the Incarnation" rather than "the Puritan religion of the Atonement."[91] For Stubbs, Hunt's combination of style and subject was a theological statement, one that made the spiritual visible precisely as part of a movement, a "modern Christian theology" that sought to enlarge the meaning of Christianity and its applicability to the secular world.[92]

For both Stubbs and Ruskin, the message of the picture was clear—the truth of the Resurrection and the afterlife, and, as Stubbs said, "the reality of that spiritual kingdom of God that underlies all our daily life"—and this was closely connected to its realistic style. For Stubbs, the "devout carefulness and pious accuracy [with which] the painting is painted" is part of this vision of a faith and a redemption that come through daily work. In the printed edition of the sermon, the printer made perhaps a "Freudian" typographical error: "The picture is the work of a lifetime consecrated to the workship [*sic*] of the beauty of Truth."[93] Similarly, for Ruskin, who called the painting "the greatest religious picture of our time," the conception of the painting's subject was its principal success: "in this English picture all the story of escape, as of the flight, is told in fulness of peace and yet of compassion."[94] Like Stubbs, Ruskin found the painting's story inseparable from Hunt's particular skills: "the painter's . . . better than magical power of giving effects of intense light, has aided the effort of his imagination, while the passion of his subject has developed in him a swift grace of invention which, for my own part, I never recognised in his design till now."[95] He concluded in terms not of the painting's technique, but of its spiritual message: that the picture's "happy vision of conquered death" would bring hope to the bereft.[96] Indeed, the painting participates in a particularly Victorian concern with the death of children, rescuing the innocents from death in vain and picturing them as the first to achieve immortal life through Christ.[97]

If part of Hunt's precision lay in his Protestant vision of the reality of redemption, however, part of it also came from an imperialist vision of the East, particularly Jerusalem (where he began the painting), as unchanging and therefore offering a direct vision of biblical landscapes, people, and even animals.[98] This was a common aspect of imperial ideology, and Hunt articulated it very clearly in a letter: "Since I first knew the East, the opportunities of illustrating old events by existing customs and traditions has enormously decreased, and in another fifty years the world will wonder why, when the mood of European manners had not destroyed primitive forms, painters had not fully worked to perpetuate these."[99] Indeed, in his 1891 sermon Stubbs quoted Hunt's own words on his purpose in going to Palestine—"to prove, so far as my painting can, that Christianity is a living faith"[100]—and read from a personal letter from Hunt that laid out in detail how he had decided on the particular location and how his researches in and around Bethlehem had found their way into the picture.[101]

The Walker Art Gallery catalogues of 1896 and 1901 used Hunt's own description of the picture, which focuses on the work's subject, precisely in terms of the balance between the real and the supernatural.[102] Hunt lists a series of specific decisions that he made about the painting based on his perception that his late 1870s journey revealed to him the actual conditions of the biblical flight into Egypt. He notes that the journey would have been in April, that the family is about thirty miles from Gaza, that there is a declining moon, that Mary is riding a particular breed of ass, and that "the foal follows its mother, as is seen to this day in the east."[103] He decided on Joseph's particular pose based on his observation of Syria: "Signal fires, still lit in Syria in time of trouble, are burning on the slope looking down from the tableland. St. Joseph is watching these fires, intent on discovering any signs that may present themselves of a movement of soldiery upon the road." Hunt has placed his figures in a specific temperature: "Having left the colder climate of the high country, then thickly populated and well-cultivated, the fugitives have descended into the rich and more balmy atmosphere of the plain."[104] In all of these comments, Hunt evinces his belief that nineteenth-century Palestine could reveal the scenes of biblical events, that realism would bring the event to life, and that these facts could be adequately known and then portrayed.

Hunt also included clues about his own interpretation of the experience and emotions of the participants, showing that he hoped his reconceived flight would lead viewers to a deeper spiritual awareness of sacrifice and redemption through a naturalistic portrayal of the supernatural.[105] For instance, he describes his painting's distinctions between the real water (ruffled only by Joseph's footsteps) and the "flood, upon which the spiritual children advance . . . mystically portrayed as ever rolling onward." This spiritual wave, unlike the real water, "dissipate[s]" into "airy globes, which image [*sic*] the Jewish belief in the millennium that is to follow the advent of the Messiah."[106] In Hunt's description, then, and thus in the Walker Art Gallery catalogues, the painting brings together an argument for the living reality of ancient biblical time in the Middle East with one for the close relationship between observable reality and a deeper spiritual reality of Christian redemption. For Hunt, it would seem, his style and his message were intimately linked, making a bridge between the seen and the unseen, bringing the supernatural into the same visual field as the natural. As we have seen, however, for some observers, Hunt's Pre-Raphaelite attention to a meticulous, detailed realism worked against his larger spiritual meaning.

In both of these examples from the Walker Art Gallery, we find again a catalogue compiler struggling to make sense of the contradictions inherent in works that aimed to bridge the material and the transcendent in complex and contradictory ways. While curator Dyall could easily and seemingly enthusiastically describe many works in terms of subject, story, and moral, paintings within the collection resisted easy interpretation and brought with them all of the tensions and debates of late Victorian culture.

MANCHESTER: INDUSTRY, SPIRITUALITY,
AND FIDELITY TO NATURE

The Manchester City Art Gallery issued multiple catalogues of its permanent collection beginning in 1888, for prices ranging from threepence (in 1888) to one shilling (in 1908). Curator William Stanfield compiled these until 1905, when reformer and art lecturer J. E. Phythian took over and significantly reworked the catalogues' organization and approach to the collection (see Chapter 5). Stanfield combined the catalogue styles of Birmingham and Liverpool, giving information about both the subjects of the pictures and the careers of the artists. Like Dyall in Liverpool, Stanfield understood works in terms of narrative, but he also occasionally wrote about color and composition. Like Wallis at Birmingham, Stanfield gave information about the artists; however, perhaps reflecting Manchester's emphasis on "big names," the catalogue tended to spend more space on the artists' achievements than on their early training. He often used the Ruskinian phrase "fidelity to nature" to assess artists' works, judging whether or not the work was a "faithful" or "literal transcript."[107] He did occasionally make some apparent allusions to the collection's urban location, commenting, for example, that Luke Fildes's *Venetians* represented "land where the sky is clear, and poverty is not always associated with toil," or bringing out the particular elements of the experience of nature that Mancunians might notice, as the "quiet pastoral beauty" of Henry Dawson's *On the Trent, Near Nottingham* or the sea salt and fresh air of James Clarke Hook's *Under the Sea.*[108] As in Birmingham and Liverpool, the Manchester catalogues rarely engaged explicitly with any then-current art critical debates, although Stanfield did use excerpts (not always identified or credited) from various art writers in compiling his entries. The museum's paintings, representing as they did a variety of approaches in contemporary art, carried all of the tensions regarding how to portray reality, the ultimate purpose of art, and the meaning of nature that we have seen in the other collections.

Already, we have seen how the museum catalogues read paintings in terms of "art as experience," even if contemporary art criticism brought up other aspects of a painter's work. This becomes particularly clear in comparing the Manchester City Art Gallery catalogue's description of Hook's *Under the Sea* with Chesneau's discussion of it. The art gallery purchased the painting in 1891 for the considerable sum of £945. Chesneau described Hook as a painter of "Pre-Raphaelite Landscape," writing that "Mr. Hook is remarkable for the superiority of his sea and coast pieces, in which he decidedly excels." Indeed, in Chesneau's assessment of *Under the Sea,* he treats the seascape while dismissing the figures:

A jutting cliff diminishes the height of the canvas, and throws into perspective the vast waste of green waters, studded with white sails. Three miners, clothed in sacking, and wearing huge hats, in one of which is fastened a still smoking candle-end, have just been brought up by a submarine tunnel from the bottom of the sea. They are seated in a narrow railway truck, which runs on a sharply descending line of rails leading into the tunnel. The men are received on their arrival by the wife and child of one of them; but these

James Clarke Hook, *Under the Sea,* 1864. © Manchester City Galleries.

figures are of feeble and heavy execution, and although they may heighten the interest of the picture, they certainly do not add to the merit of the work.[109]

In contrast, after naming the specific mine (the Bottallack Copper Mine) and describing the scene in similar terms, Stanfield enters into the narrative unfolding among the figures in great detail:

On the iron trolley, which has just emerged from the mine and been drawn up the steep iron tramway, are a group of tired and toil-stained bread-winners, who have earned a brief cessation from their morning's labour, to enjoy in comfort and pleasant surroundings the frugal meal provided by the comely housewife, in whose arms a chubby, rosy-cheeked boy is smiling a happy greeting to the bronzed and bearded father as he alights from the wagon. Seated on the ground is the eldest born, tired out with the twofold exertion of chasing bird and butterfly and carrying father's dinner. Like other similar subjects by this painter, the salt of the sea and the freshness of the air pervades this picture.[110]

For Stanfield, as we have seen for the other catalogue compilers, the aim of the picture is to bring people into the exotic landscape—the west coast of Cornwall—in order to provide an experience—"the salt of the sea and the freshness of the air"—in distinct contrast to life in gritty Manchester. But he also enters into a portrayal of, and relationships between, the protagonists, as of primary interest and didactic use to the public. Indeed, George Shepherd noted in 1881 that Hook was "one of our most popular artists, his sense of rich colour and feeling for breezy weather being in happy accordance with the public taste," his "Devon and Cornish coast scenes [being] instinct with healthy colour and freshness of feeling."[111] In Chesneau's account, then, we read art criticism judging the work as a representation and given merit on the quality of its choices and execution; in Stanfield, as with the other museum catalogues, we see an interest in art in terms of story and subject.

Yet even this idealizing and simple picture presents its own contradictions. Hook's painting depicts labor, in the form of miners coming up for lunch, in a picturesque way; the family group bringing them their meal is well fed and well dressed, their devotion to the paterfamilias shown in both their mission and their aspects. This is not any social realism or deep commentary on labor; Hook has chosen to show the miners at rest rather than in the midst of work. The title and the image connect these workers to fishermen, while the traditional lunch in the "field" connects them to agricultural laborers. However, the precipitous descent and the dark hole make for a strong contrast with the seascape, alluding, even if obliquely, to the danger and hard labor by which Manchester's metals were procured and its engines fed. Would viewers have concentrated on the picturesque seascape, the idealized family group, or the vertiginous drop into darkness? The painting offers multiple readings in this context.

As we have seen, the Manchester City Art Gallery bought Millais's painting *Autumn Leaves* in 1892 for £1,300, while turning down both a Titian and a Rembrandt portrait for similar prices as too nude and too expensive, respectively. During his lifetime and immediately afterward, critics recognized Millais as of unique stature; Walter Armstrong wrote in 1885 that "in our living school of English painters Sir John Everett Millais enjoys by far the widest fame," and Ruskin and Shepherd compared him favorably to the old masters.[112] But his biography also posed a problem, for, as Debra Mancoff has observed, his dramatic change in artistic style—from his Pre-Raphaelite days to president of the Royal Academy just before his death—became a kind of morality tale. As Jeremy Maas has pointed out, "an estimate of Millais's work will depend to some extent on one's attitude to Pre-Raphaelitism."[113] Recently, Paul Barlow has also noted the continuation in contemporary criticism of the "equation of stylistic differences with moral worth," in this case the moral values of twentieth-century sensibilities (for example, liberalism and feminism), and observed that most recent scholarship concentrates on Millais's Pre-Raphaelite phase but ignores his later work.[114] Was his change in style a fall from grace, a squandering of God-given talent and discipline, or was it the full flowering of artistic maturity after what Millais himself described as his "artistic puberty"?[115] Millais presented a kind of litmus test for late-nineteenth-century critics on the fraught issues of beauty and truth, grace and "stern fact," symbolism and realism, and on the traditional aims of painting and the strict and moralizing ideas of Ruskin and his followers.

Cosmo Monkhouse summarized the debate clearly in his review of Millais's career in 1899:

Whether this diversion of his genius is to be regretted or not is a question upon which opinions are divided. To some it seemed a desertion of higher spiritual and intellectual aims, to others the free assertion of his own personality, the recognition of his right function of an artist. It is also a question whether he could or should have endeavoured to blend more the old Millais with the new, and employed his perfectly matured skill in realizing the conception of his finer fancy.[116]

Some tried to understand Millais's Pre-Raphaelite period in terms of the personalities of the three principals, tending to see Millais as talented but weaker minded and less dogmatic or inspired than Rossetti or Hunt; Monkhouse concluded that Millais's career path was "probably inevitable, a normal growth affected only by some extraneous conditions at its outset, not unlike that of a tree on whose robust stem some rare variety has been grafted to flourish only for awhile."[117] Others took it as an opportunity to argue against the revolutionary ideas embodied in the works of the Pre-Raphaelites and articulated by Ruskin in their defense. Armstrong explained, "I do not wish the moral, if I may call it so, of our great painter's career to be lost," wanting to use Millais's artistic development to show that "the most gifted painter, if he determines to quit the beaten road and hark back to the beginnings of things, will inevitably be led, through by-paths that are often stony, to the great and easy track prepared by ages of experience."[118] He went on to attack Ruskin directly: "Mr. Ruskin, and with him the crowd which had been fascinated by an eloquence which had never been reached in English prose, had taken up an objective theory of Art, and with it the notion that all Art should be didactic, that its deliberate and immediate aim should be to become a sort of handmaid to religion—almost to dogmatic religion."[119] Harry Quilter, in contrast, mourned what might have been: "Had he [Millais] continued as he began, and he lent to the Pre-Raphaelite school the influence of his keen sense of beauty, both of emotion and nature, it is impossible to say what the English school might not have been at the present time." Quilter intimated that the temptations of fame and riches might have influenced Millais's choices: "I do not judge of any man's motives, and I will not raise the question here, but, from one cause or another, Millais forsook his old ways, gradually turned his attention to portrait and landscape painting, became fashionable." He declared that "the change seems to me almost pathetic—that a painter should begin his work with the noblest deeds of self-sacrifice and heroism he can find for subjects" and turn to subjects without meaning, "a 'brown ulster' and a beef-eater's uniform, for those are practically the chief subjects of the two last large figure paintings of this artist!" For Quilter, this served to tell a very different moral than for Armstrong: "realism is not noble in itself, if it have no higher object."[120] As with the works of the other artists we have considered, then, Millais's paintings brought with them debates about truth and beauty, the role of the artist, and the artistic and symbolic meaning of the real, material world.

While both the Walker Art Gallery and Birmingham Museum and Art Gallery each purchased one important work by Millais at the end of the century, in the years before World War I the Manchester City Art Gallery bought five.[121] These purchases reflected Manchester's tendency to concentrate on contemporary, popular, and narrative works; indeed, as both a former Pre-Raphaelite and president of the Royal Academy, Millais boasted a unique combination of outsider and Academic credentials. These paintings included transitional works of the 1850s, *Autumn Leaves* and *Wandering Thoughts*, and his later, more mainstream phase in *A Flood*, *Victory, Oh Lord!*, and *Stella*. Contemporary observers were nearly universal in their praise for *Autumn Leaves*, and twentieth-century art historians have found in it a rich source for bringing together the multiple forces at work in Victorian art. Recently, scholars have read it as both a tribute to Ruskinian and Pre-Raphaelite truth to nature and a move toward the symbolism and search for nonnarrative beauty that characterized the aesthetic movement.[122] Paul Barlow notes how "the themes of fragility and transience . . . [are] thoroughly integrated into the style, not just the imagery" and how in the painting Millais sought "to mark time caught in suspension, and space resolving itself into glowing planes which appear as if lit from behind and within"—evidence of "the continuing influence of Ruskin's theological readings of space and light."[123]

By the end of the century, when Manchester purchased it and Stanfield catalogued it, *Autumn Leaves* was an acknowledged masterpiece, but critics differed on how to read it, with some emphasizing its pure naturalism—a simple landscape with figures—and others finding in it a deeper spiritual statement about the cycles of life and death. F. G. Stephens wrote a perceptive piece in 1856 in which he brought out the scriptural resonances of the work, in response to which Millais actually wrote Stephens a letter to express his gratitude for such perspicacity.[124] Stephens noted, "You might take it either way—as a beautiful effect of nature, such as is rarely painted, and a triumph in that way; or you might accept it as we have attempted to describe."[125] Perhaps surprisingly, Ruskin took the former route, reading the work purely in terms of Millais's remarkable depiction of the effects of twilight and his use of color in his close observation of the natural landscape.[126] Likewise, as astute an observer as Ford Madox Brown had declared *Autumn Leaves* "the finest in painting and colour he [Millais] has yet done, but the subject somewhat without purpose and looking like portraits."[127] Marion Spielmann of the *Magazine of Art* noted in 1898:

Those who ought to have known better objected that the picture told them no story, as if poetry, colour, sentiment, and composition were not enough. It shows us the effect of the poetry of landscape upon this simply yet exquisitely placed group of rather plain children—the solemnity that is upon them as much as on the scene—even while the painter draws and models every leaf with perfect truth and beauty, and places it there, a subdued glory. If all this be not story enough, there is the contrast between these young

Sir John Everett Millais, *Autumn Leaves*, 1855–1856. © Manchester City Galleries.

children in the spring of life burning at sundown the sere and yellow leaf, while "the glow within the darkness that all can see adds a significance which all must feel."[128]

Monkhouse declared: "Its freshness at the moment consisted in its absolute absence of 'subject' in what would now be called a 'literary' sense. It was a painted 'song without words.'"[129] Victorian critics thus found a variety of ways to approach the painting, both at its original exhibition and in assessments of the artist in the 1890s; in the latter, most understood *Autumn Leaves* as a landmark for the artist because of its multiple levels of meaning and interpretation.

With these ideas in mind, it is interesting that Stanfield, in the Manchester City Art Gallery catalogue of 1895, chose to incorporate the two prominent approaches to the work, quoting both Stephens (identified only as "a well-known critic") and Ruskin. The initial description of the painting gives both a detailed account of the subject and a spiritual interpretation, quoting John 9:4: "The sun has sunk, the whole valley is full of a luminous mist, out of which, at intervals, stark, denuded poplars rise sharp against the sky, which has been golden, but now fades to a dun brassiness, while in the zenith is the black and purple fringe of night—'For the night cometh when no man can work.'"[130] The catalogue also provided a detailed biography, some of which was taken directly from Shepherd's piece of 1881.[131]

Millais's *Autumn Leaves* participated in the core debates about art in the late Victorian period in three important ways. First, the painting conveyed an idea and a mood without a clear narrative, expressive of the beauty of the scene. Millais's wife Effie recorded in her journals that "he wished to paint a picture full of beauty and without subject," and, after decades of the work of Whistler, Moore, Burne-Jones, and others of the aesthetic movement, critics such as Monkhouse and Spielmann could read it in this way.[132] Second, the painting brought up all of the problems of assessing the influence of the Pre-Raphaelite Brotherhood and John Ruskin at the end of the nineteenth century, notably in the morality tale of the artist's own career, raising the ever-present debate about beauty and truth. Third, the painting spoke to a deeper spiritual interpretation; William Holman Hunt remembered Millais speaking of "the odour of burning leaves" as "the incense offered by departing summer to the sky," and Millais and others conceived of the work as a metaphorical exploration of scriptural passages on death.[133] The delicacy of the painting and its rare combinations of the literal and the figurative, harmonious coloration and closely observed detail, portraiture and beauty, meant that it achieved the rare status of an almost universally acknowledged "masterpiece."[134] These very qualities bring out the constant tension in Victorian thought between the natural and the spiritual and the narrative and the symbolic. Other paintings attempting to transcend these categories often met with criticism, but the timing of this one (after the most heated attacks on the Pre-Raphaelites had calmed) and its particular qualities seem to have given it great critical weight. The Manchester catalogue provided the various angles of interpretation, although it did not enter into any of these debates or make them explicit. Nonetheless, despite attempts to explain or contain them, like Hook's work, *Autumn Leaves* brought remarkable expressions of tension and doubt into the museum.

CONCLUSION

In 1995, in "The Origins of the Early Picture Gallery Catalogue in Europe, and Its Manifestation in Victorian Britain," Giles Waterfield examined the history of how galleries and museums sought to classify and interpret their collections. His essay connects the development of catalogue policy to debates about national schools and public access and shows the development of an art historical consciousness and education policy, notably at the National Gallery in the 1840s and 1850s.[135] Particularly important was the 1847 *Descriptive and Historical Catalogue of the Pictures in the National Gallery*, compiled by Ralph Wornum and Charles Eastlake, which began to introduce German art historical concepts such as "the development of schools within a broad political and social framework, rather than discussing particular paintings in literary terms."[136] The National Gallery subsequently reissued this catalogue at a variety of prices, for example, an 1855 version with only the names of the artists and titles and dates of the pictures, for one penny, and an abridged fourpence edition in 1858.[137] Waterfield is dismissive of the "provincial" galleries' attempts to catalogue their works—"to the modern reader, these catalogues show a chaotic lack of taxonomical expertise." He notes the educational aims in the entries, both in terms of technical training and the provision of biographical information that might inspire others to pursue the fine arts, and in terms of "patriotic and social instruction." Ultimately he concludes that

most of these municipal catalogues were non-analytical, reflecting the lack of planning in the collections themselves, and used the opportunity of communicating with the masses to introduce an improving moral discourse. . . . It is a depressing reflection on the state of art museums and of art historical knowledge in nineteenth century Britain that a century which for a brief period in the 1850s had witnessed so active an interest in the codification of works of art had by its close produced so few publications of corresponding value.[138]

Waterfield's purpose was to assess these developments from the point of view of a curator (as director of the Dulwich Picture Gallery) and art historian, not as a cultural historian. But it is instructive to consider the significant difference in his approach to my own, in that this and the preceding chapters have tried to illuminate how these museums operated along a very different set of assumptions about art and its purpose than late-twentieth-century standards. The museums' approach to their collections in terms of subject matter reflected their larger policy in collecting and indeed in justifying their very existence, namely, the understanding of art as experience, rather than in terms of the development of art as a form of representation with its own internal history. The museum advocates who pushed for and eventually influenced these institutions saw the experience of art as an essential antidote to the moral and physical ugliness of nineteenth-century industrial society, and the industrial city in particular. They explored art in terms of its subject and story in order to deepen the viewer's experience of the painting as a window, not as a lesson in art history.

Victorian art was deeply concerned with these same issues of truth and beauty, fact and poetry, the real and the ideal. However, the paintings that the museums collected contained ambivalent and complex responses to the cultural contradictions and uncertainties of their time. They brought these tensions into the museums with them, whether about, for instance, landscape and industry (East), the ugliness of modern society (Burne-Jones), the purpose of art (Moore), the possibilities of representing spiritual realities (Hunt), the contrast of industrial and traditional labor and landscape (Hook), or the spiritual meaning of nature (Millais). The art critics of the time did not approach these works in the same terms as our own art historians would today, instead debating the artistic meaning of beauty and truth, the role of the modern artist, and relationships between the seen and the unseen. Although the catalogues did not always address these issues directly, the paintings did, challenging visitors with alternative visions of the modern world, of imaginary pasts, and of religious belief.

The success of the museums at the end of the nineteenth century led to new policies to accommodate the public, including extensions, restaurants and tea rooms, temporary loan exhibitions, free admittance, and social events. However, even as they increased public accessibility, a new generation of curators and reformers transformed their approach to art, increasingly interpreting their collections in terms of art history rather than art-as-experience. As modernism, and modernist art history, redefined art and its purpose, the Victorian collections, and the Victorian approach to them, would come to seem almost incomprehensible and, eventually, even despicable.

5 A NEW NARRATIVE
From Experience to Appreciation

Now, at the beginning of the twenty-first century, we are familiar with the idea of public art museums as institutions that hover between inclusion and exclusion. The art itself is often baffling to viewers even as it embraces and critiques popular culture. Private events for members and friends become cocktail parties for the well-to-do, while outreach programs try to bring in particular, targeted categories of people deemed unable or unwilling, for whatever reasons of cultural or economic disadvantage, to visit museums. Public and private funding combine to promote art as a public good, even if art museums become, at times, private spaces. Corporate-sponsored blockbuster exhibitions and museum stores full of image-saturated merchandise—from teacups to totebags—sell art as one form of entertainment among many, but one that offers a frisson of self-improvement and high-mindedness as well as an opportunity for "retail therapy."

This confusion about art museums as class bound or universal, private or public, entertaining or educational, is not new. The preceding chapters have explored the Victorian movement to bring art to the people through public institutions. We have seen how, despite the idealistic rhetoric of some museum advocates, the origins of Manchester's and Liverpool's city galleries lay in private or commercial endeavors, and how these legacies could complicate the goals of free public access to permanent collections. In the 1880s and 1890s, the resulting municipal art museums brought in and managed increasingly mass audiences—literally hundreds of thousands of visitors. To do so, they developed new strategies such as opening tea rooms, holding large social events that could include alcoholic refreshments and dancing, selling reproductions, putting on free temporary loan exhibitions, offering greater access to their free-entry permanent collections, and giving illustrated lectures. Some of these innovations served to attract a wider public but threatened to collapse the distinction between museums and other kinds of commercial entertainment; others demarcated ostensibly public institutions as arenas for middle-class sociability.[1] Reformers imagined museums in terms that framed them as domesticated public spaces, separate and protected from the corrosive nature of industrial capitalism like the theoretical "domestic sphere" itself. But, as with suburban homes, industrial capitalist dynamics had created the art, wealth, political power, class differences, and even the social dysfunction that made the museums possible and apparently necessary. Museums only *seem* to remove objects from the market forces that define other social relations.[2]

While these museums increasingly cultivated mass audiences, at the same time new ideas about art, and new kinds of art, challenged the underlying assumptions that had fueled the nineteenth-century museum movement. These ideas generally go under the name "aestheticism" or "modernism," part of the complex series of changes in European culture often associated with the avant-garde in the years leading up to World War I and entering the mainstream thereafter. Carl Schorske has characterized modernism as essentially "ahistorical," a definition that takes into account the broad sweep of art that challenged the nineteenth-century emphasis on historicism, narrative, didacticism, and realism.[3] New art movements, whether impressionism, symbolism, or postimpressionism, brought viewers' eyes to the surface; the artworks that came out of such movements insisted on being looked *at*, rather than *through*—they constantly called attention to their own representational quality. By the years just before the Great War, art had become something entirely different from what it had been during the great museum movement. In England, the key dates were the two postimpressionist exhibitions in 1910 and 1912.[4] Orchestrated by Clive Bell and Roger Fry, the collection of works by Cézanne, Gauguin, Van Gogh, Manet, Seurat, Matisse, and others helped to establish a new modernist canon and a new mode for judging art, namely, in terms of "self-expression." As Desmond MacCarthy wrote in the introduction to the 1910 exhibition catalogue, "it is the boast of those who believe in this school, that its methods enable the individuality of the artist to find completer self-expression in his work than is possible to those who have committed themselves to representing objects more literally."[5] Art and its role had radically shifted, from the Pre-Raphaelite observation of nature, to the impressionist study of light and color, to what MacCarthy called the postimpressionist revelation of "that emotional significance which lies in things, and is the most important subject matter of art."[6] These new ideas about art as personal expression would eventually also reach Birmingham, Liverpool, and Manchester.

These three museums remained remarkably consistent in their acquisition and educational policies for more than a generation after their establishment. However, as art and ideas about it changed, so too did the museums. Even as they brought in ever-larger numbers of visitors, the city museums gradually and haphazardly began to reconceptualize their essential purpose. Around the early 1900s, lecturers began to stress art appreciation and education over the empathetic experience of subject matter, and building extensions allowed new kinds of displays that reordered the collections into a meaningful chronological narrative. In the 1920s, more radical change came with the appointments of museum directors. They established and enacted policies that would create representative historical collections, quickly issued new catalogues of permanent collections, and, in the 1930s, oversaw further extensions and rehangings. All of these changes led city art museums to rethink their most basic functions: from presenting the experience of beauty, truth, and story, the museums began to provide educational, representative collections; to seek the expert advice of directors; to hang their displays in terms of historical development; and to explain art in terms of aesthetic appreciation and artists' motivations. Two of the movements toward larger audiences could, however, become modes of more subtle class divisions: the increasing emphasis on attracting large audiences through free access, entertainment, refreshments, and consumption, and the gradual transformation of the museums into institutions for art education rather than for the simple experience of beauty.

The work of French sociologist Pierre Bourdieu, particularly his 1984 book *Distinction: A Social Critique of the Judgement of Taste*, is useful here in considering multiple kinds of inclusion and exclusion. One of his key insights is that even as museums embraced the idea of universal access as a right of citizenship; in fact, they began a new kind of cultural exclusivity. Their public nature occludes the education—the "cultural capital"—needed to appreciate the complex and abstract forms of art and art history that, since the advent of modernism, no longer speak in terms of beauty, truth, and easily readable stories.[7] Art museums emerged as public institutions that offered class-based leisure—a form of consumption through which educated elites might enjoy themselves and display their cultural capital—*and* that made educational resources potentially open to all citizens. This contradiction remains at the heart of museum use, such *apparent* accessibility being, as Bourdieu points out, the basis for the invisibility of museums' modes of exclusion.

Yet, in contrast to Bourdieu, could this new educational vision also be liberating? Perhaps, by reconceiving their work as being primarily to educate the public about art rather than as being part of a grander scheme of redeeming industrial cities, public museums became one starting point for imagining a time—still far distant, even today—when a society's heritage would be a natural right for all, through universal education and access to a full spectrum of cultural institutions and events. The question of the purpose of and audience for museums is still a profound one, addressing all of the many layers of condescension and class involved in "elite" or "high" culture, because it always ultimately asks who enjoys what kind of art, and why.

SEEKING A MASS AUDIENCE: ATTENDANCE, REFRESHMENTS, AND EXHIBITIONS

While the city art museums in Birmingham, Liverpool, and Manchester gradually came to serve mass audiences, their development differed significantly in terms of how they became accessible and attempted to educate their visitors. This is partially due to the different institutional histories of the three museums. As we have seen in the instances of collecting and opening policies, these origins carried particular legacies. The museums in Manchester and Liverpool were committed to annual exhibitions of works for sale, which limited public access to their free-entry permanent collections and determined a particular regime of opening policies, ticket pricing, and social events. In contrast, the Birmingham Museum and Art Gallery was able to emphasize its permanent collection and to develop themed free-entry loan exhibitions from an early date.[8] However, gradually all three museums placed greater emphasis on their permanent collections and developed the use of temporary free loan exhibitions, expanding the museums' free-entry areas in relation to paid-entry exhibitions of works for sale. Indeed, despite their different origins and histories, the museums became enormously popular and well attended as their permanent collections and free admissions grew. Attendance figures show that, not surprisingly, the more free access the museums offered, the higher the numbers of visits: at the always-free Birmingham Museum and Art Gallery, visits hovered around one million per year in the late 1880s, while visits to the Walker in Liverpool gradually rose to just over six hundred thousand at their height in 1892 (when it opened on Sundays), and the Manchester City Art Gallery saw a gradual growth in visits as it opened the autumn exhibition for free and then began a series of free temporary exhibitions in the early 1900s, reaching nearly one million visits in 1912.[9]

As is clear from these numbers, the archives and art museum reports record significantly large attendances, particularly when put in relation to each city's population at the time. In 1891, for instance, Birmingham's census population was 478,113, and the recorded visits to the art museum were 738,875; Liverpool's census population was 517,980, and there were 503,991 visits; Manchester's official population was 505,368, and the art gallery committee reported 331,517 visits to the City Art Gallery.[10] These figures might be high and certainly record the number of visits rather than of visitors (meaning they do not account for multiple visits by the same people), but they are remarkable and were verified by turnstiles and detailed record keeping.[11] These were clearly important and popular institutions that served the outlying regions and attracted more than the elite middle class.

As art museums developed during the nineteenth century, they began to make clearer distinctions between "pictures to see" and "pictures to sell," even though some had emerged out of exhibitions of works for sale.[12] In Liverpool and Manchester, autumn exhibitions of works for sale lay at the heart of the museums' evolution and practice, although both autumn exhibitions gradually declined in importance and attendance numbers in relation to the permanent collections. However, at their height during the 1880s, the autumn exhibitions became a primary way of bringing in larger audiences, as the municipal art museums lowered ticket prices for evening openings, sought popular works of art, provided social events and refreshments, and opened the exhibitions free on Sundays. These strategies simultaneously increased attendance and differentiated between classes of visitors.

The autumn exhibitions at the municipal art museums in Liverpool and Manchester present especially interesting evidence in terms of the parallel popularization of art and differentiation of the audience by class, with increasing emphasis on free public access by the turn of the twentieth century. The museums in both Liverpool and Manchester offered season tickets (usually costing a considerable five or six shillings) that allowed multiple visits to the autumn exhibition at any time, as well as tickets at varying prices depending on time of day and week of the exhibition: at both the Manchester City Art Gallery and the Walker Art Gallery, a day ticket was one shilling, and an evening ticket was sixpence until the last weeks of the exhibition, when the price dropped to threepence. For example, between 1878 and 1895 at the Walker Art Gallery (which kept detailed records of admittance differentiated by price), on average 72,262 people paid to attend the autumn exhibition: again on average, approximately 40 percent of the tickets sold for one shilling, 22 percent for sixpence, and 34 percent for threepence, while only 4 percent of visitors bought season tickets.[13] Despite the polarization of the city, the relatively strong sale of six-penny tickets suggests a group for whom it was indeed important to take advantage of the evening tickets available earlier in the season, perhaps the small but vigorous population of respectable low-paid clerks and other white-collar workers for whom it would have been a key means of distinguishing themselves, Leonard Bast–like, from the working-class three-penny crowd.[14] By the late 1880s and early 1890s, both museums opened their autumn exhibitions for a few Sundays for free, and these attracted large numbers of visitors, generally several thousand in a few hours of the afternoon (and correspondingly reduced the number of three-penny visitors).[15] At the Walker, free Sundays during 1893–1895 increased attendance by an average of 26 percent over the previous three years, with about twenty thousand more visits per exhibition.[16]

In addition to differentiated ticket prices, the museums also divided visitors by class through private social events that offered refreshments, music, and decorations. In 1911 Birmingham Museum and Art Gallery curator Whitworth Wallis noted, "There are many individuals who are apt to regard the Art Gallery as a fad, just as there are many well-to-do and well-informed people in this city who never enter the Art Gallery except at a Mayoral Reception."[17] Liverpool curator Charles Dyall, assessing the progress of the Walker Art Gallery in 1888, observed:

Since the opening of the Gallery in 1877, the Committee have at various times held Soirees and Receptions, principally in connection with the Autumn Exhibitions, which have afforded great pleasure to a large number of the Citizens and others invited. The fine suite of rooms is admirably adapted for entertainments of this kind, and the building being in direct communication with the Picton Reading Room, the Library and the [Natural History] Museum, a very large number of guests can be entertained at one time, as many as four thousand being present at the Conversazione give by the Medical Association in 1883, to whom the use of the buildings was granted by the Committee.[18]

The impressive architecture, central locations, connecting rooms, and high-value decorations of the municipal art museums made them ideal spaces for socializing and showing off the cities' cultural aspirations and wealth, as well as the power and importance of local government.

Programs and invitations for several events preserved in the Liverpool Central Library Archives give us a glimpse into the kinds of entertainments offered. For example, a program from a conversazione held in connection with the autumn exhibition of 1880 included a "Promenade Concert by the Band" in the upper rooms of the gallery (containing the autumn exhibition), while the Liverpool Police Band played in the lower rooms (containing the permanent collection). The connecting Picton Reading Room offered an "Exhibition of Microscopes" and "Rare Illustrated Books, &c.," while in the lecture hall above, the members of the Artists' Club presented a "Vocal and Instrumental Concert" of works by Verdi, Schumann, and Rossini, among others. Refreshments were "served in the Lower Rooms of the Walker Art Gallery, Upper Vestibule, and the Hall of the Museum."[19] An 1891 program for an "At Home, Given by His Worship the Mayor and Mayoress" for the "Visit of the Institute of Mechanical Engineers to Liverpool" shows a similar pattern of music and refreshments, with the addition of dancing in the Grosvenor Room of the Walker Art Gallery.[20] Arrangements for refreshments and entertainment during special exhibitions could become especially elaborate; again in Liverpool we find the curator obtaining a special license to allow "public dancing, singing, music or other public entertainment of the like kind in connection with the 1907 Liverpool Naval Exhibition," as well as permission to sell beer and wine. The committee also made arrangements for the exhibition to be supplied with "four trees with electric fruit" by Philip Rathbone's son Edmund, apparently to be placed "in the Entrance to the Smoking Divan."[21] These were elaborate affairs for the great and the good of Liverpool, who, by hosting private events, continued the associations between the museums and domesticated public space, as elites used the various public municipal institutions and the valuables they contained in ways not unlike the rooms of a great country estate or city villa. The public spaces of the municipal art museums became private, by invitation only, during these events, and this separate status was highlighted by the special entertainments available: music, food, and dancing—not to mention trees with electric fruit.

As with the autumn exhibitions' differentiated ticket prices, closed social events meant that these public institutions still maintained or emphasized distinctions of cultural and economic class. Not only the elites, however, got to use the museums as social spaces; in Manchester, at least, other groups used the art museum as well. The Recreative Evening Classes Association, whose committee was elected from the Trades Council of Manchester and Salford and the Working Men's Clubs Association, took advantage of what the curator promised would be a "really good tea" and half-price tickets to the autumn exhibition at the Manchester City Art Gallery in 1889 for a "social gathering of the friends and teachers of the Association."[22]

However, by the turn of the twentieth century, the museums increasingly emphasized free public access, to both temporary exhibitions and their permanent collections. Rotating exhibits could draw new visitors in; for instance, in 1910 the Manchester City Art Gallery Committee urged "pursuing the policy of arranging Temporary Exhibitions in such a way as to stimulate and educate public interest in various forms of Art Work."[23] One way that municipal art museums could enhance their resources and collections watts by displaying works on loan, for which to a great extent they relied on the generosity of the great local collectors.[24] However, another important method of putting temporary exhibitions together was through loaning works to each other, and the minutes and reports of all three art museums are filled with requests from other municipal art museums for loans of specific works.[25] Until 1883, municipal museums had to get approval from the National Gallery Trustees each time they wished to borrow even works in storage such as the Turner watercolors. Through the 1880s and 1890s, Liverpool and Manchester especially vied to reach the Royal Academy first each year to request the loan of the latest Chantrey Bequest picture.[26]

Perhaps not surprisingly, Birmingham, with its early recognition of the importance of themed exhibitions and the display of historical works of art, led the effort to get municipal institutions greater access to the vast national collections in London. In 1877, Mayor George Baker (Companion of Ruskin's Guild of St. George, who would bring Ruskin to Birmingham later that year) and Liberal councilor Jesse Collings (chairman of the Free Libraries Committee, who had led the effort to open the art museum on Sundays) called a meeting of "Representatives of Municipal Corporations" to discuss how they could get London to share the artistic wealth.[27] In two meetings, first in July 1877 with the Prince of Wales and the Royal Commissioners of the Exhibition of 1851, then in November of that year with the National Gallery Trustees, the municipal deputations stated their case for greater access to London's public art collections.[28] As a result, Parliament ultimately passed the National Gallery Loan Act of 1883, an acknowledgment of cultural centers north of the Watford gap.[29] Such national support aided local art museums in attracting larger audiences through free temporary loan exhibitions and began to create a national system of cultural institutions out of the ad hoc development of regional museums.

It is striking that from as early as 1885, the Birmingham Museum and Art Gallery put together themed exhibitions around artists or subjects (for example, "Edward Burne-Jones and George Frederick Watts," "David Cox," "Old Masters,"

"Modern French," "The Pre-Raphaelite Brotherhood," "Marine and Animal Painters") and that these were free exhibitions of loans, not of works for sale. In 1891, the Birmingham Museum and School of Art Committee recorded an interesting contemporary commentary from a report presented to the Ministère de l'Instruction et des Beaux-Arts by M. Marius Vachon. He wrote: "To-day the Birmingham Museum is the finest museum which exists in the provinces, and the one which throughout the whole of England, the British Museum excepted, receives the greatest number of visitors. These figures (the attendances) have greatly astonished me."[30] Vachon attributed these high attendance figures to the nature of the city as well as to specific museum policies.[31] He connected the "general municipal pride," the "old traditions of Liberalism," and the power and proaction of the "governing bodies" with the advanced state of "public instruction" in the city. He observed that "thanks to the system of loans and gifts, the museum is constantly filled with new collections, so that the interest in it is always being renewed." He commented on the "remarkable" organization of the museum and praised the numerous cheap catalogues and extensive labeling of exhibits.[32] The Birmingham Museum and Art Gallery thus impressed at least one outside (and French, no less) observer as to its large audience and active educational policies.

Gradually, all three art museums began to attract larger audiences by emphasizing free entrance to their permanent collections and loan exhibitions, rather than by using the differentiated ticket pricing and limited access of paid-entry exhibitions of works for sale. A national system of loans from the capital meant new acknowledgment of the success and importance of regional institutions. Private events still shut off the galleries, but sometimes incentives or benefits for the few became amenities for the many, as refreshments moved from being served only at private social events to being available at paid-entry exhibitions, and finally to being part of public museum spaces. Eventually, museum committees began bringing refreshments daily into the art museums for everyone. These kinds of activities complicated the status of the art museums as primarily for contemplation, social reform, or moral education and made them both more accessible and more clearly in a continuum with other, commercial forms of leisure. However, even as they sought and acquired mass audiences with new modes of consumption and free admittance, museums also slowly began to place new emphasis on art education and appreciation, rather than on the experience of subject, beauty, and story. These haphazard changes paralleled and reflected the increasing professionalization and specialization of the museum world, as well as changes in art and ideas about its social role.

FROM SUBJECT, STORY, AND MORALITY TO ART APPRECIATION: CATALOGUES AND LECTURES

At the founding of these three municipal art museums and for several decades thereafter, in their reports, catalogues, lectures, pamphlets, and other means— their acquisition policies, their architecture, the organization of their collections, their opening hours—the museums' governing committees articulated a commitment to the idea of art as the experience of beauty, truth, and story, which were understood as essential antidotes to industrial society. However, little by little, the language of art appreciation for its own sake entered the museums' publications and organization. In contrast to late-nineteenth-century catalogues that encouraged visitors to "read" paintings for their subjects and stories, in the decade after World War I the museums put out new permanent catalogues that instructed viewers to consider the color, light, composition, and painting techniques of the paintings on display. Using the examples from Chapter 4, we can follow the changes in subsequent catalogues and trace the remarkable shift toward a new type of art interpretation. This new approach emphasized the appreciation of artworks' modes of representation and understood art as education, rather than encouraging an empathetic appreciation of the paintings' subjects that positioned art as experience.

As we have seen, the descriptions in the late-nineteenth-century catalogues of all three city art museums emphasized story, subject, and moral readings, even in comparison to contemporaneous art critical debates over the relative merits of beauty and truth in painting. In general, the new, early-twentieth-century catalogues increasingly interpreted the art in terms of a new overarching narrative, that of art history, rather than the individual narratives presented by each painting. To this end, catalogues gave more standardized information about each work: dimensions, medium, dates of creation and acquisition, exhibition history; and about each artist; training, background, approach, and movement or school. Of course, as the collections were still overwhelmingly made up of British art from the nineteenth century to the present, and as the Victorian era itself was coming into historical focus, the collections took on a historical character in some sense by the simple passage of time. However, as can be seen in the catalogues, lectures, extensions, and appointment of dedicated directors, the art museums were becoming progressively more autonomous from city government, operated as sites of artistic appreciation and the education of a democratic citizenry. At the same time, as with the formation of other disciplines and professions at the end of the nineteenth century, the study of art and its history was becoming increasingly specialized. "Art history" as an academic discipline would not become truly established in Britain until the founding of London's Courtauld Institute, opened in 1932.[33] However, already the Slade Professorship of Fine Art at Oxford (begun in 1870 with John Ruskin) had placed art and its study within the academic establishment, and later generations of art critics had begun to approach their subject in a broader context. By the early twentieth century, new critics such as D. S. MacColl, Clive Bell, and Roger Fry would become important national voices for understanding art without Ruskin's moralizing interpretive approach. As this sea change in criticism and aesthetics swept through the British art world, the Victorian nature of the regional collections remained, and the museums' catalogues gently began to place them in a more historical perspective.

In Birmingham, curator Wallis formulated unusually clear and directed policies in acquisition and interpretation, partially through his control of the Art Gallery Purchase Committee and partially through the rare convergence of his own ideas and those of the wider municipal reform of which the art museum formed an important part. Wallis worked as curator in Birmingham for a remarkable forty-two years, and his longevity no doubt contributed to the continuity of many of the Birmingham Museum and Art Gallery's policies. However, even here, the catalogues gradually changed, cutting out many descriptions altogether and rewriting what had been long, empathetic accounts, as of Edward Burne-Jones's *The Star of Bethlehem*. By 1912 the entry for Alfred East's *Hayle, from Lelant* only notes that East was a "living artist" and details the medium, dimensions, exhibition history, and purchase information of the work.[34] Parts of the 1923 description of *The Star of Bethlehem* remain nearly word for word as they appeared in 1899, but the entry omits the long, imaginative discussion of the scene. Instead, the catalogue contains a history of its commission and design, a paragraph on the history of the subject (taken from the 1899 version), and some quotations from Georgiana Burne-Jones's *Memorials of Edward Burne-Jones* about the making and import of the work.[35] Together with the detailed information provided on the painting (medium, dimensions, exhibition, and reproduction history), and without the literary narrative, the entry thus emphasizes the work as part of the

artist's oeuvre, and the history of portrayals of the subject, rather than presenting it as a new experience of the nativity.

In Liverpool, the Walker Art Gallery did not publish a new catalogue to the
permanent collection from 1901 until 1927, by which time the curatorship had
changed several times.[36] Not surprisingly, the 1927 catalogue took out Dyall's
imaginative literary and moralizing interpretations, for instance, of Arthur
Stocks's *Motherless* and Stanhope Forbes's *A Street in Brittany*, replacing these
with only standardized information about the medium and dimensions of each
work.[37] Albert Moore's *A Summer Night* received an illustration but no description. The 1927 entry for William Holman Hunt's *Triumph of the Innocents* used
the same description (Hunt's own), but introduced this discussion of the artist's
treatment: "The subject of the [flight into Egypt] is here treated with remarkable originality, and made fresh and significant; the artist having combined with
his vivid conception of the scene an infinitude of symbolical suggestion. The
picture and its meanings are well explained in Mr. Holman Hunt's description
written at the time it was painted."[38] In this way the catalogue comments on
both the picture and the description, underlining the realistic treatment and use
of symbolism and highlighting the fact that what makes the piece interesting is
its original interpretation of a familiar biblical subject. The work is thereby put
into a larger history of representation.

In Manchester, the catalogues' first change from describing subjects to analyzing artists and their works in terms of art historical importance, style, and influences came about when art enthusiast J. E. Phythian replaced curator William
Stanfield (who had no specialized art training) as compiler of the catalogue.[39]
Still an ardent Ruskinian, however, Phythian continued to give his own interpretations of works in what would seem today a rather idiosyncratic manner
(he noted of Herkomer's *Hard Times*, "Here is art on the way to make Socialists
of us!"[40]). In many ways Phythian's catalogue is a transition from the art-as-
experience model to the new art education model that would later come into
vogue—understandable, given his background. Thus for James Clarke Hook's
Under the Sea and John Everett Millais's *Autumn Leaves*, Phythian rewrote Stanfield's entries to assess the two men's influence as artists and their treatments of
their subjects. For Hook's picture, he brings up the issue of labor, compares it
with other works in the collection, and emphasizes how the picture approaches
its subject, but—unlike Ernest Chesneau (see Chapter 4)—he still interprets
the meaning of the figures rather than examining their execution. His discus-

sion of Millais's *Autumn Leaves* uses a more clearly art historical or art critical framework, grouping the museum's seven works by Millais together, discussing his evolution as an artist, and reiterating much of the art critical debate over the fifteen years since the artist's death.[41]

The more significant transition came to the Manchester City Art Gallery with the 1914 appointment of the art museum's director, Lawrence Haward, from London, who began to reinterpret the collection in significant ways. In a 1925 book of reproductions from the collection, for example, Haward introduced the collection in terms of its representativeness: "old masters and foreign artists, though not unrepresented, are less in evidence than the modern British School, the reason being that as examples of all schools of painting are undesirable, even when obtainable, the collection has aimed primarily at illustrating the chief phases of British art, more especially in the last hundred years."[42] What is particularly interesting about this is that Haward turns the nature of the art gallery's Victorian collecting—based on very different principles, as we saw in Chapter 3—and the constraints on its purchasing, closely connected to its autumn exhibitions, into deliberate policy. He does, however, notice the particular emphasis in purchases: "But the pictures of this period [the early and middle part of the Victorian era] for which the Gallery is best known are a group of works by the four men who were most intimately connected with the Pre-Raphaelite Brotherhood."[43] Noting the works of Rossetti, Hunt, Millais, and Brown, Haward does not try to explain this specialization. He does not make any grand claims for the overall purpose or urban role of the art gallery, noting only that it is part of a larger city complex of cultural institutions.[44] This absence of wider institutional claims is itself part of the more general change from social reform to education.

As we have seen, one method of simultaneously educating and entertaining audiences in order to popularize the art museums was through the provision of illustrated lectures. As with the changing catalogue entries, by the early years of the twentieth century lecturers increasingly emphasized aesthetic and art historical education over the experience of the subject or moral of pictures. For example, in contrast to Liverpool councilor and art advocate Rathbone's 1890 lecture on impressionism, which used the Ruskinian idea of truth to nature,[45] two lectures given at the Walker Art Gallery by the Reverend T. W. M. Lund in 1909 and 1912 present visual art in new terms, emphasizing mode of representation over subject matter. In the first of these, "A Picture Gallery Through a Layman's Eyes," Lund explicitly argued for a more lenient view of new styles of art and for artists to explain themselves to the public, because, as he saw it, most did not rise above children in a narrative view of art:

The child's next step is to put a story into his picture. A man rides to market on the horse, the soldier fights the foe, the dog hunts a hare. The child, whether in years or in education, rarely passes the point of a subject picture. That is why Frith's "Derby Day" and "Railway Station," *et hoc genus omne* [and all those like it], arrested the attention of thousands. . . . That is why the picture, before which crowds stand in a Gallery, is sure to be one, which is a tale of life, an episode of experience, in which we can see ourselves or our friends, or the types that we know, in some corner or other.[46]

However, Lund recognized that artists had come to understand art in a new way, in terms of "Idealism," in which the "story-telling is forgotten" and "the drawing, the grouping, the colour, the values, the atmosphere, the types, the brush-work, these become everything. The human romance, or tragedy, or idyll, becomes 'A Study in Mauve' or 'A Dream in Yellow' or 'Satin Slippers.'" Lund bemoaned the fact that after Idealism came Conventionalism, which "means soulless Art, or rather the bare bones of Art, out of which all, that made it Art, has gone." He took pains to state that while he had come to "make the subject secondary," it was still a key part of painting and was "not a negligible quantity for anyone."[47] In his 1912 lecture at the Walker, "Some Uses of an Art Gallery," he reiterated that the subject was secondary to mode of representation.[48] Echoing MacCarthy's 1910 postimpressionism catalogue, in this lecture Lund told the audience that they should understand works in terms of the artist's individuality and hinted that the technological innovations of the nineteenth century in photography had influenced this new understanding of art:

In Art, the thing to be represented must pass through the medium of the artist's soul, and it comes out, as he sees it. *We are seeing him even more than we are seeing Nature.* If the correctness of outline were Art, Photography would do as well, or even if accuracy of colour were enough, since Colour Photographs can give exactness of colour better than the brush. We want the genius of the artist, his individuality, to give us just the quality, which compensates for what he cannot copy from Nature.[49]

Again, Lund said, one of the chief pleasures of viewing art was "deciphering what the artist is trying to tell us about himself. He wants to convey to us his own impression about the thing he is painting." The visitor should be asking, "'What is this man wanting to tell me? . . . He may want to tell you about Colour, or Light, or Values, or the soul shining in a face, or a bit of history,—but he will tell it in his own way, and will have his interpretation of it, and that is what you and I have to find out."[50] By 1912, that is, visitors were not being taught to judge works on their truth to nature, but in a new interpretive mode that saw the artist's impression and experience as central to the art itself. Although Lund named Ruskin, and not Roger Fry, his theory brought the radical reinterpretation of art in terms of self-expression to Liverpool.

In Manchester, in 1903, J. E. Phythian began the sort of educational outreach that T. C. Horsfall had advocated twenty years before, instituting midday talks and "Half Hours at the Manchester City Art Gallery" to help visitors appreciate and comprehend the collections. However, he emphasized a new understanding of art: "A picture should be a beautiful thing independently of what it represents. The lines, shapes and colours in a picture should be beautifully arranged, as words are arranged in a poem." Using the examples of Edward Lear's nonsense poetry, and pointing out that "music, for the most part, does not imitate anything" (one is reminded of Whistler's "Nocturnes" or the art critical discussion of Albert Moore's works), Phythian emphasized the decorative aim of painting and visual representation, arguing that art's fundamental purpose was to be beautiful. He then encouraged his audience to look at the paintings in the art gallery (pointing out specific examples) in terms of line, composition, and color and to notice the effect these made upon them:

Having once obtained the idea of this kind of beauty in works of art, one of the best ways, indeed the best way, of increasing our knowledge and our pleasure is to observe carefully for ourselves the differences between one work and another, and between the impressions they make upon us. One picture we may call pretty; another, beautiful; another, grand or solemn. Why by what varying use of line, light and shade, and colour are these different impressions made upon us, and different emotions raised within us? Our permanent collection now gives plenty of scope for such interesting study.[51]

Thus, in these public lectures, Phythian emphasized art as providing a particular kind of individual aesthetic experience, rather than as serving larger social aims. Like Lund in Liverpool, Phythian highlighted the pleasure that a deeper understanding could give to art museum visitors.

In its public lectures and collecting decisions, in contrast to the museums in Liverpool and Manchester, the Birmingham Museum and Art Gallery somewhat defensively maintained the connections between art, morality, craft, production, and the development of the municipality well into the early twentieth century. Indeed, despite changes in the approach in the catalogues and the hanging of the collection, lectures and pamphlets published in association with the Birmingham Museum and Art Gallery took pains to reject the new aesthetic ideas and the influence of impressionism. For instance, in 1897 Birmingham exhibited J. T. Middlemore's copy of Hunt's *Triumph of the Innocents* (later given to the gallery). In a pamphlet that Hunt put together for the occasion, he included a comment by Arts and Crafts designer Walter Crane: "I am old-fashioned enough to think it of some consequence what a picture says, and what is its spirit and aim, as well as what it represents and how it represents it."[52] Note the use of "old-fashioned"—and the new assumption that "how it represents it" was of primary interest. Likewise, in a 1908 lecture William Rothenstein consistently made strong links between truth to nature, elevated themes for art, the essential morality of art, fine artisanry, and the health of a nation and its arts, in explicit defiance of new trends in art and art criticism. He reiterated the principles of art, craft, a healthy society, beauty, and morality, reassuring art students that "if you will search sufficiently deeply, in solitude and with unflinching faith in the belief that every reality is essentially a part of the great idea of God, I think you will in time discover the secret it carries within," urging them to remember that "an ideal, then, may only be wrested in single combat with nature . . . working with that sense of reverence which is common, I think, to all true craftsmen."[53] Indeed, echoing ideas that might have been said by the Reverend George Dawson fifty years before, Rothenstein emphasized that "the greatest value of art lies in its power of stimulating men in the direction of hope and courage," so that "no thoughtful men, who sit in place of authority, can neglect the serious claim of an art school and an art gallery, and sound craftsmen of every kind have upon the life of the city for whose welfare they are acting."[54]

Thus, in Manchester and Liverpool especially, catalogues, lectures, and pamphlets began to emphasize surface—the mode of visual expression—over subject and to incorporate new ideas about artists and their relationship to nature and to art history. The Birmingham Museum and Art Gallery showed enormous continuity, largely due to the longevity of its energetic curator Wallis, who died still in his post in 1927.[55] Even in Birmingham, however, the catalogues became more and more professionalized, and diehards such as Rothenstein and Crane had to defend their increasingly "old-fashioned" ideas about art.

A NEW DIRECTION: EXTENSIONS AND DIRECTORS

Thus we see two major developments in city art museums at the turn of the twentieth century: the increasing emphasis on free access through temporary loan exhibitions and permanent collections, and the new educational approach to art that understood it in terms of historical development, personal expression, and formal internal analysis rather than larger social meaning or empathetic narrative. Both of these trends combined in gallery expansion and administrative centralization. By the end of the nineteenth century, all three museums needed significant extension to show their collections. This did not simply mean extra wall space, however; it meant not having to move the permanent collection for temporary exhibitions, and it meant being able to hang the collection in the new, single-line "aesthetic" style popularized the generation before at the Grosvenor Gallery (opened in 1877), if possible in some kind of order (chronological or otherwise). At the same time, by the second decade of the twentieth century, facing a new raison d'être and increasing criticism of the Victorian collections and organization, the long-standing debate over how to best manage city art collections—by city committee or specialist expert—received new interest, and the museums appointed directors who could run the institutions with greater autonomy than could city council committees. Taken together, these changes moved the art museums away from the reforming aims of their original advocates—as antidotes to industrial society—and toward a new vision of culture as education, an essential right of citizenship as part of the national patrimony.

Whether paid or free, temporary exhibitions conflicted with the permanent collections. As attendance figures and the permanent collections grew, paid exhibitions of works for sale especially became difficult for the museums to justify because they necessitated the removal of the free-entry permanent collections. All three galleries faced such conflict and overcrowding and therefore recognized the need for extensions as their holdings increased.[56] For example, during the early years of the Manchester City Art Gallery, the autumn exhibition was an important focus, but as the permanent collection grew in size and importance, continual free access to the public collections became a priority. As soon as it opened, W. E. A. Axon noted that "any one who visited the Liverpool Art Gallery must be struck by the crowds that thronged it," while "so far as the working classes were concerned, the present arrangements practically debarred them from seeing the pictures" in Manchester, because of the inaccessibility of the free-entry permanent collection.[57] Indeed, from 1884 to 1889, during the autumn and spring exhibitions, the permanent and any loan collections were removed into what Manchester artists described in a letter to the gallery as the "bare[,] gloomy, and repellent" lower floors.[58] This constant moving also meant that during the hanging of the temporary exhibitions, the collections were inaccessible to the public.[59] The installation of electric lighting improved matters somewhat, at least in the evenings when the lights were turned on.[60] However, as the artists' letter pointed out, without artificial light the ground-floor galleries remained too dark to be useful during the day—their inadequate natural light apparently being caused by having only a limited number of sash windows and by the city's smoke-filled skies.[61]

The Birmingham Museum and Art Gallery and the Manchester City Art Gallery at first solved these difficulties through internal structural renovations in 1892 and 1893, respectively, with both museums creating continuous galleries that provided a circuit of movement through the building and exhibits.[62] However, these modifications were not sufficient, and under the pressure of growing attendance and the increasing importance and size of the permanent collections, all three municipal art museums sought local government funding for major extensions: Liverpool in 1884 and 1912; Birmingham in 1898, 1904, and 1911; and Manchester in 1892, 1899, and 1912 (the last plan, however, was stymied by the war[63]). In Liverpool and Birmingham, the city councils approved funding (1884 and 1904, respectively), but the costs were in fact defrayed by private gifts and bequests (1884 and 1905). The Manchester City Art Gallery did not receive additional space until 1933, when it took over the old Athenaeum building next door.

The three municipal art museums and their respective city councils dealt with the problem of space in ways consonant with the development of the original museums. For the extension of the Walker Art Gallery, the Liverpool City Council approved the expenditure of £6,000 in 1881 and of £5,500 in 1883, but in 1884 the original donor, Andrew Barclay Walker, defrayed the full cost with a gift of £11,720.[64] In 1899, the Birmingham City Council bought land behind the Council House, and then five years later—as in the decision to build the original museum and art gallery above the Gas Department—agreed to incorporate new art galleries into a plan to extend the offices of the Council House.[65] Then in 1905, after work on this had already begun, *Birmingham Daily Post* proprietor John Feeney died and left a bequest of £50,000 for the erection of a new art gal-

No.	I.	GALLERY :	WATER COLOURS......	NOS.	1–237
,,	II.	,,	OIL PAINTINGS	NOS.	238–294
,,	III.	,,	OIL PAINTINGS	NOS.	295–359
,,	IV.	,,	OIL PAINTINGS	NOS.	360–450
,,	V.	,,	OIL PAINTINGS	NOS.	451–576
,,	VI.	,,	OIL PAINTINGS	NOS.	577–614
,,	VII.	,,	OIL PAINTINGS	NOS.	615–702
,,	VIII.	,,	PERMANENT PICTURES NOS.		
,,	IX.	,,	PERMANENT PICTURES NOS.		
HALL :		PERMANENT PICTURES.............. NOS.			

Plan of Exhibition Galleries,

Plan of the Manchester City Art Gallery showing continuous galleries, 1892, from Corporation of Manchester Art Gallery, Royal Institution, Autumn Exhibition Catalogue (Manchester, 1892), front matter. Manchester Local Studies 759.2 M23. Courtesy of the Greater Manchester County Record Office (with Manchester Archives).

lery (twenty years before, Feeney had given the Birmingham Museum and Art Gallery a large collection of Japanese and Chinese enamels). Because the Council House/art gallery extension project was already well under way, the council and the Feeney trustees agreed to use the bequest to defray the costs for the new galleries.[66] The ten new galleries thus acquired opened in 1912, and a further six new galleries opened in 1914. The municipal art museums in Liverpool and Birmingham received extensions as they had originally been built, as a combination of municipal effort and private capital.

Like the Birmingham City Council, in 1899 the Manchester City Council approved the expenditure of £25,000 to purchase the land behind the original building for an extension to the gallery. However, this extension did not actually open until the *twenty-first* century, in 2002.[67] Part of this delay came from a movement to relocate the City Art Gallery, along with the Central Reference Library, to the site of the old Royal Infirmary in Piccadilly Gardens, a scheme that led to several grandiose plans—and the reelection campaign for city council by Art Gallery Committee Chairman Walter Butterworth, who lost—but eventually came to nothing.[68] Because the Manchester City Art Gallery did not receive additional space after 1892, the museum's autumn exhibitions of work for sale took place on a much-reduced scale, with free entry to boost attendance after 1902, and the exhibitions ended altogether after 1908.

These extensions and changes meant that in the early decades of the twentieth century, the municipal art museums could begin to rearrange their collections into chronological and grouped displays. Instead of fitting paintings into every available space on the wall, in typical Victorian fashion, they could hang works in a single line, with greater space between paintings. Thus the organization and architecture of the museums began to play that central role of shaping circulation and experience which had been a feature of some earlier museums (notably the Louvre during the French Revolution) and became a recognized part of twentieth-century museum architecture and design.[69] For example, in

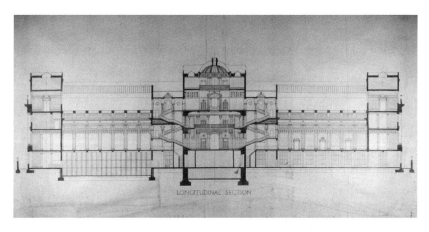

Elevation of the proposed gallery for the site of the old Royal Infirmary, early twentieth century. Courtesy Greater Manchester County Record Office (with Manchester Archives), Archives GB.24. MISC/921.2.

1885, the Library, Museum, and Arts Committee in Liverpool reported that "the recent extension of the Gallery having obviated the necessity of the disturbance of the Collection for the Autumn Exhibition, the Curator has been able to make a more definite and systematic arrangement of the works of Art." However, the committee did not mention chronology or schools of art, only that "the importance of the Collection, both numerically and artistically, has thus been brought into fuller prominence."[70] Indeed, a systematic, chronological hang would not emerge until the extension and reorganization in the 1930s, when the city council finally voted to approve an annual acquisitions fund (up to that point acquisitions had been funded solely through receipts from the autumn exhibitions) and a remodel that doubled the gallery's exhibition space.[71] In 1898, the Manchester City Art Gallery Committee reported that it had "rearranged the pictures forming the Permanent Collection in Galleries 1 to 5, with regard, for the first time, to chronological order, so far as such arrangement was compatible with the satisfactory exhibition of the individual pictures."[72] In the 1913 one-penny guide to the Feeney Galleries, the extension of the Birmingham Museum and Art Gallery, curator Wallis noted that visitors

will find that, for the first time in the history of the Art Gallery, the pictures forming the permanent collection of paintings can be seen to the best possible advantage, for the lighting of the new rooms is in remarkable contrast to the frequent gloom of the old ones. The greatly increased wall space, too, has permitted a certain amount of classification and arrangement impossible until now, which, it is to hoped, will be of advantage to students of English painting.[73]

Thus, the growth of the permanent collections, and of attendance figures, encouraged the development of new methods of educational work, as each municipal art museum gradually changed from a series of small galleries filled with fairly random displays of contemporary art into continuous galleries showing more representative collections, which attempted to use organization and display to teach the history of English art. At the same time, new ideas about the proper display of art gradually came into the museums; for example, the Birmingham Museum and Art Gallery's Pre-Raphaelite room in the new Feeney Galleries showed a unity of design, the single-line hang, and space between paintings reminiscent of aesthetic interiors.[74]

By the early years of the twentieth century, then, the Victorian museums were increasingly conceptually and even physically transforming into institutions that emphasized an aesthetic and intellectual purpose, rather than an experiential and empathetic one. As catalogues, lectures, extensions, and rehangings changed the museums, many began to call for hiring directors who would be able to run them more autonomously and with a view to following deliberate and long-term acquisition policies. This was not actually new; in fact, Ruskin back in 1880 had advised the town of Leicester that only a single person could create a collection effectively.[75] Throughout the 1890s, these calls became more frequent, but they were generally not enacted until during or after the Great War.

Already in Manchester in 1889, William Arnold connected the extension, collecting, display, and directorial policies into one plan for reform: he suggested hiring "a highly competent director," creating a new site and design for the museum, and instituting a policy of collecting representative historical art (including casts of ancient sculpture), prints, and design (primarily textiles), rather than solely acquiring paintings by contemporary artists.[76] In Birmingham in 1893, Joseph Chamberlain, member of Parliament, former mayor, early advocate for the Birmingham Museum and Art Gallery, and a trustee of the Public Picture Gallery Fund, wrote to Thomas Martineau (a trustee of the Public Picture Gallery Fund since 1881), "My view is that it is a mistake to use the funds to buy the pictures of living artists unless their position is so absolutely assured as to make the purchase a certain investment." Instead, Chamberlain advocated purchasing "some picture of a dead master of the English School" so that the gallery would form "a public illustration of English art." He feared, he wrote, that the works of living artists "will not hereafter be considered representative and a small collection like ours should, as far as possible, consist of works having real representative value."[77] Chamberlain's suggestions were heeded to some extent in subsequent Public Picture Gallery Fund purchases, as the fund acquired works by Reynolds, Turner, Prout, Ruskin, and William Henry Hunt (although it also bought works by contemporaries Watts, Legros, Whistler, Henry Moore, Lawson, and Francis Cotman).[78] Birmingham curator Wallis articulated a more definite policy of specialization in the Pre-Raphaelite Brotherhood, but he always wielded more power than the average curator and aimed at a more definite and representative acquisitions policy.[79]

In 1922, Director Haward of the Manchester City Art Gallery gave a talk at the Royal Society of Arts in London, which was followed by a discussion that included many of the major players in the world of arts administration, such as the chair, Sir Charles John Holmes, director of the National Gallery; Sir Whitworth Wallis, curator of the Birmingham Museum and Art Gallery; J. Bailey, formerly part of the Department of Circulation at the Victoria and Albert Museum; Professor Arthur M. Hind, who held the Slade Professorship of Fine Art at the University of Oxford; and A. F. Kendrick, of the Department of Textiles at the Victoria and Albert Museum.[80] As reported in the *Journal of the Royal Society of Arts*, Wallis argued to this group that "certainly in great cities like Liverpool, Manchester and Birmingham the museum should have a *raison d'être*, and if they specialised they would draw the public from a distance. They would come to see, he [Wallis] would not say ten masterpieces, but they would come to visit collections formed with a definite purpose." Wallis noted that "Birmingham made up its mind to specialise, and with all due deference to the Tate Gallery and other galleries, he advised those who wished to study English Pre-Raphaelite art to go to Birmingham for that purpose."[81] Thus although in the late nineteenth century Wallis articulated the museum's goals as informed by Ruskin and Morris, precisely because these were clear policies of acquisition and display, they also fit with the new ideas about museums in the early twentieth century, and he apparently reframed them in terms of changing expectations.

In Manchester, Arnold's call for these sorts of reforms in acquisitions was repeated and referenced in an official Manchester City Art Gallery report in 1905 and again in a work by Bernard Taylor in 1912.[82] These documents reiterated the growing sense that even provincial art institutions should aim at some kind of rational organization and representation of various periods and schools of art. The 1905 report ("Report of the Art Gallery Committee Visit to Art Galleries and Museums in Belgium, Holland, Germany, and Great Britain") reiterated what Arnold had pointed out sixteen years before, namely, that "the permanent collection has hitherto been limited, as regards exhibition in the Mosley Street Galleries, to modern British paintings and water-colour drawings, with a little sculpture in marble and bronze, and a few plaster casts." Like Arnold, the report advocated a more historical and representative acquisitions policy:

The contents of this Gallery and Museum should illustrate, by means of original works, copies, reproductions, models, casts, etc., most, if not all, of the following branches of art. In each case the general history and development, and in most cases the present condition of the art should also be illustrated: 1. Pictorial Art, including oil painting, water-colour drawing, engraving, etching, etc. A local portrait gallery should be included in this section. 2. Sculpture, including Wood Carving. 3. Architecture. 4. Furniture. 5. Textiles, Lace, Embroidery. 6. Ironwork. 7. Bronze. 8. Numismatics. 9. Gold and

Silver Plate. 10. Jewellery and Enamels. 11. Ivories. 12. Bookbinding. 13. Illumination. 14. Pottery and Porcelain. 15. Glass.[83]

The sheer catholicity of this list shows the extent to which the museum ideal had changed, and the evident one-dimensionality of the collection as it then existed.

In Liverpool, a controversy over Rathbone's supervision of the purchase of E. A. Hornel's *Summer* and other works by the then-young "Glasgow Boys" school led to a public debate in 1892 over the administration of the gallery.[84] When novelist and art critic George Moore called for a professional director in the *Speaker*, Rathbone defended his legacy and in fact the ability of a city council to develop a public collection better than an art expert:

George Moore is himself not satisfied with the selection of the Chantrey purchases, and yet they are selected by professional artists chosen for their eminence in art, whether justly deserved or not. Now the great safeguard in our administration is its impartial ignorance, which leads it to seek the very best advice of the very best authorities, and to select according to that advice. . . . No doubt an ideal autocracy might avoid making mistakes but it would have this danger . . . the public, having no voice in the purchase of pictures, would lose all interest. Now, municipal galleries are not museums, but educational institutions for the citizens generally, and a popular interest is a necessary element of their success in this direction.[85]

Crucially, for Rathbone the Walker Art Gallery was *not* a "museum"—that is, aiming at broad representation—but a gallery to interest people in art. Those, like Moore, who proposed a different role for the institution—a clear acquisitions policy, developed and enacted by a professional director—attempted again to change the gallery on curator Dyall's resignation in 1904, when they unsuccessfully tried to get modernist proponent D. S. MacColl appointed.[86] Liverpool did not see any real change until the period of extensions and the new acquisition fund in the 1930s, when Frank Lambert became the Walker's first director (in 1932) and began to create a comprehensive collection of British art.[87]

In Haward's 1922 Royal Society of Arts talk, "The Problem of Provincial Galleries and Art Museums, with Special Reference to Manchester," he outlined the main obstacles facing the director of a "provincial" art museum, namely, having to reject unacceptable or accommodate unreasonably large gifts, the lack of good lighting, the lack of planning for clear circulation and movement of visitors, the absence of a clear acquisitions policy, and the lack of space. However, he also offered solutions: a director to establish and enact clear policies, more space, occasional rehanging of the permanent collection to maintain public interest, temporary exhibitions with clear catalogues and associated lectures, school programs (he noted the success of programs instituted during the war because of the loss of school space for hospitals), study rooms, independent advisers, and coordination among all of the city's art institutions.[88] He also articulated a clear understanding of the purpose of such institutions: to "become a really vital influence in the town, setting standards of reference for students, artists, and craftsmen, and acting generally as cultural centres for the whole community."[89] Gone was the moral uplift and social purpose of the Victorians.

In the discussion after Haward's talk, National Gallery director Holmes also argued in favor of a new kind of educational role for art museums, one predicated on Britain's being a "democracy, which was in perpetual danger from want of knowledge on the part of the voting population." He went on to explain that museums could help bring citizens "into touch with the great achievements of the past, so that they recognised that they were not merely dwellers in this or that village or city, but were part of a universal citizenship which had a history of many thousand years."[90] Here is the purposive role for art, again—but this time connected not to spiritual development (as in Horsfall's Ruskinian formulation), but to democratic citizenship. Not surprisingly, the assembled experts all argued in favor of appointing expert directors to pursue definite acquisition and display policies, but Professor Hind of Oxford noted the lack of a degree in art history, which was hindering the development of a professional class of museum directors.[91] In all three museums, in fact, the new ideas about art, and about the purpose of the museum—as educational rather than experiential—gradually led to radical shifts in policy, ultimately resulting in significant extensions and reorganization, and institutional changes so that a professional director could develop a representative collection.

CONCLUSION: BECOMING VICTORIAN

When these city museums tried to make art popular, they did not abolish the social stratification inherent in many museum policies; at the same time, they began incremental but significant changes in the museums' intended purpose. Catalogues, lectures, and pamphlets that had once instructed viewers to look at paintings to learn about subject, story, and morality began to emphasize art history, technique, style, color, composition, and visual language. The very success and popularity of the free permanent collections and temporary exhibitions meant that these competed for space, leading to building renovations and extensions. With new space, all three municipal art museums rearranged their collections into chronological hangs, presenting their paintings in single-line, evenly spaced displays. A new understanding of the museums as primarily about intellectual education, rather than the experience of beauty, also inspired the cities to eventually appoint expert directors to develop and carry out plans to form representative historical collections. Together, these changes meant that the municipal art museums began to subtly emphasize art for its own sake, in terms of historical development, as personal enjoyment and enrichment instead of as an antidote to industrial society. (The Birmingham Museum and Art Gallery's publications continued to espouse ideas of earlier generations in its connections between art, craft, morality, and civic reform, but the physical organization of its collections changed with the Feeney extension of 1912.)

These museums originally developed out of a confluence of certain kinds of visual language—realism, Pre-Raphaelitism, narrative, genre—popular in the late nineteenth century, particular ways of "reading" paintings, and a movement to make art useful to society in a variety of ways that would uniquely suit urban, industrial, capitalist Britain. This convergence was brief, and even at its height, the municipal art museum movement was challenged by new ideas about art. As radical new movements emerged at home and abroad, art styles and subjects changed; to new generations of artists, critics, and patrons, narrative and historicist painting especially seemed to embody all of the instrumental and class-bound uses of art of the late nineteenth century.

The city art museums of Birmingham, Liverpool, and Manchester depended for their limited government funding on the understanding that art was useful. This understanding rested on a particular kind of art and a particular way of reading art. When these foundations shifted, however, the museums did not fall; indeed, only small structural, institutional, and interpretive changes were necessary to redefine the municipal art museums to fit the new paradigm. However, their original collections became increasingly obsolete, and the amenities they could offer in terms of entertainment generally failed to compete with the new amusements of the twentieth century. Particularly with the inclusion of abstraction and modernism after World War II, the fine arts became elite again, and cultural distinction became inscribed not by differently priced admission tickets, or when the museums were open, but by who could understand and interpret the art according to the new standards. Indeed, it is perhaps instructive

to consider that the heyday of the municipal art museum in the nineteenth century coincided with that of narrative art, and that both museums and art had to
change with the challenge of the most popular twentieth century narrative art
form: the cinema. At the same time, film was in many ways able to continue the
narrative strategies of nineteenth-century realist art, along with its ambiguous
potential for both education and entertainment. While the relationship between
nineteenth-century narrative art and early cinema lies outside the scope of this
book, the didactic uses to which nineteenth-century narrative and realist art
were put to a great extent continued in Britain with the creation of the British
Broadcasting Corporation.[92]

Now, however, blockbuster exhibitions of art—often from the nineteenth
century—have brought back mass audiences, and art museums have become,
by the beginning of the twenty-first century, central to educational and cultural
planning, to local and national government, and in particular to plans for gentrification and urban development. While the kind of art exhibited has radically
altered the idea of what art museums are for, both in the United States and in
Great Britain, many Victorian ideas about art, nature, and beauty as necessary
antidotes to industrial society continue to shape policy and even our everyday
lives, even if the underlying natural theology or Ruskinian reasoning has been
lost. The need for beauty, and for morality, amid the ugliness of industrial capitalism continues. It still remains, however, to fully utilize the museums we have
inherited, and to make their collections truly accessible and meaningful to all
through universal education.

EPILOGUE

This book has attempted to make connections between the mid-nineteenth-century revolution in art practice and aesthetics brought about through the Pre-Raphaelite Brotherhood and its articulate defender, John Ruskin, and the subsequent museum movement that sought to transform industrial culture and society through the experience of beauty and truth. By changing the terms of the debate in art—by redefining Keats's famous dictum that "Beauty is truth, truth beauty"—artists and critics transformed art into a force for moral regeneration. This redefinition of art got to the heart of critiques of industrial society, and the industrial city in particular, and understood the experience of beauty, truth, and story as essential in combating the moral and physical ugliness of industrial capitalism. Reformers pushed through museum projects in Birmingham, Liverpool, and Manchester, running into different obstacles and opportunities depending on each local context. Despite these differences, however, there was remarkable consistency as museum supporters sought inspiration, and often received remonstrance, from Ruskin. Supporters in all three cities reconceived museums as forms of domesticated public space, whose founders relied on gendered ideas about the ideal middle-class home to imagine a public alternative to the public house or gin palace that would offer beauty, refuge, and decorum. The three institutions collected art on the understanding that they were providing essential experiences rather than representative historical or educational collections. They interpreted the art in terms of beauty, truth, and story, highlighting experience over art criticism or education. At the same time, however, the art resisted these descriptions and engaged wider Victorian tensions about representation, labor, beauty, truth, nature, industry, and the spiritual meaning of the seen world. In the early twentieth century new ideas gradually transformed the museums, as a new generation of directors and city councils reconceived of the collections as primarily existing to educate citizens rather than to provide an antidote to industrial ugliness.

Meanwhile, despite innovations in France—about which the British in general remained highly skeptical—modern art and British art at this time seemed synonymous, and the achievements of the Royal Academy as well as the New English Art Club were celebrated as national triumphs.[1] In 1899, the Tate Gallery's first catalogue could boast of the achievements of modern British artists, especially in comparison to those in France.[2] However, just one generation later the art and ideas that had supported the museum movement would seem hopelessly outdated and frankly risible.[3] For instance, several monarchs and a world war later, in 1934, the official guide to the National and Tate galleries could categorically state, "The most significant developments in the history of painting during the nineteenth century took place in France," and hail "Monet, Manet, Renoir, Sisley, and Pissarro" as the leaders of impressionism, the "one original development in modern art."[4] This complete turnaround, however, meant a radical redefinition of what art meant, the standards by which it was to be judged, and even the uses to which it could be put.

We can hear some of the struggle involved in this transformation in a 1938 collection of essays from the BBC journal the *Listener*, published simply as *Art in England*. In the introduction, editor R. S. Lambert explains the volume's appearance: "Oddly enough, there is no easily accessible and up-to-date book on Art in this country for the general reader." He notes in particular that existing guides to modern art "do not meet the needs of that large and increasing section of the public which is becoming more and more interested in the visual arts and perhaps, at the same time, more and more puzzled about their present development." In fact, introducing the essay by Bloomsbury art critic Clive Bell, Lambert points out that Bell "offers clues to the art habits of the Victorian age which we are just learning to discard."[5]

As it happens, Bell's essay "Victorian Taste" leaves the reader in no doubt of his feelings about the differences between Victorian and contemporary aesthetic standards. "What the Victorians made and called art," he declared, "was almost always rubbish . . . [and] Victorian taste was almost always vile. . . . [It was the] imitation of something that was alive once. These Victorians are as men who should disinter the mummies of beauties long dead and take them for brides. Their art is necrophilous."[6] Clearly, Bell had nothing but scorn for Victorian artists' attempts to copy the past, or nature, or both, and blasted Victorian patrons—from Prince Albert to the new multitudes of ignorant middle-class collectors—who "conceived of [art] . . . as something with not quite a place of its own somewhere between religion and hygiene."[7] If Victorian art—so recently lauded across Britain for its high achievement and even higher morality—could be so condemned, what of the many museums throughout the nation founded to bring it to the British people?

As we saw in Chapter 1, some Manchester museum supporters had great confidence that art would be able to prove *both* their own willingness to give back to the community and the greatness of the industrial era. The reformers who eventually succeeded in establishing a city art museum there did so on the understanding that art had social benefits for all classes, while some of the more radical art enthusiasts believed art could serve to help transform industrial capitalism. Ultimately these ideas combined in the city museums of Birmingham, Manchester, Liverpool, and elsewhere to create contradictory monuments. On the one hand, these museums became monuments to the wealth of the cities' elites and the accomplishments of the industrial era; on the other, they embodied a larger cultural critique which hoped that beauty might redeem or reduce the squalor and misery that the industrial system created among the working classes. Similarly, the museums are simultaneously testaments to both the lost hope of improving industrial design with examples of historical artisanship and the now-abandoned idea that such objects might inspire artisans to make finely wrought goods that would bring them joyful labor. Ultimately, from Bell's perspective, Victorian art itself was a kind of conceptual mausoleum, containing the remains of past glories but unable to revive them.

These brief examples begin to illustrate how completely art and its uses came to be redefined in Britain after the Great War. This enormous shift can help illustrate the connections between dominant ideas about art and its resulting social role. More than thirty years ago, in her 1977 book *The Nationalization of Culture*, Janet Minihan showed that in contrast to continental Europe, the British arts establishment embraced centralized arts administration and funding only after World War II.[8] In doing so she noted, but did not explore, an aspect of this change, namely, that the British government after World War II explicitly stopped supporting art in order to reform the underprivileged and began supporting it as a more basic life-enhancement for an educated populace. She hinted, also, that there might have been a "relationship between artistic trends and Treasury funding."[9] Space does not permit me to pursue the history of these three institutions through the twentieth century, but I end this book by noting how nineteenth-century art museums, under the challenge of modernism, came to be monuments to an earlier age of ideas about the public role of art. I also want to try to understand Bell's vitriolic statements about Victorian art—in particular, his perceptions of its mimeticism and earnestness—and how these very qualities helped establish those museums in the first place. This requires briefly exploring further the complex relationship between the nineteenth-century search for a living art, the "imitative" nature of Victorian aesthetics—as seen in the debate between beauty and truth—and how justifications for public art changed in the twentieth century.

We can see this connection between a style of art and its perceived public purpose most clearly in the municipal art museums founded in the last quarter of the nineteenth century; as we have seen, Birmingham, Liverpool, and Manchester established their museums with help from reformers heavily influenced by the Ruskinian idea of bringing beauty to the masses. As Bell wryly noted, Victorians believed that art was good for society ("somewhere between religion and hygiene"). Nineteenth-century municipal governments justified expenditure on art museums through the conceptual "use-value" of art—its efficacy in social reform—and that efficacy was precisely based on art's status as "imitation," expressing both beauty and truth, which contemporaries believed allowed art to communicate the wonder of nature and God's work to a wide audience. This was often in explicit reaction to the ugliness of industrial cities.

At the same time, nineteenth-century artists and art critics were particularly concerned about finding a style of art appropriate to the constantly changing modern age and about the relationship between art, design, and mechanization. Henry Cole and Prince Albert hoped to improve British industrial design as a way to stay competitive in the international marketplace. John Ruskin and later William Morris rejected mechanized production as dehumanizing both workers and consumers, advocating instead, as Morris put it, that everyday objects should be "art made by the people and for the people as a joy both to the maker and the user."[10] Although clearly contradictory—improving or undermining industrial production—the arguments of both Cole and Ruskin led reformers to advocate strongly for museums, since both seemed to be saying that people needed contact with examples of good design from the past. In an 1880 lecture at the Birmingham Town Hall, Morris explained how past ages had enjoyed this close connection between meaningful work and daily beauty:

So much is now known of the periods of art that have left abundant examples of their work behind them, that we can judge of the art of all periods by comparing these with the remains of times of which less has been left us; and we cannot fail to come to the conclusion that down to very recent days everything that the hand of man touched was more or less beautiful: so that in those days all people who made anything shared in art, and all people who used the things so made: that is, *all* people shared in art.[11]

For Morris, following Ruskin's famous essay "The Nature of Gothic," the glory of the art of past ages consisted as much in the implied social conditions of the workforce as in the accomplishment of its design.

Like the South Kensington Museum and other public art museums designed to educate workers, the Birmingham Museum and Art Gallery took this principle to mean that Italian stonework and iron balustrades, medieval stained glass, Majolica ware, Japanese enamels, Indian carving, and Chinese porcelain might have a considerable effect on the local population. Indeed, the 1885 six-penny Birmingham museum catalogue urged its readers to view these objects of applied art in clearly Morrisian terms—although inflected with a certain Henry Cole–ish practicality.[12] The *Birmingham Daily Times* picked up the cry; celebrating the Birmingham Museum and Art Gallery's new building in 1885, the paper quoted Ruskin, who had once argued that the "arts and sciences will tend . . . to exalt the strength and quicken the soul of every nation which employs them to increase the comfort of lowly life, and grace with happy intelligence the unambitious courses of honourable toil."[13] Even in the midst of the Second Industrial Revolution, many seemed to hope that somehow production might *not* involve turning workers into mere accessories to machines.

However, there was a fundamental contradiction in the attempt to use handmade crafts as the basis for industrial design, and in subsequent years this would haunt British production and design museums alike. Indeed, using the finely wrought artisanry of other periods and countries as sources for new and better-manufactured designs led to precisely the kind of "vulgar Victorianism" that Bell and others so despised. Moreover, by the 1870s and 1880s the vast majority of industries in Birmingham and elsewhere were abandoning skilled artisanal workshop-style production in favor of factory, machine-driven, and highly specialized processes. The problem of the design revolution of the Arts and Crafts movement and the design dicta of Ruskin and Morris came back to this essential point: they depended on the gradual elimination of machine production, but that was beyond reform. Instead of inspiring a revolution of happy, fulfilled workers making goods by hand, the collections of applied art amassed in local museums contributed to the tendency that both Cole and Ruskin so despised of using completely inappropriate decoration on every conceivable mass-produced item—the very definition of kitsch.

Morris himself, of course, realized the basic contradiction between his own attempts at craft revival and the sad reality that the clientele of Morris & Co. could never include the workers whose lives he hoped to beautify; ultimately, he came to feel that there would be no true artistic renaissance until social revolution had remade the conditions of production. The Arts and Crafts movement, however, took on all sorts of variations as different cultures embraced it. In the early years of the twentieth century, particularly in Germany and Scandinavia, new groups of artist-reformers adopted the idea of good design for the masses, with the important caveat that they *accepted* mass production as a basic social reality and the foremost tool of social progress. (Bauhaus brought this to a high standard; IKEA is certainly the most omnipresent contemporary example of this particular idea.) Meanwhile, in Britain, by the time of Lambert's 1938 volume of essays *Art in England*, the nineteenth-century reformers' hope for a new combination of fine art and fine craft that would "bring joy to both user and maker" had been completely transformed, and the idea of handicraft or applied arts as the great hope of British manufacturing had been abandoned. Mass-produced commercial art now seemed as important as other kinds of artisanship, and *Art in England*'s section on "Patronage in Art To-day" includes a piece by the publicity manager for Shell-Mex and B.P. Ltd. Another of the essays on arts patronage notes that "the natural reaction from the aestheticism of nineteenth-century art is responsible for the now familiar paradox that true aesthetic qualities are to-day mainly found in objects not designed by professional 'artists' at all: in aeroplanes, motor-cars, suit-cases, tennis-rackets, and so forth."[14] This was the machine aesthetic of Bauhaus, of the futurists and vorticists. Nineteenth-century collections of highly finished handmade goods to inspire industrial design or a revitalization of traditional crafts had become the sad testimonials to a vanished critique of the industrial age.

Next to the collections of textiles, stone carving, and wrought ironwork remained those nineteenth-century paintings and sculptures about which Bell despaired in 1938 that "when they were not imitating things of the past, they were imitating nature, which is worse."[15] Yet as we have seen, that very quality, what Ruskin called truth to nature, had been the argument for bringing art to the people in the first place. The many movements that combined to produce modernism fundamentally transformed the idea that paintings should or could be judged in these terms. In looking back across the cultural fault lines created by modernism and deepened by World War I, Bell could make his pronouncement: Victorian art was rubbish and led nowhere.

In developing their acquisition, education, and opening policies, the three municipal art museums explored in this book based their decisions on the idea that art existed for broad social purposes. However, gradually and tentatively the museums came to embrace a new, art historical framework in their purchases, publications, and organization. In contrast to late-nineteenth-century catalogues that encouraged visitors to "read" paintings for their subjects and stories, by the early years of the twentieth century, catalogues instructed viewers to consider the color, light, composition, and painting techniques of the paintings on display. When possible, rather than the dense Victorian hang that filled each wall with paintings from floor to ceiling, museum extensions allowed them to show their collections in single lines that highlighted the uniqueness of each artist's vision. The museums in Birmingham, Liverpool, and Manchester gradually gave their paintings chronological organization, emphasizing the extent to which the museums had become instruments to instruct visitors in art history. Indeed, during the nineteenth century these had been museums of contemporary art, often purchasing from annual exhibitions of new work; the basis of the collections thus had been formed in the last decades of that century. However, purchases and gifts in the early twentieth century began to emphasize building up the collection of Victorian art. Although the museums still bought some contemporary works by war artists such as Muirhead Bone, or by Camden Town painters such as Augustus John, purchases and gifts also began emphasizing the art-historical past, particularly the nineteenth century. Drawings by the acknowledged masters of the period—Brown, Burne-Jones, Rossetti, Ruskin, Morris—or bequests of collections formed years earlier began to make up the most substantial gifts and purchases. Increasingly, however, this was framed as creating a representative historical collection rather than in the Ruskinian hope that a meticulous realism and commitment to idealizing narrative might reach the masses through the universal language of beauty.

In 1945, as the Labour Party envisioned the world after the war, party leaders began to publish prospectuses on their plans, such as *The Old World and the New Society* and *Plans for an Arts Centre*. In the latter of these, drawn up by none other than John Maynard Keynes, the committee devoted to making a national policy on arts provision—the Arts Council of Great Britain—attacked the basis of aesthetic judgment and arts policy that had dominated British thinking since the days of Ruskin. "We must rid ourselves," Keynes wrote, "of the false idea that art is a palliative for social evils or a branch of welfare work."[16] The axis of visual representation had shifted. In the years after World War II, through national arts acquisition funds and other means, the municipal art museums of Birmingham, Liverpool, and Manchester came to own more recent twentieth-century art and began to expand into nineteenth-century foreign works. They embraced white-wall modernism and began to think about their audiences as made up of individuals whose lives should be enriched with art, rather than hoping art would substitute for dirty and decaying houses, the pub, the music hall, or atheistic or socialist tendencies. Indeed, by the 1960s, the Victorian world had fallen so far out of favor that it began to be fashionable again, when a series of exhibitions of Ford Madox Brown, William Holman Hunt, and John Everett Millais at Liverpool's Walker Art Gallery, the Royal Academy, and the Victoria and Albert Museum reintroduced these forgotten artists to new audiences.[17] The Walker now framed them in art historical terms and sought to understand them in their historical context. Yet to eyes conditioned to see cubism or pop art, the Pre-Raphaelites could seem strange and even beautiful, and the art and idealism of the nineteenth century could become an inspiration for a new generation of those who would again seek to challenge industrial capitalism through art and craft and, explicitly this time, social and sexual revolution. Although they never lived up to the hopes of their more idealistic founders, art museums always hold that potential, as art itself does, to change the way we see the world, and perhaps—as some of those Victorian reformers hoped—to thus galvanize us to change it.

Reference Matter

ABBREVIATIONS USED IN
NOTES AND BIBLIOGRAPHY

BCLLS   Birmingham Central Library Local Studies

BCP   Birmingham Council Proceedings (Borough of Birmingham and City of Birmingham, *Proceedings of the Council*)

LCRL   Liverpool Central Reference Library

MCAG   Manchester City Art Gallery

MCLA   Manchester Central Library Archives

MCP   Manchester Council Proceedings (City of Manchester, *Proceedings of the Council*)

NGA   National Gallery Archives

RMI   Royal Manchester Institution

WAG   Walker Art Gallery

NOTES

INTRODUCTION

1. Whistler, *Mr. Whistler's "Ten O'Clock,"* 9. Emphasis in original.

2. Ibid.

3. For more on Sadler, see Higginson, "Centenary"; "Michael Sadler Memorial Exhibition"; Cohen, "Sir Michael E. Sadler," 282.

4. Sadler, *Pictures in a Great City*, 6.

5. Whistler, *Mr. Whistler's "Ten O'Clock,"* 20–21. In 1878, Whistler famously sued Ruskin for libel for comments about his painting *Nocturne in Black and Gold: The Falling Rocket*. On that trial, see, for example, Merrill, *A Pot of Paint*.

6. For a seminal work on the nineteenth-century intellectual movement connecting aesthetics, labor, and morality, see Williams, *Culture and Society*.

7. See, for example, Ruskin, Letter 80, July 16, 1877, *Fors Clavigera*, 7:142, discussed in Chapter 1.

8. Ibid., Letter 88, February 8, 1880, 8:63.

9. On the St. George's Museum in Sheffield, see Swan, *Preliminary Catalogue*. Tim Hilton discusses the guild in *John Ruskin*, 588–591.

10. See Gandhi, *My Autobiography*, esp. chaps. 18–20, 264–269, and chap. 23, 275–277.

11. Tim Hilton argues that Ruskin's influence was "limited" rather than "vast" and that "all these tendencies in British life would have been present had Ruskin never written" (Hilton, *John Ruskin*, xx). However, many museum advocates explicitly understood themselves to be following Ruskin's ideas.

12. Particularly important in this regard has been the work of art historians Timothy Barringer and Elizabeth Prettejohn.

13. See, for example, John Tosh's pithy discussion of domesticity in *A Man's Place*, esp. 4.

14. As Susan Pearce writes in *On Collecting*, museums have developed an identity based on separating goods from the marketplace and placing them outside of capitalist relations, even as they depend on market values for their collections' "pricelessness."

15. Wallis, "The Museum and Art Gallery," 491.

16. On art as a window, see Woodson-Boulton, "A Window onto Nature."

17. See, for example, Foucauldians such as Bennett, *The Birth of the Museum*, and Hooper-Greenhill, *Museums and the Shaping of Knowledge*.

18. Morris, *News from Nowhere*, 149.

19. On Reynolds's influence on Keats, see Dean, "Some Quotations in Keats's Poetry"; Keats, "Ode on a Grecian Urn," lines 17–20, http://englishhistory.net/keats/poetry/odeona grecianurn.html.

20. Keats, "Ode on a Grecian Urn," lines 46–50.

21. Reynolds, "Discourse VII," 32. On Reynolds's influence on Keats, see Dean, "Some Quotations in Keats's Poetry"; on the relationship between Locke, Shaftesbury, and the

idea of universal taste, see Dowling, *The Vulgarization of Art*. This was the basis of theories of assimilation—that exposure to beauty would lead to moral development—which justified most Victorian efforts to bring art and beauty to the masses. See Schmiechen, "The Victorians."

22. On the nude in Victorian culture, see, for example, Nead, *The Female Nude*, and Smith, *The Victorian Nude*.

23. A point made well in the introduction to Aldington, ed., *The Religion of Beauty*, esp. 13–14. I am grateful to Bill McKelvy for this reference. Portions of the following discussion are reprinted by permission of the publishers from Woodson-Boulton, "A Window onto Nature"; excerpted sentences appear on pp. 148–150. Copyright 2008.

24. Hewison, "The Beautiful and the True," 13. My understanding of the relationship between Ruskin's background, his ideas on art, and his political and economic ideas has also been inspired by Williams, *Culture and Society*; Hilton, *The Early Years* and *The Later Years*; Barringer, *Men at Work* and *Reading the Pre-Raphaelites*; and the teaching of Debora Silverman.

25. For a good discussion of how Pugin's and Ruskin's ideas played out in practice, see Macleod, *Style and Society*.

26. "We may indeed perceive, as far as we are acquainted with the nature of God, that we have been so constructed as in a healthy state of mind to derive pleasure from whatever things are illustrative of that nature" (Ruskin, *Works of John Ruskin*, 2:51, quoting a passage of Ruskin's *Modern Painters*, vol. 1).

27. Ibid., 5:171–172.

28. Ibid., 11:49.

29. Ruskin, "The Nature of Gothic," in Rosenberg, ed., *The Genius of John Ruskin*, 170–196.

30. Horsfall, *The Government of Manchester*, 33.

31. See, for instance, Woodson-Boulton, "Temples of Art"; Waterfield, *Art for the People*; Borzello, *Civilising Caliban*; Wilson, "'The Highest Art'"; Harrison, "Social Reform"; Harrison, "Art and Social Regeneration"; Harrison, "Art and Philanthropy"; and Koven, "The Whitechapel Picture Exhibitions."

32. A longer version of this argument appears in Woodson-Boulton, "A Window onto Nature."

33. For more on the relationship between the New Museology and recent historical scholarship on museums, see Woodson-Boulton, "Victorian Museums."

34. Hewison, "The Beautiful and the True," 11. For more on the effects of middle-class art patronage, see Williams, *Culture and Society*; Ladd, *The Victorian Morality of Art*; Landow, "There Began to Be"; and Roberts, "Exhibition and Review." For a recent reperiodization of the change in British collecting patterns from old masters to contemporary British art to the late eighteenth century, see Hoock, "'Struggling Against a Vulgar Prejudice.'"

35. Macleod, *Art and the Victorian Middle Class*, 30, and Roberts, "Exhibition and Review," 88. Andrea Geddes Poole, in *Stewards of the Nation's Art*, makes a similar argument about arts patronage, noting differences of standards and stewardship between aristocratic and bourgeois trustees of, and donors to, London art institutions.

36. Aldington, *The Religion of Beauty*, introduction; Roberts, "Exhibition and Review"; and Landow, "There Began to Be."

37. Landow, "There Began to Be," 125–126.

38. As Frances Borzello writes in his study of "art philanthropy" in London, "By employing art to civilise, [Samuel Barnett and others] were adding an artistic solution to all the other solutions which emerged after 1870 to deal with the problem of the poor" (*Civilising Caliban*, 5). I would add regional city art museums to the "art philanthropy" movement. For a more recent discussion of that movement, see Maltz, *British Aestheticism*.

39. See Liverpool Central Reference Library Archives, *Minutes of the Libraries, Museums, and Arts Committee*. As we will see in Chapter 1, the art gallery existed administratively long before an actual gallery was built.

40. For an excellent discussion of the technological and cultural upheavals of the years before World War I, see Kern, *The Culture of Time and Space*.

41. See Bailey, *Leisure and Class*; Bailey, "'Will the Real Bill Banks'"; Bailey, "Leisure, Culture and Historian"; Thompson, "Social Control"; and Thompson, *The Rise of Respectable Society*.

42. See Hobsbawm, *The Age of Empire*, esp. chap. 2, and Matthew, "The Liberal Age," 5:16. On the rise of department stores in particular, see Rappaport, *Shopping for Pleasure*.

43. On the visual culture of the late nineteenth century in the context of print journalism, see, for example, Beegan, *The Mass Image*.

44. The Second Reform Act of 1867 expanded the vote to include around two-thirds of the male urban population, thereby doubling the electorate; the Education Act of 1870 established local school boards to run mandatory primary schools; the Education Act of 1880 made school attendance mandatory; the Third Reform Act of 1884 extended male household suffrage to the countryside, doubling the English and Welsh electorate again to more than four million; and the Redistribution Act of 1885 continued to fix old inequities and corruption in voting by creating uniform single-member constituencies for Parliament.

45. Early historians such as Josef Redlich and Francis W. Hirst (*The History of Local Government*) crafted a Whiggish narrative of the steady march toward democracy in the nineteenth century. Later scholars such as E. P. Hennock (*Fit and Proper Persons*) and Derek Fraser (*Urban Politics*) have emphasized the extent to which local elites—albeit of the industrial and merchant classes, rather than the old landowning gentry—preserved authority through the new government structures.

46. See Woodson-Boulton, "Local Government."

47. See House of Commons debates, March 6, 1845, and March 13 and April 10, 1850, in *Hansard's Parliamentary Debates, Third Series*, vol. 78, 381–394, and vol. 109, 838–850 and 154–164, respectively.

48. See, for example, studies on prostitution, degeneration, and the London poor, such as Walkowitz, *City of Dreadful Delight*; Pick, *Faces of Degeneration*; and Stedman Jones, *Outcast London*.

49. Britain was not alone in its use of art in social reform; indeed, both Ruskin and Morris were highly influential on the Continent. See Herbert, *The Artist and Social Reform*.

50. Jerome Buckley has argued that the "central attribute" of the Victorian era was "a double self-consciousness, public as well as private . . . an awareness of the personal self in time and of the whole era itself as perpetual transition" ("Victorian England," 5). I previously published a longer version of this idea, and portions of the following paragraph, in Woodson-Boulton, "Victorian Museums and Victorian Society," 112–114.

51. Cohen, *Household Gods*, 3.

52. See Pearce, *On Collecting*, for an excellent discussion of collecting practices as a measurement of a society's valuations and values.

53. Randolph Starn makes this point in connection with multiplying museums at the beginning of the twenty-first century ("A Historian's Brief Guide," 89).

54. Some of this derives from the multidisciplinary nature of museum studies, so that the language of, for example, sociologists' work on museums, while historically informed, tends to work with abstract categories. See, for example, Fyfe, *Art, Power and Modernity*, particularly chap. 8, 160–182.

55. See, for example, Black, *On Exhibit*, 4–5.

56. Kriegel also makes this point in "Review Essay," 684.

57. Contrast the highly centralized French model presented in Sherman, *Worthy Monuments*.

58. Compare, for example, Bailkin, *The Culture of Property*; Hill, *Culture and Class*; and Kriegel, *Grand Designs*.

59. Short accounts of the founding of the museums have been published in collection catalogues; see Davies, *By the Gains of Industry*; Morris, *Victorian and Edwardian Paintings*; and Morris, "Philip Henry Rathbone." Dean, "Private Patrons and Public Art," has a chapter on the Manchester City Art Gallery.

CHAPTER 1

Portions of this chapter were previously published in Woodson-Boulton, "'Industry Without Art Is Brutality': Aesthetic Ideology and Social Practice in Victorian Art Museums," *Journal of British Studies* 46, no. 1 (January 2007): 47–71. © 2007 by The North American Conference on British Studies. All rights reserved.

1. For greater detail on the founding of these art museums, see Woodson-Boulton, "Temples of Art," chaps. 1–3.

2. I am using Simon Gunn's sense of "ritual" as part of the "visualisation of social position, and with it the affirmation of collective [middle-class] identity" ("The Middle Class," 122) that included such Manchester practices as commuting, meeting at the High Exchange, and "Doing the Square" on Saturday mornings. He further elaborates these ideas in *The Public Culture of the Victorian Middle Class*.

3. For good case studies in the British context, see, for example, Hill, *Culture and Class*; Bailkin, *The Culture of Property*; and Taylor, *Art for the Nation*.

4. See Duncan, "Putting the 'Nation' in London's National Gallery."

5. On the role of culture in the formation of urban government and as a response to urbanization, see, for example, Meller, *Leisure and the Changing City*; Hennock, *Fit and Proper Persons*; Joyce, *Visions of the People*; and Hunt, *Building Jerusalem*.

6. See Hennock, *Fit and Proper Persons*, 31–34, 105–107. The Birmingham Town Council became the Birmingham City Council in 1889. Throughout this book, the use of "town council" or "city council" follows the year in which each town became a city: Manchester in 1854, Liverpool in 1880, and Birmingham, as noted, in 1889.

7. Dale, *The Life of R. W. Dale*, 401–402.

8. See Dale, "George Dawson"; Hennock, *Fit and Proper Persons*, 61–79; and Dale, *The Life of R. W. Dale*.

9. Crosskey, *A Hand-Book of Rational Piety*, 123; see also Crosskey, *A Citizen of No Mean City*, 5, quoted in Hennock, *Fit and Proper Persons*, 96.

10. Dale had attended Dawson's sermons as a young man and only stopped going to the Church of the Saviour when his own duties as minister at Carr's Lane Chapel prevented him. Hennock, *Fit and Proper Persons*, 154. For an interesting recent assessment of Dale's influence, see Binfield, *The Cross and the City*.

11. The *Spectator*, December 2, 1876, quoted in Hennock, *Fit and Proper Persons*, 68.

12. No date is given in the text published in 1888, but Dawson died in 1876: Dawson, "Beauty and Purity in Towns."

13. See, for example, Ruskin, in *Works of John Ruskin*, 5:171–172.

14. Dawson, "Beauty and Purity in Towns," 495.

15. Ibid.

16. Ibid.

17. For an excellent study of Birmingham's civic culture and the tradition of "self-improvement," see Rodrick, *Self-Help and Civic Culture*.

18. Dawson's congregants who were also chairmen of the Free Libraries Committee included E. C. Osborne, William Harris, Jesse Collings, and G. J. Johnson; others involved in art education included Samuel Timmins, J. A. Langford, and H. S. Pearson (Hennock, *Fit and Proper Persons*, 94 nn38–39). The committee overseeing the municipal libraries, museums, art gallery, and art school in Birmingham went through a number of names as its remit expanded. The committee was constituted and issued its first report in 1860 as the Free Public Libraries and Museums Committee and subsequently issued reports under a variety of names, including the Free Libraries and Industrial Museum Committee, the Free Libraries and Museums Committee, and the Free Libraries and Art Gallery Committee, until the council created a separate committee to oversee the art museum and school of art in 1884. For ease of reference, I refer to the committee that combined oversight of the libraries and early iterations of the art museum as the Free Libraries Committee.

19. Brothers Joseph, Arthur, and Richard Chamberlain, their brother-in-law William Kenrick, and R. F. Martineau were all part of Crosskey's congregation. On Crosskey and the membership of these men in his Church of the Messiah, see Hennock, *Fit and Proper Persons*, 94.

20. *The Sunday Question Again*, 4.

21. Hennock, *Fit and Proper Persons*, 131. What was innovative about the Liberal Association was its use of a subscription membership to control candidates for the council at the ward level; with the expansions of the franchise in 1867 and 1885 this kind of political organizing became increasingly powerful.

22. See Collings, *On the State of Education in Birmingham*, and Francis Adams, *History of the Elementary School Contest in England* (1882), in Hennock, *Fit and Proper Persons*, 86 n23. See also Hennock, *Fit and Proper Persons*, chap. 2.

23. Hennock notes that soon after the Liberals took control, it was not the Conservatives but the older Liberals who fought the pro–municipal action party (*Fit and Proper Persons*, 135). See also Briggs, *The History of Birmingham*, esp. 7, 165. For new, critical perspectives on these same developments, see Jones, "Public Pursuit of Private Profit?," and Leighton, "Municipal Progress."

24. The Liberal Party would of course split in 1885 over the issue of Irish Home Rule. Joseph Chamberlain is not simply important for his time as the mayor of Birmingham, but as the voice for an imperial Britain, a potential leader of the Liberal Party who instead led the Unionist secession in national politics.

25. There was a close relationship between Dale and Joseph Chamberlain, both real and perceived. A. W. W. Dale cites criticism at the time of Joseph Chamberlain's candidature for Parliament: "Better men, [a London newspaper] asserted, had been passed over, simply because 'Mr. R. W. Dale has nominated Mr. Chamberlain, and the will of Mr. Dale is the will of Birmingham'" (Dale, *The Life of R. W. Dale*, 421).

26. Timmins, *A History of Warwickshire*, 207. Asa Briggs noted J. H. Chamberlain's influence in the suburbs in introducing Gothic redbrick decorated architecture (*The History of Birmingham*, 23). See also Brooks, *John Ruskin and Victorian Architecture*, and Weiner, *Architecture and Social Reform*. On Timmins, Chamberlain, and George Baker as prominent Birmingham Ruskinians, see Hilton, *John Ruskin*, xix.

27. In 1886, J. A. Cossins wrote of Chamberlain's design for the School of Art that it "is in the very original modern Gothic style, almost created by the late J. H. Chamberlain, and practised with such great success by the firm to which he belonged. The School is perhaps the finest of their works, and possesses a rare grace and refinement in every detail" ("Architecture," 125).

28. Chamberlain, *Exotic Art*, 15, 34. And yet he worked to establish a municipal industrial museum and gallery of art that would encourage the imitation of historical styles!

29. Ibid., 23–24.

30. Ibid., 26, 31, 33.

31. Ironically, A. B. Chamberlain had to leave because of illness in the same year his superior, Whitworth Wallis, died, having been assistant curator for thirty-seven years. See Wallis, "The Museum and Art Gallery," 516–518, and "The Late Sir Whitworth Wallis, F.S.A., 1855–1927," 185–186. I am grateful to Victoria Emmanuel of the Birmingham Museum and Art Gallery for providing me with a copy of the latter.

32. See Tangye, *My Library Catalogue*, 218–220, and letter dated November 5, 1881, from Tangye to Mayor Richard Chamberlain, read before the town council meeting, BCP 1880–1890, November 9, 1881, 10.

33. Victoria and Albert Museum, "Panelled Room from The Grove in Harborne," http://collections.vam.ac.uk/item/O10987/room-panelled-room-from-the-grove/, accessed February 15, 2011. Joseph Chamberlain lived in Highbury from 1879 to 1914.

34. Victoria and Albert Museum, "Watercolour" (interior of The Grove, probably by Kenrick himself), http://collections.vam.ac.uk/item/O78178/watercolour/?print=1, accessed February 15, 2011.

35. Compare Weiner, *Architecture and Social Reform*.

36. Morris, *Address Delivered at the Town Hall*, and *"Labour and Pleasure,"* later published in Morris, *The Collected Works*, 28–50, 51–80.

37. Morris, *"Labour and Pleasure,"* 6, 8, 28 (emphasis in original).

38. On the improvements of the 1860s, see Briggs, *History of Birmingham*, 9–11, 72–82, and Hiley, "Birmingham City Government," 102–103. Following earlier historians J. T. Bunce and E. V. Hiley, Briggs also emphasizes the importance of Joseph Chamberlain's mayoralty (*History of Birmingham*, 69). Denys P. Leighton calls Joseph Chamberlain and

his followers the "New Radicals," emphasizing the extent to which they centralized municipal government in the town council ("Municipal Progress," 128–129).

39. R. W. Dale in Armstrong, *Henry William Crosskey*, 402.

40. Hiley, "Birmingham City Government," 102–103; Briggs, *History of Birmingham*, 72–82.

41. Letter dated April 26, 1875, from Chamberlain to Collings, printed in the Free Libraries Committee Report, May 11, 1875, BCP 1871–1879, 419.

42. On the resulting centralization of municipal government in the town council, largely doing away with an earlier system of "submunicipal" government at the ward and parish levels, see Leighton, "Municipal Progress," 128–129.

43. Michael Stratton has come to the same conclusion, noting the "relatively consistent architectural image" of Martin and Chamberlain's new Board Schools: "During the 1870s terracotta became closely associated with Birmingham's Civic Gospel, a concerted movement to improve the political administration and fabric of the city. Schools were designed as corporate expression of the ideals of the Board and the city's councillors" ("Architectural Terracotta in Birmingham," 23). See also Tim Hilton's memories of attending a Birmingham Board School and J. H. Chamberlain's role as Ruskinian architect, in *John Ruskin*, xvii–xix.

44. Chamberlain, *Six Years of Educational Work*, 11.

45. Ruskin, *The Seven Lamps*, 7. I am grateful to Debora Silverman for pointing out the similarities between Chamberlain's statements and Ruskin's ideas about ornament in that book.

46. Weiner, *Architecture and Social Reform*.

47. Tim Hilton mentions this meeting between Baker, Ruskin, and the (unnamed) "fathers of the city" in *John Ruskin*, xix–xx, 639–640.

48. Ruskin, Letter 80, July 16, 1877, *Fors Clavigera*, 7:142.

49. Ibid.

50. Ibid., Letter 88, February 8, 1880, 8:65.

51. Ibid., Letter 87, undated, 8:52. Ruskin was reacting to Dale's obituary of Dawson published in *Nineteenth Century* (August 1877).

52. The council discussed, moved, and approved the creation of the "Free Public Libraries and Museums Committee" on March 6, 1860, BCP 1859–1871, 122–123.

53. Free Libraries Committee Report, May 15, 1860, BCP 1859–1871, 195.

54. Langford, *The Birmingham Free Libraries*, 4; Free Libraries Committee Report, September 5, 1865, BCP 1859–1871, 350; J. T. Bunce, "Address Delivered at the Annual Meeting of Members, 10th January 1876," in *Addresses* (1876), 8–9. See also Free Libraries Committee Report, April 9, 1861, BCP 1859–1871, 197.

55. See Free Libraries Committee Report, August 6, 1867, BCP 1859–1871, 399; Chamberlain, *The Corporation Museum*, 3; and Free Libraries Committee Report, May 11, 1875, BCP 1871–1879, 423. On the collection, see *Report of the Free Libraries and Museum Committee* (Birmingham, 1867), 5–6.

56. The semipublic bodies included the Industrial Art Museum Committee and the Public Picture Gallery Fund, which included members of the council and the Free Libraries Committee as well as art-reforming citizens. Annual attendance in the thirty-by-seventy-foot room was 145,761 in 1872, when the gallery first opened on Sundays. By

1877, in the same space, attendance was an astonishing 393,645. Attendance figures from the Museum and Art Gallery Committee Report, May 6, 1913, BCP 1901–1914, 418 (see also Woodson-Boulton, "Temples of Art," 36–42, apps. 3 and 4).

57. Meeting of the Town Council, May 7, 1872, BCP 1871–1879, 405, and May 11, 1876, BCP 1871–1879, 424–425.

58. As the council tried to find ways to house it adequately, the art gallery had an itinerant existence from 1877, when it moved into temporary rooms on Paradise Street, until 1880, when it in fact became only an administrative reality and the collections went into storage until 1885.

59. After Council House architect Yeoville Thomason declared the land behind that building unsuitable for the new Assize Courts, the General Purposes Committee recommended that site for the new permanent Art Gallery and Museum, the bottom floors to be used for municipal offices. This was recommended in the Report of the General Purposes Committee, August 3, 1880, and approved in Resolutions on the same date (BCP 1880–1890, 373, 375–377). According to a report in the *Birmingham Daily Post* (July 20, 1881) of the speech given by the chairman of the Gas Committee, Councilor Marris, at the laying of the inscription stone of the art gallery on July 19, 1881, "the suggestion of the exact manner in which the Free Libraries Committee and the Gas Committee should join in doing this work emanated from the Mayor." The mayor at the time was Richard Chamberlain.

60. Joseph Chamberlain apparently anticipated that the profits from the gasworks would be of a magnitude to allow for ambitious building or other improvement schemes (see letter to Jesse Collings dated September 12, 1875, in University of Birmingham Library Special Collections).

61. Gas Committee Report, March 7, 1882, BCP 1880–1890, 362–363. The former Gas Offices, as well as the former Water Department, are now administration and temporary exhibition spaces.

62. Museum and School of Art Committee Report, December 8, 1885, BCP 1880–1890, 34–37.

63. Museum and School of Art Committee Report, December 2, 1884, BCP 1880–1890, 76. Whitworth's brother and nephew were also prominent art museum curators, at Nottingham and Bath (and later the Whitworth Institute, Manchester), respectively. See Baird, "The Knights of Museums," and Sharman, "George Wallis."

64. The Art Gallery Purchase Committee noted (*Report of the Art Gallery Purchase Committee, 9th November 1882,* 10) that they were compiling a report on categories of works to be collected; Wallis completed this when he arrived three years later. Wallis, *Report of the Curator.*

65. *Cooper and Co.'s Penny Guide,* 12.

66. See Dale, *The Life of R. W. Dale,* 412–413.

67. The following summary of Liverpool politics and history is gathered from Collins, *Politics and Elections in Nineteenth-Century Liverpool;* Belchem, *Popular Politics;* Muir, *A History of Liverpool;* Neal, *Sectarian Violence;* Simey, *Charity Rediscovered;* Waller, *Democracy and Sectarianism;* Walton and Wilcox, eds., *Low Life and Moral Improvement;* and White, *A History of the Corporation of Liverpool.* I am indebted to Edward Morris for recommending several Liverpool histories, especially the Waller book.

68. See Waller, *Democracy and Sectarianism*, 2, and Rawley, *The Transatlantic Slave Trade*, esp. chap. 9.

69. Waller, *Democracy and Sectarianism*, 2.

70. For descriptions of the poverty in Victorian Liverpool and city planning to ameliorate it, see Sharples, *Liverpool*, esp. 8 and 25.

71. The alignments of Anglican/Conservative and Catholic/Nonconformist/Liberal were solidified during a crisis over the municipality's provision of education in the early period of municipal government after the Municipal Corporations Act of 1835; riots broke out over Liberal councilors' attempts to establish a compromise by which corporation schools would be acceptable to Catholic as well as Protestant children. See Collins, *Politics and Elections*, 27–28; Waller, *Democracy and Sectarianism*, 11–12; White, *A History of the Corporation of Liverpool*, 21–24; and Fraser, *Urban Politics in Victorian England*, 134–135.

72. See Simey, *Charity Rediscovered*. In addition, the town council controlled only limited sources of municipal income (taxable property or municipal trading) that might have allowed a greater extension of and confidence in municipal projects. The Liverpool Town Council lost control of the dock revenues to a merchant-controlled board in 1857 but did ultimately take over tramways and electricity companies in the 1890s. White, *A History of the Corporation of Liverpool*, 78, 160–166; Harris, *Municipal Self-Government*, 183–184.

73. Compare Wilson, "'The Florence of the North'?"

74. Picton, *Sir James A. Picton*, 68.

75. In the field of culture, the Nonconformist community in Liverpool had been particularly important from the early years of the nineteenth century, with the Radical intellectual circle around the Unitarian, abolitionist, member of Parliament, Renaissance scholar and collector William Roscoe. Waller, *Democracy and Sectarianism*, 13; White, *A History of the Corporation of Liverpool*, 151; Collins, *Politics and Elections*, 198–199; Walton, *Lancashire*, 138; and Holt, *The Unitarian Contribution*, 18. On the Renshaw Street Unitarians, B. Guinness Orchard wrote in 1893 of the Rathbones' "dogged ardour" in "promot[ing] national education, middle-class culture, public parks, free libraries and museums." Orchard, *Liverpool's Legion of Honour* (Liverpool, 1893), quoted in Simey, *Charity Rediscovered*, 17–18. See also Waller, *Democracy and Sectarianism*, 14–15.

76. Waller, *Democracy and Sectarianism*, 18–19.

77. See the *Twenty-first Annual Report of the Committee of the Free Public Library, Museum, and Gallery of Art, of the Borough of Liverpool, for the Year 1873* (1873), 7. Note that after its constitution in 1850, the name of this committee changed numerous times to reflect its changing resources and responsibilities, and the town council often used different names interchangeably at the same time. For clarity, throughout this book I will refer to the committee governing Liverpool's public libraries and museums by one of its many iterations, the Library, Museum, and Arts Committee.

78. I have been unable to trace any writings by Edward Samuelson. Edward Morris describes Samuelson attempting to secure the support of other Conservatives for the gallery, while Rathbone eventually became the main impetus and controller of art policy on the Arts and Exhibitions Sub-Committee. See Morris, *Victorian and Edwardian Paintings*, 2, 7–8. Samuelson publicly split with Picton and Rathbone over the Walker's acquisitions policy and accounts in 1886.

79. For example, see Rathbone, *The Political Value of Art*, 24, 32.

80. Morris discusses Rathbone's biography and influence on the Walker Art Gallery in *Victorian and Edwardian Paintings*; on his family background, see ibid., 8.

81. See Picton, *Sir James A. Picton*, 4; "The Two Pictons (Sir James A. Picton and His Son)," *Liberal Review*, January 11, 1879, 3 and 4; and "In Memoriam (Sir James A. Picton)," *Liverpool Review*, July 20, 1889, 9–11.

82. Picton, *Sir James A. Picton*, 68.

83. *Liberal Review*, April 30, 1881. See also Lund, *The Ideal Citizen*.

84. Rathbone, *The Political Value of Art*, 22.

85. William Rathbone V had been a member of Parliament and mayor. William Rathbone VI (Philip's older brother) was Liberal member of Parliament for Liverpool 1868–1895.

86. Picton, *Liverpool Improvements*, 5. Compare Ruskin, *The Seven Lamps*, 14.

87. Picton, *Liverpool Improvements*, 20–21; Picton, *Our Municipal Institutions*, 20, 24.

88. "The commercial cities of antiquity, Carthage, Tyre, Palmyra, Alexandria, erected magnificent monuments, many of which remain to this day, to attest their greatness. The cities of the middle-age commerce, Venice, Florence, Genoa, expended their wealth in vying with each other in adorning their cities in the spirit of honourable rivalry" (Picton, *Liverpool Improvements*, 24).

89. Ibid.

90. Picton, *Our Municipal Institutions*, 24.

91. Speech given October 18, 1852, at the opening of the municipal library, museum, and art gallery, quoted in Picton, *Sir James A. Picton*, 215.

92. P. H. Rathbone, "Sir James A. Picton (a poem)," in Rathbone, *Varying Moods*, 113. Often rebuffed in his efforts by the Liverpool City Council, in his tribute poem Rathbone could not help noting that Picton was "a faithful citizen / Of no mean city—not mean as to size— / But little conscious where real greatness lies" (ibid.).

93. As Ruskin argued in *The Stones of Venice*, first published in 1853.

94. Rathbone, *The Political Value of Art*, 32, 38, 36.

95. For example, Rathbone argued against "the coarse vulgarity which has characterised some forms of modern democracy, which has impeded the civilization of America and threatens to endanger our own. I mean the vulgarity which treats culture as an enemy, and refinement as an insult" (ibid., 24).

96. Ibid., 42. "Unfortunately the Reformation in too many instances repressed rather than encouraged Art, and even succeeded in associating the idea of it with that of moral corruption—its necessary antithesis" (ibid., 24).

97. Many thanks to the editors of *Victorian Review* for permission to reprint parts of my essay "John Ruskin, Letters to James Allanson Picton; the Ruskin Society in Manchester (1880s)," *Victorian Review* 35, no. 1 (Spring 2009), 60–64.

98. Picton, *Sir James A. Picton*, 373.

99. Ibid., 374. According to curator Charles Dyall, Ruskin did eventually visit the Walker (*First Decade of the Walker Art Gallery*, 19).

100. Picton, *Sir James A. Picton*, 375. Similarly, two years later, when Picton was working on the proposed new Liverpool Cathedral (ultimately begun in 1904 from a design by Giles Gilbert Scott and completed twenty years later), he evidently asked Ruskin for his advice but received the following remonstrance: "I must reply that the only cathedrals I care for in England are her mountains, and the only facts I trust her books—that she can't

now build a cathedral if she would, and shouldn't till she has unbuilt nearly everything else on her ground" (January 13, 1886; ibid).

101. Influential collector of early Italian and German art William Roscoe had helped to found the Liverpool Royal Institution, and Roscoe's friends had bought his collection and presented it to the institution on his bankruptcy in 1816. See Ormerod, *The Liverpool Royal Institution*, 32–33; Walker Art Gallery, *The Walker Art Gallery*, 8; and Wilson, "'The Florence of the North'?," 41. Probably also around the year 1849, Picton apparently negotiated with the Liverpool Academy to display its diploma works in the Royal Institution, according to B. H. Grindley, "on the condition that they should be the nucleus of a Permanent Gallery of Art"; see Grindley, *History and Work*, 14–15. On the 1849–1850 transfer scheme, see Royal Institution Minutes of June 29 and July 2, 1850, quoted in Ormerod, *The Liverpool Royal Institution*, 43. On the successful 1892 transfer, see *Library, Museum, and Arts Committee Report on the Transfer* in City of Liverpool, *Proceedings of the Council 1892–1893*, 1631–1637. Compare this to the 1883 transfer of the Royal Manchester Institution, below.

102. See Walker Art Gallery, *Annual Report 1937–38*, 5. On Liverpool's public library movement, see Glasgow, "The Origins of the Liverpool Public Libraries."

103. The council paid £10,000 for the land behind St. George's Hall known as Shaw's Brow (now site of the Derby Museum, Brown Library, Picton Reading Room, and Walker Art Gallery). At the time it was a slum area. Brown was Liberal member of Parliament for South Lancashire and head of the firm Brown, Shipley, and Company; Picton designed many waterside warehouses for Brown's company and probably had a role in prompting Brown's offer. See *[First] Report of the Library and Museum Committee*, 8; Libraries, Museums, and Arts Committee, *Library and Museum Rate*, 4; Picton, *Notes on the Free Library and Museum*, 692–693; and Picton, *Sir James A. Picton*, 263–265. Brown eventually spent £35,000 on the grand neoclassical building designed by the town architect and surveyor John Weightman (Picton, *Sir James A. Picton*, 268).

104. *Thirteenth Annual Report of the Committee of the Free Public Library, Museum, and Gallery of Arts, of the Borough of Liverpool* (1865), 7.

105. Ibid.

106. "A Word to Art-Maniacs, by a Free Lance, I," *Liberal Review*, October 26, 1878, 5.

107. Grindley, *Exhibitions of Pictures and Municipal Management*, 5.

108. "A Word to Art-Maniacs, I," 5, and "A Word to Art-Maniacs, by a Free Lance, III," *Liberal Review*, November 9, 1878, 5.

109. "A Word to Art-Maniacs, by a Free Lance, II," *Liberal Review*, November 2, 1878, 4–5.

110. "A Word to Art-Maniacs, I," 5.

111. Reformer and general Liverpool gadfly Hugh Shimmin became sole editor of the *Porcupine* soon after its founding in 1868. On the *Porcupine*, see Simey, *Charity Rediscovered*, esp. 53–54. On Shimmin, see Walton and Wilcox, *Low Life and Moral Improvement*, esp. the introduction.

112. "Fine Arts and Photography," *Porcupine*, July 11, 1868, 150.

113. Walker Art Gallery Archives, Art and Exhibition Sub-Committee Minutes 1871–1872, WAG Box 1.

114. The exhibition attracted more than twenty-three thousand paying visitors and grossed more than £6,000, allowing the expenditure of £500 on works of art. *Nineteenth Annual Report of the Committee of the Free Public Library, Museum, and Schools*, (1871), 6.

The committee bought *Elaine*, by Mrs. Anderson, for £315; *Snowdon*, by John Finnie, for £80; and *Starry Eyes*, by J. M. Jopling, for £100. See *Statement of the Works of Art*, 3.

115. Gallery of Arts Report City of Liverpool, *Proceedings of the Council* (1873), 850–856; and Meetings of the Council of the Borough of Liverpool held on Wednesday the 6th day of August 1873 and Wednesday the 3rd day of September 1873, Libraries, Museum, and Arts Committee Minute Book, April 1872–October 1874, LCRL Archives, 352 MIN/LIB 1/9, 257 and 272.

116. Walker donated £20,000: Council Proceedings, November 10, 1873, in Libraries, Museum, and Arts Committee Minute Book, April 1872–October 1874, 301.

117. The Conservative Party's use of social and religious divisions, as well as beer and liquor, as voting incentives, ensured continued dominance less through local issues than through encouraging loyalty to pub, church, and queen. On the Conservatives' larger political strategy, see Waller, *Democracy and Sectarianism*, 18–19. On the use of liquor in elections, see Collins, *Politics and Elections*, 86–87.

118. On December 3, 1873, Picton resolved, Samuelson seconded, and the council unanimously approved the name Walker Art Gallery. City of Liverpool, *Proceedings* of the *Council* (1874), 32–33. The council allocated £1,200 for purchases; *Statement of the Works of Art*, 5.

119. See Simey, *Charity Rediscovered*.

120. Dyall, *First Decade of the Walker Art Gallery*, 17. For more on the use of the municipal institutions, see Chapter 5.

121. On the development of their siting and architecture, see *Twenty-first Annual Report of the Committee of the Free Public Library, Museum, and Gallery of Art*; Gallery of Arts Report, 855–856, and "The Proposed Fine Art Gallery," *Porcupine*, February 22, 1868, 468.

122. For example, as Eric Hobsbawm writes, "Whoever says Industrial Revolution says cotton. When we think of it we see, like the contemporary foreign visitors to England, the new and revolutionary city of Manchester" (*Industry and Empire*, 56).

123. Important works on Manchester include Kidd and Roberts, eds., *City, Class, and Culture*; Archer, ed., *Art and Architecture in Victorian Manchester*; Wolff and Seed, eds., *The Culture of Capital*; Hewitt, *The Emergence of Stability*; and Gunn, *The Public Culture*.

124. Rose, "Culture, Philanthropy, and the Manchester Middle Classes."

125. On the importance of the RMI and other voluntary institutions in the formation of middle-class identity, see Morris, *Class, Sect and Party*. For the history of the RMI, see Cleveland, *The Royal Manchester Institution, Its History from Its Origin to 1882* and *The Origin of the Royal Manchester Institute*; Macdonald, "The Royal Manchester Institution"; Seed, "'Commerce and the Liberal Arts'"; and Hewitt, *The Emergence of Stability*, 144–145, 161–162, and *passim*.

126. Seed, "'Commerce and the Liberal Arts,'" 52; Hewitt, *The Emergence of Stability*, 161.

127. Hewitt, *The Emergence of Stability*, 161.

128. Macdonald, "The Royal Manchester Institution," 30.

129. RMI Minutes of First Meeting, October 1, 1823, quoted in ibid., 31.

130. Hereditary governorships sold for 40 guineas, life governorships for 25 guineas, and annual ones for 2 guineas per year; when the society had raised £11,000 within two months, the new governors took steps to receive royal patronage. Ibid., 32; Cleveland, *The Royal Manchester Institution, Its History from Its Origin to 1882*, 6–7.

131. S. D. Cleveland notes that a site "bounded by Dickinson, Cooper and Peter Streets, part of the site where the new Reference Library is now in process of erection, however, was very seriously considered. It had several advantages, but it was finally turned down because 1) its situation was too much at the extremity of the town; 2) it was in the vicinity of several factories; and 3) as a matter of taste its proximity to St. Peter's Church might be objectionable. Perhaps the last reason is the most difficult to appreciate to-day" (*The Royal Manchester Institution, Its History from Its Origin to 1882*, 8).

132. The RMI developed relationships with other cultural bodies, renting out space from the opening of the building in 1838 and creating departments of affiliated institutions in 1853. Ibid., 16. Other sectional departments included the Manchester Academy of Fine Arts, which joined in 1859 and ended its official affiliation in 1862, although it continued to hold exhibitions and meetings in the RMI building; and the Medical Society, which joined in 1855. This role of renting out meeting space continued as the Manchester City Art Gallery.

133. The annual exhibitions benefited from gas lighting installed in 1838 and increased attendance through six-penny Saturday-evening openings beginning in 1845, which extended to every weekday evening for the last four weeks of the exhibition beginning in 1849. Ibid., 15. The permanent collection became accessible for a six-penny ticket to the public three days a week in the room formerly occupied by the defunct Choral Society, and the RMI published a catalogue to the permanent collection in 1848. On the opening of the permanent collection, see ibid., 16. See also the RMI, *Catalogue of the Permanent Gallery of the Royal Manchester Institute* (1848).

134. For an extensive study of the changing collecting habits of the industrial Victorian middle class, see Macleod, *Art and the Victorian Middle Class*. See also Roberts, "Exhibition and Review"; Waldfogel, "Narrative Painting"; and Landow, "There Began to Be a Great Talking About the Fine Arts." After the corporation acquired the collection, many of the old masters were reattributed; further research is necessary to determine what happened to these. See the first permanent catalogue published as a municipal art museum, Stanfield, *Descriptive Catalogue of the Permanent Collection of Pictures*. On the RMI collection, see Dean, "Private Patrons and Public Art Endeavors in Victorian Manchester," 21–22.

135. On Fairbairn, see Wolff and Arscott, "'Cultivated Capital,'" 23; Arscott, "Employer, Husband, Spectator," 162–165; and Macleod, *Art and the Victorian Middle Class*, 90.

136. *Free Art Gallery and Museum for Manchester*, 14–15.

137. During the height of the Cotton Famine, November 1862, the Poor Law guardians or the relief committees gave aid to fully one-half of all workers in the cotton district. Redford, *The History of Local Government in Manchester*, 266; see also Walton, *Lancashire*, 241.

138. Redford, *The History of Local Government in Manchester*, 252–267.

139. Rowley, *Fifty Years of Work Without Wages*, 32–33.

140. Also active were city librarian, journalist, and antiquarian W. E. A. Axon; lithographer George Falkner; manufacturer George Milner; and banker Thomas Read Wilkinson. These men participated in various combinations in the Manchester Art Museum (founded 1878), the Ruskin Society (founded 1879), the Ancoats Recreation Society (founded 1880), the Royal Manchester Institution (founded 1823), and the governing committee of the Manchester City Art Gallery (founded 1883). Information on occupations from the list of signatories in agreement between the Royal Manchester Institution and the City of

Manchester, dated November 16, 1881, Appendix to Special Meeting of the Governors, December 2, 1881, RMI, General Meetings of Governors. Annie Holt Dean also includes useful information about some of these men and their collecting habits in her thesis "Private Patrons and Public Art Endeavors in Victorian Manchester."

141. Letter from Morris to Horsfall, undated (ca. February 12, 1881), in MCLA, Skinner, *T. C. Horsfall*, 71. According to Michael Harrison, there are no extant versions of this correspondence ("Art and Philanthropy," 145 n55).

142. Harrison, "Art and Philanthropy," 120–121.

143. T. C. Horsfall to Councilor F. Todd, January 17, 1918, quoted in ibid., 121.

144. Rowley, *Fifty Years of Work Without Wages*, 36–37.

145. Ibid., 43.

146. Ibid., 52. See also Treuherz, "Ford Madox Brown," esp. 168–170.

147. I am basing the following synopsis largely on the work of Anthony J. Pass (*Thomas Worthington*).

148. Thomas Worthington, "On the Homes of the Poor and the Means of Improving Their Condition," *Manchester Statistical Society Transactions* (1860–1861), 92–114, quoted in Pass, *Thomas Worthington*, 106–107. Sir Michael Sadler (see the Introduction) took note of Worthington's work in his introduction to *Continuation Schools in England and Elsewhere* (1907), quoted in Pass, *Thomas Worthington*, 72.

149. See MCLA, Pooley, Letters; MCLA, RMI Sub-Committee Minutes; MCLA, RMI Council Minutes; MCLA, RMI Transfer Documents; MCLA, RMI, Rough Minutes; MCAG Archives, Art Gallery Committee Minutes; and MCAG Archives, Art Gallery Curator's Letter Book.

150. Approved Art Gallery Committee Meeting, MCAG Archives, Art Gallery Committee Minutes, vol. 1, January 22, 1885.

151. J. E. Phythian, Extract from "Reminiscences" (about his interest in Ruskin), n.d., MCLA M270/9/26/8.

152. MCLA, Phythian, Miscellaneous Correspondence, Letter from Ruskin to Phythian, January 10, 1880, MCLA M270/9/49/6.

153. Originally printed in the *Manchester Guardian*, February 27, 1877, reprinted as a separate pamphlet, *An Art Gallery for Manchester* (Manchester, 1877). Shelagh Wilson notes Horsfall's importance as the "founding figure" of the art philanthropy movement that famously included Canon Samuel Barnett's later exhibitions in Whitechapel, in London's East End ("The Highest Art," 173).

154. Ruskin, Letter 79, June 18, 1877, *Fors Clavigera*, 7:119–130.

155. Horsfall, *The Art Museum, Manchester*, 3.

156. Ruskin, Letter 79, June 18, 1877, *Fors Clavigera*, 7:124 n(a); 7:124–125 (quoting Horsfall); 7:124–125 n(c); 7:130.

157. As the first and "central" Ruskin Society, Manchester established branches in Glasgow, Liverpool, Birkenhead, Sheffield, and London (which became an independent society in 1881). Ruskin, *Works of John Ruskin*, 38:124; MCLA, Ruskin Society Scrapbook; Hilton, *The Later Years*, 269, 440.

158. Aims of the Society, Preliminary Statement of the Ruskin Society, undated, although presumably from the First General Meeting of the Society held on January 15, 1879; in MCLA, Ruskin Society Scrapbook.

159. Ibid.; Phythian, "Reminiscences."

160. On the Ancoats Recreation Society's art exhibitions, see Rowley, *Fifty Years of Work Without Wages*, 174, 197; *Catalogue of the Exhibition of Works of Art in the New Islington Public Room, Ancoats*; *Exhibition of Works of Art, Ancoats*; and *Exhibition of Industrial Art, Etc., Ancoats*. The first exhibition included engravings after William Holman Hunt and Edward Burne-Jones; works by Ford Madox Brown, including designs for the Town Hall murals and two paintings commissioned by Charles Rowley; drawings by Frederic Shields; copies of J. M. W. Turner, Jan Van Eyck, and Leonardo da Vinci; and British watercolors. See *Catalogue of the Exhibition of Works of Art in the New Islington Public Room, Ancoats*.

161. Ruskin, quoted on frontispiece of *Catalogue of the Exhibition of Works of Art*, 1880 and 1881.

162. Letter from Thomas Worthington to Council of the Royal Manchester Institution, December 2, 1879, in MCLA, RMI Transfer Documents, M183/3. In this letter, Worthington suggested changes to the internal layout of their building to create a series of seven galleries on the top floor, "so that, when there is a crowd of visitors, they may enter on one side, pass through the whole of the rooms and make their exits on the opposite side, without retracing their steps." On Worthington's Ruskinian, redbrick architecture, see Pass, *Thomas Worthington*.

163. Letter from Thos. Worthington, George Falkner, W. A. Turner, and C. J. Pooley to Chairman and Council of the Royal Manchester Institution, March 1, 1880, printed copy (six copies printed, Strictly Private and Confidential), in MCLA, RMI Transfer Documents, M183/11. Emphasis in original.

164. I summarize the transfer of the RMI to the city council from the published minutes of the City Council, City of Manchester, *Proceedings of the Council* (November to November, printed January of following year), hereafter MCP, and the manuscript RMI minutes and documents held in the MCLA. For the city council's transactions in relation to the transfer, see MCP 1880–1881, 39, 52, 543–548, 633–637, 733–736; 1881–1882, 33–38, 79–80, 106–111, 260–262; and 1882–1883, 25–26. For the RMI's transactions relating to the transfer, see MCLA, RMI Rough Minutes; MCLA, RMI Sub-Committee Minutes; MCLA, RMI Transfer Documents; MCLA, RMI Council Minutes; and MCLA, RMI, General Meeting of Governors.

165. Letter from Worthington, Falkner, Turner, and Pooley to RMI, March 1, 1880. The Manchester City Council would, for example, be able to afford Worthington's proposed changes to the RMI building.

166. Ibid.

167. This change was first made by the [City] Council Sub-Committee as to the Royal Manchester Institution at a meeting on July 1, 1881, and approved by the RMI Transfer Scheme Committee on July 15, 1881; MCLA, RMI Sub-Committee Minutes. The city council approved this agreement on the limitation of the £2,000 annual grant to twenty years at a special meeting of the [City] Council, September 7, 1881, MCP, 1880–1881, 543.

168. In preparing for the first municipally run autumn exhibition, curator William Stanfield reported to W. A. Turner, chairman of the Art Sub-Committee, that they had invited more than one thousand London "big names" to submit works. Note from Stanfield to Turner, MCAG Archives, Art Gallery Curator's Letter Book, vol. 1, June 7, 1883, 18, and August 2, 1883, 46.

169. Frederic Shields to C. J. Pooley, December 31, 1883, in MCLA, Pooley, Letters; see Chapter 3.

170. Charles Rowley, "Art Food and Art Poison, by Charles Rowley (a paper read before the Manchester Atheneum Graphic Club)," in MCLA, *Odds and Ends*, 530–556; Horsfall, "Neglected Pictures."

171. See Picton, *Sir James A. Picton*, 214–215.

CHAPTER 2

1. Collings, *Speech*, 7.

2. Snell and Ell, *Rival Jerusalems*, chap. 1, "The 1851 Census of Religious Worship."

3. A huge literature is devoted to the debate over secularization. On the one hand are those who argue that the evidence of declining religion among urban workers led to a considerable organizing effort and religious revival (for example, see Jones, *The Christian Socialist Revival*, 58). On the other hand are those who emphasize the increasing secularization of nineteenth-century society: "The mantle of moral rectitude, sanctimonious piety, and austere recreations lugubriously endured, had shrunk until it no longer fitted any but the lower middle class, their ultimate weapon of respectability in the struggle to distance themselves from the seaside-postcard vulgarity of the better-off workers, with whom they might otherwise have become confused" (Thompson, *The Rise of Respectable Society*, 260). For a good discussion of the historiography, see Green, *Religion in the Age of Decline*, esp. 1–30. See also McLeod, *European Religion in the Age of Great Cities.*

4. See, for example, Greenwood, *Museums and Art Galleries*, esp. 177–178, 200–201.

5. Green, *Religion in the Age of Decline.*

6. Recently, Diana Maltz has argued that the social movement to open museums and galleries on Sundays "was affiliated with the Aesthetic movement," part of what she calls "missionary aestheticism." For Maltz, aestheticism and the search for beauty included philanthropic and missionary aspects, such as opening art galleries in slums or the organizing efforts to beautify working-class homes. Her study is a welcome addition to the literature on ideas about beauty and industrial society at the end of the nineteenth century, and makes an important corrective to more limited definitions of aestheticism that approach the movement only from the point of view of the search for beauty and art for art's sake. However, it is important to note that the related "art for art's sake" movement could conflict explicitly with those attempts to bring beauty to the masses (as in James McNeill Whistler's "10 O'Clock" speech discussed in the introduction). Maltz, *British Aestheticism*, esp. chap. 4, "The Museum Opening Debate and the Combative Discourses of Sabbatarianism and Missionary Aestheticism."

7. "Better dwellings, therefore, for the labouring classes are suggested as a most essential aid and introduction to the labours of the Christian agent" (Mann, *Census of Great Britain*, 95).

8. Meyer wrote: "I have a number of palms for decoration and shall try to procure one or two canaries to make the surroundings as comfortable and homelike as possible. Babies will have to be given up at the door, and for them we have our crèche, where feeding-bottles, rattles and other toys will be provided, and our kind amateur nurses will set the mothers free for an hour of quiet self-culture and social intercourse. I hope

to read them selections from Tennyson and Longfellow" (Meyer, "The People's Drawing Room," *Bristol Christian Leader* [1894], 132, quoted in Kent, "The Role of Religion," 161).

9. See Kent, "The Role of Religion," esp. 165.

10. Ibid., 158.

11. Horsfall, *The Government of Manchester*, 32–33.

12. F. W. Robertson, quoted in *The Sunday Question Again*, 8.

13. Butler, *Victorian Doubt*, 2.

14. See, for example, letters to provincial galleries regarding gas lighting, Meeting of the Board of National Gallery Trustees, December 14, 1885, NGA, NG7/79/1885 and NG7/80/1885; and Letter from Mr. Whitworth Wallis assenting to the conditions on which the National Gallery Board had agreed to lend to the Birmingham Art Gallery a collection of Turner's sketches, January 24, 1891, read at board meeting, February 3, 1891, NGA, NG7/136/1891; requests from provincial galleries for loans, September–October 1892, NGA, NG7/146/1892.

15. For an excellent discussion of the complex political history of the Sunday observance movement, see Wigley, *The Rise and Fall of the Victorian Sunday*. In his dissertation ("Life, Liberty, and Leisure"), Dan Eshet argues for the profound effect of the French Revolution on evangelical attitudes toward work and leisure, using a Weberian understanding of Protestant culture and practice. Two recent works also deal with the Sunday-opening debate and Sunday observance, respectively: Maltz, *British Aestheticism and the Urban Working Classes*, and Miller, *The Peculiar Life of Sundays*.

16. Wigley, *The Rise and Fall of the Victorian Sunday*, 7–12. Much of the Victorian literature on the proper observance of the Sabbath used both early church history and detailed biblical exegesis.

17. Ibid., 12. This is in contrast to Christopher Hill's argument that the suppression of saint's days corresponded to an early capitalist impulse to maximize labor and minimize disruptions to production and distribution schedules. See Hill, *Society and Puritanism in Pre-Revolutionary England* (London, 1964), discussed in Eshet, "Life, Liberty, and Leisure," 24.

18. See Hobsbawm and Ranger, eds., *The Invention of Tradition*.

19. The Lord's Day Observance Society was known at first as the Society for Promoting the Due Observance of the Lord's Day and was founded by the evangelical Clapham Sect in 1831, under the influence of Sabbatarian Daniel Wilson (Wigley, *The Rise and Fall of the Victorian Sunday*, 34). It was primarily an Anglican movement that sought to achieve a stricter interpretation of the Sabbath through legislation restricting Sunday trade.

20. Such questions reverberated through other debates as well, notably over the 1870 Forster Education Act.

21. Wigley, *The Rise and Fall of the Victorian Sunday*, 183, positions this as class insecurity. Expanding on Wigley's work, Eshet has argued that the combined effect of the French and Industrial Revolutions, and English fears of the loss of traditional controls, led evangelicals such as Daniel Wilson to take a new, more aggressive approach to Sunday observance, which helped create the "gloomy Victorian Sunday" between the 1830s and 1850s ("Life, Liberty, and Leisure," x).

22. Wigley, *The Rise and Fall of the Victorian Sunday*, 34.

23. Ibid., 68.

24. See the Lord Chancellor's summary of previous votes in his response to the question raised by Lord Thurlow in the House of Lords, March 26, 1878, "Opening of National Museums and Galleries on Sundays. Question. Observations," in *Hansard's Parliamentary Debates, Third Series*, vol. 239, 401–402.

25. See *The National Sunday League*, title page.

26. Wigley, *The Rise and Fall of the Victorian Sunday*, 125–126.

27. An anti-Sunday-opening pamphlet argued that "this town, its government, and institutions were being rapidly given up unto the hands of the Unitarians, the members of Mr. Dawson's congregation, and others, holding what are called 'advanced opinions'" (*The Sunday Question Again*, 3–4). On Dawson and the influential ministers R. W. Dale and H. W. Crosskey, see Chapter 1.

28. Vincent, *Notable Pictures*, 3. Minutes of the Council Meeting, March 26, 1872, BCP 1871–1879, 6; and Free Libraries Committee Report, Meeting of the Council, April 15, 1873, in BCP 1871–1879, 331.

29. Davies, *By the Gains of Industry*, 17.

30. Wigley, *The Rise and Fall of the Victorian Sunday*, 131; *Annual Report of the Free Libraries Committee*, 1872, list of committee members and officers, n.p.; Collings and Green, *The Life of the Right Hon. Jesse Collings*, 93.

31. Collings and Green, *The Life of the Right Hon. Jesse Collings*, and *Annual Report of the Council of the National Sunday League* (1877), 2.

32. Ibid., 91, 119. For an example of his reforming educational ideas, see Collings, *On the State of Education in Birmingham*. Collings was a founding member and honorary secretary of the National Education League, formed in 1868, which agitated for free universal education to be administered by a national system of school inspections, with mandatory attendance, nonsectarian or secular teaching, and local rates.

33. Collings and Green, *The Life of the Right Hon. Jesse Collings*, 93–94.

34. See Minutes of the Meeting of the Council, January 2, 1872, BCP 1871–1879, 96–112, and March 26, 1872, BCP 1871–1879, 281–284; for approval, see April 2, 1872, BCP 1871–1879, 349.

35. See Collings, *Speech*. At the meeting on January 2, the Lord's Day Defence Association deputation presented fifty-four memorials against Sunday opening from religious organizations. The memorials were from members of Congregationalist, Church of England, Baptist, Methodist New Connection, Primitive Methodist, United Free Methodist, and Presbyterian churches and chapels, as well as from the Church of England Young Men's Association, the Christian British Workmen Public House, Church of England Sunday Schools, Wesleyan Sunday Schools, and Methodist Sunday Schools. See Minutes of the Meeting of the Council, January 2, 1872, BCP 1871–1879, 97. On the workers' representation in favor of Sunday opening and an additional memorial against from a Methodist congregation, see Minutes of the Council Meeting, March 26, 1872, BCP 1871–1879, 284.

36. See Collings, *Speech*, 7, and below.

37. See *The Sunday Question Again* and the speeches by Rev. Spooner and Mr. Vince in Collings, *Speech*, 4–7.

38. *The Sunday Question Again*, 8.

39. Ibid.

40. Collings, *Speech*, 4.

41. Ibid., 5.

42. *The Sunday Question Again*, 7. Intriguingly, the pamphlet's author argued for the sacredness of the day of rest precisely because of the benefits it brought: "there must have been a God to create this blessed law of Sunday rest: it is too grand, too generous an arrangement for man to have invented it" (ibid., 6).

43. Ibid., 6. The municipal library was open three nights a week, while the art museum was open only on Saturday evenings from the beginning of 1872, as there were concerns about the effects of gas lighting on the artwork. The art museum opened on two nights a week beginning in 1873 and, after the installation of electricity in the new art museum building, was open four nights beginning in July 1886. See Minutes of the Council Meeting, March 12, 1872, BCP 1871–1879, 218; April 15, 1873, BCP 1871–1879, 332; and Museum and School of Art Committee Report, January 4, 1887, 3; report is printed in BCP 1880–1890, 47. See also Woodson-Boulton, "Temples of Art," app. 3.

44. *The Sunday Question Again*, 5; Rev. Spooner in Collings, *Speech*, 4.

45. "It was curious to hear Mr. Spooner quoting just one part of the law which seemed to suit his case, and ignoring other parts which are set aside with impunity and without rebuke, by the clergy and the people generally. The command, for instance, which forbade a man to light a fire on the Sabbath, under the penalty of death, was equally a part of the law, and equally binding as the portion quoted by Mr. Spooner. I most cordially agree—every member of this Council will agree with Mr. Spooner's statement—'that no advantage, real or permanent, can accrue either to communities of individuals from any violation of God's law;' but the question is—Will any law of God be violated by carrying out the proposal of the Committee?" (Collings, *Speech*, 8).

46. "There are congregations in this town who would willingly send deputations in favour of the proposals of the Committee, but as far as my influence goes, I have discouraged that step, because the theological views are generally founded on 'authority' and not argument, and cannot therefore be debated in this assembly. Besides I have never been able to see, I cannot see now, what special connexion the question has with religious societies; and I prefer to treat it, as I hope the Council will treat it, as a matter of municipal government affecting the comfort and convenience of our fellow citizens as such" (ibid., 9).

47. Ibid.

48. Ibid., 10.

49. Ibid., 12.

50. Ibid., 11.

51. Ibid., 15.

52. Ibid.

53. Ibid., 19.

54. Minutes of the Council Meeting, May 7, 1872, BCP 1871–1879, 404.

55. See Chapter 1. I am grateful to Edward Morris for sharing with me his extensive knowledge of the history of Liverpool and the Walker Art Gallery.

56. See Waller, *Democracy and Sectarianism*.

57. Recall that the Walker Art Gallery's new building, which opened to the public in 1877, was gifted to the town by the brewer and Conservative mayor Andrew Barclay Walker.

58. Aked, in *Proceedings of the First National Council of the Evangelical Free Churches* (London, 1896), 199–200, quoted in Kent, "The Role of Religion," 159–160.

59. Waller writes, "The Conservatives pandered to Orange convictions, from sympathy and expediency. Sabbatarianism, for instance, was integral to the Orangemen's code and furnished opportunities of inter-class co-operation. . . . Anti-Sabbatarian Conservatives mostly avoided the question" (*Democracy and Sectarianism*, 92). On the growing weakness of the Conservatives during this period, see ibid., 97–121.

60. The museum of the Earl of Derby's natural history collection opened in temporary quarters in 1853, moving into the building provided by merchant William Brown in 1860. This was augmented in 1867 with goldsmith and antiquarian Joseph Mayer's gift of his collection of antiquities, some of which were later transferred to the Walker Art Gallery. See Hill, "Municipal Museums," 115–116.

61. Liverpool Museums Minutes, December 8, 1870, quoted in ibid., 129.

62. The committee wrote, "Some years since a similar attempt [at Monday evening opening] was made, but owing to the disorderly conduct of some of the visitors, it had to be abandoned. It is gratifying to find that at present the utmost order and propriety prevail, indicating an advance and improvement in popular feeling. In connection with this movement addresses or short lectures have been given illustrative of the collections by voluntary lecturers, which have been highly appreciated" (*Thirty-sixth Annual Report of the Committee of the Free Public Library, Museum, and Walker Art Gallery, of the City of Liverpool* [1889], 4). The 1889 report noted that "the visitors were of all classes and ages, working men predominating. Their demeanour was all that could be desired, and no instance has occurred of the levity and boisterousness which led to the discontinuance of the first experiments in Monday evening openings which were commenced in October, 1863, and were terminated in March, 1871" (ibid., 18).

63. See Bailey, "'Will the Real Bill Banks Please Stand Up?,'" and Hill, "'Roughs of Both Sexes.'"

64. Spier, "Among the Pictures," 195.

65. Most of those calling for Sunday opening, however, did not connect this to ending the hold of the autumn exhibition on the resources and space of the art gallery; indeed, many of the Liberal papers that most often railed against the Sabbatarian interests keeping the municipal institutions closed on Sundays also fiercely attacked any attempt to expand the gallery as unnecessary expense (physical expansion being in Liverpool, as in Manchester, the only thing that could allow the exhibitions and the permanent collection to coexist; see Chapter 5).

66. On the Congress, see Axon, "The Social Science Association and the Sunday Question." On the formation of a local Society, see the *Liberal Review*, November 8, 1879, 4, and the *Liverpool Review*, January 27, 1894, 3–4.

67. *Liberal Review*, July 12, 1879, 10.

68. Ibid., 9–10.

69. "How soon will Liverpool tread in the footsteps of Manchester? How long will it be before the many Liberal and prominent citizens who are well known to agree with the action of the Manchester Town Council and the authorities of the Royal Institution make up their minds to display the courage of their opinions[?]" (*Liberal Review*, November 8, 1879, 4). See also *Liverpool Review* (which incorporated the *Liberal Review* in

1883), Saturday, September 15, 1883, 4. See also the *Liberal Review*, February 26, 1881, 3–4, and the *Liverpool Review*, September 19, 1885, 10.

70. See *Annual Report of the Council of the National Sunday League* (1885), 5; *Liverpool Review*, September 19, 1885, 10; and City of Liverpool, *Sunday Opening of Libraries, Museums, and Art Galleries*, 1285–1295. In the report presented to the town council, the librarian summarized the findings: "The total number of Institutions sent to was 142, and 122 have returned the Circular with more or less of the questions answered. The Circulars herewith submitted, have been divided as follows: 17 from Institutions now open on Sunday. 4 from Institutions which have been open, but are now Closed. 22 from Institutions Closed, but in connection with which there have been local efforts made to open them. 79 from Institutions Closed, and no efforts made to open them" (1287).

71. Those galleries that were open on Sundays hardly would have been inspiring to the Conservative council in Liverpool: Radical Birmingham and Manchester, Catholic Dublin, Liberal Stoke-upon-Trent and Stockport, and old London institutions such as Kew, Hampton Court, and Greenwich.

72. Wigley, *The Rise and Fall of the Victorian Sunday*, 146. Following Jesse Collings's line of argument, the Sunday Society campaigned to show that the Sabbatarian stance of the Trades Union Council was unrepresentative of working people in general. Ibid., 137–138. The head of the Trades Union Council at this time was Henry Broadhurst, whom Wigley characterizes as a "social Sabbatarian" and one of only two working-class men in the House of Commons.

73. On the 1890 election, see Waller, *Democracy and Sectarianism*, 112–119; on John Lea, 113. On the Conservatives' control, Waller writes: "This might not have been admirable but it was legal. Although in the County Councils aldermen [senior councilors] were elected by councillors alone, in borough councils, until the Municipal Corporations Amendment Act, 1910, aldermen were elected by councillors and non-retiring aldermen. The Conservative majority in the Liverpool Council was preserved by this device until 1892, when eight aldermen retired" (114).

74. Ibid., 92.

75. Ibid., 135, 137.

76. *Thirty-ninth Annual Report of the Committee of the Free Public Library, Museum, and Walker Art Gallery, of the City of Liverpool, for the Year Ending 31st December, 1891* (1892), 4.

77. Ibid., 26. This and other elements of the report were reported in the *Architect*, April 1, 1892, 213.

78. On November 14, 1892, the subcommittee "read a circular . . . from the Bishop of Coventry, Secretary of Committee of Bishops and Clergy appointed by Convocation of Canterbury, requesting answers to questions, referring to Sunday opening of the Gallery to which the Curator was instructed to reply" (WAG Archives, Art and Exhibition Minutes, 1892–1894 WAG Box 2). Likewise—this time requesting information for the opposing side—the meeting of the same subcommittee the following month recorded receipt of a request for information from Mark H. Judge, honorary secretary of the Sunday Society, wanting to *disprove* claims of "failure" made by the Lord's Day Observance Society about the Walker Art Gallery's opening on Sundays. Minutes of the Meeting of the Arts and Exhibitions Sub-Committee, December 12, 1892, ibid. I have found no record of the replies that the subcommittee sent.

79. For the decision to close during the summer months, see Minutes of the Arts and Exhibitions Sub-Committee, May 23, 1892; May 15, 1893; and April 23, 1894, ibid. For "cleaning and other purposes," see, for example, *Fortieth Annual Report of the Committee of the Free Public Library, Museum, and Walker Art Gallery* (1893), 26, and *Forty-first Annual Report of the Committee of the Free Public Library, Museum, and Walker Art Gallery* (1894), 26.

80. See MCLA, Skinner, *T. C. Horsfall*, 60.

81. Minutes of a Special Meeting of the Council, September 4, 1878, MCP 1877–1878, 354. In 1873, according to the city council minutes, a "memorial was presented from inhabitants of the city requesting that the Reference Library and Reading-rooms of the several Free Libraries should be opened on Sundays, from two o'clock to eight o'clock p.m." (Meeting of the City Council, February 19, 1873, MCP 1874, 148). However, "numerous memorials were presented from the members of religious denominations, and from other bodies within the city, against the proposal," and the motion was defeated by an amendment that kept them closed, conceding only that "the Free Libraries Committee be requested to ascertain what additional time can be given on week-day evenings for the accommodation of readers" (April 2, 1873, ibid., 173).

82. In Liverpool, the *Liberal Review* reported that on Tuesday, November 4, just over two weeks after the first Sunday opening at the RMI, the Manchester Presbytery—claiming to represent eighty congregations—held a meeting against the RMI's action. The *Review* quoted the resolution moved by Rev. W. McCaw and passed at the meeting: "The Presbytery having had their attention called to the fact that since their last meeting the Council of the Royal Institution in this city have opened their exhibition of paintings and statuary to the public on Sabbath afternoons resolve to express their deep regret at what they cannot but regard as a grave official violation—however unintentional on the Council's part—of the divine sanctity of the Lord's Day. Following, moreover, within a few months, as it does, the act of the City Council in throwing open the Free Libraries on the Sabbath, this Presbytery views it with all the greater apprehension as another indication of the tendency of the times to pervert the Sabbath from a day of sacredness and rest to one of recreation and work eventually" (November 8, 1879, 8).

83. RMI, *Exhibition of the Works of Modern Artists, 1880*, 5.

84. Skinner, *T. C. Horsfall*, 60. He added: "Till they do this, they have themselves to blame for much of the brutality which has shown itself in Lancashire towns."

85. Minutes of Meeting of the Council, August 7, 1878, MCP 1877–1878, 301.

86. Minutes of a Special Meeting of the Council, July 3, 1873, MCP 1872–1873, 248.

87. Jane Axon, "Sunday at the Royal Manchester Institution," *Sunday Review* 4, no. 1 (October 1879), 14.

88. Letter from Thos. Worthington, George Falkner, W. A. Turner, C. J. Pooley to Chairman and Council of the Royal Manchester Institution, March 1, 1880, printed copy (six copies; printed Strictly Private and Confidential), in MCLA, RMI Transfer Documents.

89. Axon, "Sunday at the Royal Manchester Institution," 14, 15.

90. Ibid., 15. For another supportive account of the initial opening, see Peter Cameron, "Among the Pictures on Sunday," *Momus* 4, no. 86 (October 23, 1879), 62.

91. Hill, *Would the Sunday Opening of Museums, Libraries and Places of Amusement,*

Increase or Diminish Sunday Drinking?, 4. He explained that opening any cultural institution would increase the demand for refreshment: "Whatever the recreation or amusement may be—whether it be a Sunday band, a museum, a picture gallery, or a public library—if persons are attracted from a distance, or incur any mental or physical fatigue in realising the amusement, so surely they will demand the opening of and frequent the public-house for drink to sustain them" (5).

92. Ibid., 8. Even more damning, he adds, "There does not exist any national widespread passion for the study of works of art" (9).

93. *Daily News*, February 1, 1879, quoted in ibid., 10.

94. Snell, *Sermon Preached*, 10. See also Snell, *Second Sermon Preached*.

95. Snell, *Sermon Preached*, 10–11. Emphasis in original.

96. Ibid., 12.

97. Ibid., 14. Emphasis in original.

98. The amendment lost three votes to seven; the motion to open on Sundays lost on the deciding vote of the chairman. Minutes of the Monthly Meeting of the Council, Wednesday, October 6, 1880, MCLA, RMI Rough Minutes.

99. Three thousand tickets were distributed between noon and 2 p.m. on the Thursday, Friday, and Saturday before each Sunday the institution opened to the public. On the first Sunday 1,294 people attended in the three hours the gallery was open; on the second Sunday, 2,550 people attended; the committee increased the number of tickets to 4,000 for subsequent days. See Minutes of Meetings of the Sunday Exhibition Committee, Sunday, November 7th, and Tuesday, November 14th, MCLA, RMI Rough Minutes.

100. The next year the Sunday opening also had to be proposed and approved; see Monthly Meeting of Council, Wednesday, September 7, 1881; Wednesday, October 5, 1881, MCLA, RMI Rough Minutes. There is no record of the 1882 decision, taking place as the RMI handed itself over to the Corporation of Manchester.

101. See *Annual Report of the Representatives of the Royal Institution on the Art Gallery Committee of the Corporation of Manchester*, September 23, 1889. See also mention of the new policy in Art Gallery Committee Minutes, December 24, 1891, in a letter from a deputation from the RMI, MCAG Archives, Art Gallery Committee Minutes, vol. 3, November 24, 1891, 6: "The permanent collection, which has become by purchase and gifts very considerable and valuable, now occupies the larger portion of the gallery space, and the Art Gallery Committee have recently wisely determined that the works shall be permanently hung, and open to the public free of charge."

102. "Saturdays after 11/1/84 Autumn Exhibition tickets: 10am–2pm 6d.; 2–9pm 3d." MCAG Archives, Art Gallery Committee Minutes, vol. 1, October 20, 1884, 254. The evening's opening decision is recorded in Minutes of Council Meeting, October 6, 1886, MCP 1885–1886, 839.

103. Resolution of a Special Meeting of Governors held in the Town Hall, Manchester, on Wednesday, October 31, 1894, MCAG Archives, Art Gallery Committee Minutes, vol. 3, November 29, 1894, 220.

104. See MCLA, MCAG, House Sub-Committee Minutes, September 5, 1895.

105. See City of Manchester, *Index of Minutes of the Council*.

106. Horsfall, *The Government of Manchester*, 32. Horsfall did not imagine this oc-

curring without protest: "A great outcry at once arose in the town; it was said that the Town Council proposed measures which would desecrate Sunday. A large deputation, chiefly composed of clergymen and ministers of many denominations, sought an interview with the Mayor to protest against the carrying out of his proposals for the opening on Sundays of what they called 'places of mere amusement'" (ibid.).

107. Ibid., 3.

CHAPTER 3

1. In this chapter I concentrate on acquisitions made through purchase, rather than gifts. Bestowing gifts of single works or whole collections was an important way for wealthy individuals to influence the development of local museums, and in fact many local worthies began to collect with a view to making a gift to their municipal art museum. Like purchases, gifts carried givers' assumptions about the museums' functions and relationship to their cities. However, here I am most interested in those works acquired through the museum committees' deliberate decisions; when available, information about price and method of purchase gives a good indication of the committees' priorities and relative values. The research that informs this chapter is summarized in Woodson-Boulton, "Temples of Art," apps. 1.1–3 and 2.

2. Wallis, "The Museum and Art Gallery," 477–478.

3. Dowling, *The Vulgarization of Art*, and Woodson-Boulton, "A Window onto Nature."

4. Williams, *The Country and the City* and *Culture and Society*; Barringer, *Men at Work*.

5. Sadler, *Pictures in a Great City*, 5. As noted in the introduction, Sadler was an internationally respected expert on the sociology of education. Here, he nearly echoes, in all seriousness, Wilde's famous parody "The Decay of Lying" (1909), in which he argued that nature imitates art.

6. Ibid., 6.

7. Thomas, *Man and the Natural World*; Schivelbusch, *The Railway Journey*; and Barringer, *Men at Work*.

8. See Macleod, *Art and the Victorian Middle Class*, on the relationship between Victorian art and the formation of middle-class identity.

9. Contemporaries included a wide variety of specimens under the rubric of "applied art," from industrial products to both functional and purely decorative handmade objects, including contemporary and historical examples from British colonies and non-Western areas, such as India, China, and Japan, but also from the British Isles and the Continent. Following this multivalent usage, I will use the word "applied" to include all of these possibilities.

10. A great deal of Greenwood's correspondence survives in the Manchester Central Library Archives; he seems to have sent copies of his books to many influential cultural and political leaders, including Ruskin, Andrew Carnegie, and many prominent Liberals, including William Gladstone. See Greenwood, MCLA holdings.

11. Greenwood, *Museums and Art Galleries*, 5.

12. Ibid., 175–176.

13. Ibid., 174.

14. John Ruskin, "A Museum or Picture Gallery: Its Functions and Its Formation," in Ruskin, *Works of John Ruskin*, 34:259. These letters were first published in *Art Journal*,

June and August 1880, and republished in *On the Old Road*, 1885. See the editors' informative bibliographical note in the cited volume, 246.

15. See Hewison, Warrell, and Wildman, *Ruskin, Turner and the Pre-Raphaelites*, 11–13.

16. Ruskin, "A Museum or Picture Gallery," in *Works of John Ruskin*, 34:259.

17. Ruskin, *Fors Clavigera*, 5:310, quoted in Howard Swan, *Preliminary Catalogue*, 6–7.

18. Ruskin, "A Museum or Picture Gallery," in *Works of John Ruskin*, 34:260.

19. Ruskin notes that he made this choice in *Fors Clavigera* as "one of the four pictures I chose for permanent teaching" (ibid.).

20. Ibid., 259–260.

21. Ibid., 260.

22. "Mr. Ruskin on Contemporary Art," *Co-operative News*, February 7, 1880, in MCLA, Ruskin Society Scrapbook.

23. They also turned down a Titian (a *Danaë*) because it was "too nude." MCAG Archives, Art Gallery Committee Minutes, vol. 3, June 30, 1892, 88; see my discussion of this episode in Woodson-Boulton, "A Window onto Nature," 153–154.

24. The *Weekly Post* revealed Osler's identity soon after his death in 1877. "The Public Picture Gallery Fund," *Weekly Post*, January 20, 1877, collected in BCLLS, Osborne, *Newspaper Cuttings*. The fund's name indicated that it was for a "public picture gallery," not a "public" fund. The first gift of the fund to the gallery was *A Condottiere* by Frederick Leighton (member and later president of the Royal Academy), on February 12, 1873, which became one of the celebrated pictures of the collection. The purchase was aided by the Royal Birmingham Society of Artists and private subscription. Minutes of the Council Meeting, March 26, 1872, BCP 1871–1879, 6; and Report of the Free Libraries Committee, Meeting of the Council, April 15, 1873, in BCP 1871–1879, 331. For a summary of gifts to the Birmingham Museum and Art Gallery from the Public Picture Gallery Fund, see Vincent, *Notable Pictures*.

25. For a detailed history of these committees and their memberships, see Woodson-Boulton, "Temples of Art," chap. 1, esp. 81–86, 88–93.

26. Report of interview with Mr. Whitworth Wallis at the Birmingham Museum and Art Gallery, April 25, 1894, reported at a meeting of the Special Sub-Committee re: Art Directorship, MCAG Archives, Art Gallery Committee Minutes, vol. 3, May 31, 1894, 194–195.

27. Ibid., 195.

28. Information on purchases is from Woodson-Boulton, "Temples of Art," app. 1.2, 423–431; n423 lists the multiple sources that went into creating that database.

29. *Cooper & Co.'s Penny Guide*, 2. Emphasis in original.

30. Ibid., 12.

31. Reports on Purchases to the Council in 1882 and 1883 show the Art Gallery Purchase Committee's emphasis on applied art from an early stage of its formation. Report of the Art Gallery Purchase Committee, Presented at the Monthly Meeting of the Council, November 9, 1882, and Report of the Art Gallery Purchase Committee for Presentation at the Monthly Meeting of the Council on December 11, 1883, BCP 1880–1890.

32. Wallis, *Borough of Birmingham Art Gallery Purchase Committee*. In 1911, after the Art Gallery Purchase Committee had spent its funds and ceased to exist, Wallis could report that "the object, or groups of objects, catalogued have increased from 11,124 in 1885, to 20,900 at the present time—an addition of nearly 10,000. They include examples of

jewellery, gold and silver work, Limoges enamels, ivory carvings, glass, decorative iron work, steel, carving in wood and marble, textiles, lace, majolica, porcelain, and earthenware" (Wallis, "The Museum and Art Gallery," 492–494).

33. Wallis, "The Museum and Art Gallery," 486.

34. *Cooper & Co.'s Penny Guide*, 12.

35. Wallis, "The Museum and Art Gallery," 495.

36. Dyall, *Catalogue of the Walker Art Gallery* (1900), 6.

37. Dyall, *First Decade of the Walker Art Gallery*, 5.

38. Ibid.

39. Figures are from Woodson-Boulton, "Temples of Art," 261, Table 4.1. I originally derived these data from the accounts published annually in the Proceedings of the Liverpool Council, 1871–1914.

40. Rathbone, *The Mission of the Undraped Figure in Art*.

41. For Rathbone's connections between Puritanism and iconoclasm in English culture, see Rathbone, *The Political Value of Art*, 24, 32, *passim*. For his Orientalist argument, see Rathbone, *The Mission of the Undraped Figure in Art*, 3–4. Alison Smith helpfully provides context by placing Rathbone's defense within the debates over the repeal of the Contagious Diseases Acts—the need to view women as essentially pure—and fears over conflict with the Ottomans after the Bulgarian Massacres of 1876. See Smith, *The Victorian Nude*, 207–208.

42. Rathbone, *The Mission of the Undraped Figure in Art*, 7. Rathbone's question is, of course, still relevant today in public arts institutions.

43. Ibid.

44. Walker Art Gallery, *Catalogue of the Museum of Casts* (1887).

45. Ibid., iii.

46. Ibid.

47. See Hill, *Culture and Class*, 245–246.

48. Frederic Shields to C. J. Pooley, December 31, 1883, MCLA, Pooley, Letters to C. J. Pooley.

49. Charles Rowley, "Art Food and Art Poison, A Paper Read Before the Manchester Athenaeum Graphic Club," in MCLA, *Odds and Ends* 35 (Easter 1889), 530–556; 546–547.

50. Ibid., 536, 542, 539–540, 549.

51. Ibid., 555. Note the echo of Morris's ideal of work as providing "joy to the producer and the user." See, for example, Morris, *Labour and Pleasure*.

52. Horsfall, *A Description of the Work of the Manchester Art Museum* (1895), 1. On Horsfall's art and reform projects, see Chapter 1.

53. Rowley, "Art Food and Art Poison," 547, in MCLA, *Odds and Ends*.

54. See Arnold, *The Possibilities for an Art Gallery in Manchester*; Manchester City Art Gallery, *Report of the Art Gallery Committee Visit*; and Taylor, *Municipal Art Galleries and Art Museums* (discussed in Chapter 5).

55. See Woodson-Boulton, "Temples of Art," app. 1.3, 433.

56. See MCAG Archives, Art Gallery Committee Minutes, vols. 1–3.

57. Sadler, *Pictures in a Great City*, 6.

58. Arnold, *The Possibilities for an Art Gallery in Manchester*, 7–8. Arnold includes (page 9) an "unintentionally droll" guide to the historical collections at Chetham College,

Manchester, published in the *Manchester City News*, November 13, 1886, as an example of the "first stage," of which (sadly) space allows me to quote only a few lines:

That's the Head of a Wild Albatross.

That Gun was taken from the dead body of a Frenchman at the Battle of Waterloo, in the year 1815.

That is part of Oliver Cromwell's Stone Tankard.

Those two are Indian Nuts.

That is the Skeleton of a Male Child.

That is the Hand of an Egyptian Mummy.

That Boot once belonged to Queen Elizabeth.

And so on.

CHAPTER 4

1. Parkes, *The Pre-Raphaelite Movement*, 37.

2. See, for instance, South Kensington Museum, *A Guide to the Collections*, 20–21, and Cook, *A Popular Handbook to the National Gallery*, 390–392.

3. Richmond, *Leighton, Millais and William Morris*, 17. Richmond himself noted that "the subject of a picture may be delightful; it has nothing to do with its merits," a position very different from the general interpretation of art at the city art museums (ibid.).

4. Landow, "There Began to Be."

5. Cust, ed., *Catalogue of the National Gallery of British Art* (1899), 10.

6. See Ruskin, *Academy Notes, 1856*, quoted in Stanfield, *Catalogue of the Permanent Collection* (1895), 100.

7. Burne-Jones was elected an associate of the Royal Academy in 1885 but resigned in 1893. Wallis, *Museum and Art Gallery. Catalogue* (1897), 15.

8. Cook, *A Popular Handbook to the National Gallery*, 387–388. Cook added a footnote on the term "English": "The term 'English School' seems permissible in the National Gallery, inasmuch as there are also national galleries for Scotland and for Ireland. Moreover, the number of Scottish pictures here is inconsiderable, and though several of the painters represented were Irishmen, they all settled early in life in London" (387 n2).

9. South Kensington Museum, *A Guide to the Collections*, 21, 19–20.

10. Parkes, *The Pre-Raphaelite Movement*, 37, 52.

11. Morris, *Address on the Collection of Paintings*, 8.

12. Ibid. Burne-Jones put beauty above all; as he wrote about the nativity (a subject that he painted for the Birmingham Museum and Art Gallery in 1887 as *The Star of Bethlehem*—see below), "It is too beautiful not to be true"—a notably aesthetic justification for the sacred and his particular answer to the debate, that is, that beauty itself implies truth (a rather Platonic intervention). Georgiana Burne-Jones, *Memorials of Edward Burne-Jones*, vol. 2, quoted in Birmingham Museum and Art Gallery, *Illustrated Catalogue* (1912), 16.

13. Morris, *Address on the Collection of Paintings*, 8.

14. Ibid., 6.

15. Monkhouse, *British Contemporary Artists*, 53–54.

16. Chesneau, *The English School of Painting*, x.

17. Ibid., 180.

18. Ibid., 204.

19. Ford, *Rossetti*, 2; see also Parkes, *The Pre-Raphaelite Movement*, 40, and South Kensington Museum, *A Guide to the Collections*, 25–26.

20. Quoted in Parkes, *The Pre-Raphaelite Movement*, 40.

21. Richmond, *Leighton, Millais and William Morris*, 27.

22. Spielmann, *Millais and His Works*, 13.

23. See, for example, Landow, "There Began to Be"; Macleod, *Art and the Victorian Middle Class*; and Hoock, "'Struggling Against a Vulgar Prejudice.'"

24. Horsfall, "Neglected Pictures," 236.

25. Axon, *Art in Lancashire*, 175–183.

26. See, for example, Phythian, MCLA, "How to Enjoy Pictures."

27. For example, Wallis gave a lantern-illustrated lecture titled "Art of Pompeii" in the Liverpool municipal lectures series in 1894; see *Forty-first Annual Report of the Committee of the Free Public Library, Museum, and Walker Art Gallery, of the City of Liverpool, for the Year Ending 31st December, 1893* (1894), 18. The RMI also hired Wallis to give a series of three lectures on Pompeii and a magic lantern–illustrated lecture on William Holman Hunt, as reported in the Meeting of the RMI Council, Wednesday, December 7, 1892, and Wednesday, November 27, 1895, MCLA, RMI, Council Minutes.

28. See, for example, *Thirty-seventh Annual Report of the Committee of the Free Public Library, Museum, and Walker Art Gallery, of the City of Liverpool, for the Year Ending 31st December, 1889* (1890), 13. Dyall gave a lecture titled "Pictorial Art: Its Value as a Record of Men and Manners," illustrated by oxyhydrogen light (a magic lantern).

29. See, for instance, Morris, *Address on the Collection of Paintings*. (This was published by the museum for one penny.) See also Caine, *Disquisition*.

30. I have found no records of sales of the Manchester City Art Gallery's permanent collection catalogue, but estimated returns from sales are close to those reported from Liverpool (roughly £30 annually from sales of the three-penny catalogue, meaning an approximate annual sales figure of 2,400 catalogues). "Catalogues Sold, £30." Estimates 1889–1890, MCAG Archives, Art Gallery Committee Minutes, vol. 2, January 23, 1889, 154. The average annual sales of all catalogues, 1887–1913, in Birmingham hovered at around 13,700; in Manchester the number of autumn exhibition catalogues sold (six-penny and three-penny versions), 1884–1892, averaged 12,200, in addition to the 2,400 permanent collection catalogues noted above; in Liverpool the number of six-penny autumn exhibition catalogues sold averaged a remarkable 19,250, while sales of all other catalogues (including the three-penny permanent collection catalogue and those for temporary exhibitions) averaged 1,300. The highest reported figures for the three museums were 41,358 at Birmingham for all of its catalogues in 1892; 26,610 at Liverpool for all of its catalogues in 1884; and 26,240 at Manchester in 1890. See Woodson-Boulton, "Temples of Art," Table 6.3, 375.

31. Compared to attendance figures in the years of highest sales, only 5 percent of attendees in Birmingham and Liverpool bought catalogues (although numbers at individual exhibitions might have been higher), while in Manchester 11 percent of attendees did (23 percent bought autumn exhibition catalogues, 6 percent bought three-penny catalogues to the First Arts and Crafts Exhibition, and only 2 percent bought catalogues to the permanent collection).

32. Indeed, all but one of the works with descriptions in the catalogues of 1897 and

1899 had been purchased by the Art Gallery Purchase Committee. See Chapter 3 on the various funds available for acquisitions at the Birmingham Museum and Art Gallery.

33. Report of interview with Mr. Whitworth Wallis at the Birmingham Museum and Art Gallery, April 25, 1894, reported at a meeting of the Special Sub-Committee re: Art Directorship, MCAG Archives, Art Gallery Committee Minutes, vol. 3, May 31, 1894, 194–195.

34. See Birmingham Museum and Art Gallery, *Catalogue (with Notes)* (1888); Wallis and Chamberlain, *Illustrated Catalogue (with Descriptive Notes)* (1899); and Birmingham Museum and Art Gallery, *Catalogue (with Descriptive Notes) of the Permanent Collection* (1901).

35. In later one-penny editions (e.g., 1897 and 1900), a note instructed readers to see the sixpence *Illustrated Catalogue of the Permanent Collection of Paintings* "for fuller descriptive notes of the Pictures and Memoirs of the Artists." See Wallis, *Museum and Art Gallery. Catalogue* (1897), 5; and Wallis, *Museum and Art Gallery. Catalogue* (1900), 4. In the first, 1886 penny edition of the handbook, curator Wallis stressed what could be learned in terms of design and craft from the industrial art objects on display, describing the Italian gallery as "a room full of objects which should be of the greatest interest to the workers in nearly all branches of Birmingham trade" (*Cooper and Co.'s Penny Guide*, 5). At the same time, he noted that "we speak to masters (if they will buy the penny guide), as well as men, for it is their fault more than the men's that modern work is as ugly and uninteresting as it is" (ibid., 10).

36. His recent biographers refer to him as the "most significant figure in English landscape painting"; see Johnson and McConkey, *Alfred East*. On East's trip to Japan, see Fine Art Society, *The Fine Art Society Story*, 32.

37. Wallis, *Museum and Art Gallery. Catalogue* (1897).

38. On ekphrasis, see, for example, Liz James's discussion of this mode of engagement with art in the Byzantine context in "Senses and Sensibility in Byzantium." I am grateful to Timothy Barringer for this reference.

39. Wallis and Chamberlain, *Illustrated Catalogue* (1899), 49.

40. The watercolor is 101⅛ × 152 inches.

41. Bell, *Sir Edward Burne-Jones*, 80–82. Bell argued against those who called Burne-Jones a "pessimist," an "essentially modern" painter who yet avoided painting anything real, and against those who criticized his recognizable style of idealized figures.

42. Ibid., 83. For Bell, Burne-Jones combined imagination and observation to accomplish the goal of painting; as he approvingly quoted painter and critic E. J. Poynter, "the true object of art is to create a world, not to imitate what is constantly before our eyes" (79).

43. Chesneau, *The English School of Painting*, 235.

44. Wildman and Christian, *Edward Burne-Jones*, 313. Wildman explains this in current art historical terms: "Perhaps no other Victorian artist was so vividly aware that he was engaged in the business of creating pictorial fictions. . . . Increasingly he sought to forge a new pictorial language in accordance with an inner vision, to cut loose from the trammels of representation in a way that hovers on the brink of modernism" (ibid.).

45. Ibid. Henry James admired this quality in Burne-Jones's works at the 1878 Grosvenor Gallery exhibition; he wrote that they had "the great and rare merit that they are *pictures* . . . conceptions, representations. . . . No English painter of our day has a tithe of his 'distinction'" (James, *The Painter's Eye: Notes and Essays on the Pictorial Arts*, ed. John

Sweeney [London, 1956], 162–164, quoted in Wildman and Christian, *Edward Burne-Jones*, 214). However, James later criticized this "artificial[ity]" in familiar terms: "The things he does in these [studio] conditions have exceeding beauty—but they seem to me to grow colder and colder—pictured abstractions, less and less observed" (letter to Charles Eliot Norton, n.d., quoted in Wildman and Christian, *Edward Burne-Jones*, 313).

46. For an excellent recent discussion of this that challenges the received idea of Burne-Jones as a "dreamer" whose works are primarily escapist, see Rager, "'Smite This Sleeping World Awake.'" I am grateful to Timothy Barringer for this reference.

47. Ady, *The Life and Work of Sir Edward Burne-Jones*, 1–2.

48. Ibid., 2.

49. Morris, *Address on the Collection of Paintings*, 11.

50. Wildman and Christian, *Edward Burne-Jones*, 317. Wildman wonders, but does not answer, whether this is "primarily escapism" or whether "the modern psyche . . . responds to an art of nervous irritability," which reflects "a troubled and transitional age" (319–320).

51. Rager, "'Smite This Sleeping World Awake,'" 441. Rager also notes what we will recognize as the art-reforming nature of this project: Burne-Jones stipulated that the *Briar Rose* paintings had to be shown at the Whitechapel exhibitions in London before going to their final purchaser, and in general she points out that he "sought primal themes that could speak to any audience, from the working classes to the privileged classes, from the urban poor to the rural peasant, from youth to old age" (444). Rager convincingly reconnects the series to the poem William Morris wrote for it (which was published in the exhibition catalogues) and to Morris's use of dreams in *A Dream of John Ball* (1886) and *News from Nowhere* (1890) as a mode to galvanize readers into action. Hence we can understand Burne-Jones's work as closely connected to Morris's project of using art and beauty to, as Morris wrote to Horsfall, "Educate your workmen into general discontent!" (see Chapter 1).

52. Bell, *Sir Edward Burne-Jones*, 94.

53. Ady, *The Life and Work of Sir Edward Burne-Jones*, 25.

54. Blackburn, *New Gallery 1891*, 10.

55. *Art Journal*, June 1891, 185, quoted in Wildman and Christian, *Edward Burne-Jones*, 295.

56. Wildman and Christian, *Edward Burne-Jones*, 293–294.

57. In another context Wildman also discusses the particular "fascination" that drapery held for Burne-Jones, "its inert substance offering the perfect vehicle of those linear rhythms that lay at the heart of his tendency to abstraction" (ibid., 315).

58. Wallis, *Museum and Art Gallery. Catalogue* (1897), 15–16; and Wallis and Chamberlain, *Illustrated Catalogue* (1899), 20–21. Intriguingly, in both catalogues this entire narrative section is in quotation marks, but it is not attributed, and I have not been able to locate the source for this description.

59. Ibid.

60. The foundation stone of the Birmingham Museum and Art Gallery reads, "By the Gains of Industry We Promote Art."

61. See, for example, his discussion of Stanhope Forbes's *A Street in Brittany*: "One of the most pleasing features of continental towns is the contented and happy appearance of the humbler classes; simple in their living, dressed in neat but inexpensive clothing, scrupulously clean, industrious, and sober, they show that real happiness is not con-

fined to the powerful and wealthy" (Dyall, *Descriptive Catalogue* [1883], 52). On Alfred Stocks's *Motherless*, Dyall wrote that it was "a touching picture of sorrowing affection for the departed wife,—showing, with undoubted truth and power, that the finer feelings of human nature are shared by all classes" (Dyall, *Descriptive Catalogue* [1896], 57). The same descriptions also appeared in Dyall, *Descriptive Catalogue* (1901).

62. Rathbone, *Impressionism in Art*, 6, 7. Rathbone assumes an audience that is at least fairly hostile to impressionism, whose "minds" need "train[ing] to understand these things," and presents the analogy that even to the drinker of "the best port wine," it will "have a very disagreeable taste" if he thinks it is "red hock" (ibid.).

63. Ibid., 8–9.

64. Asleson, *Albert Moore*, 188. Moore's only other purchaser (who offered £1,000) backed out because he feared the painting's seminude women might offend his hotel patrons, so the artist was forced to take the Walker's very low price (which nonetheless offered the prestige of the work being in a public collection) (189).

65. In his 1881 book *A Short History of the British School of Painting*, George Shepherd included Moore as a "painter of incident" and listed a few titles of his works to that date, clearly not deeming him important enough for even a paragraph of his own (150). George Moore (no relation) wrote in an 1892 review, "No difference exists even in Academic circles as to the merits of Mr. Albert Moore's work. Many Academicians will freely acknowledge that his non-election is a very grave scandal; they will tell you that they have done everything to get him elected, and have given up the task in despair. . . . The two greatest artists living in England [Moore and Whistler] will never be elected Academicians; and artistic England is asked to acquiesce in this grave scandal" ("The Royal Academy," *Fortnightly Review*, 57 [June 1892]: 828–839, quoted in Asleson, *Albert Moore*, 188). See also Asleson, "Nature and Abstraction," 115.

66. Robyn Asleson notes that Moore's use of Ruskin's ideas was always "discriminating and specific": "The vital narratives and ethical analogies that the critic associated with nature's formal properties were obviously antithetical to his [Moore's] mature views, but even in his youth he appears to have rejected them" ("Nature and Abstraction," 118).

67. Prettejohn, *Art for Art's Sake*, 127. In her chapter on Moore, Prettejohn explores in detail his use of grid patterns, depiction of "flesh," and deliberate anachronisms, finding his work to be "a remarkably early example of a systematic use of abstract geometry to supersede mimesis as the basic aesthetic principle" (ibid.). I am grateful to Timothy Barringer for this reference.

68. For example, critic Sidney Colvin wrote in 1870 of Moore's "power of arranging and combining the lines of the human form into a visible rhythm and symmetry not less delightful than the audible rhythm and symmetry of music" ("English Painters of the Present Day. II.—Albert Moore," *Portfolio* 1 [1870], 6, in ibid., 126). More recent critics have agreed; a 1978 catalogue describes Moore as carrying Leighton's classicism "even further," as he "replaced even the most blandly traditional subjects with subjectless subjects bearing frivolous or misleading titles" (Allen Staley, "Post-Pre-Raphaelitism," in Minneapolis Art Institute, *Victorian High Renaissance*, 25). In her 1999 interpretation, Asleson characterized Moore's work as a "lifelong enquiry into the abstract formal properties of beauty" ("Nature and Abstraction," 121). More recently, Prettejohn has argued that "a progressive abandonment of narrative or expressive content" in Moore's works went "hand-in-hand with increasing

systematization of a compositional procedure based on the abstract geometry of the grid" (*Art for Art's Sake*, 104). Further, she connects Moore's grids to later examples of modernist abstraction: "While [Moore's paintings] are fully representational in one sense, in another they are fully abstract, and on much the same terms as those of the great abstractionists of the early twentieth century. . . . The pictures' value does not lie in the female figures they represent, nor even in the accuracy or beauty of the representation, but rather in the abstract formal harmonies of the paintings themselves, considered for their own sake alone" (126).

69. The inclusion of even seminude figures shows the influence of Rathbone, then chair of the Library, Museum, and Arts Committee, who had defended his inclusion of Alma-Tadema's *The Sculptor's Model* back in 1878 and attempted to put nude sculpture on St. George's Hall in the center of the city. See Chapter 3 and Rathbone, *The Mission of the Undraped Figure in Art*. On the composition of Moore's works and his use of grids, see Prettejohn, *Art for Art's Sake*, 101–127.

70. Prettejohn, *Art for Art's Sake*, 120. My emphasis.

71. Review of *A Summer Night* at the Grafton Gallery exhibition, 1894, in *Magazine of Art* (1894), xvii, in Morris, *Victorian and Edwardian Paintings*, 315 n9. Prettejohn discusses the controversy over the depiction of "flesh" among artists in the 1860s in *Art for Art's Sake*, 108–109.

72. Baldry wrote, "The flesh tones are warm and full, creamy rather than silvery, and are juxtaposed with the pale primrose yellow of the draperies wrapped round the legs of the seated figures and thrown over the cushions upon which the centre girl reclines" (*Albert Moore: His Life and Work* [London, 1894], 63–64, quoted in Morris, *Victorian and Edwardian Paintings*, 313). The *Art Journal* called *A Summer Night* "a partial reversion to the emotional motives of his earlier works. The *Summer Night* was an awakening from the sublime unconsciousness of the dozen years immediately preceding" (*Art Journal* [1894], 89, quoted in Morris, *Victorian and Edwardian Paintings*, 314 n2).

73. He continues that the painting "betrays to a slight extent the care and ingenuity that he always lavished upon his productions, but which in other pictures are better concealed" (Baldry, in Morris, *Victorian and Edwardian Paintings*, 313). Similarly, the critic of the *Athenaeum* wrote of the work, "His notions of composition seldom rise above the principles of design inevitable in bas-relief" (May 3, 1890, in ibid., 315 n7).

74. Rathbone, *Impressionism in Art*, 9. Strangely, he contrasts this with the Dutch painter Peter de Hooch: "The object of the first painter [Moore] is to make you feel you are in a beautiful room surrounded by beautiful walls; the object of the second [de Hooch] to make you feel that you are not cramped in the little room he has painted, but that there is a large, great world outside full of brightness, and therefore he generally manages to introduce a half-open door with the sun glinting through it" (ibid.).

75. Morris, *Victorian and Edwardian Paintings*, 313.

76. Asleson, *Albert Moore*, 185.

77. Dyall, *Descriptive Catalogue* (1896), 71.

78. Ibid.

79. Milner, *The Pre-Raphaelites*, 62. Milner notes that Hunt was persuaded because of the support he had received early in his career from the Liverpool Academy and because the Walker Art Gallery already contained two important works by the other founding members of the Pre-Raphaelite Brotherhood, Rossetti (*Dante's Dream*, purchased in 1881

for £1,575) and Millais (*Lorenzo and Isabella*, bought in 1884 for £1,050), so that the three paintings together would be "a permanent memorial to the Pre-Raphaelite Brotherhood" (ibid.). The total purchase price for Hunt's work, easily the most expensive painting that the Walker bought in the years 1877–1910, was made up from a one-time grant from the council, the museum's regular purchase funds (provided by autumn exhibition receipts), and a special fund raised by subscribers. See *Thirty-ninth Annual Report of the Committee of the Free Public Library, Museum, and Walker Art Gallery, of the City of Liverpool, for the Year Ending 31st December, 1891* (1892), 4.

80. Chesneau, *The English School of Painting*, 194–195.

81. Shepherd, *A Short History*, 109–110.

82. For a good discussion of this, see Jacobi, *William Holman Hunt*, particularly the introduction.

83. Milner, *The Pre-Raphaelites*, 61.

84. Michaela Giebelhausen (*Painting the Bible*) connects Hunt's work to the controversy over biblical criticism in the 1860 volume *Essays and Reviews* and the subsequent push to imagine Christ as a historical figure: "*The Finding of the Saviour in the Temple* shared with *Essays and Reviews* the complex problems of representation based on historical research. . . . Hunt emerged as the true innovator—intrepid historian, explorer and ethnographer—who presented mid-Victorian audiences with a fully orientalized image of Christ that was both realistic and seemingly authentic" (175). In reimagining "Christ for the current age," as she puts it, Hunt responded to a pervasive cultural absence in the wake of the crisis of faith provoked by both biblical criticism and Darwinian evolutionary theory. Hunt aimed, she writes, "to make the biblical story 'live as history,'" supplying his own complex vision of an historical, yet divinely inspired Christ" (179). See esp. her chap. 4, "The Making of William Holman Hunt as the Painter of Christ," 127–187. I am grateful to Timothy Barringer for this reference.

85. Stephens, "The Triumph of the Innocents," *Portfolio* 16 (1885): 81, in Landow, *William Holman Hunt and Typological Symbolism*, 136.

86. "Mr Holman Hunt: His Work and Career," *Blackwood's Edinburgh Magazine* (1886), in Landow, *William Holman Hunt and Typological Symbolism*, 137.

87. Forsyth, *Religion in Recent Art*, 3rd ed. (London, 1905), 178, in Landow, *William Holman Hunt and Typological Symbolism*, 136.

88. Landow, *William Holman Hunt and Typological Symbolism*, 137–138.

89. Jacobi, *William Holman Hunt*, 83.

90. Stubbs, "'The Triumph of the Innocents,'" 101, 103. Stubbs had referred to Jean-François Millet on that painter's famous evening prayer painting *Angelus*, "The Infinite Must Be Perceived" (103).

91. Ibid., 106. Stubbs found in both "the poet Browning and the painter Holman Hunt, this new spirit of the Incarnate and the Risen Christ, the great social Emancipator and Redeemer of the world, penetrat[ing] all they either write or paint, and in its turn reveal[ing] to the blunter sense and duller insight of more commonplace souls the signs of the kingdom of God verily present in our midst" (ibid.).

92. Ibid. He described this new theology as one "that tends to enlarge the sphere of the Church, to draw closer her ties with the best secular life of the world, and to widen our conceptions of Christianity from a mere narrow scheme of personal salvation into a

religion of world-wide redemption, in which the cosmical significance of the Incarnation implied the re-consecration of the whole universe to God" (ibid.).

93. Ibid., 113–114. Indeed, Stubbs exhorted his congregation: "Let us consecrate our work, whatever it might be, to some noble service" (115).

94. Ruskin, "Art in England, Lecture I: Realistic Schools of Painting: D. G. Rossetti and W. Holman Hunt," delivered March 9, 1883, in Ruskin, *Works of John Ruskin*, 33:277; reference from, and quoted in, Coleridge, *The Leaders of the English Pre-Raphaelites*, 48.

95. Ruskin, "Art in England," in Ruskin, *Works*, 33:278.

96. Ibid.; also quoted in Stubbs, "'The Triumph of the Innocents,'" 112.

97. See Stubbs's discussion of the painting as comfort for "every deathbed scene" ("'The Triumph of the Innocents,'" 113).

98. Francesca Vanki Altman notes that "the Middle East epitomized both symbolism and reality as no other part of the world could. It combined the aims of newness, realism, tradition, and historical verisimilitude." Altman interprets Hunt's trips to the East as therefore not "blatantly and simplistically Orientalist in the Saidian sense of the word," because she sees them as part of his wider search for "scientific or historical fact" ("William Holman Hunt, Race, and Orientalism," 47, 49). Although she gives a detailed and nuanced account of Hunt's racial and religious attitudes in relation to European imperialist and Orientalist culture, I see this instance of Hunt's understanding of the East as unchanging (and therefore a repository of biblical "facts") as a typical expression of late Victorian Orientalist attitudes. For a good historical interpretation of ideas about the "East" in relation to nineteenth-century European ideas about time and progress, see Adas, *Machines as the Measure of Men*.

99. Letter to Harold Rathbone (brother to Philip), quoted in Milner, *The Pre-Raphaelites*, 61.

100. Stubbs, "'The Triumph of the Innocents,'" 104.

101. "On this journey I met many native parties, in all of which there were features to be gathered up of use for my object, as, for instance, in the manner of leading the ass, the objects forming the load, and the posture adopted by women in riding, the fashion of carrying the tools used for a man's trade—when he was a handicraftsman—and the habit of saving the shoes when the traveller was not in a place where his feet might be defiled, the way of wearing the costume, which, with clothes supplied in a studio, no artist could think of applying properly without such study of the proper habits." He mentions, also, that the "group of trees over the water-wheel, which is in the central part of the picture," he painted over three nights of a full moon, having found it on his journey. Letter from Holman Hunt to Charles Stubbs, n.d., quoted in ibid., 108. Giebelhausen also notes how Hunt used these reports on his paintings' creation to reinforce the realism and accuracy of his biblical scenes, an Orientalist trope that worked alongside his painterly technique of painstaking mimeticism (*Painting the Bible*, 181–182). Both of these sources of verification also received a wider cultural currency and deeper meaning because they "paralleled the methods of historical research favoured by liberal Protestantism" (187).

102. The catalogue from a June 1890 exhibition at the London Guildhall also used Hunt's description of his picture.

103. Dyall, *Descriptive Catalogue* (1896), 72.

104. Ibid.

105. For example, he describes the emotional experience of the Virgin: "Conscious of the divine mercy the heart of Mary rejoicing over her rescued son, feels compassion for the murdered Innocents and for the childless mothers less happy and honored than herself. It is at this moment . . . that Jesus recognises the spirits of the slain Innocents" (ibid).

106. Ibid., 73.

107. See, for example, entries on Whaite, *The Heart of Cambria*; Meredith, *Homewards, Conway Marsh*; and Brett, *The Norman Archipelago*, in Stanfield, *Descriptive Catalogue* (1888), 41, 51–52, and 52, respectively. See also the descriptions of Davies, *Young Poachers*, and Cole, *The Heart of Surrey*, in Stanfield, *Catalogue of the Permanent Collection* (1895), 76 and 120–121, respectively.

108. On Fildes, see Stanfield, *Descriptive Catalogue* (1888), 53; on Dawson and Hook, see Stanfield, *Catalogue of the Permanent Collection* (1895), 95–96 and 103–104, respectively.

109. Chesneau, *The English School of Painting*, 238, 240.

110. Stanfield, *Catalogue of the Permanent Collection* (1895), 103.

111. Shepherd, *A Short History*, 47.

112. Armstrong in Lang, *The Life and Work of Sir Frederick Leighton*, 1. See also Ruskin's *Academy Notes, 1856*, quoted in Stanfield, *Catalogue of the Permanent Collection* (1895), 100, and Shepherd, *A Short History*, 111.

113. Jeremy Maas, *Victorian Painters* (London, 1968), 128, quoted in Mancoff, ed., *John Everett Millais*, 5. Jason Rosenfeld also notes the changing fate of Millais's reputation, in a "supranational" context, looking in particular at his perhaps unexpected influence on Vincent Van Gogh and Salvador Dalí ("Millais in His Time and Ours," in Rosenfeld and Smith, eds., *Millais*, 10–13).

114. See Barlow, "Millais, Manet, Modernity," 51. See also Barlow, *Time Present and Time Past*, 1. I am grateful to Timothy Barringer for these references. Barlow has convincingly argued that Millais's late work in particular has remained a challenge to established modes of art history that define the "modern" in terms of the French avant-garde; as Barlow has described, Millais's late works are "deliberately *accommodating*," allowing for interpretations on "multiple levels of consciousness, intellectuality and emotional engagement" ("Millais, Manet, Modernity," 61; emphasis in original). For Barlow, late-twentieth-century critics have missed the tensions and complexities in Millais's works precisely because of this very accessibility.

115. Millais quoted in Spielmann, *Millais and His Works*, 29.

116. Monkhouse, *British Contemporary Artists*, 74–75.

117. Ibid., 75. Even Baldry, his hagiographic biographer, admitted that "he might even be said to be wanting in imagination, if by imagination is understood the capacity to evolve things curious and unusual out of the inner consciousness" (*Sir John Everett Millais*, 21). Spielmann was even more critical: "In a few short years these supports [Rossetti and Hunt] were withdrawn from Millais's art, in which we find the execution still, but where—at least in the same degree—the intellect or the imagination?" (*Millais and His Works*, 24; see also 25). On the relationship with the original Brotherhood, see also Monkhouse, *British Contemporary Artists*, 50–51, and Parkes, *The Pre-Raphaelite Movement*, 47–48.

118. Armstrong in Lang, *The Life and Work of Sir Frederick Leighton*, 7. Likewise, Chesneau viewed Millais as having tempered the errors of his youth: "The Pre-Raphaelite,

who had formerly so strictly followed the rules of the school, that the faithful carrying out of detail had been almost an infatuation for him, had now freed himself from so slavish a yoke, without losing the respect he bore it, or failing to recognise the worth of the system. Since that time the years have rolled on, carrying the master, step by step, to a fuller realisation of his artistic aspirations" (*The English School of Painting*, 220–221).

119. Armstrong in Lang, *The Life and Work of Sir Frederick Leighton*, 8.

120. Quilter in Parkes, *The Pre-Raphaelite Movement*, 40–41.

121. See Woodson-Boulton, "Temples of Art," app. 2.

122. See in particular Warner, "John Everett Millais's 'Autumn Leaves,'" and Bowdler, "Ars Longa, Vita Brevis." The 2007 Tate catalogue lists this as the first work in its "Aestheticism" section, and Jason Rosenfeld connects it with his other "proto-Aestheticist works of the late 1850s." See Rosenfeld and Smith, eds., *Millais*, 132–133.

123. Barlow, *Time Present and Time Past*, 73.

124. Millais, letter to F. G. Stephens, in Stephens Papers, Bodleian Library, quoted in Warner, "John Everett Millais's 'Autumn Leaves,'" 127–128.

125. F. G. Stephens, *The Crayon*, III, November 1856, 324, quoted in Warner, "John Everett Millais's 'Autumn Leaves,'" 128.

126. Ruskin, *Academy Notes, 1856*, in Stanfield, *Catalogue of the Permanent Collection* (1895), 100.

127. Quoted in Spielmann, *Millais and His Works*, 90.

128. Ibid., 92. Quotation unidentified in the original text.

129. Monkhouse, *British Contemporary Artists*, 63. He also noted that "it puzzled the critics, but is a joy forever" (64).

130. Stanfield, *Catalogue of the Permanent Collection* (1895), 99.

131. Compare ibid., 101–102, with Shepherd, *A Short History*, 111.

132. Effie quoted in Barringer, *Reading the Pre-Raphaelites*, 139.

133. Hunt quoted in ibid.

134. See, for example, Spielmann, *Millais and His Works*, 90; Ruskin in Stanfield, *Catalogue of the Permanent Collection* (1895), 100; and Baldry, *Sir John Everett Millais*, 46.

135. Waterfield, "The Origins of the Early Picture Gallery," 59–64.

136. Ibid., 61; see also Wornum and Eastlake, *Descriptive and Historical Catalogue*.

137. Waterfield, "The Origins of the Early Picture Gallery," 62. Waterfield explains that Eastlake imagined an even more comprehensive catalogue, in a Treasury Minute of 1855, that would give all relevant information about each work, including its "place in a larger scheme if appropriate, its subject, dimensions, support, medium and inscription, the location of associated works, versions, copies, engravings, associated drawings, and a 'General History,' meaning primarily a detailed provenance" (63). This would have been a notable change from the earlier narrative approach to a more scientific and professionalized one but was not carried out in the nineteenth century.

138. Ibid., 67, 68, 70–71.

CHAPTER 5

1. Nick Prior has written about the "ambiguities" of museums, pulling between exclusion and inclusion, and between cultural capital as a form of social distinction on the one hand and public admittance as a legitimation of the nation-state on the other. He

connects "nationalization" to the development of "increasingly public and heterogeneous leisure regimes," but not explicitly to capitalism. See Prior, "Museums," 40.

2. As Richard Brettell has written, "Museums were among the few places of display in modern culture apparently free from the pressures of commodity markets, and this very status gave them immense power," the key word here being "apparently" (Brettell, *Modern Art*, 69). See also Pearce, *On Collecting*.

3. Schorske, *Thinking with History*, introduction, "The Book: Theme and Content."

4. Tillyard, *The Impact of Modernism*.

5. MacCarthy, "The Post-Impressionists," 174.

6. Ibid., 175.

7. For a longer discussion of Bourdieu's ideas in relation to Victorian museums, see, for example, Woodson-Boulton, "Victorian Museums and Victorian Society," 115–116.

8. In Birmingham, the Society of Artists complained that the Birmingham Museum and Art Gallery's free temporary loan exhibitions were "powerful counter attractions" to the society's own paid-entry autumn exhibition of works for sale. Letter dated December 14, 1892, printed in Report of the Museum and School of Art Committee, March 28, 1893, in BCP 1890–1900, 245–247.

9. See Woodson-Boulton, "Temples of Art," app. 4.

10. Census data for 1891 from Online Historical Population Reports (UK Data Archive, University of Essex), http://www.histpop.org. For attendance figures, see Woodson-Boulton, "Temples of Art," app. 4. Admission to the permanent collection of each museum was free.

11. For more information on turnstiles and visitor records, see Woodson-Boulton, "Temples of Art," 351–352.

12. Patricia Mainardi, in *The End of the Salon*, stresses the distinction between the two modes of appreciating art (seeing or selling) in her discussion of the French salon. For a discussion of the same tensions at the Grosvenor Gallery, see Denney, *At the Temple of Art*, 46.

13. *Annual Reports of the Committee of the Free Public Library, Museum and Schools, of the Borough of Liverpool* (Liverpool, 1876–1895), summarized in Woodson-Boulton, "Temples of Art," app. 3.2.

14. Compare the discussion of respectability and "moral rectitude" in Thompson, *The Rise of Respectable Society*, 260.

15. For detailed attendance figures, see Woodson-Boulton, "Temples of Art," chap. 6 and apps. 3.1–3 and 4.

16. Ibid., app. 3.2.

17. He added, "These people are ignorant of the great amount of good work being done by this institution in cultivating the powers of observation amongst all classes" (Wallis, "The Museum and Art Gallery," 512).

18. Dyall, *First Decade of the Walker Art Gallery*, 17.

19. LCRL, Autumn Exhibition of Pictures, bound with *Libraries, Museums and Arts Committee. Second Autumn Exhibition: Report of Fine Arts Committee, 1873* (Liverpool, 1873).

20. *Visit of the Institute of Mechanical Engineers*, 1–2.

21. Walker Art Gallery Archives, Arts and Exhibitions Sub-Committee Minutes, January 21 and 25, and February 8 and 15, 1892, WAG Box 2.

22. MCAG Archives, Art Gallery Committee Minutes, vol. 2, February 28, 1889, 153–154.

23. Art Gallery Committee Report for the Year 1909–1910, in MCP 1854–1914, 1909–1910, 2 (report begins at Council Proceedings page 525).

24. See Macleod, *Art and the Victorian Middle Class*, for a discussion of the importance of middle-class collectors of contemporary British art in the northern and midlands cities, especially Birmingham and Manchester.

25. For example, in the 1888 Birmingham Museum and Art Gallery Report the committee noted that they "have pleasure in stating that several of the most important of these works [for a temporary loan exhibition] were lent to the Corporation of Birmingham by the Corporation of Manchester; and, while recording their thanks, they desire to point out the valuable assistance which leading Corporations may thus render each other by occasional interchanges by way of loans of fine works in their possession" (Report of the Museum and School of Art Committee, January 3, 1888, BCP 1880–1890, 4 [report begins at Council Proceedings page 123]).

26. The Chantrey Bequest was the only national fund for the acquisition of contemporary art, administered by the Royal Academy. On requests to the National Gallery for loans from the Turner Collection from the Glasgow Corporation Galleries of Art, Oxford School of Art, Hartley Institution, Walker Art Gallery in Liverpool, and National Gallery of Ireland, see NGA, Trustees of the National Gallery Meetings, NG7/4/1878, NG7/8/1879, NG7/3/1878, NG7/29/1882, NG7/30/1882, NG7/31/1879, and NG7/32/1879. After the National Gallery Loan Act of 1883 passed, the cities quickly took advantage of it; the National Gallery trustees maintained strict standards in terms of security, fire precautions, and lighting apparatus (no gas lighting) and required the municipalities to provide a good deal of information about their premises before agreeing to lend works. For example, see ibid., NG7/39/1882, NG7/41/1883, NG7/45–48/1883, NG7/50–51/1883, and NG7/53/1884. On Birmingham, Liverpool, and Manchester requests to the Royal Academy for loans of Chantrey pictures, see Royal Academy Archives, Royal Academy Council Minutes, vol. 18: May 15, 1883; June 17, 1884; July 3, 1884; May 12, 1885; November 17, 1885; July 8, 1886; May 10, 1887; July 7, 1887; vol. 19: July 19, 1888; March 11, 1890; June 16, 1891; July 9, 1891; December 15, 1891; vol. 20: July 12, 1894; June 18, 1895; July 11, 1895.

27. Letter dated December 18, 1876, from George Baker, mayor of Birmingham, to "Mayors and Chairmen of Committees of Corporations of Towns possessing Galleries of Art and Museums," in *Free Libraries and Museums. Conference of Representatives*, 5–6.

28. See Deputation of Representatives of Municipal Corporations to the Royal Commissioners of the Exhibition of 1851, Marlborough House, July 20, 1877.—Statement submitted to His Royal Highness the Prince of Wales in explanation of the object of the Deputation, BCLLS LP31.83 502249, and NGA, Minutes of the Meeting of the Trustees of the National Gallery, November 26, 1877, NG1/5/89.

29. The deputation to the National Gallery resulted in a written request: a letter from Birmingham, dated January 1, 1878, which was read at a trustees board meeting March 4, 1878. (See also NGA, Minutes of the Meetings of the Trustees of the National Gallery, August 6, 1877, NG1/5/1877, 86, and NGA, Trustees of the National Gallery Minutes, Statement of Deputation from Municipal Corporations, requested by the Trustees of the National Gallery, read at Meeting of the Board February 4, 1879, NG7/7/1879.) This is generally a restatement of Collings's arguments from the January 1877 conference and

includes interesting information on the eighteen corporations involved. At that meeting of February 4, 1879, the trustees resolved that they could not comply with the deputation's requests, NGA, NG1/5/1879, 119–120; the main difficulty was the need to get an act of Parliament to override the specific terms of gifts and bequests to the National Gallery, which the trustees eventually sought and obtained in 1881; see NGA, NG1/5/1881, 185.

30. Quoted in Report of the Museum and School of Art Committee, May 5, 1891, in BCP 1890–1900, 7 (report begins at Council Proceedings page 373). Parenthetical expression in original.

31. He noted the "social and economic position of the population of Birmingham, which lives and prospers solely by its artistic industries," and the strong city government that worked to educate its citizens (ibid.).

32. Ibid.

33. On the Courtauld see, for example, Poole, *Stewards of the Nation's Art*, 13.

34. Birmingham Museum and Art Gallery, *Illustrated Catalogue* (1912). The 1923 version adds a fuller description of the artist (Birmingham Museum and Art Gallery, *Illustrated Catalogue* [1923], 93–94).

35. Birmingham Museum and Art Gallery, *Illustrated Catalogue* (1923), 27; compare to the 1899 edition, 17–21. The only change in the history section is from "Sir Edward" in 1899 to "Burne-Jones" in 1923. The 1930 edition is even more brief, taking out the paragraph on the artist's experience painting the picture and shortening the discussion of the painting's subject (Birmingham Museum and Art Gallery, *Catalogue of the Permanent Collection* [1930], 27).

36. Morris, *Public Art Collections*, 90, 152. See also *Historical Summary of the Walker Art Gallery*, in Walker Art Gallery, *Annual Report, 1937–1938*, 6.

37. Walker Art Gallery, *Illustrated Catalogue* (1927). For Dyall's descriptions, see Chapter 4, note 61.

38. Ibid., 100.

39. For example, in contrast to earlier exegeses of Ford Madox Brown's painting *Work* written by the artist himself, Phythian assessed Madox Brown in relation to his influence on the Pre-Raphaelite Brotherhood. Phythian, *Handbook to the Permanent Collection* (1910), 10–11.

40. Ibid., 53.

41. Ibid., 55, 81–82.

42. Manchester City Art Gallery, *Reproductions from the Collection*, 6.

43. Ibid.

44. Ibid., 7.

45. Rathbone, *Impressionism in Art*.

46. Lund, *A Picture Gallery*, 3.

47. Ibid., 4, 5.

48. Lund, *"Some Uses of an Art Gallery,"* 8–9.

49. Ibid., 9. My emphasis.

50. Ibid., 13, 14.

51. Phythian, *Half Hours at the Manchester City Art Gallery*, 3, 4.

52. In Hunt, *A Description of the Picture*, 15–16.

53. Rothenstein, *An Address by Mr. W. Rothenstein*, 12–13.

54. Ibid., 4. On Dawson, see Chapter 1.

55. "The Late Sir Whitworth Wallis, F.S.A., 1855–1927," 185.

56. In 1879, just two years after the Walker Art Gallery opened, the Library, Museum, and Arts Committee suggested "erecting additional galleries at the rear of the present building" to accommodate the permanent collection and the annual exhibition, and the city council allowed the committee "to obtain plans and estimates for the proposed extension" (*Twenty-seventh Annual Report of the Committee of the Free Public Library, Museum, and Walker Art Gallery, of the Borough of Liverpool* [1880], 25). In 1889, the RMI members of the committee noted that "the question as to whether the Permanent or the Annual Exhibition shall have preference is one which has therefore been already too long delayed" (C. J. Pooley, Deputy-Chairman, Art Gallery Committee, Manchester City Art Gallery, in *Report of the Representatives of the Royal Institution on the Art Gallery Committee of the Corporation of Manchester*, September 23, 1889 [Manchester, 1889], unpaginated). As Birmingham assistant curator Chamberlain wrote, "it became necessary to place in store many interesting specimens and collections, and the series of annual loan exhibitions had in the end to be abandoned, owing to the lack of room. . . . These conditions . . . naturally had a detrimental effect on the generosity of donors, for new gifts could not be adequately shown without putting away others of equal value, [and] it became evident that a new building, or a large extension of the old one, had become absolutely necessary" (Chamberlain, *The Corporation Museum and Art Gallery*, 7–8).

57. W. E. A. Axon, comment reported in Horsfall, "Neglected Pictures," 236.

58. During the first autumn exhibition in 1883, the permanent collection was not shown at all. See Corporation of Manchester Art Gallery, Royal Institution, *First Autumn Exhibition Catalogue*, 1883, 5. On the art community's view of the lower rooms, see Resolution of the Art Club, Manchester, November 3, 1886, in letter from Robert Edward Johnson and 56 other artists, MCAG Archives, Art Gallery Committee Minutes, vol. 2, January 6, 1887, 15.

59. "The constant removal of the Permanent Collection to make way for the Periodical Exhibitions must in time have a deleterious effect on the valuable collection already acquired, and it is also desirable that it should be at all times accessible, free of charge, to the public" (*Report of the Representatives of the Royal Institution*).

60. The subcommittee recommending the use of electricity cited one reason for its adoption that "the rooms on the ground floor could be better utilised and made more attractive for the permanent exhibition." See Report of the House Sub-Committee, July 23, 1885, in Report of the Art Gallery Committee, presented to the City Council, August 12, 1885, MCP 1884–1885, 408.

61. Johnson's letter urged that if this policy was continued, the lower galleries should be opened only at night when the lights were on. MCAG Archives, Art Gallery Committee Minutes, vol. 2, January 6, 1887, 15.

62. In Manchester this caused considerable controversy, as the RMI members of the Art Gallery Committee accused the City Art Gallery Committee and the city council of "sacrilege" to the work of architect Sir Charles Barry. The *Architect* followed the debate closely and lamented the Art Gallery Committee's decision to remove corridors in order to create more space. The journal argued that "a corridor is an important feature in an art gallery, for the rooms assume interest as they are approached by one," and concluded, "The gallery is looked at as if it were a wall for advertisements, and so long as

some more square feet can be found all other considerations have to be set aside" ("The Week," March 4, 1892, *Architect,* January–June 1892, 149). See Letter to the City Council of Manchester dated November 24th, 1891, recorded in Appendix, Meeting of Council, Wednesday, January 6th, 1892, in MCLA, RMI, Council Minutes. MCLA M6/1/1/5 also contains the RMI Council's reaction to the renovation plan; the Art Gallery Committee's response is recorded in Report of the City Art Gallery Committee, April 13, 1892, 373. On the Birmingham renovation, see Report of the Museum and School of Art Committee, June 6, 1893, BCP 1890–1900, 394.

63. See Haward, "The Problem of Provincial Galleries and Art Museums," 635.

64. See Minutes of the Council Meeting, July 6, 1881, in City of Liverpool, *Proceedings of the Council* (1881), 275–276; *Twenty-ninth Annual Report of the Committee of the Free Public Library, Museum, and Walker Art Gallery, of the City of Liverpool* (1882), 3; *Thirty-first Annual Report of the Committee of the Free Public Library, Museum, and Walker Art Gallery, of the City of Liverpool* (1884), 3; *Thirty-second Annual Report of the Committee of the Free Public Library, Museum, and Walker Art Gallery, of the City of Liverpool* (1885), 3.

65. This was in part at least prompted by an offer of paintings to the Birmingham Museum and Art Gallery. On November 14, 1898, the Museum and School of Art Committee read a letter from local collector J. T. Middlemore offering a collection of works by G. F. Watts, William Holman Hunt, and Edward Burne-Jones "if our city will build what I consider a suitable gallery for the proper display of the works of Art which it possesses, and hopes to possess." Reported in *Birmingham Daily Mail*, "A Generous Offer to the Birmingham Art Gallery," November 15, 1898. Additional articles in local papers about the offer and extension are preserved in BCLLS, Osborne, *Newspaper Cuttings.*

66. For summaries, see Chamberlain, *The Corporation Museum and Art Gallery,* and Wallis, "The Museum and Art Gallery"; see also Letter from the Feeney Trustees, January 25, 1906, read and entered on the Council Minutes, February 6, 1906, BCP 1901–1914, 69–70; Report of the Museum and School of Art Committee, May 3, 1910, BCP 1901–1914, 307–308; Report of the Museum and School of Art Committee, May 2, 1911, BCP 1901–1914, 228–229; Report of the Museum and School of Art Committee, May 7, 1912, Minutes of the Council, June 25, July 22, and October 15, 1912, BCP 1901–1914, 536–537, 822–823, 948–949, and 1268–1269, respectively. Curator Wallis felt this was an abrogation of Feeney's wishes: "Personally, I am quite positive that Mr. Feeney never contemplated any such arrangement, for he frequently attacked the present building for being above the Gas Department. Mr. Feeney intended his gift to be used for a building devoted to the arts alone and erected on an independent site" (Wallis, "The Museum and Art Gallery," 506).

67. The Manchester City Council borrowed the necessary funds of £25,125 through the Manchester Corporations Act, 1882, on the City Fund and City Rate. See Report of the City Art Gallery, May 3, 1899, MCP 1898–1899, 535, and Resolution, August 2, 1899, 1435.

68. See MCLA, election addresses, 1912, MCLA M266/1/2/21–26, and MCLA, Butterworth, Letters. Posters from this election survive at MCLA M266/1/2/23–24; one for Butterworth compares the cost of using the infirmary site for an art gallery and library to erecting a new Exchange, proclaiming:

The Reference Library and Art Gallery will be OPEN TO ALL. The Exchange, 70 to 75 per cent of whose members reside outside the City, will be open only to Subscribers.

Is the Art Gallery an Expensive Luxury? No! Certainly not! The whole annual cost is equal to only one half-penny Rate.

ELECTORS, do not be deluded by vague promises, but Vote for Butterworth, AND SOUND FINANCE.

69. For some important discussions of the Louvre and the idea of movement through museums, see Duncan, "Putting the 'Nation' in London's National Gallery"; Duncan and Wallach, "The Museum of Modern Art as Late Capitalist Ritual"; Deutsche and Ryan, "The Fine Art of Gentrification"; Hooper-Greenhill, *Museums and the Shaping of Knowledge*; and Sheehan, *Museums in the German Art World*, 70.

70. *Thirty-third Annual Report of the Committee of the Free Public Library, Museum, and Walker Art Gallery, of the City of Liverpool* (1886), 32.

71. Morris, *Public Art Collections in North-West England*, 91.

72. Report of the City Art Gallery Committee, 1898, MCP 1897–1898, 2294.

73. Wallis, *The Feeney Galleries*, 3.

74. See Wallis, *The Feeney Galleries*.

75. "Mr. Ruskin on Contemporary Art," *Co-operative News*, February 7, 1880, in MCLA, Ruskin Society Scrapbook. See discussion of Ruskin's advice in Chapter 3.

76. Arnold, *The Possibilities for an Art Gallery in Manchester*, 13–27.

77. University of Birmingham Special Collections, Letter from Joseph Chamberlain to [Thomas] Martineau.

78. See Woodson-Boulton, "Temples of Art," app. 1.2.

79. See "Discussion" following a talk given by Lawrence Haward in 1922 at the Royal Society of Arts, included at the end of Haward, "The Problem of Provincial Galleries and Art Museums," 639–640, addressed in greater detail below.

80. See "Discussion" included at the end of Haward, "The Problem of Provincial Galleries and Art Museums," 638–642.

81. Ibid., 640.

82. Arnold, *The Possibilities for an Art Gallery in Manchester*, and Taylor, *Municipal Art Galleries and Art Museums*.

83. Manchester City Art Gallery, *Report of the Art Gallery Committee Visit*, 5, 2.

84. See Edward Morris's discussion of this debate in *Victorian and Edwardian Paintings*, 11–17.

85. Philip Rathbone, *Speaker*, November 5, 1892, 563, quoted in ibid., 14. Rathbone also noted that this ignorance "has saved us from being run away with by preconceived prejudices, and has given us the necessary courage to select pictures without regard to name, and by unknown artists who have since risen to unquestioned eminence." Of course, in most cases (for example, Manchester) the opposite tended to be the case, as in fact happened in Liverpool after Rathbone's death in 1895.

86. Morris, *Victorian and Edwardian Paintings*, 16. MacColl led the charge against the Royal Academy's control of the Chantrey Bequest and was appointed director of the Tate Gallery in 1916. See Fyfe, "The Chantrey Episode."

87. Morris, *Public Art Collections in North-West England*, 91.

88. Haward, "The Problem of Provincial Galleries and Art Museums", 633–637.

89. Ibid., 638.

90. Ibid., 638–639.

91. Ibid., 641.

92. For a seminal discussion of how the use of new technologies is largely determined by cultural assumptions, see Williams, *Television*.

EPILOGUE

1. See my discussion of this conflation of "modern" and "British" in Woodson-Boulton, "The Art of Compromise."

2. Cust, ed., *Catalogue of the National Gallery of British Art*, 10.

3. On the changing status of art and its social role in reaction to modernism, see Borzello, *Civilising Caliban*, and Tillyard, *The Impact of Modernism*.

4. Wilson, *The National and Tate Galleries*, 90; see also xxii–xxv for the established canon of French impressionists.

5. Lambert, ed., *Art in England*, 5, 6.

6. Ibid., 43–44.

7. Ibid., 45.

8. I am grateful to Vanessa Schwartz for this reference.

9. Minihan, *The Nationalization of Culture*, 167.

10. Morris, *Labour and Pleasure*, 8.

11. Ibid., 6.

12. *Cooper and Co.'s Penny Guide*, 12. See Chapter 3.

13. "The Museum and Art Gallery," *Birmingham Daily Times*, December 3, 1885.

14. Robert Hinks, "Patronage in Art To-day, (a)" in Lambert, ed., *Art in England*, 76–77. See also Jack Beddington, "Patronage in Art To-day, (c)," ibid., 82–87.

15. Bell, "Victorian Taste," 44.

16. *Plans for an Arts Centre*, 6.

17. *Ford Madox Brown, 1821–1893*; *Millais, PRB-PRA*; and *William Holman Hunt: An Exhibition*.

BIBLIOGRAPHY

ARCHIVAL SOURCES

Birmingham Central Library Archives

Chamberlain, J. H. *A Catalogue of the Works of Mr. John Ruskin, as collected by J. H. Chamberlain, prior to January the first, 1879.* (MS.) Birmingham Central Library Archives Inner Iron Room 74/78126.

"Industrial Art Museum: Copy of Committee Minutes, Accounts, 1870–71." Minutes of the Industrial Art Museum Committee. (MS.) Birmingham Central Library Archives ZZ63B 497578.

Birmingham Central Library Local Studies (BCLLS)

NAAAAI, *Third Annual Congress, Birmingham, November 4 to November 8, 1890. Preliminary Programme of Local Arrangements,* 1890. BCLLS B. HIST D/R 239488.

Osborne, G. H. *Newspaper Cuttings Relating to the Art Gallery, School of Art, Grammar School, Etc., Collected by G. H. Osborne, 1866–1905.* (Unpublished scrapbook.) BCLLS LF71-061 243127, 1866–1905.

Unpublished Report of the Free Libraries and Industrial Museums Committee for Presentation at the Monthly Meeting of the Council, April 5, 1881. BCLLS 578186.

Birmingham Museum and Art Gallery Archives

Birmingham Museum & Art Gallery Day Book 1, January 16, 1885–July 18, 1905. (Uncatalogued).

Petition from glassmakers in favor of industrial museum to the Worshipful Mayor, the Aldermen, and Members of the Town Council of the Borough of Birmingham, ca. 1875. (Uncatalogued).

British Museum

Documents relating to the 1857 Manchester Art Treasures Exhibition. British Museum 7805.e.27.

Liverpool Central Reference Library (LCRL)

At Home, Walker Art Gallery, Thursday, 3rd November 1881: Programme. LCRL Local Studies H q 708.5 LIB.

Autumn Exhibition of Pictures, Walker Art Gallery: Conversazione, Monday, December 6th, 1880: Programme. LCRL Local Studies H q 708.5 LIB.

Minutes of the Libraries, Museums, and Arts Committee, 1850–1969. (MS.) LCRL Archives 352 MIN/LIB 1/1–40.

Picton, J. A. *Notes on the Free Library and Museum of the Borough of Liverpool.* Pages 691–695 of unidentified text at the Liverpool Record Office, H 027.4 PIC. Liverpool, ca. 1858.

Manchester Central Library Archives (MCLA)

Butterworth, Walter. Letters to Walter Butterworth commiserating on the loss of his New-ton Heath Seat at the City Council Elections, November 1, 1912. MCLA M266/5/1/1–42.

Cleveland, S. D. *The Origin of the Royal Manchester Institute*. 1930. (Typed MS.) MCLA CL1/706M9.

Election addresses re: proposed use of Piccadilly site for Art Gallery and Library. MCLA M266/1/2.

Greenwood, Thomas. MCLA holdings: O17.442.M62 Vol. 8, pp. 269–277, and M137/4/2/45, M137/3/1/2 (photo), and Thomas Greenwood Correspondence 1–, 1880–1887.

MCAG. Art Gallery Committee House Sub-Committee Draft Book, 20 November 1882 to 21 December 1897. (Unpaginated MS.) MCLA M9/76/2.

———. Art Gallery Committee Letter Book, Vol. 1, 1882–1888; Vol. 2, 1888–1895. (MS.) MCLA M9/76/3/1–2.

———. House Sub-Committee Minutes. Art Gallery Committee, House Sub-Commit-tee's Draft Book, 20 November 1882 to 21 December 1897. (Unpaginated MS.) MCLA M9/76/2/1.

Odds and Ends, Magazine for the St. Paul's Literary and Educational Society, Bennett Street School. (Unpublished MS.) MCLA M38/4/2/35.

Phythian, J. E. Ancoats Brotherhood. MCLA M270/9/40/1–2.

———. "How to Enjoy Pictures." Workers' Education Association, Stockport Syllabus. Stockport, 1925. MCLA M270/9/33.

———. Letters Mostly to J. E. Phythian Relating to Art. MCLA M270/9/49/11–36.

———. Miscellaneous Correspondence: Letters relating to John Ruskin and the Ruskin Society. MCLA M270/9/49/1–10.

———. Miscellaneous Ephemera, 1879–1911. MCLA M270/9/49/37–47.

———. Newspaper Cuttings Referring to Talks by J. E. Phythian. MCLA M270/9/35/1–19.

———. Notebook with Notes on Turner's Works and Trips to Italy. MCLA M270/9/24/5.

———. Notes and Quotations from Books and Newspapers on Art, History, and Reli-gion. MCLA M270/9/25/4.

———. Notes on Sermons and Ruskin Society Meetings. MCLA M270/9/27.

———. Papers of J. E. Phythian, Art Gallery Committee 1898–1910. MCLA M270/9/43/1–19.

———. Talks and Writings by J. E. Phythian. MCLA M270/9/26/1–9.

Pooley, C. J. Letters to C. J. Pooley, 1875–1893. (MS.) MCLA MS/927.5/p111.

Proposed Art Gallery and Library for Manchester, longitudinal section and first floor plan, early twentieth century. MCLA MISC/921.

RMI. Council Minutes, 1878–1908. (MS.) MCLA M6/1/1/5.

———. General Meetings of Governors, 1835–1907, containing Annual Reports. (MS.) MCLA M6/1/2.

———. RMI Transfer Documents: Documents relating to the transfer of the RMI donated to the Manchester Central Library Archives by Lady Worthington in 1974. MCLA M183/–.

———. Rough Minutes of the Council and Committees, 1880–1889. (MS.) MCLA M6/1/3/16.

———. Sub-Committee Minutes, 1876–1885. (MS.) MCLA M6/1/8/3.

Ruskin Society Scrapbook, 1879–1904. (MS.) MCLA BR824.86.Gr.1.

Skinner, Dorothy Frances. *T. C. Horsfall [1841–1932]: A Memoir*. (Unpublished typed MS.) MCAG MISC/690/11.

Manchester Central Library Local Studies
Newspaper Clippings: Manchester City Art Gallery exhibitions, 1895–. Manchester Central Library Local Studies 708.273 Ne4.

Manchester City Art Gallery (MCAG) Archives
Art Gallery Committee Minutes. (MS.) Vol. 1: 1882–1886; Vol. 2: 1886–1890; Vol. 3: 1890–1894. (Uncatalogued).
Art Gallery Curator's Letter Book. (MS.) Vol. 1: 1883–1889; Vol. 2: 1889–1895; Vol. 3: 1895–1897. (Uncatalogued).
MCAG Acquisitions Records.

National Art Library, Victoria and Albert Museum
Liverpool Art Club: Art pamphlets, Liverpool, 1875–1878. NAL 502.F.20.

National Gallery Archives (NGA)
History Files: HF/3 1895 Correspondence, HF/5 1897 Correspondence and Papers, HF/6 1898 Correspondence.
Trustees of the National Gallery Meetings, NG7/–.

Royal Academy Archives
Royal Academy Council Minutes, 1877–1898.

University of Birmingham Special Collections
Letter from Joseph Chamberlain to Jesse Collings, September 12, 1875. Joseph Chamberlain Collection JC5/16/47.
Letter from Joseph Chamberlain to [Thomas] Martineau, April 22, 1893. Joseph Chamberlain Collection JC6/1/E5.

Walker Art Gallery Archives
Art and Exhibition Sub-Committee Minutes. (MS.) WAG Boxes 1 and 2.

PUBLISHED SOURCES
Adas, Michael. *Machines as the Measure of Men: Science, Technology, and Ideologies of Western Dominance.* Ithaca, NY: Cornell University Press, 1990.
Ady, Julia Mary Cartwright. *The Life and Work of Sir Edward Burne-Jones, Bart. / by Julia Cartwright (Mrs. Henry Ady). With Numerous Illustrations.* London: Art Journal, 1894.
Aldington, Richard, ed. *The Religion of Beauty: Selections from the Aesthetes, with an Introduction by Richard Aldington.* London: William Heinemann, 1950.
Altman, Francesca Vanki. "William Holman Hunt, Race, and Orientalism." In *Worldwide Pre-Raphaelitism,* ed. Thomas J. Tobin, 45–68. Albany: State University of New York Press, 2005.
Annual Report of the Council of the National Sunday League, with a Statement of Accounts for the Year, to Be Submitted to the General Meeting of Its Members, Held at Langham Hall, Great Portland Street, on Friday Evening, April 13th, 1877. London: William Austin, 1877.
Annual Report of the Council of the National Sunday League, with a Statement of Accounts for the Year, to Be Submitted to the General Meeting of the Members, Held at St. James' Hall (Entrance from Regent Street,) on Wednesday Evening, May 13th, 1885. London: William Austin, 1885.

Annual Reports of the Committee of the Free Public Library, and the Derby Museum, of the Borough of Liverpool. Presented to the Town Council. Liverpool: D. Marples, 1855–1862, 1864.

Annual Reports of the Committee of the Free Public Library, Museum, and Gallery of Art, of the Borough of Liverpool. Liverpool: Henry Greenwood, 1873–1876.

Annual Reports of the Committee of the Free Public Library, Museum, and Gallery of Art, of the Borough of Liverpool. Presented to the Town Council. Liverpool: Liverpool Printing and Stationery, 1867, 1870–1872.

Annual Reports of the Committee of the Free Public Library, Museum, and Gallery of Arts, of the Borough of Liverpool. Presented to the Town Council. Liverpool: George McCorquodale, 1863, 1865, 1866.

Annual Reports of the Committee of the Free Public Library, Museum, and Schools, of the Borough of Liverpool. Liverpool: D. Marples, 1869, 1870, 1871.

Annual Reports of the Committee of the Free Public Library, Museum, and Walker Art Gallery, of the Borough of Liverpool. Liverpool: Henry Greenwood, 1878–1891.

Annual Reports of the Committee of the Free Public Library, Museum, and Walker Art Gallery, of the City of Liverpool. Liverpool: J. R. Williams, 1892–1896.

Annual Reports of the Free Libraries Committee, Birmingham. Birmingham, 1867–1885.

Annual Reports of the Liverpool Royal Institution. Liverpool: J. Richardson and Son, 1860–1893.

Annual Reports of the Manchester Art Museum. Manchester, 1888–1906.

Annual Reports of the Manchester City Art Gallery. Manchester, 1901–1914.

Annual Reports of the Representatives of the Royal Institution on the Art Gallery Committee of the Corporation of Manchester. Manchester and London: G. Falkner and Sons, 1887–1891, 1895, 1907.

Archer, John H. G., ed. *Art and Architecture in Victorian Manchester: Ten Illustrations of Patronage and Practice.* Manchester: Manchester University Press, 1985.

Armstrong, Richard Acland. *Henry William Crosskey, LL.D., F.G.S.: His Life and Work.* Birmingham: Cornish Brothers, 1895.

Arnold, Dana. *Rural Urbanism: London Landscapes in the Early Nineteenth Century.* Manchester: Manchester University Press, 2005.

Arnold, William Thomas. *The Possibilities for an Art Gallery in Manchester, with Appendix on Cambridge.* Manchester, 1889.

Arscott, Caroline. "Employer, Husband, Spectator: Thomas Fairbairn's Commission of *The Awakening Conscience.*" In *The Culture of Capital: Art, Power and the Nineteenth-Century Middle Class*, ed. Janet Wolff and John Seed, 159–190. Manchester: Manchester University Press, 1988.

Asleson, Robyn. *Albert Moore.* London: Phaidon, 2000.

———. "Nature and Abstraction in the Aesthetic Development of Albert Moore." In *After the Pre-Raphaelites: Art and Aestheticism in Victorian England*, ed. Elizabeth Prettejohn, 115–134. Manchester: Manchester University Press, 1999.

Axon, Jane (Mrs. W. E. A. Axon). "The Social Science Association and the Sunday Question." *Sunday Review* 4, no. 1 (October 1879): 1.

Axon, William E. A. *Art in Lancashire.* Manchester, 1884.

Bailey, Peter. *Leisure and Class in Victorian England: Rational Recreation and the Contest for Control, 1830–1885.* London: Routledge and Kegan Paul, 1978.

————. "Leisure, Culture and the Historian: Reviewing the First Generation of Leisure Historiography in Britain." *Leisure Studies* 8 (1989): 107–127.

————. "'Will the Real Bill Banks Please Stand Up?' Towards a Role Analysis of Mid-Victorian Working-Class Respectability." *Journal of Social History* 12 (1979): 336–353.

Bailkin, Jordanna. *The Culture of Property: The Crisis of Liberalism in Modern Britain.* Chicago: University of Chicago Press, 2004.

Baird, Olga. "The Knights of Museums: The Wallis Family and Their Memorabilia in the Collection of the Wolverhampton Art Gallery." *Birmingham Historian* 32 (Summer 2008): 23–29.

Baldry, A. L. *Sir John Everett Millais.* London: George Bell and Sons, 1908.

Barker, Emma, and Colin Cunningham. "Case Study 8: Art in the Provinces." In *Academies, Museums and Canons of Art*, ed. Gill Perry and Colin Cunningham, 238–256. New Haven, CT: Yale University Press, 1999.

Barlow, Paul. "Millais, Manet, Modernity." In *English Art 1860–1914: Modern Artists and Identity*, ed. David Peters Corbett and Lara Perry, 49–63. Manchester: Manchester University Press, 2001.

————. *Time Present and Time Past: The Art of John Everett Millais.* Aldershot: Ashgate, 2005.

Barringer, Timothy. *Men at Work: Art and Labor in Victorian Britain.* New Haven, CT: Yale University Press, 2005.

————. *Reading the Pre-Raphaelites.* New Haven, CT: Yale University Press, 1999.

————. "Victorian Culture and the Museum: Before and After the White Cube." *Journal of Victorian Culture* 11, no. 1 (2006): 133–145.

BCP. Birmingham Council Proceedings. See Borough of Birmingham and City of Birmingham, *Proceedings of the Council.*

Beavan, Brian. *Leisure, Citizenship and Working-Class Men in Britain, 1850–1945.* Manchester: Manchester University Press, 2005.

Bebbington, D. W. *Evangelicalism in Modern Britain: A History from the 1730s to the 1980s.* London: Unwin Hyman, 1989.

————. *The Nonconformist Conscience: Chapel and Politics, 1870–1914.* London: George Allen and Unwin, 1982.

Beegan, Gerry. *The Mass Image: A Social History of Photomechanical Reproduction in Victorian London.* New York: Palgrave Macmillan, 2008.

Belchem, John. *Popular Politics, Riot and Labour: Essays in Liverpool History, 1790–1940.* Liverpool: Liverpool University Press, 1992.

Bell, Malcolm. *Sir Edward Burne-Jones: A Record and Review.* 3rd ed. London: Bell, 1894.

Bennett, Tony. *The Birth of the Museum: History, Theory, Politics.* New York: Routledge, 1995.

Binfield, Clyde. *The Cross and the City: Essays in Commemoration of Robert William Dale, 1829–1895.* Cambridge: United Reformed Church History Society, 1999.

Birmingham Museum and Art Gallery. *Catalogue of Burne-Jones and Rossetti Collections of Drawings Etc Presented to the City, 1903.* Birmingham, 1903.

————. *Catalogue of the Permanent Collection of Paintings in Oil, Tempera, Water-Colour, Etc./City of Birmingham, Art Gallery. Price One Shilling.* Birmingham: Hudson, 1930.

————. *Catalogue (with Descriptive Notes) of the Permanent Collection of Paintings in Oil and Water-Colours and the Collection of Statuary.* Birmingham, 1901.

———. *Catalogue (with Notes) of the Collection of Paintings in Oil and Water Colours, by Living and Deceased Artists.* Birmingham: E. C. Osborne and Son, 1888.

———. *Illustrated Catalogue (with Descriptive Notes) of the Permanent Collection of Paintings in the Art Gallery and in Aston Hall and Elsewhere.* Birmingham: Hudson and Son, 1909, 1912, 1923.

Black, Barbara J. *On Exhibit: Victorians and Their Museums.* Charlottesville: University Press of Virginia, 2000.

Blackburn, Henry. *New Gallery 1891: A Complete Illustrated Catalogue of the Summer Exhibition, with Notes by Henry Blackburn.* London: Chatto and Windus, 1891.

Borough of Birmingham. *Proceedings of the Council.* Birmingham: B. Hunt and Sons, 1859–1871.

———. *Proceedings of the Council.* Birmingham: George Jones and Son, 1871–1879, 1880–1890, 1890–1900.

———. *Proceedings of the Council.* Birmingham: Percival Jones and Son, 1901–1914.

Borough of Manchester. *Proceedings of the Council, from November, 1851, to November, 1852.* Manchester: Cave and Sever, 1853.

Borzello, Frances. *Civilising Caliban: The Misuse of Art 1875–1980.* London: Routledge and Kegan Paul, 1987.

Bourdieu, Pierre. *Distinction: A Social Critique of the Judgement of Taste,* trans. Richard Nice. Cambridge, MA: Harvard University Press, 1984.

Bourdieu, Pierre, Alain Darbel, and Dominique Schnapper. *The Love of Art: European Art Museums and Their Public.* Stanford, CA: Stanford University Press, 1991.

Bowdler, Roger. "Ars Longa, Vita Brevis: Life, Death and John Everett Millais." In *John Everett Millais: Beyond the Pre-Raphaelite Brotherhood,* ed. Debra N. Mancoff, 207–233. New Haven, CT: Yale University Press, 2001.

Brettell, Richard R. *Modern Art, 1851–1929: Capitalism and Representation.* Oxford: Oxford University Press, 1999.

Briggs, Asa. *The History of Birmingham, Vol. 2: Borough and City, 1865–1938.* London: Oxford University Press, 1952.

———. *Victorian Cities.* New York: Harper and Row, 1963.

Brooks, M. W. *John Ruskin and Victorian Architecture.* New Brunswick, NJ: Rutgers University Press, 1987.

Buckley, Jerome H. "Victorian England." In *The Mind and Art of Victorian England,* ed. Josef L. Altholz, 3–16. Minneapolis: University of Minnesota Press, 1976.

Bunce, J. T. *Addresses to the Midland Institute.* Birmingham, 1876, 1877, 1892.

———. *A History of Birmingham with a Sketch of Its Earlier Government.* Birmingham: Cornish Brothers, 1878.

Burton, Anthony. *Vision and Accident: The Story of the Victoria and Albert Museum.* London: V&A, 1999.

Butler, Lance St. John. *Victorian Doubt: Literacy and Cultural Discourses.* New York: Harvester Wheatsheaf, 1990.

Caine, T. H. Hall. *A Disquisition on Dante Gabriel Rossetti's Painting in Oil, Entitled "Dante's Dream," in Possession of the Corporation of Liverpool, Delivered at the Request of His Worship the Mayor, on the Occasion of a Reception Given by Him and Mrs. W. B.*

Forwood, at the Walker Art Gallery, on the Evening of Thursday, November 3rd, 1881, by T. H. Hall Caine. Liverpool: Printed at the "Daily Post" and "Echo" Offices, 1881.

Catalogue of the Exhibition of Works of Art in the New Islington Public Room, Ancoats. Manchester: A. Ireland, 1880.

Catalogue of the Objects of Art and Art Manufactures in the Corporation Free Art Gallery, Ratcliff Place, with Notes Descriptive, Historical, Biographical, &c., on the Pictures, Statues, Busts, &c., Exhibited Therein; Including a Guide to the East India Collection, Selected from the India Museum, Whitehall Place, London, Under the Authority of the Secretary of State for India, and Now Being Exhibited by the Committee of the Birmingham School of Art. Birmingham: Free Art Gallery Committee, 1870.

Chamberlain, Arthur Bensley. *The Corporation Museum and Art Gallery.* Birmingham: Cornish Brothers, 1913.

Chamberlain, John Henry. *Exotic Art: A Lecture to the Birmingham and Midland Institute.* Birmingham: Cornish Brothers, 1883.

Chamberlain, Joseph. *Progress of Birmingham Improvement Scheme. Speech at a Special Meeting of the Council, 11th June 1878.* Birmingham: Improvement Committee, 1878.

———. *Six Years of Educational Work in Birmingham. An Address, Delivered to the Birmingham School Board, by the Chairman, Joseph Chamberlain, Esq., M.P., November 2, 1876.* Birmingham: "Journal" Printing Offices, 1876.

Chesneau, Ernest. *The English School of Painting; Translated by Lucy N. Etherington; with a Preface by [J.] Ruskin.* 4th ed. London, 1884.

City of Birmingham. *Proceedings of the Council.* Birmingham: George Jones and Son, 1890–1900.

———. *Proceedings of the Council.* Birmingham: Percival Jones and Son, 1901–1914.

City of Liverpool. *Proceedings of the Council.* Liverpool, 1871–1914.

———. *Sunday Opening of Libraries, Museums, and Art Galleries. Report of the Librarian and Answers from Various Institutions to the Questions Issued by the Library, Museum, and Arts Committee.* Liverpool: Henry Greenwood, 1885.

City of Manchester. *Index of Minutes of the Council, from Incorporation of the Borough, 23rd October, 1838, to the End of the Municipal Year Ended 31st October, 1900.* Manchester, 1901.

———. *Proceedings of the Council.* Manchester: Henry Blacklock, 1854–1914.

Cleveland, S. D. *The Royal Manchester Institution, Its History from Its Origin to 1882, when the building and contents of the Institution were presented to the Manchester Corporation and became the City Art Gallery.* Manchester: Printed by direction of the [RMI] Council, 1931.

Cohen, Deborah. *Household Gods: The British and Their Possessions.* New Haven, CT: Yale University Press, 2006.

Cohen, Sol. "Sir Michael E. Sadler and the Sociopolitical Analysis of Education." *History of Education Quarterly* 7, no. 3 (Autumn 1967): 281–294.

Cole, Henry. *Fifty Years of Public Work of Sir Henry Cole, Accounted for in His Deeds, Speeches and Writings.* London: G. Bell, 1884.

Coleridge, Mary E. *The Leaders of the English Pre-Raphaelites: Holman Hunt, Rossetti, Millais, with My Grandfather, His Wives and Loves, by Diana Holman-Hunt.* Vol. 1. London: T. C. and E. C. Jack, 1908.

Collings, Jesse. *On the State of Education in Birmingham: A Paper Read at the Social Sciences Meeting in Birmingham, October, 1868.* Birmingham: Cornish Brothers, 1869.

———. *Speech of Mr. Councillor Jesse Collings, in the Birmingham Town Council, on the Resolution to Open the Public Art Gallery, and Free Reference Library, on Sundays.* London and Birmingham: National Sunday League, 1872.

Collings, Jesse, and John L. Green. *The Life of the Right Hon. Jesse Collings, with an Introduction by the Right Hon. Austen Chamberlain, M.P.* London: Longmans, Green, 1920.

Collins, Neil. *Politics and Elections in Nineteenth-Century Liverpool.* Aldershot: Scolar, 1994.

Concise Catalogue of British Paintings, Vol. 1: British Artists Born Before 1850. Manchester: Manchester City Art Gallery, 1976.

Conn, Stephen. *Museums and American Intellectual Life, 1876–1926.* Chicago: University of Chicago Press, 1998.

Cook, E. T. *A Popular Handbook to the National Gallery, with Preface by John Ruskin.* 2 vols. London: Macmillan, 1888.

Cooper and Co.'s Penny Guide to the Birmingham Art Gallery and Museum with a Plan of the Building, and List of Pictures. Birmingham: Cooper and Co., 1886.

Corbett, David P. *The Modernity of English Art, 1914–1930.* Manchester: Manchester University Press, 1997.

———. *The World in Paint: Modern Art and Visuality in England, 1848–1914.* University Park: Pennsylvania State University Press, 2004.

Corporation of Liverpool. *Council Proceedings.* Liverpool: Henry Greenwood, 1874.

———. *Liverpool Naval Exhibition, 1892.* Liverpool: C. Tinling, 1892.

Cossins, J. A. "Architecture." In *Handbook of Birmingham, Prepared for Members of the British Association.* Birmingham: Hall and English, 1886.

Crook, J. Mordaunt. *The British Museum.* New York: Praeger, 1972.

———. *The Dilemma of Style.* Chicago: University of Chicago Press, 1987.

Crosskey, H. W. *A Citizen of No Mean City: Discourse in Memory of Thomas Phillips.* Birmingham, 1876.

———. *A Hand-Book of Rational Piety.* London: Philip Green, 1893.

Cust, Lionel, ed. *Catalogue of the National Gallery of British Art, Tate Gallery.* London: Eyre and Spottiswoode, 1899.

Dagognet, François. *Le musée sans fin.* Seyssel: Éditions Champ Vallon, 1993.

Dale, A. W. W. "George Dawson." In *Nine Famous Birmingham Men: Lectures Delivered in the University,* ed. John H. Muirhead, 75–108. Birmingham: Cornish Brothers, 1909.

———. *The Life of R. W. Dale of Birmingham.* London: Hodder and Stoughton, 1898.

Darcy, Cornelius P. *The Encouragement of the Fine Arts in Lancashire, 1760–1860.* Manchester: Manchester University Press, 1976.

Dark Doings at the Royal Institution, Manchester. Manchester: Isaac W. Petty and Son, 1879.

Davies, Stuart. *By the Gains of Industry: Birmingham Museums and Art Gallery 1885–1985.* Birmingham: Birmingham Museums and Art Gallery, 1985.

Dawson, George. "Beauty and Purity in Towns." In *Shakespeare and Other Lectures,* ed. George St. Clair, 494–499. London, 1888.

Dean, Annie Holt. "Private Patrons and Public Art Endeavors in Victorian Manchester." MA thesis, University of California, Davis, 1988.

Dean, Dennis R. "Some Quotations in Keats's Poetry." *Philological Quarterly* 76 (Winter 1997): 69–85.

Denney, Colleen. *At the Temple of Art: The Grosvenor Gallery, 1877–1890.* Cranbury, NJ: Associated University Presses, 2000.

Deutsche, Rosalyn, and Cara Gendel Ryan. "The Fine Art of Gentrification." In *October: The First Decade, 1976–1986*, ed. Annette Michelson, 151–171. Cambridge, MA: MIT Press, 1987.

Dickens, Charles. *Address Delivered at the Birmingham and Midland Institute on the 27th of September, 1869.* Birmingham: Josiah Allen, Jr., 1869.

Dowling, Linda. *The Vulgarization of Art: The Victorians and Aesthetic Democracy.* Charlottesville: University Press of Virginia, 1996.

Duncan, Carol. "Putting the 'Nation' in London's National Gallery." In *The Formation of National Collections of Art and Archaeology*, ed. Gwendolyn Wright, 101–111. Washington, DC: National Gallery of Art, Washington, and University Press of New England, 1996.

Duncan, Carol, and Alan Wallach. "The Museum of Modern Art as Late Capitalist Ritual: An Iconographic Analysis." *Marxist Perspectives* 4 (Winter 1978): 28–51.

Dyall, Charles. *Catalogue of the Walker Art Gallery; Ed. with Introduction and Notes by Charles Dyall: Gems of the Galleries, No. 3.* Illustrated. Liverpool, 1900.

———. *Descriptive Catalogue of the Permanent Collection of Pictures.* Liverpool, 1901.

———. *Descriptive Catalogue of the Permanent Collection of Pictures; comp. by Charles Dyall*, 1896.

———. *Descriptive Catalogue of the Permanent Collection of Pictures. Compiled by Charles Dyall.* Liverpool, 1883.

———. *First Decade of the Walker Art Gallery: A Report of Its Operations from 1877 to 1887.* Liverpool, 1888.

———. *Library, Museum and Arts Committee. Walker Art Gallery: Report on the Transfer of the Roscoe Collection of Paintings, Sculpture, Etc., by the Trustees of the Royal Institution to the Liverpool Corporation, and on the Necessity for Enlarging the Walker Art Gallery, by Charles Dyall. Dec. 15, 1892.* Liverpool, 1892.

Dyall, Charles, and Clarence G. Dyall. *The Walker Art Gallery: Sketch of the Rise and Progress of the Institution and Catalogue of the Permanent Collection.* Liverpool, 1895.

Ellis, Edith Lees. *The Masses and the Classes. A Plea. A Lecture Given in Ancoats.* Manchester, ca. 1890.

Engels, Frederick. *The Condition of the Working-Class in England.* New York: International Publishers, 1975.

Eshet, Dan. "Life, Liberty, and Leisure: Sunday Observance in England and the Cultural Ideology of Modern Leisure." PhD diss., University of California, Los Angeles, 1999.

Exhibition of Industrial Art, Etc., Ancoats, June and July 1881. Manchester, 1880.

Exhibition of Works of Art, Ancoats. Manchester: James Ashton, 1881, 1882, 1884.

Farago, Claire, and Donald Preziosi. *Grasping the World: The Idea of the Museum.* Aldershot: Ashgate, 2004.

Fine Art Society. *The Fine Art Society Story: 125 years, 1876–2001.* London: Fine Art Society, 2001.

[First] Report of the Library and Museum Committee, to the Town Council, of the Borough of Liverpool, October, 1853. Liverpool: Robert H. Fraser, 1853.

Flint, Kate. *The Victorians and the Visual Imagination.* Cambridge: Cambridge University Press, 2000.

Ford, Ford Madox. *Rossetti: A Critical Essay on His Art, by Ford Madox Hueffer.* London: Duckworth, 1902.

Ford Madox Brown, 1821–1893. Exhibition organized by the Walker Art Gallery, Liverpool, 1964. Liverpool: Walker Art Gallery, 1964.

Fraser, Derek. *Urban Politics in Victorian England: The Structure of Politics in Victorian Cities.* Leicester: Leicester University Press, 1976.

Free Art Gallery and Museum for Manchester: Report of a Meeting Held in Manchester Town Hall, March 5th, 1860. Manchester, 1860.

Free Libraries and Museums. Conference of Representatives of Municipal Corporations, Held in the Council Chamber, Birmingham, Friday, the 5th Day of January, 1877. Birmingham: "Journal" Printing Offices, 1877.

Fyfe, Gordon. *Art, Power and Modernity: English Art Institution, 1750–1950.* Leicester: Leicester University Press, 2000.

———. "The Chantrey Episode: Art Classification, Museums and the State, c1870–1920." In *Art in Museums*, ed. Susan M. Pearce, 5–41. London: Athlone, 1995.

Gandhi, Mahatma. *An Autobiography: The Story of My Experiments with Truth, with a Foreword by Sissela Bok*, trans. Mahadev Desai. Boston: Beacon, 1993.

Giebelhausen, Michaela. *Painting the Bible: Representation and Belief in Mid-Victorian Britain.* Aldershot: Ashgate, 2006.

Gilbert, Alan D. *Religion and Society in Industrial England: Church, Chapel and Social Change, 1740–1914.* London: Longman, 1976.

Girouard, Mark. *The Return to Camelot: Chivalry and the English Gentleman.* New Haven, CT: Yale University Press, 1981.

Glasgow, Eric. "The Origins of the Liverpool Public Libraries." *Library Review* 46, no. 4 (1997): 262–267.

Godlee, Arthur. "The Birmingham and Midland Institute." In *Birmingham Institutions: Lectures Given at the University*, ed. John H. Muirhead, 317–362. Birmingham: Cornish Brothers, 1911.

Green, S. J. D. *Religion in the Age of Decline: Organisation and Experience in Industrial Yorkshire, 1870–1920.* Cambridge: Cambridge University Press, 1996.

Greenwood, Thomas. *Museums and Art Galleries.* London: Simpkin, Marshall, 1888.

Grindley, B. H. *Exhibitions of Pictures and Municipal Management. Lecture by B. H. Grindley, Delivered at the Free Public Library, Museum and Gallery of Art, Liverpool, March 9th, 1875.* Liverpool: Gilbert G. Walmsley, 1875.

———. *History and Work of the Liverpool Academy of Arts. Lecture by B. H. Grindley, Delivered at the Free Public Library, Museum and Gallery of Art, Liverpool, February 9th, 1875.* Liverpool: College Lane Steam Printing Works, 1875.

Gunn, Simon. *History and Cultural Theory.* Edinburgh: Pearson Education, 2006.

———. "The Middle Class, Modernity and the Provincial City: Manchester, c. 1840–1880." In *Gender, Civic Culture, and Consumerism: Middle-Class Identity in Britain, 1800–1940*, ed. Alan Kidd and David Nicholls, 112–127. Manchester: Manchester University Press, 1999.

———. *The Public Culture of the Victorian Middle Class: Ritual and Authority and the English Industrial City, 1840–1914.* Manchester: Manchester University Press, 2000.

Haertinger, Pia. *John Ruskin und das Museum: Portrait eines Pioniers und einer Museumsepoche.* Frankfurt am Main: P. Lang, 1996.

Halkett, George R. *Notes to the Royal Society of Artists' Autumn Exhibition, Birmingham, 1878.* Birmingham: Hudson and Son, 1878.

———. *The Royal Manchester Institution Notes, 1878.* Edinburgh: St. Andrew's Steam Printing Works, 1878.

———. *The Walker Art Gallery Notes, Liverpool—By Special Permission of the Council. Containing 112 Illustrations of the Chief Works, from Drawings by the Artists. By the Editor of "Royal Scottish Academy Notes," "Notes to the Glasgow Institute of Fine Arts," &c., &c.* Liverpool: W. H. Smith and Son, 1878.

Hansard's Parliamentary Debates, Third Series, vols. 78, 109, 239. London: Cornelius Bruck, 1845, 1850, 1878.

Harris, George Montagu. *Municipal Self-Government in Britain: A Study of the Practice of Local Government in Ten of the Larger British Cities.* London: P. S. King and Son, 1939.

Harrison, Michael. "Art and Philanthropy: T. C. Horsfall and the Manchester Art Museum." In *City, Class, and Culture: Studies of Social Policy and Cultural Production in Victorian Manchester,* ed. Alan Kidd and K. W. Roberts, 120–147. Manchester: Manchester University Press, 1985.

———. "Art and Social Regeneration: The Ancoats Art Museum." *Manchester Region History Review* 7 (1993): 63–72.

———. "Social Reform in Late Victorian and Edwardian Manchester with Special Reference to T. C. Horsfall." PhD diss., University of Manchester, 1987.

Hartnell, Roy. "Art and Civic Culture in Birmingham in the Late Nineteenth Century." *Urban History* 22, no. 2 (August 1995): 229–237.

Hauser, Arnold. *The Social History of Art, Vol. 4.* London and New York: Routledge, 1999.

Haward, Lawrence. "The Problem of Provincial Galleries and Art Museums, with Special Reference to Manchester." *Journal of the Royal Society of Arts* 70, no. 3636 (1922): 631–642.

Hennock, E. P. *Fit and Proper Persons: Ideal and Reality in Nineteenth-Century Urban Government.* London: Edward Arnold, 1973.

Herbert, Eugenia. *The Artist and Social Reform: France and Belgium, 1885–1898.* New Haven, CT: Yale University Press, 1961.

Hewison, Robert, "The Beautiful and the True." In *Ruskin, Turner and the Pre-Raphaelites,* ed. Robert Hewison, Ian Warrell, and Stephen Wildman, 11–20. London: Tate Gallery, 2000.

Hewitt, Martin. *The Emergence of Stability in the Industrial City: Manchester, 1832–67.* Aldershot: Scolar and Ashgate, 1996.

Higginson, J. H. "The Centenary of an English Pioneer in Comparative Education: Sir Michael Sadler (1861–1943)." *International Review of Education* 7, no. 3 (1961): 286–298.

Hiley, E. V. "Birmingham City Government." In *Birmingham Institutions: Lectures Given at the University,* ed. John H. Muirhead, 87–144. Birmingham: Cornish Brothers, 1911.

Hill, Charles. *Would the Sunday Opening of Museums, Libraries and Places of Amusement, Increase or Diminish Sunday Drinking?* London: Partridge, 1879.

Hill, Kate. *Culture and Class in English Public Museums, 1850–1914.* Aldershot: Ashgate, 2005.

———. "'Roughs of Both Sexes': The Working Class in Victorian Museums and Art Galleries." In *Identities in Space: Contested Terrains in the Western City Since 1850*. Ed. Simon Gunn and Robert J. Morris, 190–203. Aldershot: Ashgate, 2001.

Hill, Katherine Sian. "Municipal Museums: Social Reproduction and Cultural Activity in Liverpool and Preston, 1850–1914." PhD diss., Lancaster University, 1996.

Hill, Octavia. *The Manchester Art Museum, Ancoats Hall, Great Ancoats Street. Address by Miss Octavia Hill, Delivered at the Annual Meeting, May 7th, 1897*. Manchester: H. Rawson, 1897.

Hilton, Tim. *John Ruskin*. New Haven, CT: Yale University Press, 2002.

———. *John Ruskin: The Early Years*. New Haven, CT: Yale University Press, 2000 [1995].

———. *John Ruskin: The Later Years*. New Haven, CT: Yale University Press, 2000.

Hobsbawm, Eric. *The Age of Empire, 1875–1914*. London: Weidenfeld and Nicolson, 1997.

———. *Industry and Empire from 1750 to the Present Day*. New York: Penguin, 1990.

Hobsbawm, Eric, and Terence Ranger, eds. *The Invention of Tradition*. Cambridge: Cambridge University Press, 1993.

Hollis, Patricia. *Ladies Elect: Women in English Local Government, 1865–1914*. New York: Oxford University Press, 1987.

Holt, Raymond V. *The Unitarian Contribution to Social Progress in England*. London: George Allen and Unwin, 1938.

Hoock, Holger. "'Struggling Against a Vulgar Prejudice': Patriotism and the Collecting of British Art at the Turn of the Nineteenth Century." *Journal of British Studies* 49, no. 3 (July 2010): 566–591.

Hooper-Greenhill, Eilean. *Museums and the Shaping of Knowledge*. New York: Routledge, 1992.

Horne, Charles Silvester. "R. W. Dale." In *Nine Famous Birmingham Men: Lectures Delivered in the University*, ed. John H. Muirhead, 253–292. Birmingham: Cornish Brothers, 1909.

Horsfall, T. C. *An Art Gallery for Manchester*. Manchester, 1877.

———. *The Art Museum, Manchester. I. The Scheme and History of the Committee. II. Pamphlet on the Scheme, by T. C. Horsfall. III. Relation . . . to the Elementary Schools and Workmen's Clubs*. Manchester: A. Ireland, 1878.

———. *A Description of the Work of the Manchester Art Museum*. Manchester: J. E. Cornish, 1891.

———. *A Description of the Work of the Manchester Art Museum*. Manchester, 1895.

———. *The Government of Manchester. A Paper Read to the Manchester Statistical Society, November 13th, 1895, with Additions*. Manchester: J. E. Cornish, 1895.

———. *Handbook by T. C. Horsfall, to the Manchester Art Museum*. Manchester: A. Ireland, 1888.

———. *The Need for Art in Manchester: An Address, Given May 2nd, 1910, at the Annual Meeting of the Governors of the Manchester Royal Institution*. Manchester: Charles H. Barber, 1910.

———. "Neglected Pictures" (report of a meeting of the Manchester Literary Club). *The Architect*, October 20, 1883, 236.

———. *The Place of "Admiration, Hope & Love" in Town Life: Reply by T. C. Horsfall to an Address Presented to Him on 30th June, 1910, by Nearly Three Hundred of His Fellow-Citizens*. Manchester: Charles H. Barber, 1910.

———. *Ruskin on Religion & Life, a Paper Read to the Manchester Ruskin Society.* Manchester: J. E. Cornish, 1902.

———. *Statement of the Aims and Objects of the Manchester Art Museum.* Manchester, 1886.

———. *The Study of Beauty, and Art in Large Towns. Two Papers by T. C. Horsfall, with an Introduction by John Ruskin, D.C.L., LL.D., Honorary Student of Christ Church, and Honorary Fellow of Corpus-Christi College.* London: Macmillan, 1883.

———. *Suggestions for a Guide-Book to Life. A Lecture Delivered to the Chorlton-cum-Hardy Mutual Improvement Society in 1886.* Manchester: Sherratt and Hughes, 1905.

———. *The Use of Pictures and Other Works of Art in Elementary Schools. A Paper Read at the International Conference on Education, Held in London, in 1884.* London: John Heywood, 1887.

———, ed. *Proceedings of the Manchester Conference on Education Under Healthy Conditions.* London: John Heywood, 1885.

Hunt, Tristam. *Building Jerusalem: The Rise and Fall of the Victorian City.* London: Weidenfeld and Nicolson, 2004.

Hunt, W. Holman. *An Address Delivered by Mr. W. Holman Hunt, at the Distribution of Prizes to Students of the Birmingham Municipal School of Art, on the 22nd of February, 1893.* Birmingham, 1893.

———. *A Description of the Picture "The Triumph of the Innocents," by W. Holman Hunt, Lent by Mr. John T. Middlemore. (Written by the Artist.)* Birmingham: Birmingham Guild of Handicraft, 1897.

Jacobi, Carol. *William Holman Hunt: Painter, Painting, Paint.* Manchester: Manchester University Press, 2006.

James, Liz. "Senses and Sensibility in Byzantium." *Art History* 27, no. 4 (2004): 522–537.

Johnson, Paul, and Kenneth McConkey. *Alfred East: Lyrical Landscape Painter.* London: Samson, 2009.

Jones, J. Beaumont. *General Index to the Proceedings of the Council, from 28th September 1852, to 16th October, 1900, Inclusive (Minutes 1 to 18,285).* Birmingham: Percival Jones, 1901.

Jones, Linda J. "Public Pursuit of Private Profit? Liberal Businessmen and Municipal Politics in Birmingham, 1865–1900." *Business History* 25, no. 3 (November 1983): 240–259.

Jones, Peter d'A. *The Christian Socialist Revival, 1877–1914: Religion, Class, and Social Conscience in Late-Victorian England.* Princeton, NJ: Princeton University Press, 1968.

Joyce, Patrick. *Visions of the People: Industrial England and the Question of Class 1848–1914.* Cambridge: Cambridge University Press, 1991.

Keith-Lucas, B. *English Local Government in the Nineteenth and Twentieth Centuries.* London: Historical Association, 1977.

Kenrick, William. *Modern British Painters: A Lecture Delivered by Alderman William Kenrick, M.P., Chairman of the Museum and School of Art Committee, to the Students of the Birmingham Municipal School of Art, on the 26th of October, 1894.* Birmingham: George Jones and Son, 1894.

———. *On Some Art Books in the Reference Library, by Alderman William Kenrick.* Birmingham: Midland Educational, 1885.

Kent, J. H. S. "The Role of Religion in the Cultural Structure of the Later Victorian City." *Transactions of the Royal Historical Society, Fifth Series* 23 (1973): 153–173.

Kern, Stephen. *The Culture of Time and Space 1880–1918.* Cambridge, MA: Harvard University Press, 1983.

Kidd, Alan, and K. W. Roberts, eds. *City, Class, and Culture: Studies of Social Policy and Cultural Production in Victorian Manchester.* Manchester: Manchester University Press, 1985.

Klein, Rachel N. "Art Museums and Public Life in Historical Perspective." *Intellectual History Newsletter* 23 (2001): 35–43.

Koven, Seth. "The Whitechapel Picture Exhibitions and the Politics of Seeing." In *Museum Culture: Histories, Discourses, Spectacles,* ed. Daniel J. Sherman and Irit Rogoff, 22–48. Minneapolis: University of Minnesota Press, 1994.

Kriegel, Lara. *Grand Designs: Labor, Empire, and the Museum in Victorian Culture.* Durham, NC: Duke University Press, 2007.

———. "Review Essay: After the Exhibitionary Complex: Museum Histories and the Future of the Victorian Past." *Victorian Studies* 48, no. 4 (2006): 681–704.

Ladd, Henry Andrews. *The Victorian Morality of Art: An Analysis of Ruskin's Esthetic.* New York: Octagon Books, 1968.

Lambert, R. S., ed. *Art in England.* Harmondsworth: Penguin, 1938.

Landow, George P. "There Began to Be a Great Talking About the Fine Arts." In *The Mind and Art of Victorian England,* ed. Joseph L. Altholz, 124–145. Minneapolis: University of Minnesota Press, 1976.

———. *William Holman Hunt and Typological Symbolism.* New Haven, CT: Yale University Press, 1979.

Lang, Lenora Blanche. *The Life and Work of Sir Frederick Leighton . . . ; and, the life and Work of Sir John E. Millais . . . [by Walter Armstrong].* London: Art Journal, 1885.

Langford, John Alfred. *The Birmingham Free Libraries, the Shakspere [sic] Memorial Library, and the Art Gallery.* Birmingham: Hall and English, 1871.

Laqueur, Thomas. *Religion and Respectability: Sunday Schools and Working Class Culture, 1780–1850.* New Haven, CT: Yale University Press, 1976.

"The Late Sir Whitworth Wallis, F. S. A., 1855–1927. *Connoisseur* 77 (1927): 185–186.

Law, John [Mary Harkness]. *A Manchester Shirtmaker.* West Yorkshire: Northern Herald Books, 2002 [1890].

Leighton, Denys P. "Municipal Progress, Democracy and Radical Identity in Birmingham, 1838–1886." *Midland History* 25 (2000): 115–142.

Lethaby, W. R. *"Morris as Work-Master": Address Delivered by W. R. Lethaby at the Birmingham and Midland Institute on the 13th of February, 1901.* Birmingham: Cornish Brothers, 1901.

———. *"The Study and Practice of Artistic Crafts": An Address Delivered by W. R. Lethaby at the Birmingham and Midland Institute on the 15th of February, 1901.* Birmingham, 1901.

Libraries, Museums, and Arts Committee. *Accounts. In Epitome of the Accounts of the Corporation of Liverpool (Ex Health and Water).* Liverpool: Henry Greenwood, 1874–1914.

———. *Library and Museum Rate: Report of the Gardens, Library, and Museum Committee, in Reference to and Consequent upon the Decision of the Court of Queen's Bench on the Library and Museum Rate.* Liverpool, 1862.

Lorente, Jesús Pedro. *Cathedrals of Urban Modernity: The First Museums of Contemporary Art, 1800–1930.* Brookfield, VT: Ashgate, 1998.

Lund, T. W. M. *The Ideal Citizen: An Appreciation of Philip Rathbone.* Liverpool, 1896.

———. *A Picture Gallery Through a Layman's Eyes: An Address Delivered at the Walker Art Gallery, on 29th October, 1909.* Liverpool: Henry Young and Sons, 1909.

———. *The Religion of Art in Three Pictures: "An Idyll" "S. Elizabeth of Hungary's Great Act of Renunciation" and "The Doctor."* Liverpool: Edward Howell, 1891.

———. *"Some Uses of an Art Gallery," A Friday Afternoon Talk at the Autumn Exhibition, Liverpool, 1912.* Liverpool: Lee and Nightingale, 1912.

MacCarthy, Desmond. "The Post-Impressionists." In *Modernism: An Anthology of Sources and Documents,* ed. Jane Goldman, Vassiliki Kolocotroni, and Olga Taxidou, 174–178. Chicago: University of Chicago Press, 1998.

Macdonald, Stuart. "The Royal Manchester Institution." In *Art and Architecture in Victorian Manchester: Ten Illustrations of Patronage and Practice,* ed. John H. G. Archer, 28–45. Manchester: Manchester University Press, 1985.

MacDonald, Susan, and Gordon Fyfe, eds. *Theorizing Museums: Representing Identity and Diversity in a Changing World.* Cambridge, MA: Blackwell, 1996.

Macleod, Dianne Sachko. *Art and the Victorian Middle Class: Money and the Making of Cultural Identity.* Cambridge: Cambridge University Press, 1996.

Macleod, Robert. *Style and Society: Architectural Ideology in Britain 1835–1914.* London: William Clowes and Sons, 1971.

Mainardi, Patricia. *The End of the Salon: Art and the State in the Early Third Republic.* Cambridge: Cambridge University Press, 1993.

Maleuvre, Didier. *Museum Memories: History, Technology, Art.* Stanford, CA: Stanford University Press, 1999.

Maltz, Diana. *British Aestheticism and the Urban Working Classes, 1870–1900: Beauty for the People.* New York: Palgrave Macmillan, 2006.

Manchester City Art Gallery. *Catalogue of Ruskin Exhibition.* Manchester, 1904.

———. *Catalogue of the Museum Arts and Crafts Exhibitions, City Art Gallery.* Manchester, 1891, 1895.

———. *Exhibition of Drawings and Examples of Craftsmanship.* Manchester: John Heywood, 1911.

———. *Loan Exhibition of Works by Ford Madox Brown and the Pre-Raphaelite Brotherhood.* Manchester, 1911.

———. *Report of the Art Gallery Committee Visit to Art Galleries and Museums in Belgium, Holland, Germany and Great Britain, 1905.* Manchester, 1905.

———. *Reproductions from the Collection of the Manchester City Art Gallery, with an Introduction by Lawrence Haward.* London: Eyre and Spottiswood, 1925.

Manchester City Art Gallery/Royal Manchester Institution. *Catalogues of Annual Autumn Exhibitions.* Manchester, 1860–1913.

Mancoff, Debra N., ed. *John Everett Millais: Beyond the Pre-Raphaelite Brotherhood.* New Haven, CT: Yale University Press, 2001.

Mandler, Peter. *The Fall and Rise of the Stately Home.* New Haven, CT: Yale University Press, 1997.

Mann, Horace. *Census of Great Britain, 1851. Religious Worship in England in Wales, Abridged from the Official Report Made by Horace Mann, Esq. to George Graham, Esq., the Registrar-General.* London: George E. Eyre and William Spottiswoode, 1854.

Marcus, Steven. *Engels, Manchester, and the Working Class.* New York: Norton, 1985.

Matthew, H. C. G. "The Liberal Age, 1851–1914." In *The Oxford History of Britain*, vol. 5, ed. Kenneth O. Morgan. Oxford: Oxford University Press, 1984.

McClellan, Andrew. *Inventing the Louvre: Art, Politics, and the Origins of the Modern Museum in Eighteenth-Century Paris.* Cambridge: Cambridge University Press, 1994.

McConkey, Kevin. *Memory and Desire: Painting in Britain and Ireland at the Turn of the Twentieth Century.* Aldershot: Ashgate, 2002.

McLeod, Hugh, ed. *European Religion in the Age of Great Cities, 1830–1930.* London: Routledge, 1995.

MCP. Manchester Council Proceedings. See City of Manchester, *Proceedings of the Council.*

Meller, H. E. *Leisure and the Changing City, 1870–1914.* London: Routledge and Kegan Paul, 1976.

Memorandum on the Relations Existing in February, 1885, Between the Committee of the Manchester Art Museum and the Parks and Cemeteries Committee of the Town of Manchester. Manchester: A. Ireland, 1885.

Merrill, Linda. *A Pot of Paint: Aesthetics on Trial in Whistler v. Ruskin.* Washington, DC: Smithsonian Institution Press, 1992.

"The Michael Sadler Memorial Exhibition." *Burlington Magazine for Connoisseurs* 84, no. 490 (January 1944): 24–25.

Millais, PRB-PRA: An Exhibition Organized by the Walker Art Gallery Liverpool and the Royal Academy of Arts London, January–April 1967. London: William Clowes and Sons, 1967.

Miller, Stephen. *The Peculiar Life of Sundays.* Cambridge, MA: Harvard University Press, 2008.

Milner, Frank. *The Pre-Raphaelites: Pre-Raphaelite Paintings and Drawings in Merseyside Collections.* Liverpool: Bluecoat, 1995.

Minihan, Janet. *The Nationalization of Culture: The Development of State Subsidies to the Arts in Britain.* New York: New York University Press, 1977.

Minneapolis Art Institute. *Victorian High Renaissance: G. F. Watts, Lord Leighton, Albert Moore, Sir Alfred Gilbert. An Exhibition Organised by the Minneapolis Institute of Arts. Manchester City Art Gallery, 1st Sept.–15 Oct. 1978.* Minneapolis: The Art Institute, 1978.

Minogue, Martin, ed. *Local Government in Britain.* Cambridge: Cambridge University Press, 1977.

Monkhouse, W. Cosmo. *British Contemporary Artists.* New York: C. Scribner's Sons, 1899.

Morley, J. Cooper. *The Newspaper Press and Periodical Literature of Liverpool.* Liverpool: Egerton Smith, 1887.

Morris, Edward. "Philip Henry Rathbone and the Purchase of Contemporary Foreign Paintings for the Walker Art Gallery, Liverpool, 1871–1914." In *Annual Report and Bulletin of the Walker Art Gallery, Liverpool, 1975–1976*, vol. 6 (1975–1976): 59–67.

———. *Public Art Collections in North-West England: A History and Guide.* Liverpool: Liverpool University Press, 2001.

———. *Victorian and Edwardian Paintings in the Walker Art Gallery and at Sudley House: British Artists Born After 1810 but Before 1861.* London: Her Majesty's Stationery Office, 1996.

Morris, R. J. *Class, Sect and Party: The Making of the British Middle Class, Leeds 1820–1850.* Manchester and New York: Manchester University Press and St. Martin's Press, 1990.

Morris, R. J., and Richard H. Trainor, eds. *Urban Governance: Britain and Beyond Since 1750*. Aldershot: Ashgate, 2000.

Morris, William. *Address Delivered at the Town Hall, Birmingham, on the 19th of February, 1879 by William Morris, President*. Birmingham: E. C. Osborne, 1879.

———. *An Address Delivered by William Morris, at the Distribution of Prizes to Students of the Birmingham Municipal School of Art, on the 21st of February, 1894*. Birmingham, 1894.

———. *Address on the Collection of Paintings of the English Pre-Raphaelite School*. Birmingham: E. C. Osborne and Son, 1891.

———. *The Collected Works of William Morris, with an Introduction by His Daughter May Morris. Vol. 22: Hopes and Fears for Art, Lectures on Art and Industry*. London: Longmans, Green, 1914.

———. *"Labour and Pleasure, Versus Labour and Sorrow," an Address by William Morris in the Town Hall, Birmingham, 19th February, 1880*. Birmingham: Cund Brothers, 1880.

———. *News from Nowhere or an Epoch of Rest, Being Some Chapters from a Utopian Romance*. London: Longmans, Green, 1910.

Muir, Ramsay. *A History of Liverpool with Maps and Illustrations*. East Ardsley: S. R. Publishers, 1970.

Muirhead, John H. *Birmingham Institutions: Lectures Given at the University*. Birmingham: Cornish Brothers, 1911.

———. *Nine Famous Birmingham Men: Lectures Delivered in the University*. Birmingham: Cornish Brothers, 1909.

National Gallery of British Art. *Illustrated Catalogue, Loan Collection of Works by English Pre-Raphaelite Painters Lent by the Art Gallery Committee of the Birmingham Corporation. Open December, 1911 to March, 1912*. London: His Majesty's Stationery Office, 1911.

National Sunday League to Obtain the Opening of the British Museum and Other National Institutions on Sunday Afternoons; also, the Repeal of the Law Which Compels the Closing of the Crystal Palace and Other Collections for Instruction and Rational Recreation on That Day. London: J. Kenny, 1856.

Naylor, Gillian. *The Arts and Crafts Movement: A Study of Its Sources, Ideals and Influence on Design Theory*. London: Trefoil, 1990.

Nead, Lynda. *The Female Nude: Art, Obscenity and Sexuality*. London: Routledge, 1992.

Neal, Frank. *Sectarian Violence. The Liverpool Experience, 1819–1914: An Aspect of Anglo-Irish History*. Manchester: Manchester University Press, 1988.

Official Guide to Aston Hall and Park, and Its Exhibition of Fine Arts and Manufactures, Inaugurated by Her Most Gracious Majesty the Queen, on Tuesday, the 15th Day of June, 1858. Birmingham: M. Billing, 1858.

150th Anniversary Exhibition: The City Art Gallery, Past, Present and Future, May 17th–June 16th 1973. Manchester, 1973.

Ormerod, Henry A. *The Liverpool Royal Institution: A Record and a Retrospect*. Liverpool: The University Press, 1953.

Parkes, Kineton. *The Pre-Raphaelite Movement, by Kineton Parkes*. London: Reeves and Turner; Birmingham: W. Downing, 1889.

Parry, J. P. *Democracy and Religion: Gladstone and the Liberal Party, 1867–1875*. Cambridge: Cambridge University Press, 1986.

Pass, Anthony J. *Thomas Worthington: Victorian Architecture and Social Purpose.* Manchester: Literary and Philosophical Publications, 1988.

Pearce, Susan M. *Art in Museums.* London: Athlone, 1995.

———. *On Collecting: An Investigation into Collecting in the European Tradition.* London: Routledge, 1995.

Perry, Gill, and Colin Cunningham. *Academies, Museums and Canons of Art.* New Haven, CT: Yale University Press, 1999.

Pevsner, Nicolaus. *A History of Building Types.* Princeton, NJ: Princeton University Press, 1976.

Phythian, J. E. *Half Hours at the Manchester City Art Gallery.* Manchester: Sherratt and Hughes, 1903.

———. *Handbook to G. F. Watts Memorial Exhibition.* London: Sherratt and Hughes, 1905.

———. *Handbook to the Frederic J. Shields Exhibition.* Manchester: Taylor, Garnett, Evans, 1907.

———. *Handbook to the Permanent Collection of the Manchester City Art Gallery.* Manchester: City of Manchester, 1910.

———. *Handbook to the William Holman Hunt Exhibition.* Manchester, 1906.

———. *Reproductions from MCAG.* Manchester, 1910.

Pick, Daniel. *Faces of Degeneration: A European Disorder, c.1848–c.1918.* Cambridge: Cambridge University Press, 1989.

Picton, J. A. *Liverpool Improvements, and How to Accomplish Them.* Liverpool: E. Howell, 1853.

———. *Memorials of Liverpool Historical and Topographical Including a History of the Dock Estate.* Liverpool: Longmans, Green, 1875.

———. *Notes on the Origin and History of the Congregational Churches in Liverpool.* Liverpool: Benson and Holme, 1877.

———. *Notes on the Proposed Cathedral for Liverpool, Read Before the Literary Philosophical Society of Liverpool, February 9th, 1885.* Liverpool: D. Marples, 1885.

———. *Our Municipal Institutions in Their Past and Future.* Liverpool: Gilbert G. Walmsley, 1882.

Picton, J. Allanson, *Sir James A. Picton: A Biography.* London: Gilbert G. Walmsley, 1891.

Pointon, Marcia, ed. *Art Apart: Art Institutions and Ideology Across England and North America.* Manchester: Manchester University Press, 1994.

Poole, Andrea Geddes. *Stewards of the Nation's Art: Contested Cultural Authority, 1890–1939.* Toronto: University of Toronto Press, 2010.

Prange, F. G. *Art Criticism in Three Hours. On the Principle of French Before Breakfast.* Liverpool: C. Hossfeld, 1875.

Prest, John. *Liberty and Locality: Parliament, Permissive Legislation, and Ratepayers' Democracies in the Nineteenth Century.* Oxford: Clarendon Press, 1990.

Prettejohn, Elizabeth. *Art for Art's Sake: Aestheticism in Victorian Painting.* New Haven, CT: Yale University Press, 2007.

———, ed. *After the Pre-Raphaelites: Art and Aestheticism in Victorian England.* Manchester: Manchester University Press, 1999.

Preziosi, Donald. *Brain of the Earth's Body: Art, Museums, and the Phantasms of Modernity.* Minneapolis: University of Minnesota Press, 2003.

Prior, Nick. "Museums: Leisure Between State and Distinction." In *Histories of Leisure,* ed. Rudy Koshar, 27–44. Oxford: Berg, 2002.

Rager, Andrea Wolk. "'Smite This Sleeping World Awake': Edward Burne-Jones and the Legend of the Briar Rose." *Victorian Studies* 51, no. 3 (Spring 2009): 438–450.

Raimbach, David W. *A Guide to the Collection of Specimens of Art Workmanship on Loan from the South Kensington Museum Now Exhibiting at the Corporation Art Gallery.* Birmingham: Henry Wright, 1868.

Rappaport, Erika Diane. *Shopping for Pleasure: Women in the Making of London's West End.* Princeton, NJ: Princeton University Press, 2000.

Rathbone, Philip H. *Art Department. The Object and Scope of an Art Professorship.* Liverpool, n.d.

———. *The English School of Impressionists, as Illustrated in the Liverpool Autumn Exhibition.* Liverpool: Andrew Russell, 1883.

———. *Impressionism in Art: A Lecture by Mr. P. H. Rathbone at the Walker Art Gallery, Reprinted from 'The Liverpool Citizen.'* Liverpool: Porcupine Steam Printing Works, 1890.

———. *The Mission of the Undraped Figure in Art: A Defense of the "Sculptor's Model."* Liverpool, 1878.

———. *The Place of Art in the Future Industrial Progress of the Nation.* Liverpool: Lee and Nightingale, 1884.

———. *The Political Value of Art to the Municipal Life of a Nation: A Lecture Delivered at the Free Library, Liverpool.* Liverpool: Lee and Nightingale, 1875.

———. *Realism, Idealism, and the Grotesque in Art: Their Limits and Functions.* Liverpool: Lee and Nightingale, 1877.

———. "Section of Museums and National and Municipal Encouragement of Art. The Presidential Address." *Transactions of the NAAAAI, Birmingham Meeting, 1890.* London, 1891.

———. *Varying Moods Expressed in Various Verse.* Chilworth and London: Unwin Brothers, The Gresham Press (for private circulation), 1891.

Redford, Arthur. *The History of Local Government in Manchester.* London: Longmans, Green, 1940.

Redlich, Josef, and Francis W. Hirst. *The History of Local Government in England, Being a Reissue of Book I of Local Government in England, by Josef Redlich and Francis W. Hirst, Edited and with Introduction and Epilogue by Bryan Keith-Lucas.* London: Macmillan, 1958.

Regulations of the Royal Manchester Institution for the Advancement of Literature, Science and the Arts. Manchester: James Collins and Kingston, 1902.

Reid, S. J. *Sir Richard Tangye.* London: Duckworth, 1908.

Report of the Art Gallery Purchase Committee, for Presentation at a Special Meeting of the Council. Birmingham: George Jones and Son, 1882, 1883, 1885.

Reports of the Representatives of the Royal Institution on the Art Gallery Committee of the Corporation of Manchester. Manchester: G. Falkner and Sons, 1888.

Reynolds, Sir Joshua. "Discourse VII, Delivered to the Students of the Royal Academy, on the Distribution of Prizes, December 10, 1776." In *Discourses on the Fine Arts Delivered to the Students of the Royal Academy*, 27–34. London: William and Robert Chambers, 1853.

Richards, Thomas. *The Commodity Culture of Victorian England: Advertising and Spectacle, 1851–1914.* Stanford, CA: Stanford University Press, 1990.

Richmond, W. B. *Leighton, Millais and William Morris: A Lecture Delivered to the Students of the Royal Academy, by Sir William Blake Richmond.* London, 1898.

Roberts, Helene E. "Exhibition and Review: The Periodical Press and the Victorian Art Exhibition System." In *The Victorian Periodical Press: Samplings and Soundings*, ed. Joanne Shattuck and Michael Wolff, 79–105. Leicester: Leicester University Press; Toronto: University of Toronto Press, 1982.

Rodrick, Anne B. *Self-Help and Civic Culture: Citizenship in Victorian Birmingham.* Aldershot: Ashgate, 2004.

Rodway, Alfred. *Handbook to Aston Hall, Museum and Park, Cannon Hill, Calthorpe, Adderley, Highgate, Summerfield, and Small Heath Parks; and Burbury Street Recreation Ground.* Birmingham: Hall and English, 1877.

Rose, Michael E. "Culture, Philanthropy and the Manchester Middle Classes." In *City, Class, and Culture: Studies of Social Policy and Cultural Production in Victorian Manchester*, ed. Alan Kidd and K. W. Roberts, 103–119. Manchester: Manchester University Press, 1985.

Rosenberg, John D., ed. *The Genius of John Ruskin: Selections from His Writings.* Charlottesville: University of Virginia Press, 1998 [1964].

Rosenfeld, Jason, and Alison Smith. *Millais.* London: Tate Publishing, 2007.

Rothenstein, W. *An Address by Mr. W. Rothenstein, on the Occasion of the Distribution of Prizes to the Students of the Municipal School of Art, February 13th, 1908.* Birmingham, 1908.

Rowley, Charles. *Fifty Years of Work Without Wages (Laborare Est Orare).* London: Hodder and Stoughton, 1912.

Royal Manchester Institution. *Catalogue of the Permanent Gallery of the Royal Manchester Institute.* Manchester, 1848.

———. *Exhibition of the Works of Modern Artists, 1880, Sixtieth Exhibition.* Manchester: John Heywood, 1880.

———. *Exhibition of Works Comprised in the Permanent Gallery of the Institution, and a Loan Collection of Paintings and Drawings, May 1882.* London and Manchester: John Heywood, 1882.

Rushton, J. I. "Charles Rowley and the Ancoats Recreation Movement." MA thesis, University of Manchester, 1959.

Ruskin, John. *Fors Clavigera: Letters to the Workmen and Labourers of Great Britain.* 8 vols. New York: John Wiley and Sons, 1886.

———. *"A Joy For Ever" (and Its Price on the Market) Being the Substance (with Additions) of Two Lectures on the Political Economy of Art, Delivered at Manchester, July 10th and 13th, 1857.* London: George Allen, 1906.

———. *The Seven Lamps of Architecture.* New York: John Wiley and Son, 1866 [1849].

———. *The Stones of Venice*, ed. J. G. Links. New York: Da Capo, 1960 [1853].

———. *The Works of John Ruskin.* Ed. Edward Tyas Cook and Alexander Wedderburn. 39 vols. London and New York: George Allen, 1903–1912.

Sadler, M. E. *Pictures in a Great City: A Paper Read by Professor M. E. Sadler, M.A., LL.D., at a Special Meeting of the Governors of the Royal Manchester Institution, on Thursday, March 16, 1911.* Manchester: H. Rawson, 1911.

Schivelbusch, Wolfgang. *The Railway Journey: The Industrialization of Time and Space in the 19th Century.* Berkeley: University of California Press, 1986.

Schmiechen, James A. "The Victorians, the Historians, and the Idea of Modernism." *American Historical Review* 93, no. 2 (April 1988): 287–316.

Schorske, Carl E. *Thinking with History: Explorations in the Passage to Modernism.* Princeton, NJ: Princeton University Press, 1998.

Seed, John. "'Commerce and the Liberal Arts': The Political Economy of Art in Manchester, 1775–1860." In *The Culture of Capital: Art, Power and the Nineteenth-Century Middle Class,* ed. Janet Wolff and John Seed, 45–81. Manchester: Manchester University Press, 1988.

Sharman, Frank. "George Wallis: Pioneer of Industrial Art: George Wallis' Family." Wolverhampton History and Heritage website. Accessed February 15, 2011. http://www.local history.scit.wlv.ac.uk/genealogy/wallis/wallis13.htm.

Sharples, Joseph. *Liverpool.* New Haven, CT: Yale University Press, 2004.

Sheehan, James. *Museums in the German Art World: From the End of the Old Regime to the Rise of Modernism.* Oxford: Oxford University Press, 2000.

Shepherd, George A. *A Short History of the British School of Painting.* London: Sampson Low, Marston, Searle, and Rivington, 1881.

Sherman, Daniel J. *Worthy Monuments: Art Museums and the Politics of Culture in Nineteenth-Century France.* Cambridge, MA: Harvard University Press, 1989.

Silverman, Debora. *Art Nouveau in Fin-de-Siècle France: Politics, Psychology, and Style.* Berkeley: University of California Press, 1989.

———. *Van Gogh and Gauguin: The Search for Sacred Art.* New York: Farrar, Straus and Giroux, 2000.

Simey, Margaret. *Charity Rediscovered: A Study of Philanthropic Effort in Nineteenth-Century Liverpool.* Liverpool: Liverpool University Press, 1992.

Sizes of Rooms in Royal Academy, National Gallery, and South Kensington Galleries, Prepared for Birmingham Art Gallery Committee, 1880. Birmingham: C. Whitwell and Sons, 1880.

Smith, Alison. *The Victorian Nude: Sexuality, Morality, and Art.* Manchester: Manchester University Press, 1996.

———, ed. *Exposed: The Victorian Nude.* London: Tate Publishing, 2001.

Snell, Bernard Joseph. *Second Sermon Preached by Rev. Bernard J. Snell, M.A., B.Sc., on the Sunday Question.* Manchester: John Heywood, 1888.

———. *Sermon Preached by Rev. Bernard J. Snell, M.A., B.Sc., Richmond Chapel, Salford, on the Sunday Opening of Free Libraries.* Manchester: John Heywood, 1888.

Snell, K. D. N., and Paul Ell, eds. *Rival Jerusalems: The Geography of Victorian Religion.* Cambridge: Cambridge University Press, 2000.

South Kensington Museum. *A Guide to the Collections of the South Kensington Museum. Illustrated with Plans and Wood Engravings.* London: Spottiswoode, 1888.

Spalding, Frances. *The Tate: A History.* London: Tate Gallery Publishing, 1998.

Spielmann, M. H. *Millais and His Works, with Special Reference to the Exhibition at the Royal Academy 1898 / by M. H. Spielmann; with a Chapter "Thoughts on Our Art of To-day," by J. E. Millais.* London, 1898.

Spier, K. C. "Among the Pictures: The Permanent Collection in the Walker Art Gallery, by a Bohemian." *Liverpool Lantern* 4 (1880): 195–196.

The Sport of Civic Life or, Art and the Municipality. Liverpool: Handley Brothers, 1909.

Stanfield, William. *Catalogue of the Permanent Collection of Pictures in Oil and Water Colours with Descriptive Notes and Illustrations.* Manchester: Henry Blacklock, 1895, 1896.

———. *Descriptive Catalogue of the Permanent Collection of Pictures, Compiled by William Stanfield.* Manchester: Guardian Printing Works, 1888.

Starn, Randolph. "A Historian's Brief Guide to New Museum Studies." *American Historical Review* 110, no. 1 (February 2005): 68–98.

Statement of the Works of Art, Purchased by or Presented to the Corporation of Liverpool. Ordered by the Library, Museum and Arts Committee to Be Printed, 24th June, 1875. Liverpool: Henry Greenwood, 1875.

Stedman Jones, Gareth. *Languages of Class.* Cambridge: Cambridge University Press, 1983.

———. *Outcast London: A Study in the Relationship Between Classes in Victorian Society.* New York: Penguin, 1984.

Stratton, Michael. "Architectural Terracotta in Birmingham." In *Made in Birmingham: Design & Industry, 1889–1989,* ed. Barbara Tilson, 21–34. Birmingham: Design History Society, 1989.

Stubbs, Charles Williams. "'The Triumph of the Innocents,' 1891." In *Pro Patria: Sermons on Special Occasions in England and America,* 100–116. London: Elliot Stock, 1901.

The Sunday Question Again: Shall the Free Libraries and Art Gallery Be Open on Sunday? Birmingham: William Watson, 1871.

Swan, Howard. *Preliminary Catalogue of the St. George's Museum, Walkley, Sheffield. Compiled by Howard Swan.* Sheffield: W. D. Spalding, 1888.

Tangye, Richard. *My Library Catalogue.* London: Headley Brothers, 1904.

Taylor, Bernard Douglas. *Municipal Art Galleries and Art Museums: Their Scope and Value: With Special Reference to the Needs and Opportunities of Manchester, and Containing Plans of the Present and Proposed Manchester Art Galleries.* Manchester, 1912.

Taylor, Brandon. *Art for the Nation: Exhibitions and the London Public, 1747–2001.* New Brunswick, NJ: Rutgers University Press, 1999.

Thomas, Keith. *Man and the Natural World: A History of the Modern Sensibility.* New York: Pantheon Books, 1983.

Thompson, E. P. *The Making of the English Working Class.* New York: Pantheon, 1963.

Thompson, F. M. L. *The Rise of Respectable Society: A Social History of Victorian Britain, 1830–1900.* London: Fontana, 1988.

———. "Social Control in Victorian Britain." *Economic History Review* 34, no. 2 (1981): 189–208.

Tillyard, Stella K. *The Impact of Modernism 1900–1920: Early Modernism and the Arts and Crafts Movement in Edwardian England.* New York: Routledge, Chapman and Hall, 1988.

Timmins, Samuel. *A History of Warwickshire.* London: Elliot Stock, 1889.

Tosh, John. *A Man's Place: Masculinity and the Middle-Class Home in Victorian England.* New Haven, CT: Yale University Press, 1999.

Treuherz, Julian. "Ford Madox Brown and the Manchester Murals." In *Art and Architecture in Victorian Manchester: Ten Illustrations of Patronage and Practice,* ed. John H. G. Archer, 162–207. Manchester: Manchester University Press, 1985.

———. *Hard Times: Social Realism in Victorian Art.* Manchester: Manchester City Art Galleries, 1987.

———. *Pre-Raphaelite Paintings from the Manchester City Art Galleries.* Manchester: Manchester City Art Galleries, 1993.

Upton, Chris. *A History of Birmingham*. Chichester: Phillimore, 1993.

Vernon, James. *Politics and the People: A Study in English Political Culture, c. 1815–1867*. Cambridge: Cambridge University Press, 1993.

Vincent, Eric W. *Notable Pictures. The Contribution of the Public Picture Gallery Fund to the Birmingham Art Gallery*. With illustrations. Birmingham: Cornish Brothers, 1949.

Visit of the Institute of Mechanical Engineers to Liverpool. 28th July, 1891. At Home Given by His Worship the Mayor and Mayoress (Miss Morgan) at the Walker Art Gallery and Liverpool Free Library and Museum. Liverpool: D. Marples, 1891.

Waldfogel, Melvin. "Narrative Painting." In *The Mind and Art of Victorian England*, ed. Joseph L. Altholz. Minneapolis: University of Minnesota Press, 1976.

Walker Art Gallery. *Annual Report, 1937–1938*. Liverpool, 1938.

———. *Catalogue of the Museum of Casts, Architectural and Sculptural*. Liverpool: C. Tinling, 1887.

———. *Catalogues of the Autumn Exhibition of Works of Art, Walker Art Gallery, Liverpool*. Liverpool: 1871–1912.

———. *Collective Exhibition of the Art of W. Holman Hunt Catalogue*. Liverpool, 1907.

———. *Decorative and Applied Art Exhibition (Catalogue)*. Liverpool, 1889.

———. *Illustrated Catalogue of the Permanent Collection*. Liverpool: C. Tinling, 1897.

———. *Illustrated Catalogue of the Permanent Collection, Price One Shilling*. Liverpool: C. Tinling, 1927.

———. *The Walker Art Gallery, Liverpool*. London: Scala Books, 1994.

Walkowitz, Judith R. *City of Dreadful Delight: Narratives of Sexual Danger in Late-Victorian London*. Chicago: University of Chicago Press, 1992.

Waller, P. J. *Democracy and Sectarianism: A Political and Social History of Liverpool, 1868–1939*. Liverpool: Liverpool University Press, 1981.

Wallis, Whitworth. *Borough of Birmingham Art Gallery Purchase Committee. Report of the Curator on the Various Classes of Art Work Desirable to Be Procured for the Museum and Art Gallery. Private and Confidential. For the Use of the Special Selection Sub-Committee*. Birmingham: George Jones and Son, 1885.

———. *Catalogue of the Loan Collection of Pictures and Drawings by J. M. W. Turner, R.A. with Descriptive and Biographical Notes*. Birmingham: George Jones and Son, 1899.

———. *The Feeney Galleries, and What to See in Them. A Short Guide to the Principal Pictures*. Birmingham: Journal Publishing Offices, 1913.

———. *Handbook, with Descriptive Notes, to the Collections of Industrial Art Objects in the Museum and Art Gallery*. Birmingham: George Jones and Son, 1886, 1888.

———. *Illustrated Catalogue (with Descriptive Notes) of the Permanent Collection of Paintings in Oil and Water-Colours, and the Pictures at Aston Hall*. Birmingham: George Jones and Son, 1892.

———. "The Museum and Art Gallery." *Birmingham Institutions: Lectures Given at the University*, ed. John H. Muirhead, 477–521. Birmingham: Cornish Brothers, 1911.

———. *Museum and Art Gallery. Catalogue (with Descriptive Notes) of a Permanent Collection of Paintings, in Oil and Water-Colours, and the Collection of Statuary*. Birmingham: E. C. Osborne and Son, 1897, 1900.

———, ed. *Catalogue (with Descriptive Notes and Illustrations) of the Collection of Paintings, in Oil and Water Colours, and a Special Collection of Works by David Cox*. Birmingham: E. C. Osborne and Son, 1890.

Wallis, Whitworth, and Arthur Bensley Chamberlain. *Catalogue, with Descriptive Notes and Illustrations, of the Permanent Collection of Paintings in Oil and Water Colours and a Special Loan Collection of Modern Pictures, Compiled by Wallis, Sir Whitworth and Arthur Bensley Chamberlain.* Birmingham: E. C. Osborne and Son, 1891.

————. *Illustrated Catalogue (with Descriptive Notes) of the Permanent Collection of Paintings in Oil and Water-Colours, and the Collection of Statuary, and the Pictures at Aston Hall.* Birmingham: Guild Press, 1899.

Wallis, Whitworth, and Alfred Saint Johnston. *Official Catalogue of the Contents of the Birmingham Museum and Art Gallery, with Notes upon the Industrial Exhibits and Short Biographical Notices of Deceased Artists Compiled by Wallis, Sir Whitworth . . . and Alfred St. Johnston.* Birmingham, 1885.

Walton, John K. *Lancashire: A Social History, 1558–1939.* Manchester: Manchester University Press, 1987.

Walton, John K., and James Walvin. *Leisure in Britain, 1780–1939.* Manchester: Manchester University Press, 1983.

Walton, John K., and Alastair Wilcox, eds. *Low Life and Moral Improvement in Mid-Victorian England: Liverpool Through the Journalism of Hugh Shimmin.* Leicester: Leicester University Press, 1991.

Warner, Malcolm. "John Everett Millais's 'Autumn Leaves': 'a picture full of beauty and without subject.'" In *Pre-Raphaelite Papers*, ed. Leslie Parris, 126–142. London: Tate Gallery, 1984.

Waterfield, Giles. *Art for the People: Culture in the Slums of Late Victorian Britain.* London: Dulwich Picture Gallery, 1994.

————. "The Origins of the Early Picture Gallery Catalogue in Europe, and Its Manifestations in Victorian Britain." In *Art in Museums*, ed. Susan Pearce, 42–73. London: Athlone, 1995.

————. *Palaces of Art: Art Galleries in Britain 1790–1990*, catalogue from Dulwich Picture Gallery exhibit held 27 November 1991–1 March 1992. Sudbury: Lavenham, 1991.

Weiner, Deborah E. B. *Architecture and Social Reform in Late-Victorian London.* Manchester: Manchester University Press, 1994.

Whistler, James McNeill. *Mr. Whistler's "Ten O'Clock."* New York: Ernest Dressel North, 1888.

White, Brian D. *A History of the Corporation of Liverpool, 1835–1914.* Liverpool: University Press, 1951.

Wiener, Martin J. *English Culture and the Decline of the Industrial Spirit, 1850–1980.* Cambridge: Cambridge University Press, 1995.

Wigley, John. *The Rise and Fall of the Victorian Sunday.* Manchester: Manchester University Press, 1980.

Wildman, Stephen. *Visions of Love and Life: Pre-Raphaelite Art from the Birmingham Collection, England.* Alexandria, VA: Art Services International, 1995.

Wildman, Stephen, and John Christian. *Edward Burne-Jones, Victorian Artist-Dreamer.* New York: Metropolitan Museum of Art, 1998.

William Holman Hunt: An Exhibition Arranged by the Walker Art Gallery. Exhibition Catalogue: Walker Art Gallery Liverpool, March–April 1969; Victoria and Albert Museum, May–June 1969. Liverpool: Elliott Brothers and Yeoman, 1969.

Williams, Raymond. *The Country and the City.* New York: Oxford University Press, 1973.

———. *Culture and Society: 1780–1950.* New York: Columbia University Press, 1983.

———. *Television: Technology and Cultural Form.* New York: Schocken Books, 1975.

Wilson, Arline. "'The Florence of the North'? The Civic Culture of Liverpool in the Early Nineteenth Century." In *Gender, Civic Culture and Consumerism: Middle-Class Identity in Britain, 1800–1940,* ed. Alan Kidd and David Nicholls, 34–46. Manchester: Manchester University Press, 1999.

Wilson, R. N. D. *The National and Tate Galleries, with One Hundred Plates in Colour.* London: T. Nelson and Sons, 1934.

Wilson, Shelagh. "'The Highest Art for the Lowest People': The Whitechapel and Other Philanthropic Art Galleries, 1877–1901." In *Governing Cultures: Art Institutions in Victorian London,* ed. Paul Barlow and Colin Trodd, 172–186. Aldershot: Ashgate, 2000.

Wise, Alexander Gordon Hay. *Notes on the Pictures of Mr. Holman Hunt: Exhibited at the Rooms of the Fine Art Society 1886, with Criticisms by John Ruskin . . . And Other Comments.* London, 1886.

Witcomb, Anne. *Re-Imagining the Museum: Beyond the Mausoleum.* London: Routledge, 2003.

Wolff, Janet, and Caroline Arscott. "'Cultivated Capital': Patronage and Art in 19th-Century Manchester and Leeds." *History Today* 37 (March 1987): 22–28.

Wolff, Janet, and John Seed, eds. *The Culture of Capital: Art, Power and the Nineteenth-Century Middle Class.* Manchester: Manchester University Press, 1988.

Woodson-Boulton, Amy. "The Art of Compromise: The National Gallery of British Art, 1890–1892." *Museum and Society* 1, no. 3 (November 2003): 147–169.

———. "'Industry Without Art Is Brutality': Aesthetic Ideology and Social Practice in Victorian Art Museums." *Journal of British Studies* 46, no. 1 (2007): 47–71.

———. "John Ruskin, Letters to James Allanson Picton; the Ruskin Society in Manchester (1880s)." *Victorian Review* 35, no. 1 (2009): 60–64.

———. "Local Government." In *The Encyclopedia of the Victorian Era,* ed. Tom Pendergast and Sara Pendergast, 2:399–404. 4 vols. Danbury, CT: Grolier Academic Press, 2004.

———. "Museums." In *The Encyclopedia of the Victorian Era,* ed. Tom Pendergast and Sara Pendergast, 3:78–81. 4 vols. Danbury, CT: Grolier Academic Press, 2004.

———. "Temples of Art in Cities of Industry: Municipal Art Museums in Birmingham, Liverpool, and Manchester, c. 1870–1914." PhD diss., University of California, Los Angeles, 2003.

———. "Victorian Museums and Victorian Society." *History Compass* 6, no. 1 (2008): 109–146.

———. "A Window onto Nature: Visual Language, Aesthetic Ideology, and the Art of Social Transformation." In *Visions of the Industrial Age, 1830–1914: Modernity and the Anxiety of Representation,* ed. Minsoo Kang and Amy Woodson-Boulton, 139–161. Aldershot: Ashgate, 2008.

Wornum, Ralph, and Charles Eastlake. *Descriptive and Historical Catalogue of the Pictures in the National Gallery.* London: W. Clowes and Sons, 1847.

Wright, Gwendolyn, ed. *The Formation of National Collections of Art and Archaeology.* Washington, DC: National Gallery of Art, Washington, and University Press of New England, 1996.

INDEX

Italic page numbers refer to figures.